The Broadway Musical

THE BROADWAY MUSICAL

Collaboration in Commerce and Art

Bernard Rosenberg and Ernest Harburg

NEW YORK UNIVERSITY PRESS
New York and London

New York University Press books are printed on acid-free paper,
and their binding materials are chosen for strength and durability.

Library of Congress Cataloging-in-Publication Data
Rosenberg, Bernard, 1923–
    The Broadway musical : collaboration in commerce and art / Bernard
Rosenberg and Ernest Harburg.
        p.   cm.
    Includes bibliographical references and index.
    ISBN 0-8147-7433-4
    1. Musicals—New York (N.Y.)—History and criticism.   I. Harburg,
Ernest.   II. Title.
ML1711.8.N3R67   1993
792.6'09747'1—dc20   93-22380
                                CIP
                                MN

Manufactured in the United States of America

10   9   8   7   6   5   4   3   2   1

For Deena and Ben.
May they always flourish.

Good Old Reliable Broadway

Why it's good old reliable Broadway,
Broadway, Broadway, Broadway, New York.
If you're looking for action we'll furnish the spot,
Even when the heat is on it's never too hot.
Not for good old reliable Broadway,
For it's always just a short walk
To the oldest established permanent floating crap game in New York.

There are well-heeled shooters ev'rywhere, ev'rywhere,
There are well-heeled shooters ev'rywhere,
And an awful lot of lettuce for the fella who can get us there.
If we only had a lousy mil, we could be a billionaire.

That's good old reliable Broadway,
Broadway, Broadway, Broadway, New York.
If the size of your bundle you want to increase,
We'll arrange that you go broke in quiet and peace
In a theater provided by Broadway
Where there are no neighbors to squawk.
It's the oldest established permanent floating crap game in New York.

Where's the action, where's the game?
Gotta have the game or we'll die from shame.
It's the oldest established permanent floating crap game in New York.

—parody of "Good Old Reliable Nathan,"
Guys and Dolls (1950),
lyrics and music by Frank Loesser

Contents

Illustrations

Figures and Charts

Preface

This is a book that neither of us could have written by himself. Its subject matter is collaboration in the Broadway musical theater. The method by which we gathered and analyzed material for this study demanded our own collaboration every step of the way. The enthusiasm, the conflict and the complementarity, the give and take, the exasperation and resolution or tension and release inherent in any collaborative effort bestowed a greater measure of insight into the phenomena we set out to understand and report.

These phenomena will never be fully understood. How could they be? If X works well with Y and Z this time and next time, but not the time after that or ever again, then what? The mystery—or the chemistry that obeys no law—abideth. To unscramble all the leads in such a mystery with additional, indeed an infinite number of, combinations and permutations would seem to be too much for anyone. It is. Yet that fact leaves us undismayed. For among the countless pieces of the puzzle, there are clues to certain tentative "constants" of collaboration. Those clues came to us over a period encompassing most of the 1980s.

Early in the 1980s we personally conducted interviews that were really more like three-way conversations among at least forty creators involved in the making of Broadway musicals. These in-depth interviews were taped, transcribed, studied, and placed into many categories and subcategories that arose time and again. As faithfully as possible, we have quoted and interpreted the impressions and experiences, the agreements and disagreements, biases, claims, and preferences of those who know best what they have done, what they are doing, and what they hope to do. These theatrical specialists provided us with matchless information about the techniques they used. But techniques change, often because the economy and its technology change. So individuals at any given moment find themselves of more than one mind about their jobs, how best to perform them, and where they fit in relation to others.

Harold Prince, who figures prominently in these pages, wrote a valuable memoir about his life in the musical theater. It is suitably titled *Contradictions.*[1] Any extended account of human action—which is also inevitably an account of human interaction—could bear such a title. Occupational socialization (or in everyday English, learning your job) is never totally consistent or all of a piece. Producers, directors, composers, lyricists, bookwriters, designers, actors, and other artistic and business collaborators: these are our dramatis personae. We have taken care to include younger and older practitioners, relative newcomers, and, whenever possible, an equal number of old-timers. No two are alike. Each is heir to a variety of traditions. All belong to a small Broadway community transmitting skills and attitudes that are constantly transformed. Part of our story turns on the growth of that community. While its members speak for themselves, the data they yield say more. Those data need to be put in a larger context toward which we hope to have taken a step or two.

The respondents with whom we talked and to whom we returned when, with the passage of years, further clarification appeared to be in order, taught us a great deal. There was also a body of altogether useful biographical and autobiographical literature. But the spoken or the written word always took us in an historical direction. "How are things now?"—when "now" seldom lasted a whole season—was a meaningful question only in relation to how "things" had been. It proved impossible to stay on top of every development. For instance, just when director-choreographers could be confidently described as in the ascendant, several died—and there never were many of them—while others withdrew. We had to keep a close eye on the daily press and on trade magazines simply to count, say, the number of theaters that comprised Broadway in New York City, let alone Broadway's national and international expansion.

In our own modest project—microcosmically similar to the far more complex musical theater projects we have tried to anatomize—every source was a resource. Almost all of our data are qualitative, but we did not neglect the quantitative data generated by others. Conclusions drawn from survey research we were able to lay our hands on are incorporated in the text. Most quantitative research is market research sponsored by theatrical executives who naturally want to know which of their products will go down best with what audiences. Their frame of reference is that of conventional economics, which we do not wish to disparage.

But, while *homo economicus* might be a valuable abstraction to economists, it is rarely our abstraction. We have found it more fruitful to place the artificially isolated realm of economic activity within an institutional environment. Thus, a purely economic issue like rising costs is embedded in several extraeconomic considerations. It is with such an issue that part 1 (chapters 1 and 2) is concerned. By plunging directly into the cost question, we begin to see how it includes but transcends the confines of classical economic theory. Skyrocketing cost is uppermost in the minds of Broadway backers and producers, especially those who have a stake in the musical theater, Brodway's most lucrative or financially disastrous sector. A single production can enrich or impoverish its backers. At the same time, everyone else in the project will rise or fall as part of a venture that at best is very chancy.

Why start with the question of cost? Because everybody interested in Broadway musicals is and has always been more or less obsessed with it. Because it affords us an opportunity for an historical and contemporary overview of those musicals from an angle that can neither be finessed nor sidestepped. Cost allows and constrains every element of musical theater. And, finally, because even cost management, duly considered, suggests the conceptual framework of what is to follow. The business of musical theater is as collaborative as the art of creating musicals. What follows revolves around the many sides of a genre that is inconceivable without creative interaction, cooperation, or, the near-synonym that pops up everywhere, collaboration.

Broadway shows are nothing if not commercial. But those who support and admire them at their best also claim that these shows are works of art. Parts 1 and 2 of this book are accordingly entitled "The Business of Musical Theater" and "Creating the Musical Show." There is collaborative conflict ideally leading to cohesion between and within these two spheres; everything merges with the cash nexus, the basic wherewithal. However, show biz and its top executives fit their intricate functions together with artistic skills to give a project its initial impetus. *To us, top executives are not only business people but, in a musical, are also producer, director, composer, lyricist, and bookwriter.* Within a volatile budget, creative teams are formed, story and song are merged, a musical fabric comes into being. Then, sifted through critics, it is passed on to audiences. We describe these processes with all the specificity various sources place at our command. Part 3, "Collaboration in the Musical," is an overall exploration of how these processes work—when they work—and how they much more commonly fail to work.

No venture can be a success without good collaboration, but whether collaboration in any specific case is good or bad cannot be known beforehand. The collaborative concept, with its element of unpredictability, is known to us as social scientists. The data that do not speak for themselves speak for us through some such concept. If the total result is less than all-inclusive, as any result must be, we hope that this necessarily unique treatment of an American art form, as it falls and rises, will contribute its bit to the general pool of knowledge about all human projects—how they are initiated, organized, and brought to completion. But only a limited picture is possible; the rest seems to us to be unfathomable.

Acknowledgments

The authors wish to thank the following for their assistance in preparing this book: George Wachtel, director of research, League of American Theatres and Producers, for his infinite knowledge, patience, and generosity of spirit; for their countless hours of assistance in ferreting out information, Dorothy Swerdlove, former curator, Bob Taylor, current curator, and the staff of the Billy Rose Theatre Collection, New York Public Library; Lynn Doherty, curator, and Kathy Mets of the Theatre Collection, Museum of the City of New York; Maryann Chach, archivist, Shubert Archive; and to those who responded graciously when called upon—Otis L. Guernsey, Jr.; Betty Spitz and Mary Assandri of the Shubert Organization; the late Richard Hummler and Sylvester Joachim, *Variety;* Brian Kell, 42nd Street Development Project; Michael Young and Melissa Wohl, Harlequin Dinner Theatre; and to all the unnamed producing organizations, general managers, and their staffs for providing information on many of the musicals mentioned in this book. Our thanks also to Robert Forrest for making initial lists of Broadway musicals.

For special appreciation because of the constant involvement in the long-term work of birthing and raising this book, our thanks to Peggy Brooks (who twice edited early drafts); Penney Hills and Robert Lilienfeld (who also edited early drafts); Camille Croce Dee and Fred Carl, who assisted in all the research details; and Nick Markovich, who labored long over the whole nine years of effort doing the days' work of organizing us and the book. And then, our thanks to all those musical theater professionals and artists who gave freely of their time and intelligence.

We wish to thank the following interviewees for their kind cooperation:

Occupation

1. Theater Owner	Gerald Schoenfeld
2. Producer	Gail Berman
	Nicholas Howey
	John Flaxman
	Claire Nichtern
3. Company Manager	Robert Buckley
	Peter Neufeld
4. Director	Martin Charnin (also lyricist)
	Arthur Masella
	Harold Prince
5. Director-Choreographer	Michael Bennett
	Geoffrey Holder
	Tommy Tune
6. Musical Playwright	Arthur Laurents
	Peter Stone
	John Weidman, Jr.
7. Lyricist and/or Composer	Carol Hall
	Sheldon Harnick
	Burton Lane
	Stephen Schwartz
8. Conductor-Musical Director	Paul Gemignani
9. Orchestrator	Anonymous
10. Musician-Union Official	John Glasel
11. Set Designer	Oliver Smith
12. Lighting Designer	Jules Fisher (also producer)
13. Costume Designer	Carrie Robbins
14. Casting Director	John Lyons
15. Actor	Anonymous
	Lonny Price (also director)
16. Press Agent	Merle Debuskey
17. Theatrical Lawyer	Donald Farber
18. Writers' Agent	Anonymous
19. Cast Album Producer	Thomas Z. Shepherd
20. Administrator	Harvey Sabinson
21. Critic	Walter Kerr
	Frank Rich
22. Actors Equity Official	Anonymous

The Broadway Musical

Broadway Crowds, 1992

In the history of musical stories-with-song, controlled by the "aristos" in ancient Greece, and by the church and the monarchs in Western Europe, the American musical is today politically free, secular, and commercial; the public decides the success or failure of a show as befits a democratic society. Broadway theater audiences on 44th Street, 1992. (Photo credit: Mark Jenkinson)

I

The Business of Musical Theater

1. Broadway Musical Show Biz and Rising Costs

F ew people would deny that a musical play presented on a stage before a live audience is an authentic art form. Nor would a bolder assertion provoke much controversy: a musical play so conceived involves a combination of all the arts. Less well known, perhaps, is the fact that theater of this kind—musical theater—was invented in ancient Greece and flourished throughout the fifth century B.C. In the fourth century, an unfinished but still unsurpassed analysis of that theater was written to such good effect that well over two thousand years later no student of musical theater can safely overlook Aristotle's *Poetics*. Do the reflections of a classical philosopher have any bearing on so worldly and modern, so "vulgar" or "demotic" a phenomenon as Broadway musical theater? We think so. In the pages that follow we will from time to time refer to the *Poetics*, as we will to any available source of light on the subject of Broadway musical theater.

But not even Aristotle enlightens his readers on the problem of patronage. Who subsidized the festivals at which works by Aeschylus, Sophocles, Euripides, Aristophanes (the last two exceedingly subversive), and many others who are forever lost to us, were performed? Surely it was the Athenian city-state with Pericles at its pinnacle. But the festivals were religious occasions. Church and state were one. The first actor, no matter how many masks he wore, must also have been a priest. No doubt such a man (and all actors were men) was handsomely rewarded in the worldliest way, but about this the written record is barren.

Documents do exist, however, about the competitive nature of tragic and comic playwriting. The festivals were contests. For tragedies, only a small group of substantial citizens—the *aristos*—judged trilogies along with a lighter, shorter satyr play, which were submitted with them. Each playwright—then called poet—created, performed, and directed his one-person presentation before the aristos. If accepted, the work was later enacted before a larger live audience in a production by two or more persons, with an indispensable chorus that chanted and danced, helped by various artisans who created the spectacle. Prizes went annually to the winner, and wealthy men of the polis paid for them. Cash transactions took place of whose details very little is known.

For over a millennium, throughout the era of Christendom, the great tradition of religious musical drama persisted. The church paid for it. The marketplace economics of theater only began to be visible as church and state were separated and pulverized, that is, after the Reformation and the Renaissance had remade the face of Western civilization. Premodern theater was then the property of popes and clerics, and of monarchs, princes, high public officials like chamberlains, and the upper aristocracy. While in the Elizabethan period a magnificent playwright like Shakespeare could own and operate a theater for his plays (which had music) and sell tickets to the public, royal favor and subsidies were still required for prosperous survival. Later, European opera, at home and when transplanted to America, tended to be sustained by the rich who a short while before had been the *nouveaux riches.*

In the United States today there is little institutional support for theater, musical or straight. Now the consumer is king. The public—the *demos*—is the final patron. In that sense, it may be said that twentieth century musical theater has been democratized, secularized, and commercialized. For better or worse, today's Broadway musicals carry the full weight of this heritage.

The art of Broadway musical theater, therefore, is anchored in both its crafts and its marketplaces. This art is always basically constrained and influenced by the limits of capital *and* by the budget, a truism that holds even for the largest productions, such as *Miss Saigon* (1991), capitalized at $10 million.

Deems Taylor, a composer and critic, knew whereof he spoke decades ago:

After all, there have only been three forms of musical stage entertainment in the history of Western culture that in their day have been huge money-makers and also perfected art forms. These three are Italian grand opera, the Viennese operetta, and the American musical.[1]

The Business of Theater

Alfred Bernheim, an historian of American theater early in this century, launched an investigation into *The Business of the Theatre* in 1931.[2] It showed, probably for the first time, an intelligible socioeconomic structure to that part of the American musical theater known as Broadway. This basic business structure persisted through the decades. It also evolved slowly until the 1980s, which is the focus of our story.

Bernheim noted that Broadway musical theater business mirrored expansionism and oligopoly as manifested in other industries with corporations like U.S. Steel, Standard Oil, or Metro-Goldwyn-Mayer. Indeed, between 1900 and 1910, the Erlanger-Klaw syndicate held a monopoly on practically all bookings of stage events in the United States, a stranglehold until the Shubert brothers helped to break up "the trust" and secure control, lately with the Nederlanders, over the Broadway establishment.[3] This duopoly survived through the 1980s, leaving some room for a third party called Jujamcyn. In the 1980s, more so than ever, New York's Broadway musical theater developed very rapidly into a national and international industry. The art of Broadway musical theater generates and sustains big business. No doubt it always will.

The necessity for a merger of art and commerce, Bernheim maintains, is built into Western civilization and its development as a large-scale capitalist industrial economy. While the aesthetic of musical shows remained in the service of religion until the Renaissance, its power then came to be expressed in dramatic theater (always with music), usually exploited in the marketplace or protected by the crown. Of all art forms, and unlike works of art by individuals (fiction, poetry, painting, sculpture), the musical theater requires materials, tools, and talent drawn collectively from many or all other art forms, and thus demands relatively larger sums of capital. To be produced before the public, every musical requires the full collaboration of artistic and business professionals.

The only other collaborative art form, according to Arthur Laurents, that is also musical, also American, but without any great need for large capital outlays, is the jazz ensemble. In both musical theater and jazz groups, the organizing of public performance allows exploitation in the marketplace and therefore requires the collaboration of artists and businessmen. And collaboration, all our interviewees tell us, is in Oscar Hammerstein's phrase, "the largest word in [musical] theater."[4] While that word is conventionally applied to the collective work of artistic craftsmen and women, the word obviously also must include the work of professionals who organize "the business of theatre."

For to create a musical, the artistry of story and song must first merge into a musical play, which exists in manuscript or on cassette until brought from page to stage by actors in a theater before a live audience. For a musical to exist, as the director Harold Prince succinctly observed, "It must be up there live." Production requires large outlays of money, not to speak of intricately organized business and legal arrangements. Musical productions, with their base in scarce and expensive real estate on which theaters repose, struggle continuously for existence in the commercial world. The true meaning of "American musical theater" in its recent origins and early development until today is synonymous with New York commercial Broadway theater, and like any large-scale commercial enterprise, Broadway show biz requires strong management.

In 1931 Bernheim wrote:

If commercialism in the theater is inevitable, efficient commercialism should permit the freest development of art. This does not mean that the most prosperous theatrical enterprise would be the most worthwhile. It does mean, however, that the theatre as a whole would have a better chance to flourish if it had a sound economic base on which to operate, than if it were left to flounder amidst the chaos of economic atrocities.[5]

Gerald Schoenfeld, chairman of the board of the Shubert Organization since 1972, sounds a similar note in the 1980s from the vantage point of a theater owner:

It's very important to have theaters in strong financial hands, the stronger the better, because theater owning today is an extremely expensive and precarious business. It's always been precarious. But right now the costs are very high and you need to have theaters in strong financial hands due to the vagaries of the business, the economic upturns and downturns, scarcities of shows, and other periodic situations.

[However] if people were interested only in wealth in this business they would sell off all their theaters and put their money into more productive, less precarious ventures. . . . A theater is a limited use piece of property.

If Thorstein Veblen, the father of institutional economics, had turned his attention to musical theater, he would have said much the same thing.

The Business Structure of American Musical Theater: An Overview

In the development of musical theater as a major part of the American entertainment industry, the economics of Broadway in New York City plays a decisive role. Broadway, economically speaking, is a loose confederation of theater owners whose theaters (which fluctuated between thirty and forty over this century) are grouped in a section of Manhattan where land values, and therefore taxes, are constantly rising. Income from theaters is necessarily limited by the number of seats, performances per week, and, most importantly, by the scarcity of saleable attractions, or products. Since 1932, the average number of musicals that reach production annually has remained fairly low—about fourteen—and the average percent of musicals that do not return their investment during their Broadway runs has remained 75–80 percent. All these are dominant facts of a high-risk business, especially precarious during downturns in the general economy.

Today, ongoing strength in the risky sector known as "show business" is provided by an oligopoly of three organizations that own theaters on Broadway. This group helps to regulate such chronic forces as pure speculators and fly-by-night neophytes with their glut of unsaleable products. These few theater owners act through a larger league of theater owners and producers to manage the rising costs of a labor-intensive business (both blue and white collar), the tax burdens of city and state, the demands of individual and corporate investors in shows, and the rising expense of new technologies used in today's musicals.

Indeed, starting in the late 1970s, all these costs erupted. They soared far beyond the general rate of inflation. In the last decade or so, two new factors have contributed heavily to the escalating production and operating costs of Broadway musicals. First, there are changes in the ever-developing form of the musical. Always a spectacle-oriented art, new technologically staggering musical megaspectacles burst on the scene in the 1980s, beginning with *Cats* (a hit), *Les Misérables* (a hit) and going on, for example, to *Carrie* (a flop), *The Phantom of the Opera* (a hit), *Aspects of Love* (a flop), and *Miss Saigon* (a hit). Broadway musicals of today continue "the tradition of the new" with larger productions combining music, story, and spectacle, at relentlessly rising costs.

Within this material context came an unanticipated change in the business structure of running musicals that impacted the control of costs. Cost management by a single strong executive, the producer, ceased to be the norm. Instead, three corporate roles took on joint responsibility for controlling costs: they are the newly dominant directors; the emergence of multiproducers; and the appearance of more powerful company managers. We term this division of labor and power the "corporate troika." This overall organizational change has led to a decentralized and usually less effective mode of cost control in musicals than in the past.

However, there is a steadily growing demand for Broadway musicals throughout the nation and the world. This demand greatly accelerated from the late 1970s through the 1980s. Thus, rising costs and longer recoupment time on Broadway are mitigated by the flow of profits pouring in from both national and international tours. As in other industries, internationalization is the trend and is keeping Broadway show business in the money.

Let us now examine the evolution of Broadway show biz in closer detail.

The Theaters of Broadway

As of the 1980s, the Broadway turf, according to Schoenfeld,

consists of an area twelve blocks long and two blocks wide. It is bounded on the South by the Nederlander Theater on 41st Street; on the North by the Broadway Theater on 53rd Street and Broadway; on the East by the Belasco Theater, located approximately 100 feet west of Sixth Avenue; and on the West by the Martin Beck Theater, located approximately 100 feet west of Eighth Avenue.[6] [See map of the Broadway theaters.]

As of 1992, there were thirty-six functioning full-size proscenium-stage legitimate theaters. The term "legitimate" refers in general to what contracts call "first-class" shows in "first-class" theaters. (These categories are not normative; they simply define the type of contract in effect.) All of New York's legitimate Broadway theaters were, with three exceptions, built between 1902 and 1927. The oldest is the Lyceum; the youngest, the Ethel Barrymore. By the middle nineties there will be one or more new legitimate theaters on Broadway. (See theater list in appendix 3.)

On this turf, all but one of the full-size functioning proscenium theaters are owned and/or operated by the big three theatrical companies. The Shubert Organization was, in 1991, involved in the ownership and operation of seventeen (it co-owns the Music Box) theaters (in 1984, $114 million box office gross); the Nederlander Organization occupied ten theaters ($60 million gross); and Jujamcyn Theaters is involved in the ownership and/or operation of five theaters ($40 million gross). The total Broadway gross income had risen to over $500 million in 1992, but proportions of gross are roughly similar to the 1984 figures.[7] The Shubert Organization is wealthier than the Nederlander group. These two constitute the oligarchy of the Broadway establishment. They have a dominant influence throughout the theater world. That our topic is musical theater changes nothing because straight plays do not approach the bonanzas that smash musicals can yield to those who invest in them. Musicals accounted for about 75 percent of the total box office on Broadway in 1990 and over 80 percent of the tours.

Theaters On The Broadway Turf (1992)

1. Broadway
2. Virginia
3. Neil Simon
4. Mark Hellinger
5. Gershwin
6. Circle-in-the Square
7. Winter Garden
8. Ambassador
9. Eugene O'Neill
10. Walter Kerr
11. Cort
12. Longacre
13. Palace
14. Edison

15. Ethel Barrymore
16. Brooks Atkinson
17. Lunt-Fontanne
18. Marquis
19. Richard Rodgers
20. Lyceum
21. Music Box
22. Booth
23. Plymouth
24. Royale
25. Imperial
26. John Golden
27. Martin Beck
28. Belasco

29. Minskoff
30. Shubert
31. Broadhurst
32. Helen Hayes
33. St. James
34. Majestic
35. Nederlander
36. Criterion

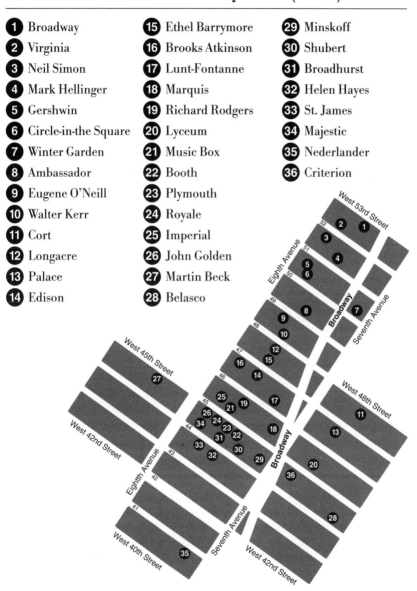

Source: *Official Broadway Theater Guide. Published by the League Of American Theaters and Producers. For other Broadway theaters, see text.*

Theater owners are well aware of their own cost pressures. Besides rising taxes—Broadway turf is inordinately valuable urban property—and rising production costs, many buildings are obsolete and cannot easily be used for nontheater purposes. Harvey Sabinson, director of special products for the League of American Theatres and Producers, notes that the Shubert Organization uses profits from its "strong" theaters to keep the "weak" ones running. The Shuberts, he says,

> would be much better off if they could sell or redevelop five theaters that are big losers, the Belasco, the Longacre, the Cort, probably even the Golden and the Booth which are so small. Their profit margins would be much higher. But they're in the business of operating theaters.

Again, Schoenfeld in the 1980s repeated what Bernheim wrote in 1931: even a hit show running for a while to full houses eventually tapers off, playing to some empty seats until it is no longer sustainable. The theater is then dark until a new show can be mounted. And while dark, it still devours tax and operating funds, as actors, stagehands, and musicians languish among the unemployed. Lost time between shows also elevates theater costs as they create debts that impinge on upcoming shows. Scarcity of saleable products seems to be an existential fact of Broadway musical business.

Where Are the Saleable Products?

When the halls are empty and the theaters dark, both producers and theater owners look desperately for product they think will sell. In 1931, Bernheim quoted a producer who kept records of his attempt to find show material:

> This firm . . . examined more than 5,000 plays over a 5–6 year period. . . . Of all these plays, only 30 were produced [or one of two hundred]; and of these thirty, only 5 were outstanding financial successes [about one out of a thousand], none, however, falling within the [smash] hit class.
>
> How can we account for such appalling results? It is not enough to say that there are inherent risks attached to production; that is self-evident. The fundamental reason seems to me to be over-expansion. I do not mean that there are too many plays produced or that the seating capacity of the theatre is too large for the population, though this may be true. I mean that there are not enough good plays written to fill all the theatres that need occupants, or to supply all the producers.[8]

The critical adjective is "good" (read, "judged by a producer to be a show that will attract audiences"); there are more than enough plays that never make it off the page. In the early 1980s during our interview, Harold Prince remarked,

There may be seventy [major regional] theaters out there in the United States, all doing [musical] work. But there is never enough real talent to create enough wondrous musicals every season to keep seventy theaters going. [In total there were about three hundred and twenty regional theaters in 1989; most do not originate musicals.][9]

Or, as Schoenfeld puts the scarcity factor, "You can't manufacture talent. You can't grind out product." The skeptic might ask, "Why not?" The lyricist Sheldon Harnick speaks to the fears of present-day Broadway writers that creation of musicals will someday be organized like filmmaking:

In Hollywood, they have a different method of putting a show together—you know, the so-called step deal. We will hire you as the first step. If we don't like what you've done, you're out. And then hire the next author, and if they don't like what he's done, get somebody else to rewrite that.

Arthur Laurents, the bookwriter and director, feels, like most of us, that because of this "step deal," the commercial studio film industry is mostly mass produced. It is devoid of artistic collaboration. What if Broadway adopted a step deal production method? We do not know if it would increase the number of shows. We do know that there is a scarcity of products deemed producible on Broadway.

The Average Number

Strikingly, the average number of new musicals—about fourteen—opening on Broadway seems to be unchanged since 1933–34. Figure 1.1 shows the data. The 1920s were the heyday of musical productions. They peaked in 1926–29, and crashed along with the stock market and the onset of talking pictures. It is not quite accurate to assert that the rise was a post-World War I phenomenon. From 1900 on, the number of new musicals climbed steadily, a trend that was briefly interrupted by the advent of motion pictures in 1914–17 (many existing theaters were converted into movie houses). By 1918, stage musicals resumed their climb and sustained it for about a decade. To be sure, in the teens and twenties, prolific creators like Kern, Hammerstein, the Gershwins, Rodgers and Hart, Victor Herbert and Sigmund Romberg, and superproducers like Ziegfeld and Garrick were on the scene. It was not unusual for a writing team or a producer to mount several shows a year. But also, in the twenties, shows that ran only a few months could be financial successes—that is, make their investment back.

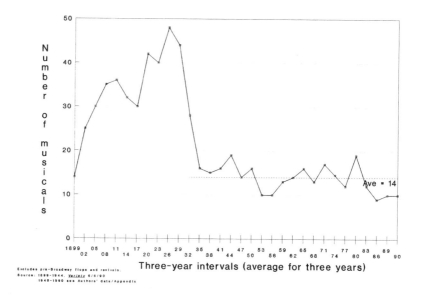

Figure 1.1 Number of Productions of New Musicals Opening on Broadway, 1899–1990[10]

The number of new musicals then slumped throughout the thirties. Strangely, musicals reached an all-time low in the fifties just when America by every conventional index was more prosperous than ever before, and Broadway was alive with great musicals in its vintage years. Clearly something else intervened (television? the bebop generation?). In any event the musical theater *since 1933* has fluctuated around a fairly constant production average. The trend is downward, its future unpredictable.

The Flop Percent

More important to theater owners and producers than number of shows per year is the average percent of *flops* and *hits*. A few smash hits will outweigh several flops. The terms "hit" and "flop" may have originated in *Variety,* the newspaper that reports on show biz (the worlds of film, television, and Broadway and regional theater) and generates its own jargon. In this book these terms are not critical judgments; they simply refer to whether or not a Broadway show returns complete investment funds during its run on Broadway.

A "flop" usually has a brief run; often no funds are returned at all to the producer or investors (who can then take a tax write-off). There is also a small number of shows that achieve artistic success *(succès d'estime)* and almost return investment while on Broadway; this is still counted here as not economically successful. For instance, *Sunday in the Park with George* (1984), which ran over seventeen months, did not quite return costs to the investors during its Broadway run. A more telling example is *Porgy and Bess* (1935), which at its opening on Broadway "flopped" after 120 performances; in 1942, however, with Ira Gershwin's permission, the opera was cut down to become more like a Broadway musical drama and had a successful run on Broadway. It then attained great success here and abroad.

A small but as yet uncounted number of shows fail to recoup on Broadway but later return investment and profit on national and foreign tours and even have substantial life over many years. Post-Broadway profits may also emerge through subsidiary sales, often to film companies, and through stock and amateur rights. Even though such shows eventually recoup, in our discussion of what happens on Broadway, they are considered flops during their Broadway run.

A hard truth about Broadway hits and flops is that any person, corporation, or private group can become an investor, even a "producer," by hiring a director and a general manager. No doubt inexperienced producers have many more flops than do professional producing agencies and theater owners whose ratio of hits to flops is not random and usually better than 50 percent.

Harvey Sabinson describes small independent producers, now being displaced, as "real working people" who are seldom affluent unless a big hit comes their way. The newcomers may join the (then) New York League of Theatre Owners and Producers, but of its 240 members early in the eighties, only thirty-five were active. "Once they're inactive for five years and haven't done a show, goodbye."

It is remarkable that the financial success-failure ratios for Broadway have remained fairly constant for the last seventy-odd years. Between 1923 and 1928, Bernheim's numbers were about 70 percent flops and 30 percent hits.[11] Bernheim found the results "appalling."[12] And yet, he wrote, there is no "elimination process." By every rule of classical economics, but not of institutional economics, inefficient firms should fall, but this so-called law is inapplicable to the theater. For as Bernheim knew:

In spite of [what] is generally known [about] the mathematical odds . . . there is never a lack of new capital for more productions. Why? In the first place because every producer and his backers think they are wise enough to beat the game. In the second, because there is a chance, however slim, to make a tremendous fortune on a small investment, and this chance is an irresistible lure.[13]

Between 1925 and 1935, the *New York Times, Variety,* and *Billboard,* using varied criteria, found about a 25–75 hit-flop ratio.[14] We decided to compile our own statistics for the years 1945–90 with a focus on musicals produced in "Broadway theaters" that returned invested funds (a "hit") or failed to (a "flop") during the post-World War II years—the immediate background to and through the 1980s. (See Figure 1.2; the reader who wishes to inspect our research criteria and lists may turn to appendix 6.) It was fascinating to learn that the success-failure ratio from 1945 to 1990 was 24 percent hits and 76 percent flops,[15] which is very close to Bernheim's results for 1923–28 and to that of the three key newspapers from 1925 to 1935.

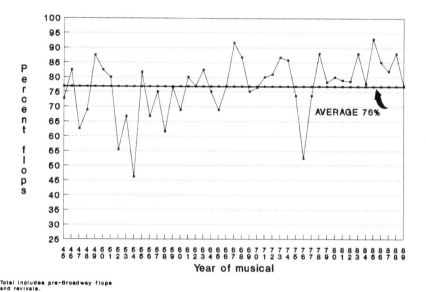

Figure 1.2 Percentage of Flops of Broadway Musicals by Years, 1945–1990

Our analysis includes revivals, which are not actually new musicals, though some revivals are reconstructions or revisions rather than exact duplications of the original shows. One still hears the usual myths about revivals bandied about: "They are old fashioned, out-of-date"—and therefore will flop—or, "The older audience wants to enjoy the old hits again" —and therefore they will succeed. We include revivals and pre-Broadway flops in Figure 1.2 because these are projects on which investors have risked their money in order to enter the Broadway arena.

Merle Debuskey, a long-time press agent for numerous shows, sums up the situation with revivals by pointing again to "the real estate":

What has happened—in terms of real wealth in the theater—is not sharp change in playwrights or directors or actors. It's the real estate—it's there year after year after year. Whether it's working or not, it exists, and that real property, which is an investment, is not profitable unless something is in it. If you and I are not producing the plays to fill these halls, then the theater owners have to do something themselves. That allows someone who doesn't have a new idea to say, "Well, I'll do a revival."

Our research indicates that revivals are a little more likely to flop—an average 78 percent—than are new musicals.[16]

The low *number* of musicals opening annually on Broadway since the 1930s (at its lowest in the 1980s) and the steady percent of *flops* (75–80 percent) since the 1920s are two of several critical facts that dominate the business of Broadway musical theater.

Why Take the Risk?

Why are "successful" established professionals so often involved in shows that do not succeed financially? We asked two theatrical lawyers about this. Alvin Deutsch said, "Partly because people in a show lie to each other. Even your best friends won't tell you," as the old soap ad put it. The other lawyer, Donald Farber, replied with a question: "Did you ever know a mother to say her baby was ugly?" Both take it for granted that truth telling in this milieu is very rare. Other explanations include critical vagaries and the fickle taste of audiences and reviewers; the lack of quality apprenticeship for writers or alternative training; the unavailability of a really good book or score, and certain specific difficulties in the art of producing musicals. Producer Nicholas Howey explains the last point:

From the producer's or the director's point of view, a straight play is arithmetic and a musical is algebra or geometry. How many more elements have to be blended: the music, the dance, the costumes which allow for the dance! You have color and light and so forth in straight shows, but in musicals it's all those elements *and* more people creating them. It's not just the author and the director. It's the author, director, choreographer, lyricist, composer, arranger, so that the chances of screwing up are much greater.

Harold Prince (now a director) and David Merrick were successful producers. The Prince production record, as set forth in his book *Contradictions,* yields a score for twenty musicals produced between 1953 and

1974: eleven financial hits and nine nonrecoupments on Broadway, a success rate of 55 percent.[17] David Merrick's record from 1954 to 1968 shows that of twenty-three productions, 39 percent were flops and 61 percent hits. These records indicate that it is possible, over the years, for a skilled producer to hit the 50–60 percent mark of financial success. We must remember that failure to recoup on Broadway does not take into account possible later long-run subsidiary payoffs like stock and amateur and film sales. Nevertheless, it is apparent that over extended periods, two of the most experienced professional producers have profited in about three out of five attempts.

Another independent producer, Arthur Cantor, is characterized in *The Learning Annex,* a bulletin describing mini-courses and their teachers to the hopeful, as follows: "Mr. Cantor has a well-deserved reputation for carefully nurturing plays—and an excellent nose for hits. 'Really, my success rate is no more than 50–60%,' he says."[18] Mr. Cantor duly notes that costs are going up, investors are harder to find, good plays are scarce. But he is not daunted because if you do get a success, "then you feel like you've put a quarter in a slot machine and hit the jackpot." The love of gambling and of musicals militates against small low-risk business sense.

Of course, the curious lapses of sound business and artistic judgment are not limited to Broadway producers. It was reported in the *New York Times* that "Hollywood still counts on the blockbuster for most of its profits. The conventional wisdom is that 8 out of 10 films will lose money."[19] Three big hits during the summer of 1984 accounted for one-third of the film box office sales. And the situation does not seem to have changed since then.

The psychic cost of a flop to its creators is also high. As Laurents remarks:

You're never sure till you go through it. You can't prepare anyone for cancer . . . or marriage, or anything else. . . . The point is that if you have enough love for what you're doing, it'll carry you through. And if you're going to be defeated, I don't have much sympathy. I have made my living, a very good one, from writing. And I figure that if I can do it, then [others] can do it. If you just say, "I am going to survive," then you survive. And if you have a failure, you say, "This is not the end. Back to work." You crawl into the back of the cave, you lick your wounds, you say, "Okay, I have to go out and get food." People are reluctant to face adversity.

A hard line from the heights about the depths.

Failure arouses even fiercer ambition in the lyricist/director Martin Charnin:

They [young writers at NYU's Musical Theatre Program where Charnin is a mentor] don't know the agony of closing a musical. Not that we ever really want them to know. But I'm not sure if you can know the fun of getting through the mine field until you blow up once on the way there.

And those who stay with it will be blown up at least several times.

Meanwhile costs keep rising. The cost of producing the average film by a major movie company was estimated at about $29 million in the early nineties; Broadway musical theater production costs are variable but they also keep defying gravity. If "one mil can get you twenty" with a smash, then Broadway musical show biz, as Thorstein Veblen wrote long ago of industrial complexes that move toward monopoly, is only constrained by the next big deal—because of widespread demand for the product.

In his 1983 pamphlet, *The Broadway Theatre,* Schoenfeld described the attraction of Broadway:

The Broadway theater is one of the essential linchpins in the economy of the City. It's the largest tourist attraction by more than twice of museums. According to a 1977 Department of Commerce study, thirty-six percent of all tourists gave the Broadway theater as their reason for coming to New York. The second choice of seventeen percent of all tourists was the City's museums. It's the place more people went for entertainment than attended the sporting events of the Mets and the Jets, the Yankees and the Giants, the Rangers and the Knicks, the Cosmos and the Nets. It's a business of $223 million in the 1981–82 theatrical season [$262 million in 1988–89 and $502 million in 1991–92].[20]

Broadway musicals, like Hollywood films, are in continuous demand at home and abroad. Risk or not, they will keep coming.

Accelerating Costs

Schoenfeld's next observation relates to the only piece of data on which all observers of Broadway evidently agree: costs have risen markedly over the years, and most especially since the 1970s:

In 1983–84, the cost of producing a large musical is between three and five million dollars [in 1989–90, five to eight million]; the cost of producing a small musical is between one and one-half million dollars [in 1989–90, two to four million], and the cost of producing a small play is between five hundred and eight hundred thousand dollars. [This has also risen in 1990–92.]

The operation of theaters has become vastly more costly and economically risky so that. . . there is practically no relationship between 1984 costs and those of 1974.

Nor between those of 1993 and 1984.

Our respondents invariably give figures for production costs "then" and "now." These are initial capitalization costs, not those of operations after a show is running. A few examples offered by theater people in the early 1980s: *Pippin,* which was produced in 1972, cost $450,000. Today the price would be more like $4.5 million. *Follies* (1971) "cost something like seven hundred and fifty thousand dollars." And now? "You couldn't even touch it for less than $5 million." "It cost two and a half million dollars to do *The Phantom of the Opera* in London. . . . It cost $8 million to place it on Broadway (1989)." "You'd have to adjust the dollar to get a fair evaluation, but given that, it's still extraordinary."

There was a sustained collective cry against the rising costs of production. It was also agreed that these costs have gone far beyond the general rate of inflation. On this point some hard evidence exists. George Wachtel concluded after study that, "As a weighted average of musicals and plays, production costs (excluding *Nicholas Nickleby*) increased 62 percent from fiscal year 1980 to 1982 while operating costs rose 45 percent."[21] And that spiral, accompanied by a "staggering" rise in ticket prices, provoked widespread criticism.

Only a few, like Michael Bennett, who moved from one success to another until his premature death, quickly got used to the rise:

In the beginning, people said, "Oh, my God, it's going to cost a million dollars." The million dollar musical was like Wow. Then a couple of years ago it was the two-million dollar musical. By now [1983] we've reached four and five, right? But it's the same million dollar musical, plus inflation.

And so is the $10 million show in the 1990s.

It's the Other Guys

Attributing higher costs and price rises to inflation alone would be laughable to most theater people—many of whom are nonetheless at first given to doing just that. However, when we originally asked theater professionals about the reasons for rising costs, their "off the top of the head" answers pointed at "local" problems. Everyone blamed everyone else, with blue-collar unions being the favorite—but not the only—target. Here are a few answers:

It's certainly the unions. The stagehands and the man who pulls the curtain making as much money as practically any actor on stage. . . . Minimums are incredible. . . . Advertising—enormous. [Why?] Its costs are much higher because the electronic media are more expensive than the print media. . . . I just think there's so much greed among theater owners. . . . It's all bad producing.

The spontaneous response to questions of cost therefore is to fix blame on one of many culprits, roughly in this order: the blue-collar unions, advertising, the greed of theater owners, production and operating expenses for new technology, and sloppy management. Elizabeth McCann, a leading company manager, writing in *U.S. News and World Report,* with appropriate wit declares that "everybody on Broadway is in total agreement that the other guy gets too much money."[22] "The other guy" can be grouped into blue-collar unions, white-collar "associations," authors, producers, and theater owners. Let us look at these alleged generators of the accelerating costs of Broadway musicals.

Blue-Collar Unions

When people refer to "the unions," they tend to mean blue-collar folk: stagehands, electricians, maybe musicians or actors. The usual charge is featherbedding. Some representative comments:

Let us say it takes five guys to move the sets. If the theater has a contract with the stagehands union, we have to hire twenty men, but who needs so many? Most of them sit around. That's how costs go up.

The unions' point of view is that if they didn't tell a producer to use twenty-four musicians, he'd do it all with piano and drums. That's bullshit. But you shouldn't force a show to pay more musicians than it needs. . . . All the craft unions have similar rules. You'll find guys who just sit around. One man's job is to move an ashtray from here to there. It's just ludicrous.

A composer/lyricist complains:

I sat down with two general managers and said, "Tell me what costs $3 million." We came to the part where one said, "ten thousand dollars for stagehands overnight." For what? He said, "That's for their hotel room and board." "Where are they staying, the Carlyle?" All these stagehands were listening to Bobby Short, drinking brandy at three in the morning. Ten thousand dollars! Why don't they drive home to New Jersey?

A top executive in the musical theater industry protests that union wages are irreversible: "On a show-by-show basis, you can effect royalty reductions, the star will take less money, the theater less rent. But you can't do anything with the unions," except that the League of American Theatres and Producers did in fact induce these same unions to take a smaller, flatter percent increase in the middle eighties.

Next come complaints about the Actors Equity Union. Merle Debuskey counters these:

They [actors] have to go out and subsidize themselves to become performing artists. Then, when the time comes, someone will pluck them out, put them on the stage and have them perform. They not only subsidize themselves. They subsidize the theater. They're not overpaid, Lord knows; they're underpaid.

Without reviewing the complications of negotiating for a "fair wage," it can be said that in the 1960s, actors were indeed relatively underpaid. But by the 1990s, those who were gainfully employed (10 to 15 percent of all thirty-five thousand actors in the New York area in Actors Equity; the rest are unemployed) now earn relatively more due to union pressures and the rising Consumer Price Index. But in a similar vein, John Glasel, a past president of Local 802 of the Musicians Union, in response to the allegation of "high wages," points out:

Actually, our wages have risen slightly *less* than the cost of living. Let's go back to the base year of the CPI [Consumer Price Index] which is 1967. Our wage scale was two hundred dollars [weekly], we had higher percentages for doubling [musicians who play more than one instrument], and slightly higher requirements for a minimum number of minutes in the theater. . . . Maybe now [1983] $570 a week sounds like a lot of money, but we don't make that 52 weeks a year. You can do a show for three weeks and then look for work for the next six months.

Whatever the actual wages were in 1990 to 1992 (they rose with the CPI), Glasel's point is still valid. In show business it is less often true that the show is on and most often the case that the show is off. Being a union member does not guarantee jobs in a risky business. As anyone knows who has ever worked the night shift or waited on tables, many of these dancers, actors, and musicians are "between engagements."

Why is the Broadway industry so highly unionized? For the same reason that several other industries are highly unionized: abusive exploitation by property owners and producers. Bernheim's 1931 book included a chapter by Alfred Harding who listed some of the principal forms of abuse once suffered by actors. These are a few examples:

There was no standard contract. Each manager wrote his own and made sure that it contained a loophole through which he could get out of anything. . . . There was no limit to the free rehearsal period. . . . Strandings were fairly frequent, and when they occurred the actors were simply abandoned to their own resources. . . . Actors were often required to furnish their own transportation. . . . Companies or individuals might be laid off without pay at any time. . . . Salaries might be cut without warning. . . . Companies could be closed without notice. . . . The manager might require up to fourteen performances a week without any increase in compensation.[23]

We are mindful that this list applies not only to actors but also to others. (One composer told us that in the "good old days," the original Shubert brothers used his songs and refused to pay him.) The formation of craft unions in the theater industry was a direct result of these and many other abuses—and without unions today, many such practices would no doubt quickly reappear.

On the other hand, one damaging charge against unions is that they too frequently overburden the development of shows before they are ready for full productions. Development entails "readings" with, perhaps, two or three week rehearsals before nonpaying audiences. An apparently legitimate grievance is that the unions impede these shows by cost demands and bureaucratic delays. Such troubles and nightmares are familiar to every one of our respondents.

However, the recurrent dream of many new producers and artists is a show that starts on a "shoestring," is permitted to develop with no unnecessary costs, and later becomes a "success." In 1983, Carol Hall described the development of *The Best Little Whorehouse in Texas* (which went on to become a huge hit):

We all worked for nothing. We didn't know what we had yet. We simply thought it seemed like a good idea. We did the whole thing over at Actors' Studio. . . . After four scenes and four songs, Actors' Studio said that they would pay the actors a hundred dollars each to mount a whole production with no set. We literally hung a Texas flag in the back—and I'm not kidding—people brought their clothes from home.

Such low-cost development is the instant-success dream of aspiring Broadway neophytes. For every such rare success, however, a myriad of undeveloped shows die aborning. It is in this early phase that every penny helps, and here, if anywhere, the unions are vulnerable to criticism for their share of rising costs—as well as impeding an artistic process (which needs time to rewrite, rehearse, and "critique") by making it prohibitively costly.

The Game of Points: White-Collar Guilds and Associations

But it is not only actors, stagehands, and musicians who have organized. So, for example, have press agents, lighting designers, directors, and choreographers. They belong to white-collar "societies," "guilds," and "associations."

In all there are at least seventeen unions and other groups that negotiate with theater owners and producers. Some contracts run several years with constrained increases in wages and salaries. But "white-collar" groups like directors and choreographers of late also obtain a percent of the gross

called "points," following in the recent trail of producers and theater owners. These points, it must be emphasized, are not from the *net* profits, but
from the weekly box office *gross* income. These ever-rising points also act
to raise costs.

The authors of shows—bookwriters, lyricists, and composers—have
received points—or royalties—for many decades. Unlike others in unions
or associations, they do not receive a salary or a fee for working on a show
—only points (sometimes given to them by the producer as a recoupable
advance). These percents have remained relatively fixed over many decades. Some complain that intransigent authors drive costs up. About this,
the composer Burton Lane remarks, "The claim that authors are getting
too much is ridiculous. In most cases the theater owners get a lot more
than they're entitled to, but authors are the first to give up their royalties
when a show isn't doing well. They may have spent five or six years
working on a show, by contrast with producers or backers just come in
with some money."

Peter Stone, bookwriter and president of the Dramatists Guild for some
time, makes this matter quite concrete:

Producers used to get half the profit. Then one day they gave themselves a half-
point of royalty. Today on our show, it's four points. What are they taking? $12,000
every week. The backers could maybe have been repaid with that money.

Stone also considers theater owners guilty of practically undetectable cor-
ruption:

It goes on all the time. The biggest area is what the theater takes in, the cash. It's
very hard to nail down what that is. Owners pay musicians and ushers, they pay
real estate taxes and insurance; they have a staff to run the house. Theirs is a very
large piece, and you don't exactly know what it is.

In a cash business, opportunities for theft are ubiquitous. Traditionally,
illicit gains from box-office theft within theater and producing organizations
have been called "ice." And the latest scandal in a long history hit in March
1992.[24]

Stone notes further:

Every group except the authors has a union. Stagehands have a union. Directors
have a guild. Writers have a guild in name, but it's not a union. It's the only group
that cannot legally bargain in the theater today because of anti-trust action brought
against it decades ago.

Theater owners have their own naturally obverse views, especially
about the guild people. Schoenfeld speaks to this point:

In many of our contracts with creative people we have no ability to negotiate freely. There is a built-in minimum. Then there's the royalty structure, which is based on a sharing of gross receipts. You have people sharing in them who have no interest whatsoever in net receipts. You have a topsy-turvy world of profit ascertainment. . . . If I'm making 10% or 5% of the gross, I have no real interest in what the net is unless someone comes to me and says, "I can't pay you your percentage any more." Since our royalty structures by and large have their roots in the past—30, 40 or 50 years ago—we are applying percentages to receipts which have far exceeded any cost-of-living or inflationary factors. [This has resulted in high operating costs.]

A vastly different view came from bookwriter John Weidman:

The lawsuit that the producers brought against the Dramatists Guild last year [1982] seemed to me to be an outrage. The piece of the pie which bookwriters get today is exactly the same as they got ten or twenty years ago. My percentage on *Pacific Overtures* (1976) is the same as my father's on *Fiorello* (1959) twenty years before me.

Actually, the precise percent is relative to the base or gross. Thus, while in the past authors did split 6 percent of the gross box office (lyricist, composer, bookwriter each receiving 2 percent), nevertheless, when in the old days the gross was lower, say a hundred thousand dollars, then 2 percent returned two thousand dollars a week. Today, when the gross is higher, maybe five hundred thousand dollars a week, 2 percent will return ten thousand dollars a week. Thus the percentage means a lot to producers, investors, and authors. The Dramatists Guild authors and the (then) New York League of Theatres and Producers negotiated in 1985 a new Approved Production Contract in which the percentage to authors starts at 4.5 percent, then remains at the "old" 6 percent—but only after investors are first paid off. (More about this in chapter 2.)

Rising Costs: The New Corporate Troika

So who controls the rising costs of Broadway musical theater? Our answer for the eighties and into the nineties is: no one person, no single group on any specific project. A cost control factor mostly overlooked by neoclassical economists arises from the application of a Veblenian idea that, in this instance, the social organization of musical production, like that of any other growing organization, undergoes basic changes that impact cost control arrangements. Each musical is a business that is managed within a corporate or company structure. Before the sixties, responsibility for cost control lay with a single executive, the producer. Since then, as we have pointed out, this solo effort has given way to a corporate troika composed of three major role groups: (1) the new directors (and their teams of designers); (2) multiproducers, and (3) the general managers. Such corporate changes and the attendant lack of central control have thus far allowed costs to take quantum jumps.

Essentially, in recent years, the *new directors* and their staffs of designers began to exert far stronger artistic leadership than in earlier times. The new director came to share financial power with the *general manager* (and staff) to whom budgetary control was delegated by multiple *coproducers* (and assorted corporate interests), who are also heavy investors. This structure replaced one in which the old-time single producer kept a dictatorial hold on both artistic and monetary matters. As the long-time producer Cy Feuer notes, "the [old] system's coming apart at the seams. . . . [Now] there's no cap on the [project] bottle."

The New Directors and Their Designers

During the sixties decade of culture shock, vintage story-based or book musicals, so dominant in the forties, fifties, and early sixties began to be replaced by musicals that emphasized "style" over "story." The smash hit *Hair* (1968) exemplified this trend. (Typically this success was followed by other "rock" musicals, mostly flops.) The change to style-dominated shows was led by director-choreographers. Thus, in the sixties there emerged a new generator of products—the new director. Into the forties, a "director" might not even get program credit. In the eighties, however, the new directors not only conceived ideas for shows but even collaborated on scripts. They now operated from a position of artistic strength, and, not incidentally, began to take a percent of the gross every week. And the kind of shows they conceived tended to cost more.

Cecil Smith and Glenn Litton, historians of the musical, write:

Company [1970], which won the Drama Critics Circle Award and a Tony for Best Musical, was. . . .typical [of] show[s] of the late 60's: its style had been determined as much by the director and choreographer as by its librettist and composer. Since the death of Oscar Hammerstein and at about the time of the dissolution of other long-standing partnerships, the style of musicals had been increasingly dictated by their directors [and] choreographers, the most active and influential of whom were Jerome Robbins, Michael Kidd, Joe Layton, Gower Champion, Michael Bennett, and Bob Fosse.[25]

Schoenfeld justifies the director's role, or the director-choreographer's increased power, by relating it to the complexities of staging recent innovative forms. So, for example, the old convention of curtains rising and falling is replaced by a continuous flow of action, with players in full view of the audience. The roles of director and choreographer sometimes fuse beyond any possibility of disengaging them.

Among those who celebrate the new director's ascendancy is the old-time producer Cy Feuer: "Michael Bennett and Hal Prince are conceptualists who deserve the total authority they get." But even Feuer adds that many directors "don't merit that designation or deserve so much power."[26]

Directors now take between 2 percent and 4-plus percent of the gross. And the new kinds of shows they dream up have also increased costs, particularly when they involve complex design. As Debuskey sees it:

These remarkable people conceived of technical equipment to produce something that was never seen before. . . . In the case of *Dreamgirls* they were able to invent light towers that did the choreography. . . . But that cost a lot of money. In *A Chorus Line*, because of computer boards, they were actually able to substitute lights for scenery.

Schoenfeld contends that directors are a *primary* source of higher cost. They

have supplanted creative producers in shaping the entire artistic package and now customarily share in authors' royalties as collaborators. *One result of the increased artistic sway of the director has been an increase in the cost and complexity of physical productions, since directors give "free rein" to designers* [emphasis added].[27]

In *The Phantom of the Opera,* according to the *New York Times,*

There are 210 lighting cues, 100 automation cues, 50 manual fly cues. They are not spread evenly throughout the performance but bunched at certain points. Two computer consoles, each manned by an operator, each two feet wide and 4 1/2 feet high, sit on an elevated bridge at stage right. They're the key to this complex automated production.

One computer handles the lighting, the other directs heavy scenic pieces such as the huge crystal chandelier, the Phantom's mirror, throne, opera box and mausoleum. All are programmed to move from a resting storage position to a targeted placement under controlled acceleration and deceleration speeds. The computer indicates what's in or out of position, with adjustments possible to one thirty-second of an inch.

But it all costs more money than the traditional set. *Phantom*'s operating costs are over four hundred thousand dollars weekly.[28] The production keeps going, however, because it consistently sells out on Broadway and around the world.

The Phantom of the Opera *(1988)*

The Phantom of the Opera (1988) represents the historical merger in the 1980s of the spectacles of early Broadway (1900s-1920s), the book-musical of the 1940s-1960s, the musical fusion of classical, operetta, and rock, the absence of "stars," and the creative use of computer-organized staging, as exemplified by the spectacular swinging chandelier. Produced by Cameron Mackintosh, directed by Harold Prince, book by Richard Stilgoe and Andrew Lloyd Webber, lyrics by Charles Hart with Richard Stilgoe, music by Andrew Lloyd Webber. (Photo credit: Joan Marcus.)

. . . And Set and Lighting Designers

The eminent set designer, Oliver Smith, observes that current fashions in set design are more architectural than they once were. Rather than use delicately painted sets, designers and their directors want to do iron and steel movable structures or just redo the theater for large effects. Now there is also motorization to move massive props or sets in perfect timing with computerized lights. This means less labor but, as Peter Neufeld, a leading general manager, says, the "little black box" may cost from ten to two hundred thousand dollars or more. Wherever this happens, set designers too will earn a percentage of the gross.

Sound Designers: A New Craft

The counterculture's electronic sounds, which nettled and unsettled an older generation in the 1960s, are now, with some modification, among the major sounds of Broadway theater. Some still bemoan this change. Again, Debuskey:

> The old theaters are acoustical marvels. I've heard of theaters built with help from the finest acoustical experts-and the sound isn't good in those places. [But] old theaters were not built for Moog synthesizers. When you have this kind of instrumentation, you have to amplify it in a way that falsifies the acoustical nature of those theaters.

But by the mid-eighties, budgets called for a sound designer with several assistants. Actors and stages were "miked"; even the audience was beginning to be wired with "rent-a-mikes."

Sound design, like costume, set, and lighting design, is now part of any Broadway show. It is not cheap. Equipment costs. Replacing it with state-of-the-art equipment at frequent intervals costs more. Doing so also gives somebody else a piece of control over how the show runs, thereby reducing the director's, the conductor's, and the orchestra's artistic input. Somewhere out of sight and out of the musicians' earshot, a sound mixer is at work. A mixer is an additional designer whose services do not come for free. Thus, the rising costs of technology are a major factor in continuous price rises and in production costs for all the labor-intensive performing arts.

The New Director as Creative Producer

Our interviewees provide abundant testimony to the effect that directors not only assist bookwriters, composers, and lyricists but now and again take the lead in seeing to it that the show is produced. Stephen Schwartz, lyricist and, at the start, also director for a new musical, indicated that he played "producing agent" not only by paying for and setting up workshop readings but also by soliciting support from theater owners, record companies, and other potential backers. Michael Bennett and Harold Prince as directors took charge of new projects in the manner described by Schwartz.

However, while the roles of producer and director usually coalesce if played by the same person, they also clash. One observer remarks that sometimes Prince, as director, says, "I need a new costume for this character," while Prince, as producer, says, "We can't afford it." More often, there is a problem between the new directors and the new multiproducers. Tommy Tune reports that the producers took his "check-writing authority" away on one show because things got out of hand.

Who are the new multiproducers and how do they affect rising costs?

The New Multiple Producers: "They Cain't Say No"

The single, sometimes creative, producer has been generally replaced by a group, often consisting of absentee business-oriented investors. This is a fact that we can hardly overemphasize. One respondent goes so far as to claim, "We no longer have *any* producers." Why did the shift to multiple producers take place?

Sheldon Harnick (along with producer Claire Nichtern and designer Oliver Smith) offers some insight. He pictures old-time producers who years ago could seek out and find many small backers willing to invest five or ten thousand dollars in a show. Occasionally, the sum might rise to fifty or a hundred thousand. "But today, if a musical's to cost $4 million, it's often necessary to approach big companies. They are sure to have deep pockets. Now, with a slew of names over the title, you find eight people each to put up five hundred thousand dollars. The number of failures is enormous. We go on. But it's almost impossible without corporate and real estate support."

And so, in the eighties, because large sums of money were needed, producers rarely turned to small private investors. Musicals became big deals running $2–10 million in production cost and up to $5 million for a tour such as that of *Starlight Express* in 1989.[29] The older producers and newer directors report struggles with the more powerful type of producer and backer. Tommy Tune: "We got *Nine* on without corporate support. Now Universal promoted *Whorehouse;* but in my dealings with another studio. . . . I find they are greedy and just want to suck off it."

Historically, film companies have periodically tried to penetrate the attractive turf of Broadway musicals. They tried in the late twenties, again in the thirties, and then in the seventies. Smith and Litton documented some of their efforts in the seventies.[30] Universal financed *The Best Little Whorehouse in Texas*. Paramount helped back *My One and Only*. But *Variety* reported in 1984 that "film companies, recently a significant source of legit investment capital, backed off collectively. MCA-Universal bankrolled two shows: *Doonesbury* and *Open Admissions*, both of which failed to attract survival attendance."[31]

These days many Broadway people are understandably wary of film companies. Martin Charnin's views resonate with others'. Speaking of Twentieth-Century Fox, he declares that because of them, "I ended up being a producer on *The First*. They pulled out some money and left us holding the bag for half a million dollars." (It flopped.)

Many investors see themselves as producers, and receive credit accordingly. But old-line producers who developed from within the Broadway milieu regard them as inept, indifferent to stagecraft, and prone to "solving a problem" by fatuously throwing money at it. Many are fly-by-night. Peter Neufeld gently dismisses them as having a "limited frame of reference for the theater."

These daring but inexperienced neophyte gamblers are characterized by a close observer:

One of the real limitations of the musical theater has a lot to do with the stupidity of producers. They get it into their heads that because something is a success every show that follows has to be like it. All of a sudden every producer wanted to do a rock musical like *Hair* and there have been forty since *Hair* opened in 1967 that have been absolute flops. . . . I loved *Hair,* I thought it was marvelous, but there was only one *Hair.* You don't create that kind of thing a second time.

Lacking theater experience as such, they are adept at raising investment capital and this, Debuskey says, is at present the prime requirement for a producer who also takes more for himself: "What happened is that instead of getting office expenses of two hundred fifty dollars, three hundred dollars, or four hundred dollars a week, producers got a percent of the box office as their producing fee."

Debuskey contrasts the old-fashioned producers who knew how to cut costs and maintain quality with contemporary executives who do not:

An estimate came in for the costumes. Cy Feuer looked at them and got the costume designer in and said, "Goddammit, this is too much money! How can you justify that?" The guy said, "Well, they were soldiers and they had piping and it cost money to sew it all in." Cy made a call. "Hey Joe, in this number how many of these soldiers are up front?" There were four. "Okay, you can put piping on the front four and for the rest of them just paint it on." If you take that and multiply it, then you know what I mean.

I've seen shows where they do a whole new set of costumes for one number. . . . Then they change the number, but it's not working, so they change the number once more and you have another whole set of costumes.

Feuer, whose career as a producer on Broadway spanned the fifties, sixties, and seventies, sees multiproducers (from the film business or other nontheater background) holding an ultimate and unfortunate veto, with a resultant looseness of cost control.

Prices are so high that the angels now get billing as producers and they have the say. If you put up two hundred and fifty thousand dollars I guess that buys you a credit. Or maybe it's up to three hundred thousand now. This is the price for being a producer. We never worked that way. . . . A show is being done that takes four weeks out of town. We used to do it in one week. You know what that means? You've got to book the theater, you've got to keep the company on. . . . Also when it [the budget] has gone up to $4 and $5 million—what difference is another two or three hundred thousand? There is no one [person] sitting there who has been with the production every step of the way, who knows where to spend money, where to pull in, what's worth doing and not worth doing.

Today's producers, lacking theatrical experience, more and more turn their project over to a director, giving him or her carte blanche. And "if that person says he needs another week's rehearsal with the entire company but he wants to get everything orchestrated tonight, it costs a lot more money for no good reason."

But it is not always so simple. Bernard Jacobs, president of the Shubert Organization, explains:

We have a degree of sophistication the British don't have. . . . You can go to plenty of London shows and they may have 70 to 100 lights. In New York you'll never see a show with fewer than 300. *Dreamgirls* had 950. The decision of where to spend money is not the producer's as much as the creative person's—whether that's Trevor Nunn or Peter Hall or Michael Bennett. And when they say something is necessary for the creative success of the show, what producer is going to say no? [32]

Maybe producers are the primary reason for higher costs?

The Theater Owner-Producers

In recent years, theater owners are often part of a producing group. As Debuskey sees it, the fact that theater owners have become producers also affects costs.

Cy Feuer and Ernest Martin, Producers (ca. 1957)

Two partners who represent the pre-1980s model "on-line" Broadway producers: Cy Feuer *(right)* wrote original scripts, rewrote others, and controlled the artistic budget closely. Ernest Martin did the corporate work. In the 1980s, multi-producers became financial backers and budget control was shared with the company manager and the director. Costs rose under this new "corporate troika." (Photo credit: Billy Rose Theatre Collection, New York Public Library.)

More often than not they bring in something that's already been done elsewhere. . . . They can't operate seventeen and a half theaters and five around the country and [be] reviewing all potential properties produced in English and raising the money for all these shows and operating every day with the creative elements helping determine what will happen the very next day. Therefore [they] are less concerned about the economics of a single project than the [old, on-line] producer would be.

The view that theater owners are loose about cost is, however, rejected by Schoenfeld, who knows that there is nothing new about the theater-owner-as-producer. On the contrary,

Up until the early forties the theater owner was a major producer of shows. The Shuberts were the largest producers of shows in the history of the American theater and still are. They produced two hundred fifty shows, five times more than anyone else ever produced. Klaw and Erlanger were large theater producers. [So were] Broadhurst, Cort, . . . Froman.

Then, in the forties, public investment was brought into the theater [through "limited partnership"]. When the war years started it was very risky just to own a theater. Producing a show and owning a theater was doubly risky. Of course, it may be doubly lucrative if you succeed. . . . Theater owners became, more or less, landlords while other people became producers.

That lasted until about 1970 when there was a recession. The urban center, especially in New York, suffered badly. The theater district became notorious. The very existence of theaters was threatened, not only by economics, but also by concentrated pornography. Traditional sources of investment capital dried up and theater owners returned to producing, not to exclude independent producers, but because they needed to fill their theaters.

Schoenfeld suggests that the theater-owners-as-producers were as canny about money, at least in the pre-World War II era, and as sensitive to good product as were the old independent producers. His version is convincing enough to make the zigzag pattern more complex and puzzling than it seems, at first blush, to be.

Theater owners also take a varying share of the box office gross. A *Variety* reporter in the mid-eighties informs us that most booking deals provide for the theater to get 25 percent of the box office take, that it remains unclear how much is "profit," that all Shubert theaters on Broadway are mortgage-free, and that all pertinent figures are very hard to come by.[33] However, when we asked Schoenfeld about a formula for theater owners, he replied that there is no uniform formula. Agreements often provide that the theater gets its cost plus about 10 percent which can be reduced if the show is not profitable. He pointed out that a theater could often return some of its percentage by providing stagehands, musicians, advertising, and other expense monies. He noted that in the eighties the Shubert Organization spent millions of dollars to refurbish older theaters, to accommodate the acoustical requirements of the new electronic sounds, and for more orchestra room as well as theater changes for the new megaspectacles. Furthermore, Schoenfeld explains, deals are not identical. Even a deal giving a theater 25 or 30 percent of the gross usually works out to net about 12 or 13 percent of the gross.

But it must also be mentioned that the theater owners traditionally keep the interest returns on advance sale of tickets. *Cats* had an advance sale of over $5 million; after two years on Broadway, *The Phantom of the Opera* still had $23 million in advance sales. In the early nineties, however, the Shubert Organization did yield a "sizeable hunk" *(Variety)* of the "float," or advance sales, to the new-style producer of *Phantom of the Opera* and *Miss Saigon.* [34]

The Effects of Multiproducers

As to quality, composer-lyricist Stephen Schwartz comments that multi-producers are not likely to have the kind of vision attributed to Leland Hayward (producer of *South Pacific*) or Harold Prince, or those who dared to stage shows like *Company* (a hit) or *Sweeney Todd* (a show that did not recoup investors' "expectations" during its first Broadway run). "A theater owner [or investor] is likely to say, 'I could sell Debbie Reynolds [a star] and so-and-so in such-and-such.' That's why you have certain second rate shows running right now." While this stereotype is too often accurate, in fairness to investor-producers or theater owners-who-produce it must be pointed out that no single "role group" (producers, authors, theater own-ers) has a prior claim to "high quality." In fact, (1) whether a show will be a hit or a flop is random, and (2) the cost of a show is not related to its artistic quality.

Prince contemplates all this:

Economics has a negative effect on the variety of musical material. It phases out the creative producer and brings in what the *New York Times* so fulsomely reported a few weeks ago, the corporate producer. Well, I don't think corporations should be producing; they should be patrons, but there's a difference. Creative producing did, in the old days, involve people who for one reason or another—generally lack of writing talent, but with great taste—wanted to be in the musical business.

The *New York Times* theater critic, Frank Rich, suggests that the multi-producer musical is simply inefficient:

There are shows like *Sweeney Todd* which won all the Tony Awards and ran over a year [fifteen months]. They do fairly good business and don't make their investment back. That's faulty producing in my mind. They let their own costs get out of control and those costs are passed on to the theatergoer.

General manager Bob Buckley (like Feuer and Debuskey) phrases his objection in different terms. He abhors "producing by committee. I think it probably escalates the cost. Decisions are not made in a timely fashion. Tight cost control is not kept. We have a new animal [with more power] called the general manager [who] becomes the line producer."

The General or Company Manager

We questioned Peter Neufeld, one of Broadway's most experienced general managers, about this new figure in the power structure:

He or she is someone hired by a producer who has optioned a property. He has to raise money, and prepare budgets for the production. . . . We have seventeen [unions], all on one- to three-year contracts. By the time you get familiar with the rules of a couple of unions, some of the others are up for renewal. . . . A lot of items on a budget are factual, but not all of them. You can't really find up front what you'll spend on orchestrations or exactly how much a set will cost. All you can do is read a script and hope to make an intelligent judgment based on what you read.

Producers often ask me, in one area or another, do you think we're making the right decision? Meaning all of us. If the show runs, all the decisions we made were right. If the show closes, all the decisions were wrong.

One of the major decisions to be made is the selection of a property. If it closes, it was a bad idea to choose that property. Each time out on a show, I don't so much mind making another mistake. I just don't want to make the same mistake.

Nevertheless, general managers are subject to periods of low income and the demands of inept producers. This may be one reason for the large number of poor shows and the high proportion of flops. The gambling attitude is common to less-than-professional producers who hire company managers and their firms to do a show.

If you have no work in your office, if you have no shows running, nothing about to go into production, and somebody walks in with a property and wants to do it, my critical eye might be somewhat more generous. Desperation will do that.

Buckley speaks concretely to cost control strategies under the old and new general managers and multi- (non-theater-professional) producers:

I think also you've got something that's unfortunate in our business: because the number of shows has gone down, the competition has dropped in construction shops. For *Show Boat,* we had a chart on the wall with thirty-two pages of drawings. Sixteen different shops bid for the show, all professional, high-class, in New York, Washington—the bids ranged from 200 to 493 thousand dollars. Same show.

And we found the two lowest bidders. One of them was a very good shop in terms of construction; the other one was a very good shop in terms of paint. We took a look and analyzed their bids and found that one was lower than the other—and construction was cheaper from the second shop. We split the show up. That takes a lot of analysis and a lot of work on the part of a producer or the general manager.

But the common process is much different these days. As Buckley puts it, "The new general manager has taken over in helping the producer. I mean, he'll take bids and go with the guy who's just within his budget and with whom he's comfortable [and avoid the hard work of cost analysis]." All of which makes us suspect that often general managers also contribute both to flops and to rising costs.

Rising Costs and Flops

This brief analysis of the new directors, multiproducers, and general managers provides a clearer view of the new business organization as it developed in the late seventies and throughout the eighties for large Broadway musicals. Even smaller shows reflect the new corporate troika pattern. We suggest that this arrangement, and the resultant corporate incompetence, was a major factor in loosening the purse strings for most of the musicals on Broadway in the seventies and eighties. Along with it went a chronic inflation, which, in a labor-intensive industry, greatly aggravates the rising costs of new technology.

But constantly increasing production and operating costs did *not* correlate with the rise and fall in flops of the eighties. It is true that the business of Broadway musicals was more fraught with financial failures in the early and middle part of that decade. Since the 1978–79 season, when twelve of fourteen musicals flopped (about 86 percent), the seasonal percentage of flops was mostly *more* than the average 76 percent (see Figure 1.2). But it is also true that in the 1989–90 season, the percentage of flops *dropped* to this average, at the same time as costs, gross box office, and, we presume, profits, rose to new heights. In the next chapter, we trace this modest epicycle from its lower point to its height—and examine the rapid evolution of Broadway musical theater as a rationalized industry in the eighties.

2. The Fall and Rise of Broadway in the Eighties

In the early eighties once again (like a doomsday prophecy) it looked to the New York City press like a time for sensationalism: "Broadway is . . . in its worst economic season in a decade. . . . What remains uncertain is whether the slump is part of Broadway's cyclical nature or the harbinger of a long-term decline." Elsewhere the public was informed that "attendance dropped 22%" from the prior year, gross receipts fell 13 percent, fifteen of thirty-nine theaters stood empty, and "11 others may go dark" in the next few weeks. A decline in the "number of new productions" and the "low quality" of shows completed the annual litany of gloom.[1] Even Harold Prince, rocked by a set of costly large-scale musicals that did not recoup, ruminated about the possible eclipse of Broadway as the "demise of the dinosaurs," and young Frank Rich echoed the old refrain dating back to the twenties in his *New York Times* article entitled "What Ails Broadway Musical Theater?"

Gerald Schoenfeld viewed the slump as part of a national recession and as a manifestation of the theater industry's cyclical nature. He noted that times were even worse in the late sixties and early seventies, followed by an "up" cycle from 1976 to 1981. And so on back to the twenties and thirties, forties and fifties, where in each decade the cries about the total collapse of the not so "fabulous invalid" resounded over and over. But the enormous adaptability, or flexibility (Bernheim's term) of Broadway entrepreneurs and the limitless public thirst for American musical theater kept the situation, as Finian (of *Finian's Rainbow*) put it, "hopeless—but not serious."

Nevertheless, recovery from the slump of the early seventies brought rapid and radical changes by the late eighties. Under severe assault about their very existence, the executives of the then League of New York Theatres and Producers followed the path·of other profit-based industries. They organized a research and development unit, attacked problems in the inner city theater neighborhood, began audience surveys, introduced more effective marketing techniques aided by computers and television, persuaded the unions to restrain their demands for several years, collaborated with authors and investors to create guidelines for a new Approved Production Contract (APC), and became the League of *American* Theatres and Producers. Independent producers, members of the League as well as nonmembers, fought back against rising costs. They raised ticket prices, searched for new material in other regions of the country and in foreign lands, increased the drawing power of their products by better marketing and introduced "megaspectacles," expanded their operations into Off-Broadway and regional theaters, and invaded world markets with high-powered touring companies. By the late eighties—'87 to '90—the flop-success ratio had fallen to its historical average and lo! the media shouted Broadway's praises. This chapter will trace the outcome of this epicycle and indicate how the American musical show biz industry moved toward a "rationalized" condition in the decade of the eighties—with every likelihood of more to come in the nineties.

The League and Survival

The League's R & D Unit. For our purposes in this book, Broadway signifies a system financially dominated by musical theater; it is also a small part of the American entertainment business. In this sense Broadway by no means consists of a single corporate structure. It is, rather, embodied in a loose confederation of executives, primarily producers and theater owners who are a major source of money. In the early part of the century, each theater owner and producer was a law unto himself. The New York League of Theatres and Producers was formed early in the thirties. In part, it owes its existence to its opponent, Actors Equity, the union that had struck against theaters and producers but simultaneously sought a mechanism for industry-wide bargaining. Thus competitive owners and producers came together.

Over the years this League was rather inchoate, but by the seventies it came to the membership that through their association they could collectively tackle a variety of problems specific to Broadway. Early in the eighties, Harvey Sabinson surveyed for us the new politics of economic survival on Broadway:

I joined the League in '76. For years many problems had impacted the theater. The League pondered these problems and decided to expand its function by creating a Department of Special Projects.

And in order to fund it they proposed a self imposed tax, each show paying a special assessment of six hundred dollars for musicals and four hundred dollars for straight plays. That program continues to this day and I became the Director of Special Projects.

City Hall was ready to write off midtown New York. . . . If it's going into the sewer [the porno business], then let it go into the sewer. . . . But we weren't ready to write it off.

We began to realize that all the things we were doing were band-aids on gaping wounds and that what would really help the area was economic development. . . . One of the first moves we made was to sponsor a study on the economic impact of the Broadway theater. The gist of our findings provided us with proof that we are an important economic resource of this city. Our impact on the metropolitan region alone is over three-quarters of a billion dollars. What happens with theater affects hotels, restaurants, the taxi cab industry, parking lots, and retail establishments in the area. We were able to show just how staggering losses were in that period [when a strike shut down theaters] and to provide data that became a significant document in the political community.[2]

Supporting Theaters and Developing Markets. Thus, New York City in the mid-eighties officially recognized that the theater district was a major asset to its economy, so that even when a theater is dark, or has run a succession of flops, its overall contribution to the district and to the city continued to be salutary. A big, so far unresolved problem persists: how to carry losing theaters. There were proposals to create a special fund for their purchase. The city then permitted sale of "air rights" over these buildings, and even moved to talk about tax relief for some theaters when they are dark. In addition, builders of new structures who put theaters into their skyscraper hotels or office buildings received special tax incentives before the "sunset provision" halted this offer. These and other such measures are traceable to constant struggle and interminable negotiation between the League and the city. Whether such effort can prevent further loss of old Broadway theaters is always uncertain. But it has fostered development of a theater in the new Marriott Hotel on Broadway, which began its operations with one long-lasting hit from England, *Me and My Gal* (1987–1990). Perfect for the tourists, who, according to Harvey Sabinson, make up two-fifths of the Broadway audience:

In 1981 when we sold 10.1 million tickets, four million of those [40 percent] went to tourists, and a million of those [10 percent] were foreign tourists [40 percent tourists, 10 percent foreign is a ratio that holds in 1992]. Our "I Love New York"

Harvey Sabinson, Executive Director; George Wachtel, Director of Research, The League of American Theatres and Producers (1992)

In the 1980s, The League of New York Theatres and Producers became The League of American Theatres and Producers because "Broadway" had become a more national and international industry. Harvey Sabinson (the first administrative head in the 1970s) became executive director of the League's considerable projects (including environmental clean-up, legislative affairs, etc.) and George Wachtel became the first director of research (market surveys for shows, trends in sales, etc.). (Photo credit: Stephanie Taddeo.)

campaign goes all over the world [showcasing Broadway as New York City's leading tourist attraction].

The Broadway Audience(s): Survey Research. What "Broadway audience" means is vague not only because of tourists but also because New York City itself provides different kinds of audiences. Knowing this, owners and producers realized that it was time for a more rigorous method with which to learn about the audience(s) attending Broadway shows. A survey ordered by the League in the late seventies[3] revealed these demographics: about half of the average audience earned well over the national income average; more than half, around 54 percent, were college graduates; the new Broadway audience was affluent, educated, professional (51 percent), and young:

The composition of the Broadway audience has changed dramatically over the last several years. The study shows a large influx of *new theatergoers*—almost one out of three have apparently become Broadway patrons within the last five years. It is significant that a vast majority of the *new* patrons are young people—almost one out of two is under 25, and close to nine out of 10 are under 35.

As a result of these trends, the composition of the Broadway audience has changed significantly in recent years. It is exceedingly young today, with *six out of 10 theatergoers being under 35 years of age.* In 1971, more than half were over 35. [In 1980, 81 percent were under fifty.][4]

The suburban areas account for 45% of the volume—almost one out of two persons in the audience.[5] The heavy theatergoers (4-plus a year) account for an estimated 70% of the total volume. A similar concentration of the audience also exists for specific types of shows.[6]

The study identified four audience segments of varying size. *Traditionalists* are veteran, more serious theatergoers who attend many times a year, and on a "let's go out" basis. *Theater Enthusiasts* have a strong interest in Broadway in general, and like musicals and plays with contemporary value and treat each outing as a "special event." *Entertainment Seekers* have been attending Broadway for many years, and prefer shows that are light, typically musicals. *Dispassionate Theatergoers* have less interest in Broadway in general, but may be attracted by a particular show.[7] Evidently, it is the older audience that decries higher and higher ticket prices, but that segment is a minority. The present generation of New York and national audiences more or less willingly pay the new prices.

Furthermore, Sabinson informs us: "We do constant audience studies that benefit each show. Show by show, we do media research which will tell them how best to spend their advertising dollars to get their audience." A case in point is *Black and Blue* (1989), an all-black musical revue; as reported in the *New York Times,* an audience survey showed that 70 percent were from outside the New York metropolitan area, and 50 percent of these were foreign visitors but only 10 percent were black. The general manager "immediately went into foreign language publications" and "there's no question that the Tony [Awards] made us." Not a hit, this musical yet wobbled on into the nineties before it closed, not quite making its money back on Broadway.[8]

The 1980 survey findings also showed that television advertising and perceptions of more choice of good shows had the most appreciable impact on consumers. A "choice of good shows" has always been the issue in any entertainment medium. Ability to charge tickets, telephone ordering, and the availability of lower-priced tickets (TKTS) also appeared to be positive factors in the high attendance of sizable consumer segments. These practices were initiated in the late 1970s and developed in the 1980s.

The Corporate Marketing of Musicals

The current corporate marketing of Broadway musicals entails use of computers, surveys, ad campaigns, and, nowadays, exposure of Broadway hits through the nationally televised Tony Awards.

Selling Tickets with Computers. Disparate interest groups—conjoined in the League—having cooperated on limited business, found more to do together, not least to facilitate the purchase of tickets. At present, tickets cost more, but they are much easier to come by.

Sabinson describes marketing methods undertaken in the eighties:

> We did a research project on the computerization of box office receipts which proved conclusively that it was feasible. The Shubert Organization did a study and all its box office and bookkeeping procedures are computerized now. Just on the purchase of tickets, [the computer] tells a customer [about] potential seats by the press of a button. And you can look ahead: "What are my advance sales like for two weeks? How can I adjust my advertising budgets to improve that situation?"

This system went nationwide in 1986. Anyone in the United States—or elsewhere in the world—became just a phone call and credit card away from a Broadway show in a Shubert house.

To be sure, selling tickets by phone and credit card for major events classified as entertainment began in the late sixties. And Broadway entrepreneurs, like most executives faced with radical innovation, resisted the change. But by the late eighties, private entrepreneurs had launched nationwide ticket services, such as Ticketmaster, which, in 1990, had a central computer (in Los Angeles) installed to spit out seventy five thousand tickets an hour, giving a phone customer the best seat available and reducing the number of available single seats (difficult to do by mere humans in box offices). By now customer lists help market additional tickets for season subscriptions and provide box office facts to theater owners that can prove very useful. During the early eighties slump on Broadway, state legislators proposed a new tax on ticket sales. However, computer analyses of marginal theaters enabled the Shuberts to persuade key legislators to drop the idea.

Surveys and census data show that an even larger Broadway market is there.

Schoenfeld is bullish:

In my opinion there is a limitless [New York] market: Seventeen to eighteen million tourists [in 1983; more like twenty million in 1990] last year and the New York megalopolis conservatively, within a narrow radius, means fifty million people. Let's say only half are potential theatergoers. Or a third. That's a third of seventy million. You have a lot out there to tap.

The Ticket Sails

In the mid-seventies everything was set for a great decision, the entrepreneurial moment of truth—to wit, a sharp increase in ticket prices. Not just a rise but the breaking of several psychological barriers. That decision was implemented around 1973 for Broadway theaters and in 1975 for the tour (see figure 2.1). The effect on box office gross was marked, and probably overwhelming even to the executives who ordered it. In the years 1974–75 to 1980–81, Broadway box office income increased from about $50 million to about $200 million and there was comparable prosperity on the road. By 1987, the yield rose to a fairly constant $8 million a week, or over $420 million a year from both Broadway and the touring companies. In 1989–90, a new record of over $650 million was recorded for Broadway and the tours.[9]

But production and operating costs continued to rise. In late 1989, major Broadway musicals raised their "top" to fifty-five dollars and *Jerome Robbins' Broadway* went to sixty dollars. It had been capitalized at more than $8 million—and failed to break even after nearly a two-year run on Broadway. *Miss Saigon* announced sixty-dollar orchestra and rear mezzanine tickets with a one-hundred-dollar front mezzanine section, and that produc-

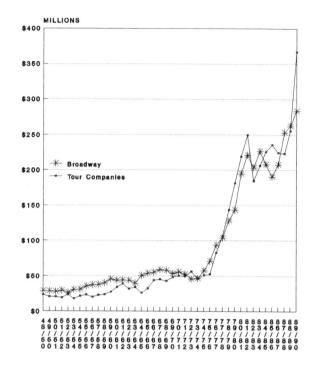

MILLIONS

Source: *Variety* 6/6/90

Figure 2.1 Season Box Office Totals (Broadway and Tour Companies, 1948–1990)

tion was capitalized at $10 million! Ticket prices and production plus operating costs constantly defy the law of gravity.

Jules Fisher (lighting designer and sometime-producer) explains:

The economics of the Broadway theater are very strange. We have a finite number of seats. Everything else escalates every year: inflation causes the price of scenery, the cloth to make costumes, taxes, plus union rates for actors, technicians, stagehands and porters to go up. We do not add another seat to the theater. There are still 1150 seats at the Broadhurst Theatre. No matter what you do, you can't get more people to see it in one evening. That's an odd fact. . . . The only way to pay for a production that has to cost more . . . [due to rising expenses for technology and personnel] is to pay for it in the ticket—unless you have a subsidy.

Schoenfeld adds context and justification:

Don't forget: theater is merely one aspect of the performing arts. It happens to be the one aspect . . . that pays taxes and is not given any benefits of non-profit status.

They [opera, dance] lose money, but they lose it in another way. They can afford to lose money knowing that they will not go out of business. They can get by on grants or subsidies. If *we* don't make it, we go out of business.

An analysis of prices by Baumol, Wolff, and Baumol, in 1986, argued that even the rapid price rise in tickets "did not fully make up for the previous erosion [during the Depression] in purchasing power . . . until the season 1982–83" and that "theater prices [over the post World War II] period" have gone up at rates similar to movies, major league baseball, and non-profit performing arts. Finally, they suggest that in spite of these rises in ticket prices, theatrical production and operating costs are still a heavy pressure, but ticket prices are within the purchasing power of present-day patrons. [10] So Broadway shows remain as glitzy as ever.

Segmental Marketing

Schoenfeld explains the system of selling tickets:

We market our tickets in many different ways. We sell them at full price, we sell them at half price through the discount ticket booth, we sell them on two-fers at one stage of the run. We sell groups at considerable discounts, we sell theater parties at discounts. We, in effect, have a mean price which is far under the price that people talk about.

But the average top ticket price also keeps rising (see figure 2.2).

The discounting of tickets, which is cited virtuously as a burden to the theater executives, is actually part of a method for increasing the volume of attendance, allowing a higher gross and more profit. One could call the system "segmental marketing."

Buckley also deals with the question of how this system works:

Bernie Jacobs reported in the *Times* the other day that if *Cats* were $100 a ticket, it would still sell out. What will happen then? There are going to be people who will pay $100. The number who pay $100 is going to be less than the number paying $50. You take those tickets, cut the price in half and make them available to another marketing segment. Then maybe cut them again—that's another group of people who will buy them. You can keep discounting and finding different markets.

We had low ticket prices on *Show Boat.* We also started the dinner-show package where for $37.50 you get dinner, parking, and an orchestra seat. And you know what? If we had charged *more* for the tickets, *Show Boat* would have run through Christmas. . . . The system licked us; we tried to fight it.

The final note (or the last blow) was struck in the mid-eighties when Off-Broadway theaters raised their ticket prices, with good financial results.

Bernard Jacobs's logic is elegant and irrefutable: "If Broadway theaters

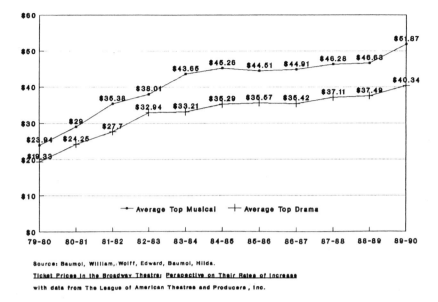

Figure 2.2 Average Top Ticket Price in Broadway Theaters, 1979–1990

slashed their prices, would we have more attendance? Probably. Less income? Yes. Could we exist? No."[11]

Ticket Prices and Attendance

Sheldon Harnick describes the social psychology of price and attendance, adding more detail about the rising expectations of the Broadway audience:

Because a show costs so much, the ticket prices have to be high, and when the ticket prices are high, I think an audience justly begins to expect something eye-popping, something so startling and so stunning that they feel they've had their money's worth; whereas, for instance, if I go to the Manhattan Theatre Club or the Circle Repertory Company Off Broadway, I've paid a much smaller price and I will be happier with a work that's interesting, but flawed.

In the early eighties a large majority of those we interviewed judged that the decrease in attendance (from a high of ten million or more in 1980–81 to about six million in 1982–83) was directly related to ticket price and a dire threat in and of itself (see figure 2.3). However, this figure also shows (1) that between 1970 and 1975, ticket prices stayed even, while attendance went down and up; (2) between 1975 and 1980, ticket prices went up and so did attendance; and (3) between 1985 and 1990, ticket prices

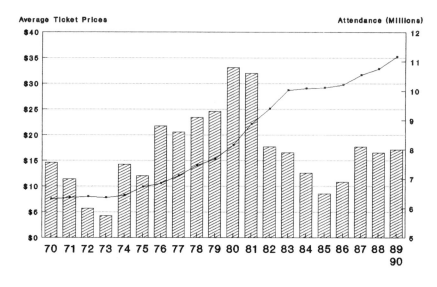

Figure 2.3 Attendance and Average Broadway Ticket Prices, 1970–1990

continued upward as attendance rose and remained the same. Other factors? Yes, like recessions in 1971–72 and 1981–82. But there is a certain constancy in one major factor—the increase of ticket prices.

The New Shows: Spectacle and Marketing

The volume of ticket sales depends to some significant extent on the strength of the "attractions" or "products." In the seventies, the "concept-musicals" of the Harold Prince-Stephen Sondheim team broke new artistic ground on Broadway, with, for example, shows like *Company* (1970), *Follies* (1971), and *Pacific Overtures* (1976); but three out of six failed to recoup the original investment, though most were *succès d'éstimes*. When Prince went to England to do *Evita* with Andrew Lloyd Webber, he doubted very much that it could leave London. But his political show—despite the experts—became a hit on Broadway in 1978. Prince himself labeled it a "revue-with-an-umbrella for a story." It also had the glow of spectacles-to-come. In 1980, Merrick went for a "revue-spectacle" with a slight semblance of a book and flashy choreography, and *42nd Street* became a smash hit for tourists and yuppies. But the spectacle of the eighties with its new musical sound (semi-"classical" and soft rock by Lloyd Webber and others) offered something different in the high-tech *Cats*—and audiences responded wildly. Even a show like *A Chorus Line*—enacted on a bare stage —projected an image in its advertising of a Broadway spectacle.

These large musicals—"revue-spectacles"—were marketed and priced in the eighties style and became lead shows for tours of regional theaters and international markets. The blockbuster, film-industry style advertising for *Cats* was especially adroit. As Claire Nichtern told us:

I saw *Cats* twice in London, and I think it was stunning, not just "Yes, it was good" —it was stunning. In the transfer there was a lot of work done. And I would say that it was glitzed to pull in New York-oriented American audiences. In London it had a quieter core. Here they've hyped it and I like the London production better. But it doesn't matter because it came in with a six and one half million dollar advance and it was marketed beautifully. The Shubert Organization did an absolutely magnificent job in the transfer.

But many other shows were shipwrecked crossing either way. And Nichtern strikes the classic chord: "Anybody who options a work can be in that position. Anybody can fall on his face. The fact that you're knowledgeable doesn't mean you're not going to have flops."

Rewards for Investors and Authors

Background. We alluded to a troubling situation in chapter 1, and it bears elaboration. By the early eighties, certain smoldering issues between playwrights, represented by the Dramatists Guild, and producers, then organized as the League of New York Theatres and Producers, led to a lawsuit. The issue was, what percentage of the box office would go to authors, producers, and investors—and in what order would they receive it? In pre-World War II days, such calculations were often made on net profit. By the eighties, a formula had evolved by which authors received a percent of the box office gross. This shift in bookkeeping to gross receipts revolutionized the business, rendering it more difficult, more complex, and more anomalous. Conventional business is run on net profit, not on gross income. The shift, consolidated in turbulent times (the sixties and seventies), made it very hard to keep money under control, especially with constantly rising costs. Now, in the nineties, reference is not made to "gross" or to "net" but to "royalty pools."

Bernard Jacobs and Gerald Schoenfeld on the Set of Cats *(ca. 1982)*

In 1982 the Shubert Organization brought in the smash hit *Cats* from London and Bernard Jacobs, president *(left),* with Gerald Schoenfeld, chairman, posed proudly with the cast. By 1991, the twenty-one productions worldwide had grossed over a billion dollars and were seen by over 40 million people. (Photo credit: The Shubert Archive.)

The New Approved Production Contract

In the mid-eighties, as we have noted, a new Approved Production Contract (1985) was accepted. Producers attained one of their major objectives, which was to arrange the "points" so that investors could recover their funds within a "reasonable time" and go on to enjoy the profits. The old small company with what might have been 250 investors, each contributing two thousand dollars, meant limited partners who at worst could lose their investment and write it off. Now, with costs steadily rising, this arrangement is much less feasible for multimillion-dollar musicals. The "joint venture" device came into corporate use for megamusicals. For a hypothetical $6 or $8 million, there may be three or four corporations in a "joint venture," which, if the show goes under, allows them to write off their losses. The economic structure of these sizable projects is also new on Broadway and the return rate on investment must be reasonable to these major players. [12]

The whole operative document was directed toward reconciliation, and did indeed abort a lawsuit between producers and playwrights, the League and the Dramatists Guild. Litigation came to an end in the settlement.

A young author who helps write a Broadway show can now walk away with twenty-six thousand dollars (a ballpark figure) in his pocket, even if the show does not open or closes the night after it opens or in two weeks. (But this could represent two to six years of work by the authors.)

When one thinks of the incredibly high earnings that come out of a smash hit, authors, with or without a fair share, get a fixed percent out of which they may be made financially comfortable for life. In the probable euphoria induced by that fact, few authors can be expected to attack investors for taking out more than they should. Not many authors are rich; when and if their ship comes in, they tend to stop grumbling. The very rich keep taking more, the professionals take more, but blue-collar union personnel do not share in the profits except to retain their temporary jobs—which, in any case, is the way our economy operates.

The Move Beyond Broadway

In the eighties, Off-Broadway and regional theaters became a shopping center and a seedbed as well as an area for workshops, all to service Broadway's continuous search for new and less expensive product. In the eighties we witnessed a growing penetration of Off-Broadway by the

Broadway establishment. Costs Off-Broadway rose, and more producers aimed at establishing a hit Off-Broadway for future transfer to Broadway.[13]

In 1983, the new Stephen Sondheim-James Lapine show, *Sunday in the Park with George,* was "workshopped" at Playwrights Horizons for about three hundred thousand dollars before moving to sell-out advance sales at the Booth Theater in 1984. (It failed to recoup fully, however, even after a seventeen-month run on Broadway.) The workshop practice is still viewed with skepticism as a cost saver by some Broadway practitioners, among them Prince and Feuer. Prince regards the musical theater as too "highly crafted" a business for workshop treatment; anything can be done informally, but real reckoning comes after the workshop stage. The only major exception, *A Chorus Line,* was unique: "They wrote it themselves along the way."

Indeed, Bennett believed workshops helped to get the musical right and then to get it on:

I support the cost of the writing of the show and the rehearsing of the show in workshop, without involving anyone else's money. At a point when I have a show that everybody can look at and we watch from the beginning to the end, it works or it doesn't work. At a point when I think the show has a really good chance, I raise the millions of dollars I'm talking about. That's very different from going to somebody and saying, "I had this idea for a show," or "Here is the score for the show," or "This is the book for the show. Now give me $4 million" [or whatever it is this year].

Bennett's workshops, which he financed, are the only evidence that this road to Broadway works both creatively and economically.

Broadway Goes National

The Regionals and the Tours. As Smith and Litton have reported, regional theater in the United States has mushroomed since the early 1960s, with "first-rate, fully professional regional companies, which can operate more cheaply than Broadway."[14] In the 1970s, they began to include musicals in their repertoire, and even to commission them. Many came to Broadway only after successful runs elsewhere. In the seventies, these included *Grease* (1972, originated in Chicago); *Cyrano* (1973, the Guthrie Theater in Minneapolis); *Raisin* (1973, Arena Stage, Washington, D.C.); and *Man of La Mancha* (1965), *Very Good Eddie* (1975), *Shenandoah* (1975), *Annie* (1977), and *Whoopee!* (1979, all from the Goodspeed Opera House in East Haddam, Connecticut).

Merle Debuskey, Press Agent; Joseph Papp, Producer (ca. 1975)

Press representative Merle Debuskey here introduces his boss, Joseph Papp (seated). Papp helped found the Public Theatre in 1967 to stimulate the Off-Broadway theater movement begun in the 1950s and 1960s. The long-running Broadway musical *A Chorus Line* was "workshopped" at the Public Theatre by Michael Bennett, and the show was a deep source of funds to the Public Theatre. Papp's work was aided for many years by Debuskey, who also has held a long tenure as president of the Association of Theatrical Press Agents and Managers. (Photo credit: courtesy Merle Debuskey.)

If institutional theaters and workshops are added to these regional companies, Smith and Litton indicate, the annual number of new musicals through the country "might well equal or surpass the statistics for any year in the '20's."[15] Nor does this include new musicals produced in college and university settings. Regional theaters serve as tryout centers for all sorts of productions that now come to Broadway already honed, if yet to be polished. Only then do they go out to the traditional road theaters that were used mostly for tryout purposes.

Prime Cities. What used to be small American towns have become small flourishing cities with cosmopolitan audiences able to support musical theater on a one-plus week level that can even surpass the gross earned each week on Broadway. It is now some while since the national urban market first began to overshadow Broadway. Total income from prime theater cities (the road) had by 1982 actually exceeded box office take from the small Manhattan turf, with a differential of $30 million. In 1989–90, the excess gross from touring companies ($367 million) again surpassed Broadway ($283 million) by $84 million. These prime cities and their box office receipts include approximately twenty-four urban areas (see charts 4.1 and 4.2 in appendix 4.).

Throughout the eighties, glitzy Broadway shows and old-fashioned stars were the big winners in prime cities. Hence, *Variety* reports that

Carol Channing in *Hello Dolly!,* Yul Brynner in *The King and I,* Mickey Rooney and Ann Miller in *Sugar Babies,* Lena Horne in her concert show and Richard Kiley in *Man of La Mancha* are the most potent examples of original stars wielding haymaker box-office clout on the road [see chart 4.2 in appendix 4.].[16]

In 1989, *Variety* reported a new record *weekly* gross for twenty-one touring Broadway shows totaling over $9 million.[17] This expansion of Broadway into a national market reveals how, in some instances, investors can recoup $5 million in less than a year, as happened with *La Cage aux Folles.* Usually, the Broadway hit show quickly forms a second road company for prime U.S. cities like San Francisco, Chicago, and Los Angeles. Income from prime city subscription audiences might then be used to offset the financing costs of a Broadway production. Tours are formed for a third company to play New Orleans and the Florida circuit, and even a fourth company in Australia or a fifth in Tokyo, and so on. Consider, for example, *La Cage aux Folles, 42nd Street, Les Misérables,* then *The Phantom of the Opera,* whose record advance sales in Chicago's Auditorium Theater surpassed $14 million even with a production cost of $10 million. *Phantom* is currently playing on Broadway and on tour in the U.S. and in cities around the world. In 1990, Bernard Jacobs told the *New York Times* that *Jerome Robbins' Broadway* (capitalized at $8 million with weekly operating cost of $424,000) would recoup only 40 percent of its investment on Broadway (where it flopped) but would recoup the remainder from national and Japanese tours. [18]

There is more evidence that "the road" (read, "the nation's cities") may come to rival Broadway—and not only in revenues. A number of shows, including *Nine, Woman of the Year, Dreamgirls,* and *Cats,* used the national tour as a second chance to fix what the original directors and writers felt needed changing all along but perhaps did not have time to fix in the heat of a pre-Broadway tryout tour. Shows may now incorporate tour changes into the New York production. Further, streamlining Broadway shows can strikingly improve some musicals on tour, while also saving on the costs of operation.

Subscription audiences on the road also provide a kind of safety net:

You know [says Buckley in the early eighties] that when you walk into the San Francisco Light Opera you've got $1.2 million spread over six or seven weeks. When you go into Denver you've got a subscription base of one hundred thirty thousand dollars. Go into Palm Beach and you've got eighty thousand dollars in the bank before you start.

Of course, regionals will want more of this big box office in the near future, thus reducing the amount of "safety."

Longer-Running Musicals. A new historical phenomenon is the increasing length of time musicals run on Broadway. Even with the same average number of new musicals on Broadway since the early 1930s (about fourteen a season), in the seventies musicals ran longer on Broadway than in any decade in its history. Since 1920, of all Broadway shows, straight and musical, only sixty-three have run more than a thousand performances, and 67 percent (forty-two) were musicals. All but six arrived after 1940. And each decade, as suggested by George Wachtel's data, shows an increased number of record breakers. (See chart 4.3 in appendix 4.) While this trend stopped in the eighties, the arrival of megaspectacles like *Phantom* now supports the prophecy for more shows with *multiyear runs,* chiefly because of the record-breaking advance sales not only in New York but also in prime American cities and in several foreign countries, among them Germany and Sweden. It appears that the longer a musical runs on Broadway, in New York City, the greater attraction it often has on tours in other prime American and foreign cities.

Hello, Dolly! is on the list of record shows for the length of its run on Broadway. And this musical, like quite a few others, still plays continuously in the United States and in foreign countries through the stock and amateur route. Since 1963, when the musical based on the play *The Matchmaker* began its pre-Broadway tryout in Detroit as *Hello, Dolly!*, Carol Channing, the lead star, has played her part 3,201 times in performances that grossed over $55 million.[19] However, most new shows (such as *Dreamgirls*) do not rely on stars; they have had interchangeable principal actors ever since the early seventies.

Regional Theaters: Broadway Centered. As we have said, by 1985 the Broadway-based New York League changed its name to reflect the realities of a growing national and international market—it became the League of American Theatres and Producers. By the end of 1990, the League had twenty officers representing more than Broadway's vested interests. According to Richard Barr, then president of the League,

We felt it necessary to take this step in order more accurately to reflect the League's widened scope of involvement nationally. For example, discussions are underway to broaden The League's membership to include presenters of commercial legitimate productions and theater operators in road cities across the country, and to provide closer communication in dealing with touring situations. Additionally, we require a national profile in Washington since we are continually involved in issues affecting the theater. Ours is much more than a local New York industry.[20]

Many prime city theaters staging musicals are owned by James Nederlander, whose family started buying theaters in Detroit before he moved to New York City.

Variety informs us that

The evolution in the touring playoff market from medium capacity theaters to huge, 3,000 plus houses, a development for which the Nederlander Organization has been largely responsible, contributes mightily to the whopping grosses accruing to the big musical tours.[21]

Furthermore, shows can tour America on the Nederlander circuit, and then come to Broadway. Speaking of *Beethoven's Tenth,* Buckley remarked that "it will have toured for seventeen weeks before coming into New York and we will have virtually recouped the investor's money." The worst case would have been terrible reviews and a closed show, with investors still receiving two-thirds return on their money. (Unfortunately, *Beethoven's Tenth* flopped in New York.)

The Shubert Organization was prevented by an antitrust decision in the

Jennifer Holliday, Sheryl Lee Ralph, Loretta Devine in Dreamgirls *(1981)*

Dreamgirls (1981), a hit musical directed by Michael Bennett, was a new kind of musical. It had a highly original lighting design and began a series of Broadway musicals that presented the lives of American blacks in a musical in a more human, less stereotyped style than before. Shown here are the dreamgirls, Jennifer Holliday, Sheryl Lee Ralph, and Loretta Devine. In 1992, George C. Wolfe's *Jelly's Last Jam* continued this trend with an original landmark musical about the life and work of Jelly Roll Morton. (Photo credit: Martha Swope.)

fifties from buying new theaters in the United States. This restriction was lifted in 1985. In buying the National Theater of Washington, D.C., the Shuberts got an early start. In the 1990s, it can be predicted with some assurance that many more first-class theaters in prime cities will be owned by the Shuberts.

Since the organizations that control most Broadway theaters have moved into the national arena, their owners not only learn to tailor advertising and publicity to local markets but they also energetically seek tax relief and subsidies on special projects. One example is a deal between the city of New Haven and the Shubert Organization to create a summer season of five Broadway musicals. We learn from *Variety* that the city provided a subsidy of five hundred thousand dollars, with the Shubert Board raising an endowment fund of four hundred thousand dollars. New Haven officials foresaw benefits deriving from musical theater for its hotels, restaurants, shops, and taxis similar to those in New York City. And they deemed the investment to be worthwhile. If such a venture attracts a stable base of subscriptions and spreads to other parts of the country, then the American theater world should outgrow Broadway in its limited geographic meaning. This trend is already fairly palpable.[22] By 1987, the Shubert Performing Arts Center of New Haven ran in the black.

A Chorus Line and *The Wiz* grossed large sums in halls as big as Chicago's Arie Crown Theater, which seats four thousand. The regional theater movement and "the increasingly sophisticated theater audiences" associated with it have demonstrated that audiences across the U.S. are willing to pay New York ticket prices "not only to see superstars but to experience glitzy special effects." But this *USA Today* article in 1984 does make a major point: "With theater audiences outside New York doubling every decade, Broadway's importance may seriously decline. . . . More sophisticated theaters-in-the-round will be built around the country, and productions will be tailored to each one. Cities outside New York should prove so lucrative. . . . that there'll be no special anxiety to go to New York."[23] Not to worry, yet. The myth of Broadway as the final arbiter is still with us.

However, in the new business of American theater, the prime cities touring companies can supplement a hit or might even save a Broadway flop like *Jerome Robbins' Broadway* or *Starlight Express*. But marketing outside the province of New York has brought the reality of regional differences into sharp relief. First, what lives in one region, even Broadway, can be sudden death elsewhere. *Tango Argentino* hits in New York but flops in Tampa, Florida; initially *Sweeney Todd* was not chosen to make it outside Broadway; *Barnum* hit in New York and died elsewhere. Conversely, many musicals of the past drew raves in New Haven, Boston, or Philadelphia and flopped on Broadway, among many, *Flahooley* (raves in Philadelphia) or *The Girl Who Came to Dinner* (big in Los Angeles).

Second, there is a lack of knowledge of many current Broadway hits in other regions. In the thirties, forties, and fifties, Broadway shows were nationally known because their hit songs were played on the radio. After the sixties, there were very few hit songs from shows. "The challenge for the nineties is to find a way to reinstate a national information distribution system for Broadway," said Susan Lee, director of Road Resources for the League of American Theatres and Producers. (*Variety* still calls non-Broadway cities "the hinterland.") In New York, she continues, you remind people to attend theater; elsewhere the ads "have to educate them" to attend. Each show requires a different marketing focus.[24] (Ads in the gay media, for instance, helped sell *Torch Song Trilogy.*)

Third, while much of the cost of tours is covered by subscription advances, in the future, costs will undoubtedly continue to increase, and so will ticket prices.[25] But the show will go on—and on—around the nation. Chart 4.1 (see appendix 4) shows the increase of cities taking in over one million dollars in box-office receipts during the eighties. One-nighters, then a one-week stand (especially in university towns), and then multiweek cities have made tours an integral part of the American musical theater industry. Still, New York's Broadway remains the flagship for the nation's musical fleet.

The term "Broadway" may now become stretched to include a national string of theaters and markets. More than 60 percent of future gross box office income could come from such cities. And a major part of the profits will derive from musicals. It might happen that the diversity of audiences will produce a more varied diet of musical theater works. We can expect, however, that the ratio of flop to success will remain as it is.

The Payoff Gets Bigger

Once more, we should be reminded that costs of production and operating costs have skyrocketed since the 1960s, and even allowing for inflation, they continue to rise. Some theater people speak of costs (and those who incur them) as "running amok." Flops are the fate of 75 to 80 percent of all musicals. The question persists, why do investors keep coming back? The New York producer of *Kean* observed that "while the price of putting on a play may be 10 times greater in New York than in London, the profit

David Merrick and Phil Silvers at Rehearsal of Do, Re, Mi *(1960)*

David Merrick's career as a highly successful Broadway producer spans many years. He is shown here with the renowned comedian Phil Silvers *(right)* during rehearsal of the long-running but unprofitable musical *Do, Re, Mi* (1960). Merrick became a living symbol in the 1980s of the old-time strong leaders of the 1920s and 1930s, like Flo Ziegfeld and Lee and J. J. Shubert. Merrick's percent of hits is about 55–60 of all his shows compared to the average 20–25 percent hits among all Broadway musicals. (Photo credit: Billy Rose Theatre Collection, New York Public Library.)

potential in New York is 20 times greater."[26] It is the translation of this potential that investors, now as ever, find so alluring.

One producer, Claire Nichtern, points out that

the shelf life of theater is eighteen years' worth of subsidiary rights. If the show doesn't make its profit immediately on the New York scene, it will go all through the country and abroad and you know it will get subsidiary rights back in time. In 1964 I produced a play called *Luv* which was capitalized at ninety thousand dollars. It paid back in three weeks as a sail-away hit.

And paid off on subsidiary rights for years after that.

A classic example is that of David Merrick's production in 1980 of *42nd Street*. Merrick was the sole investor and sole recipient of net profits, and was estimated by *Variety* to be earning about five hundred thousand dollars *net* profit per week from five companies as of early 1984. *Variety* estimated that the approximate break-even figure for this show was $225,000 a week; the Broadway production was grossing weekly about $340,000 to $350,000, with the Washington, D.C., and Los Angeles companies each grossing over $440,000.[27] A London company was still running in 1987. Beyond these immediate box office profits looms the prospect of still more from a cast record album, a film, stock and amateur production rights, including regional theaters, foreign language, radio and television productions, and videocassette sales. In 1989, *Variety* reported *Les Miz* netting six hundred thousand dollars a week with four touring companies and fourteen international companies, and grossing $450 million worldwide in 1989 (more than the total of all Broadway and national tours in 1985). *Cats,* by 1989, had become the "most profitable theatrical production in history," *netting* over the 1980s about $60 million and thereby surpassing *A Chorus Line*.[28] By 1991, the *New York Times* reported that "[*Cats*] has been seen in New York by 5.4 million people and has taken in $210,348,000 at the box office. The 21 productions worldwide have grossed more than $1 billion and have been seen by nearly 39 million people."[29] Musical smashes have a long life, and the profits arrive to investors for many years.

So even though it is inherent in the nature of Broadway musicals that three out of four shows, or eight out of ten, flop, the big payoff remains as powerful an incentive as ever. Recently, Ken Mandelbaum in *Not Since Carrie: Forty Years of Broadway Flops*[30] essentially concluded that flops are unstoppable and unknowable in advance by those who participate in them. The present authors conclude: so are successes. And so says James Nederlander, one of Broadway's leading theater owners and a coproducer of *Nick and Nora* ($4.3 plus million): "The show reads well to me. But I can't pick a hit from a flop."[31] Neither can anyone else, though as we have observed, some seasoned pros have better than average track records. (*Nick and Nora* did indeed flop.)

Skimming Away the Profits. Let us assume that we have invested in a musical show, and, *mirabile dictu,* it is a hit. Prospects are good for a long run.

But what kind of a percentage return can an investor expect? It is clear that investing in the musical theater is now and ever a high-risk capital venture. "More times than not," as Buckley distills the common wisdom, "you're going to lose. But when it pays off, it pays off well." The pertinent saying on Broadway remains: "Nothing is wrong that a smash hit won't cure," which is no more irrational than the entire investment-recoupment process—or fantasy thereof—that it mirrors.

Schoenfeld estimates that an investment of $1 million could return $20 million in the full life of a smash musical, including subsidiary rights. And if you are the only investor, like Merrick with *42nd Street,* or are a multi-smash producer like Cameron Mackintosh—*Cats, Les Misérables, The Phantom of the Opera, Miss Saigon*—then this estimate is low. Even the authors and directors who take a percentage of the gross become million-aires. Consider Andrew Lloyd Webber.

Finally, theater owners also profit from larger and longer advance sales (as well as longer-running shows). The other occupations in show biz, such as those filled by actors and stagehands, also reap added income from long-running shows and so do the "night-out" secondary businesses like restaurants, taxis, parking lots, hotels, etc. And so does the New York City tax collector.

The New Origins of Broadway Musicals

In the past, Broadway originated its own attractions and was the sole leader of new musical theater products. But then came the great divide. In 1984, *Variety* informed its readers that

during the 1963–83 period, Broadway declined from its historical position as the overwhelmingly dominant generator of its own material to runner-up to the non-profit [and foreign] theater arena, which now accounts for more Broadway shows than Broadway itself [see figure 2.4].[32]

In early 1991, six of twelve musicals on Broadway originated elsewhere.[33]

The failure to originate shows on Broadway turns out to be a bugaboo. Broadway entrepreneurs have already adapted to it. Furthermore, all this

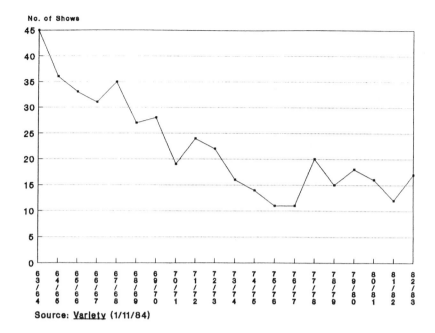

No. of Shows

Source: <u>Variety</u> (1/11/84)

Figure 2.4 Percent of All Shows with Origins on Broadway, 1963–1983

may have a salutary effect on those New York authors who are stuck in the past. Nor (as we have shown) is London the only point of origin. There is reason to anticipate that in the coming period some shows will get underway in Japan or Taiwan and any other place where show biz people can fly in and out at less expense than they suffer by opening extravagantly on Broadway. The roundabout route by which American goods are transported promotes savings. United States resources, shipped abroad, come back as finished goods, and the whole process is cheaper than doing it all at home.

The entrepreneurs on Broadway, as Bernheim said in 1931, are flexible and adaptable, else they would not have maintained the Broadway label. Musicals that originate elsewhere still must have that label, meaning in part that one cannot have a solid smash unless it runs "forever" on "Broadway." Of course, *42nd Street* ran on Broadway and in London and in Australia with a trial in Japan, where hubris took possession of it. Promoters in Tokyo tried to sell $160 tickets. Too high. But *Dreamgirls* went over there and in six weeks grossed $5.1 million on a $93 top ticket.[34] Two of the biggest hits in the Bombay theater season in 1989 were *Evita* and *Kabaret* [sic].[35] As for *La Cage aux Folles* and others, they did well in Australia and in Tokyo. Whether this development spells universal art has yet to be established, but clearly the theatergoers in highly diverse cultures respond to these shows. So what was recently deemed a failure to originate musicals on Broadway has turned into a bigger cornucopia than ever.

Looking back, then, at Broadway's fortunes, we believe their rise from the depths in the early eighties was partly due to a calculated, executive-ordered expansion of economic goals and business organization: raising ticket prices was perceived as a necessary move to support the larger executive ambition by which the Broadway cottage industry musical theater could be transformed into a national industry. Moreover, the American musical began in the eighties to have a steadily increasing international audience whose markets required serious exploitation. Not that these trends were planned. There was no conspiracy. But the aggressive and shrewd leaders of Broadway show biz were quick to create new forms of business that would help them to ride a general trend toward inflation and prosperity into the early nineties. Beyond that, the overall business cycle will have its way.

The Book-Song-Spectacle: Template for the 1990s

The "book-song-spectacle" was conceived elsewhere but became a Broadway child with *Les Misérables.* Conceived in Paris (!) by unknown authors, it had two directors, Trevor Nunn and John Caird, and the producers were lavish in their expenditures. The score has earned plaudits, and the pre-production sales guaranteed a long run. The book-song-spectacle of this type looks like something new under the theatrical sun. An original synthesis, it is not the *Ziegfeld Follies;* it is an historical subgenre, consisting of vintage book-musical elements combined with spectacle and a sung-through score. The form is plastic. It has the earmarks of a winner. Recently, Cameron Mackintosh, producer of *Les Misérables,* has fitted the template with the smash hit, *Miss Saigon,* a loose update of Puccini's *Madame Butterfly,* with "no great songs" (the *Times* of London), but "arranged with seamless operatic sweep," and with $35 million advance sales on Broadway before opening as a "critic-proof" smash hit in 1991.

At the end of the eighties, the "book, music, lyric, dance, spectacle" more or less replaced the forties template of "book, music, lyric, dance." But "book spectacle" or just plain "megaspectacle" raises the roof off the old house of costs. The deep-pocket issue is, how long does the show have to run (at what percent capacity in a fixed seat house) to make a significant profit? This was Schoenfeld's answer in 1982:

The generally desired period within which a producer should reasonably expect to recoup the costs of production of a large musical is approximately forty weeks at capacity business. . . . Since it is most likely that the attraction will not run at capacity . . . . for forty weeks, adjustments will be required in order to achieve the desired recoupment.

By 1991, the "forty weeks" had become "sixty-plus weeks," depending on production and operating costs.

Remember that with *Cats,* the production cost was $4-plus million, recouped in forty-one weeks at the Winter Garden; by January 1989, it had returned $5,800 for every thousand dollars invested.[36] But then came other shows. In the 1980s, there were twenty-six Broadway musicals with production costs over $4 million and only 69 percent were flops on Broadway, several then touring to return cost (see chart 2.1). However, the losses are also greater: *Aspects of Love* closed after an eleven-month run and an $8 million loss, believed the largest in Broadway history,[37] rivaled only by *Carrie.*[38] As Bernard Jacobs has remarked: "It was a problem when we went from 25 weeks [to recoup] to 35. And it was a problem when we went from 45, and to 55, and to 65."[39]

Many changes that loom over the Broadway musical appear to be overwhelming, but so do the changes in book publishing, in higher education, in all sorts of institutions, conventions, and conditions. And earlier transformations of American society, from the Civil War through the Great Depression to the post-World War II era, have also seemed overwhelming to those who were caught up in them. Clearly, the new techniques of computerized ticket sales, television advertising, national and world tour companies reflect changes in the larger society. They have already transformed the musical theater business.

The Future of Broadway Industry

Peering into the future requires some help from one genius who studied American industrial society. In Thorstein Veblen's words:

The standardization of industrial processes, products, services, and consumers . . . very materially facilitates the businessman's work in reorganizing business enterprises on a larger scale; particularly does this standardization serve his ends by permitting a uniform routine in accounting, invoices, contracts, etc.

The great, at the present state of development perhaps the greatest, opportunity for saving [is] by consolidation . . . in doing away with unnecessary business transactions and industrially futile maneuvering on the part of independent firms the promoter of combinations finds his most telling opportunity.

So long as related industrial units are under different business managements,

Chart 2.1 Musicals Budgeted at Over $4 Million (1980–1990)*

Title	Year	Prod. Cost	Hit/Flop	Weeks to Recoup
1. Cats	1982	4+	H	41
2. A Doll's Life	1982	4.6	F	—
3. Merlin	1983	4.9	F	—
4. My One and Only	1983	4.2	H	50
5. La Cage aux Folles	1983	5	H	52
6. Three Musketeers	1984	4.5	F	—
7. Grind	1985	4.7	F	—
8. Singin' in the Rain	1985	4.1	F	—
9. Big Deal	1986	5	F	—
10. Les Misérables	1986	4.5	H	23
11. Rags	1986	4.5	F	—
12. Me and My Girl	1986	4	H	50
13. Smile	1986	4+	F	—
14. Carrie	1987	8+	F	—
15. Phantom of the Opera	1987	8+	H	65
16. Starlight Express	1987	8+	F	—
17. Into the Woods	1987	4	F	—
18. Legs Diamond	1988	5+	F	—
19. Chess	1988	6.5	F	—
20. Black and Blue	1989	5+	F	—
21. Jerome Robbins	1989	8+	F	—
22. Three Penny Opera	1989	4.5	F	—
23. Grand Hotel	1989	4.5	H	78
24. Meet Me in St. Louis	1989	5	F	—
25. City of Angels	1989	4.4	H	51
26. Aspects of Love	1990	8	F	—

*1990 = 1989–1990 Season, 69 Percent Flops

they are, by the nature of the case, at cross-purposes, and business consolidation remedies this untoward feature of the industrial system.[40]

The motives of the businessman . . . are not simply to effect an industrially advantageous consolidation, but to effect it under such circumstances of ownership as will give him control of large business forces or bring him the largest possible gain. The ulterior end sought is an increase of ownership.[41]

Les Misérables *(1987)*

Les Misérables (1987) originated in France, went to London, and then to Broadway. It epitomizes the new template of "book-song-spectacle" that appeared in the 1980s. By 1989, four tour companies in the United States and fourteen international companies reported a net profit of $600,000 a week, grossing $450 million worldwide. It took over ten years from original idea to Broadway opening. Producer Cameron Mackintosh led the then-neophyte songwriting team of Claude Michel Schönberg (composer) and Alain Boublil (lyricist), with codirectors Trevor Nunn and John Caird. (Photo credit: Michael Le Poer Trench.)

Betty Buckley, Linzi Hateley in Carrie *(1987)*

This dramatic scene is from *Carrie* (1988). The show was nominated as the leading candidate for the most abysmal artistic and economic flop that has been viewed by Broadway audiences in the last forty-five years, as described in Ken Mandelbaum's book *Not Since Carrie: Forty Years of Broadway Flops.* (Photo credit: Peter Cunningham.)

In concise terms, applied to Broadway business, we believe that the next decade of musical show biz will include consolidation of ownership, not only of theaters around the nation, initially by the executives of the League of American Theatres and Producers, but also of management of services, that is, marketing, accounting, pay-per-view-TV, invoice services, and standardization, again, not only of product (tours of the same show) but also of contracts, salary wage scales, and control over royalties, maybe even constructed with the same computer program (as envisioned by Simon and Schuster in the book publishing industry). All of this looks like total fantasy to most old-timers, but the imperative logic of profitability in large-scale capitalist enterprises requires either expansion and consolidation or decline.

Thus, the large socioeconomic problems of musical theater are chronic and dynamic. A state of financial crisis may be perennial, and especially severe in periods of recession when musical theater is instantly affected. During those hard times, the banking and film financial wizards could start effectively penetrating the Shubert-Nederlander control over American musical theaters. Along these lines, *Variety* reported a Hollywood film producer who had bought 40 percent of the Nederlander stock in six theaters on Broadway.[42] About a quarter of American films are now being made in New York City, where not only tax breaks but also a labor force of actors, playwrights, composers, lyricists, and designers is available. Will musical theater, film, and television become more commonly owned in the future? We think so. Before such conglomerates appear, however, it is well to heed Veblen when he qualifies the "pecuniary" motive with more than one touch of irony.

Still, throughout men's dealings with one another and with the interests of the community there runs a sense of equity, fair dealing, and workmanlike integrity. . . . Business men are also, in a measure, guided by the ambition to effect a creditable improvement in the industrial processes which their business traffic touches. These sentimental factors in business exercise something of a constraint, varying greatly from one person to another, but not measurable in its aggregate results.[43]

And these are Schoenfeld's words as they echo those of Veblen regarding the "sentimental" rather than the pecuniary factors that also drive executives in large industries. "I really feel that the people who are now in the business of owning and operating theaters are committed to theater and love the theater and are determined to stay in the theater." As for the slumps and cycles and alleged demise of Broadway, Bernard Jacobs said in the midst of the 1982–83 slump:

I don't believe the theater is going to fall apart. People said the same things about the theater in 1929: ticket prices are too high, theater owners are too greedy, the economics are wrong. Everything is different, yet everything is the same. We are struggling to maintain our bearings in a very difficult economy. High production prices hurt us. Bad plays hurt us. This is a difficult business in which to function. It is fragile. But it will survive.[44]

Returning to the print media and their hyperbole, at the end of the 1989–90 Broadway season: "Broadway theater predictably set another box-office record. . . . A cluster of strong plays, a mix of new works of quality . . . outstanding revivals . . . a number of new productions . . . important stars and significant writers and directors. . . . Attendance went up to 8.03 million. . . . Broadway touring shows took a record income. . . . Long-running shows continued to run. . . . In sum, the best season in years"[45] Furthermore, only 77 percent of Broadway's musicals flopped.

II

*Creating the
Musical Show*

3. Collaboration of Top Executives: Creative Organizing of the Musical

The Broadway musical, America's grab bag of a gift to the world, is an extraordinary *mélange* of creative talent and executive courage. During its vintage years from *Oklahoma!* (1943) through *My Fair Lady* (1956) and *West Side Story* (1957), and then on through the sixties and seventies, as we have noted, 76 percent of the musicals mounted on Broadway failed to recoup their investment. In the early years Oscar Hammerstein had some seventeen flops out of twenty-six shows before *Show Boat* (1927) and eight of fifteen before *Oklahoma!* (1943), but then was involved with a very rare run of seven hits out of nine. Harold Prince, director, rising like a meteor with *Cabaret* (1966) and reveling in triumph with *Evita* (1979), must have mulled in the early eighties over his several flops. But before the decade ended, he was back on top again. In the eighties, Bennett halted a major workshop. Tommy Tune started dancing again, and then directed two major hits. Stephen Schwartz, fresh from success, struggled with a big one, and lost. Creating and organizing a Broadway show is risky business.

Each Broadway musical production requires the creation *de novo* of a large-scale organization of freelance skilled professionals to be coordinated and energized by a few top executives into a business and artistic project called "a musical." *These top executives are the producer, director, composer, lyricist, and bookwriter.* The next chapter deals more thoroughly with the other top executives, known professionally as authors. Here we will briefly analyze the generally unsung role of the producer and the director in the creative organizing of a musical. Executive action moves the project and the show through organizational phases we, by applicable analogy, call cult, sect, and church (more on this later). Line-producers not only select the play, raise funds, and take marketing action but also hire and fire the other executives, work with the director, for instance, on casting, and also resolve conflicts and try to retain objectivity in the give and take of executive decisions. Directors organize action directly at the "artistic core."

The collaborative exchange among these top executives and with their staffs generates artistic decisions that never lose sight of collective financial realities. Top executives creatively organize, motivate, coordinate, and direct the necessary transformation from page to stage. They are charged with maintaining the integrity of a show's vision, which is only potential in the original written script and score.

It is said that straight plays are written but a musical is produced. The illusion common to many beginning bookwriters that they, along with composers and lyricists, create the whole show is interesting if only because it sometimes outlasts their first few flops. If they persevere, the massive reality of organizational collaboration finally sets in. The authors then learn that the producing function in musical theater goes deeper than simply raising money. Claire Nichtern sees the problem and the pleasure:

> It is so difficult to take a group of creative people, add one to the other and come out with a sum equal to more than its parts! I call this creative organizing.

Creative organizing presupposes a battery of skills, and the human material to which they apply is fractious. But what of it if you feel, as she does, that "musical theater is enormously exciting. The whole atmosphere of our live musical theater is chilling and thrilling. What it has contributed to the world is immeasurable."

Authority and Power: Executive Functions

Decades ago, Chester Barnard, once the president of a large corporation, published a brilliant analysis of organizations called *The Functions of the Executive.*[1] Barnard's study directly illuminates the organizational analysis of a musical. Briefly, Barnard suggests that executive functions are clustered in impersonal acts funneled through central channels of communication. The executive functions act to coordinate every aspect of the organization, including activities of all who are salaried (staff, suppliers) *and* those who pay for the product (investors, ticket buyers). Executive functions (1) shape aims (the vision, the themes), (2) secure essential human efforts (the selection of personnel, hiring, firing, and resolving conflict), (3) provide a system of formal and informal communications, and (4) keep the whole

Adolph Green, Claire Nichtern, Stephen Sondheim, Betty Comden at ASCAP Music Theater Seminar (1980s)

Claire Nichtern, producer *(second from left)* is shown here at a party with lyricist/bookwriters Adolph Green and Betty Comden *(far right)* and Stephen Sondheim *(standing)*. Nichtern believes that generating a Broadway musical is a process of "creative organizing" such that the whole musical is more than the sum of its parts. The party was hosted by the American Society of Composers, Authors, and Publishers (ASCAP), an organization started by Victor Herbert in the early 1900s to protect the royalty rights of its members. (Photo credit: Courtesy Claire Nichtern.)

organization in perspective (the business end, the project's accounting and profits, and the whole artistic side). Every person in an organization carries out some of these functions, but formally, leadership rests with top executives.

Barnard's scheme helps us to understand that final authority or real power does not repose exclusively in titled positions. A widespread myth confounds authority with power and power with a person giving an order. Barnard underscores a fact too often obscured by such fables of organization. He contends that even strict command systems, such as those found in an army or church, rely on the inarticulate vote of subordinates who either consent to or defy an order issued by their superiors. Ultimately cooperation and coercion are incompatible. Commonly, daily, many orders are ignored, postponed, deflected, or actively sabotaged in any organization. The policies or orders are *deauthorized,* in Rosenberg's term.[2] A musical project is not exempt from these divisive forces.

Executives therefore constantly attempt to gauge when and under what conditions an order will be resisted (by the designer, the actor, etc.) or, conversely, when a suggestion may stimulate creative outcomes by others. A major executive function is to secure the "willingness of individuals to contribute to the organization" through collaboration. In a musical theater project, for example, the producer secures the cooperation of union and guild representatives who belong to outside organizations within which similar assent must be sought, and this requires special diplomatic skills. Such skills are also required for coping with initial conflicts about what percent of the gross box office receipts goes to whom. And so forth.

In Barnard's view, however, willingness to cooperate is never based solely on economic incentives. While pecuniary resources may limit or guide decision making, it is critical in some cases and not in others. For individuals, even in tough corporate firms, noneconomic incentives dominate inducements to perform:

Prestige, competitive regulations, social philosophy, philanthropic interests, combativeness, love of intrigue, dislike of friction, technical interest, Napoleonic dreams, love of accomplishing useful things, desire for regard of employees, love of publicity, fear of publicity. . . . Nothing but the balance sheet keeps these *non-economic* motives from running wild.[3]

The Vision of the Whole Show

Barnard does much to clarify the major executive functions, which, as he sees it, are to retain a steady sense of the whole organization, its future and its limits. "The essential aspect of the process is the sensing of the organization [project] as a whole and the total situation relevant to it."[4] In musicals, this function devolves upon a creative producer or a gifted director who is expected to monitor all decisions bearing on the integrity of a total vision. The whole *project* is primarily the responsibility of a creative line-producer; the artistic *show* is primarily a director's responsibility. Of this we are told over and over.

With a strong bond of collaboration between producer and director, a true "sharing of the vision" comes into being. If it may seldom be said to exist on Broadway in our time, the exception is also real. Nichtern: "It's the ability to bring somebody's vision, with all its demands, together." Nicholas Howey, as a creative line-producer at his dinner theater, urges a "good dose of common sense, a real good idea—and an unblinking look at the whole [show]." Charnin believes that "the director is literally the visionary in the piece. . . . Only one person, and I mean the director, can ever have . . . that kind of vision." Finally, Laurents: "What is best for the show? . . . The whole of it."

Translating the vision of a developing wholeness into cooperative action is perhaps the key Barnardian executive function:

The general executive states that "This is the purpose, this is the objective, this is the direction . . . in which we wish to move before next year." . . . The formulation and definition of purpose is then a widely distributed function, only the more general part of which is executive. In this fact lies the most important inherent difficulty in the operation of cooperative systems—the necessity for indoctrinating those at the lower levels with general purposes, the major decisions, so that they remain cohesive and able to make the ultimate detailed decisions coherent; and the necessity, for those at the higher levels, of constantly understanding the concrete conditions and the specific decisions of the "ultimate" contributors from whom executives are often insulated. . . . The function of formulating grand purposes and providing for their redefinition is one which needs sensitive systems of communication, experience in interpretation, imagination, and delegation of responsibility. . . . *Back and forth, up and down, the communications pass, reporting obstacles, difficulties, impossibilities, accomplishments; redefining, modifying purposes level after level* [our emphasis].[5]

In the creative organization of a Broadway musical project, hundreds of people are involved (we include "tryout" audiences, and Barnard would logically do the same).

Everywhere specialization of roles induces tunnel vision. Most or all of the specialty titles and jobs in a project impede one's vision so that even stage designers are liable to mistake a part for the whole show. This is true not only because the show changes with the constant input of creative ideas from everywhere in the staff but also because concentration on some single task is incompatible with a clear view of the total work. Even in heavy industry there is a price to be paid for the division of labor. Efficiency in the fulfillment of one's own role can seriously undermine the project as a whole. Tommy Tune, who wears many hats, knows what it means to wear just one:

Sometimes the choreographer goes off on his own without grasping the whole thing. Or maybe he doesn't care and is just concerned to present what comes out of him. Sometimes that happens to me when I'm directing. I have a dream to choreograph a sequence which I put in, and it's not germane.

Actors are among those least able to evaluate the whole show. When designers bring more peripheral vision to a show than that held by the director or the producer, they may miss the mark. At the other extreme, Agnes de Mille's serious and powerful dance about the meaning of the Civil War to women had a turbulent production history in the musical comedy-play, *Bloomer Girl* (1944), but it eventually was accepted as an integral part of the work.[6]

Translating Vision into Organized Action

In Barnard's judgment, and in ours, the active part of any executive process is a kind of psychic central clearance for communication that links vision to cooperation. In a musical project, the ceaseless flow of information and ideas from designers to director is well described by Arthur Masella (assistant director to Harold Prince for many years and now a successful director):

The assistant helps [the director] put it all together, keeps the channels of communication open and makes sure people know what's going on. Very often the choreographer's in that room with the dancers, the director's in this room with the two leads staging a scene, the musical director's off in a third room with a composer working out a problem, the arranger is with the conductor down the hall talking about how we're to orchestrate that, and the producer's back in his office selling tickets to theater parties. Everybody's all over the place. Someone or a small group has to be sure where everybody else is, what the others are doing and thinking . . . and that we're all working towards the same thing.

From time to time, a producer with muscle keeps a show afloat. He will not let it sink. Accordingly, those seeming to be at cross-purposes have to be jettisoned. David Merrick acted on that principle in 1956 when he barred the bookwriter, the lyricist, and the composer from *Jamaica,* a hit show. Even more drastic measures were taken in Boston in 1983 when director, musical director, and bookwriter were sacked from *My One and Only.* Again (it is believed), a producer from Paramount films with lots of muscle did it, and afterwards Tommy Tune, the new director, with several consultant bookwriters, revamped the whole show. (A hit.)

The creative organizing of a musical involves executive talent in a high-level discharge of energy and split-second timing. But powerful and successful top executives on Broadway are rare in any decade.

Development of the Idea into a Show

The vision of the show to producers and directors and authors is exciting, but it then requires that the show be prepared for development toward production. When the pure thrill of inspiration is over, come the administration, perspiration, and frustration. John Flaxman's words reverberate down Broadway's alleys and back over time for all those who have been exposed to the audition:

Anybody who's been in the musical theater business knows those evenings at composers' and lyricists' homes where everything is so fabulous, with scores that are so wonderful. . . . Then the show opens, and it's so bad you can't believe your eyes and ears. What happened?

What happened was that it got "developed." To develop an idea into a musical, one needs vitality and craft of a certain sort, of an executive sort, charged with high-powered effort and inspirational engineering, poured into a large-scale project that is itself subject to every kind of serendipity. Here is Schwartz on time, patience, and indefatigability:

Things take so long. Not that anyone wants them to. We'd all like to be finished, but it's just not right yet. If you believe in the project and think that in the end you can get it right, you just have to keep going.

I've been working a year and a couple of months on this show, and I finally have a first act I like.

Another route beckons unestablished people who, not so fancifully, might get the show running in La Jolla (as with *Big River,* which turned down the Shuberts and took Jujamcyn's offer of a Broadway theater) or in Washington, D.C., as in *Joseph and the Amazing Technicolor Dreamcoat,* which was about to close when Zev Bufman became a partner and brought it to Off-Broadway.

During the development of a show and on into rehearsal, executives get apprehensive about an impending flop. Or they totally fail to foresee it.

Passionately committed to his work, Flaxman knows what it is like to face an abyss while feeling helpless to prevent the frenetic rush into it:

It's like somebody saying, "Look, there's the cliff. Just keep walking and you'll fall off. There's nothing you can do about it." What do you tell your investors? "Look, we really should stop now. It's not working. I'm sorry, I made a mistake, but let's cut our losses now. We'll give you something back on your dollar. We haven't spent everything yet. Let's fold up." You can't do that. They'll say, "You've forgotten that *My One and Only* was in trouble in Boston. If they had shut up shop we would never have had *My One and Only*." So you keep walking. You know you're going over that cliff. And there's no stopping it.

Bennett, recalling *Ballroom,* his only flop, generalized from that experience:

Either you're sitting there very comfortably and you're pleased, or you watch it and for some reason you're very nervous. I mean, it's there. It's not an intangible thing that we're talking about—giving you a feeling that things are okay or not okay. You could even watch it a second time and not get the chills where you want to get the chills, and not be moved.

One time George Abbott called in a team after a Boston opening and closed the show. Abbott is a formidable six feet four inches and "tells it like it is" —even to the team and its backers. But how such a man's nervous system works is still a mystery.

   Even less understood is the sea change of transfer from (1) a small intimate room to a theater; (2) from Off-Broadway to Broadway; (3) and from one culture to another—most familiarly at present, Britain to America. "They both speak English, don't they?" Yes, but with different timing, inflection, dialect, allusiveness. Changes can be made, and they can do the trick. Then again, they may not.

Critique, Rewrite, Develop, Critique: Executive Exchange

With executive groups, information flows as in a circulatory system. It is funneled into executives where the heart of coordinative action must pump: messages originating at the top, lateral memos to colleagues, ideas coming up from suppliers and consumers. Executives, in developing a musical project to its optimal audience appeal, are obliged to act on both business news and artistic insight. For the musical work, these ideas are translated by authors into rewriting and by directors and actors into reinterpreting.

   A nearly unshakable postulate of show biz is that anyone can provide "constructive critique." True. But so is the opposite. Anyone can provide "destructive critique," especially when "good" material is removed for "poor/weak" material by any of the top executives. Most critique is innocuous, uninformed, something that emerges from a personal "insight" misleadingly projected onto the work. Perhaps the most damaging device for a work-in-progress can be seen when investors, outsiders, and nontheater professionals are encouraged to "talk afterwards" to the possibly callow author. In "nonprofit" quarters, at times this is experienced as institutionalized dementia. Unfortunately, it is a common device.

From conception to production on Broadway, a musical may take two to six or more years. Pros themselves perceive the phases and stages of development as "mysterious." They believe that knowing how to make the right artistic moves is "intuitive." The critique comes from within one's unfathomable self. A bookwriter-director who is also a teacher believes, as do many of his peers, that talent can be trained, but it must first be there —and this presence is also mysterious.

Prince is only a bit more analytical about how his own talent works:

You go home any time you have a session with anybody, and figure out, if you're me, why what that person said was correct, why a decision was correct. It's only after a while that you realize it wasn't necessarily correct at all. You mull it over. You commune with yourself. Beyond that, the process is inexplicable.

Collaboration in itself entails an odd critique, the creative process *à deux* (between persons in alter-roles, like lyricist-composer, producer-director, director-actor, and so forth). When two, three, or four such creators are *en rapport,* then the intrapsychic becomes interintuitive; this collaborative creativity is the basis of the musical art form. About this we shall also have more to say.

Granted that the creative process in every art (and for that matter, in every science) is wonderfully mysterious, an inward or intrapsychic phenomenon, what can we say of the musical theater, which is a quintessentially collaborative art form? Now the idea of inner psychic process gives way to "shared" process among artists, in dyads (lyricist-composer), in triads (director, author, and designer), in groups (the creative team and all the designers), and finally emerges in the mysterious collective flow of organized action integrated into a whole musical. Even directors lose perspective; many of the good ones turn to trusted outsiders. Schwartz explains: "We need an outside eye. . . . We need somebody else to shout, 'No, no, no. Look at it this way.' " Bennett also told us that he *always* called in a few trusted observers.

Another device to stir the creative juices is conventionally called upon at any point in the cult or preproject start-up phase: a "read-through" or even a "sing-through." Not strictly speaking under Equity's jurisdiction, it, too, serves to engender critique. Schwartz describes how the device operates:

Just hearing the show enables you to spot big problems—and then go back to fix them up. You do that repeatedly. At last you're . . . done: "That's it. . . . Let's go!" [This may take several years.]

After development and during previews the executive team receives a "mass critique," well-intentioned, not too technical, but full of emotion. Berman ruefully remembers:

In the preview period we were very pressured. Everybody had an opinion about something. Forty people told us to change this, and 40 other people told us to keep it. You had to listen, go home and try to sort it out or just dismiss it from your mind, which gets so cluttered! Sometimes you have to put the advice aside and go by your gut feelings.

The more experienced Prince suggests:

You must listen to everything, which means to everyone. . . . There's no way of knowing where advice that hits a responsive chord will come from. You've got to be the censor, the editor.

Others are thoroughly systematic. One writer records all comments. Weeks later she takes her hoard from the drawer (or computer) and meticulously reviews every idea, searching for any that might be useable.

As we indicate elsewhere, even regular reviewers, the mass media critics, are occasionally up to providing a constructive critique, usually in cities other than New York. The La Jolla production of *Big River* benefited from a "scathing pan" written by one Los Angeles critic who suggested a number of changes that would improve the show.[7] Invidious comparison delivered with a maximum of scorn is the rule among "clever" critics (as useless as less clever critics who admire almost anything). The witty put-down is an occupational hazard in all the prime theater cities.

The art of constructive criticism has few fine practitioners. But it tends to be a major skill of successful top executives, and is a prime factor in the creative organizing of a project. The art of critique is also mostly untrained on Broadway. For those who can learn, experience is the only teacher. But as we shall see, such criticism is at the heart of the process of collaboration.

The Project

The term "project" has a deep generic meaning. It represents mobilization of energy, commitment, involvement, and purpose. Such effort binds us as individuals into a socially constructed time and place. How much of our lives depends on any given project and its scope! The project in this meaning of the word provides more than a miniature *mise en scène* for getting married, having a baby, seeking a political office, building a house—or, in our context, creating and producing a musical. A full-fledged Promethean project suffuses the soul, body, and action of every person bound to and by it.

For each project there are requisite executive functions. For large-scale Broadway musicals, there are "prime movers," "movers," and "makers." They are the top executives. As we saw, the American musical theater industry is dominated by a handful of Broadway business leaders whose center is the Executive Committee of the League of American Theatres and Producers. Overwhelmingly, members of that committee shape the musical theater business. It bargains collectively with seventeen craft unions, guilds, and associations that speak for freelance labor. Its members, and other nonmembers, independent entrepreneurs like Harold Prince, endlessly seek new projects.

To recapitulate part of what we have already said: each musical project is a high-risk artistic and business speculation. Since 1932, fourteen new musical projects per year have, on average, reached Broadway. The large majority failed to recoup their investments. Executive skill and courage are required to "get a show on" but no more than to "close it down," to cut the losses, to give up. The print and visual mass media, through their critics, evaluate each show for its potential audience. They concentrate on story, performers, and production values, e.g., sets, lights, sound. In most reviews of a show, short shrift is made of the director's executive work, and producers are rarely if ever mentioned.

Business history, moreover, like that of all organizations, is filled with more failure than success. Not even invocation of the bottom line can prevent failure. Nor does money by itself insure the magic of high collaboration or artful intuition. Money, excitement, curiosity, prestige, and desire to contribute operate *simultaneously* to secure cooperative effort. To select any one factor as the single cause is a popular and misleading fiction. Successful executives understand the need for complex inducements and voluntary cooperation.

Only after much struggle can the bottom line turn black. For in Broadway musical ventures, the bottom line is usually red. Seldom does it directly or solely dictate individual and executive effort. More often it is an after-effect. John Flaxman, producing *Yours, Anne,* a musical play based on *The Diary of Anne Frank,* was explicit about this:

There are so many hardships you have to deal with; you realize the only reason you're there is you've *got* to be.

But now and then the thought occurs to me and I all but say, "God, I wish I could do it for the movies or for television." At least then at the end, I could support things for a long time. But money has never been my basic motivation.

Rocco Landesman, a coproducer of *Big River* (1985), calculates that "you'd have to say our chance was one in a million. God knows, common sense didn't have much to do with it."[8] Luck did, in part, and plenty of it. But executive skill and intuition are also necessary for any project to succeed. Entrepreneurs live on risk, adventure, and challenge—with which they rise or fall in each project.

Creative Organizing

A musical project can be viewed, in Nichtern's language, as the "creative organizing" by executives of a social system whose purpose is to make a musical work artistically and financially. The project may start with story ideas by an individual creator but then moves to initial outline in an authors' group that develops the outline into a script and a score (book, lyrics, and music). Collaborative directors like Bennett, Prince, Tune, Charnin, and Laurents often participate with authors to strengthen the artistic conception. But to come to life, this concept (the theme, the vision, and its execution in a musical play) must receive scarce resources that only producers can provide. It is they who take options on shows, and supply theaters with the money to illuminate and fill them.

Neither cash nor products fall from the rainbow. Martin Charnin reports that it took six years of unremitting effort to bring *Annie* to production; he scarcely twitched after the third year of hearing, "But she's got no eyes." Flaxman spent three years getting the rights to produce *Yours, Anne,* and still winces when he hears, "What? A musical comedy about Anne Frank? How can you do that? It's too depressing," or "Oh, I know, you're doing *Springtime for Hitler.*" (The answer that turned away knee-jerk stereotypes was, "It's *The Diary of Anne Frank* set to music.") Nicholas Howey never did get Nederlander's staff to agree that the antiracist musical *Finian's Rainbow* was not a racist play or out of date; his liaison man finally admitted he had neither seen nor read it, so a two-year-old option to produce was dropped. A principal recollects that no producer in New York City wanted any part of "the choreographed ethnic rumble" called *West Side Story.* He himself believed that it would flop.

Fundamentally, the project is initiated and rooted in a consensus based on faith in the vision of the show and the talents of the executive team. Script and score, contract and agreements are fashioned by a limited but heterogeneous executive team—composer, lyricist, and bookwriter, in tandem with the producer and the director. Lawyers and agents emerge to help bring a team of executives to the point of "sign-on," when a full, formal commitment is legitimized. Furious energy—a "demonic force"—is then unleashed. More than anything else, it serves to unify freelance professionals, administrators, and craftspeople whose specialized roles coalesce into a small-scale social movement. The project is going into production.

This movement foreshadows an organization similar to but not entirely identical with other organizations. For its goal is to merge corporate business authority in real estate and theater with a cooperative collectivity of artists and artisans to produce a unique product, a musical show. A large musical show can involve over a hundred different staff positions, external unions, media agencies, and as many as a dozen major investors, all bound by inflexible rules embedded in a legion of city, state, and federal regulatory bodies. Executives at this stage brim with high energy. They are, in Barnard's terminology, so channeled as to facilitate a synthesis "of contradictory forces, to reconcile conflicting forces, instincts, interests, conditions, positions, and ideals," and to stay within a volatile budget.[9] Schwartz counsels readiness: "They say, 'Okay, we like the piece. We're going to give you some money.' Now that's the point where everything has to go fast."

Viewed by a line-producer, the project looks like a hierarchical pyramid, and "the action flows from executive producers." Whether it flows down, shoots up, or moves sideways, producer Gail Berman is exhilarated by the process:

The producer's hand hits all of them simultaneously. It's what makes this job so exciting and so exhausting. I didn't know how creative it could be. You make business, artistic and conceptual decisions that allow you to use energy which might not be tapped at all if you were just a performer or a general manager.

Whether "the producer's hand" acts like Adam Smith's "invisible hand" or not, this image is suggestive. It combines the textbook metaphor (a pyramid) with "creative organizing" (of business and art), which sparks the passion for a production whose scope can be awesome.

In a musical project, the actions of everyone involved must be coordinated, and "everyone," as we noted, encompasses a large number of specialists. The division of labor is complex. *La Cage aux Folles* had over one hundred persons (some playing multiple roles) on its staff; *The Phan-*

Adolph Green, Betty Comden, Judy Holliday, Jerome Robbins, Jule Styne Discuss
Bells Are Ringing *(1956)*

The primary creative team is here represented by Adolph Green and Betty Comden (colyricists and bookwriters), the star, Judy Holliday, the director, Jerome Robbins, and composer, Jule Styne for the show *Bells Are Ringing* (1956), produced by the Theatre Guild. The days when "stars" predominated have long since gone. Contracts refer to "principal actors." (Photo credit: Billy Rose Theatre Collection, New York Public Library; photographer: B. C. Mittleman.)

tom of the Opera has over 195 (see appendix 5). Every specialist is a fragile link in the whole chain, without which a production collapses. But certain specialists are more special than others. Here collaboration becomes a sometime thing. The forces of attraction and aversion appear at every phase of a project—including the initial phase.

The Multiple Origins of a Musical Project

The metaphor of the birth of a project (or of the musical as a baby) touches a chord. The show is conceived by certain collaborative interaction ("I sense something here"). The exact date of conception is guesswork. With gestation come positive sounds ("Yeah! Let's put it on!"). The burden of carrying an idea and developing it is shared in a kind of collective couvade. But the image can be stretched only so far. We should not forget that bringing a Broadway musical production to term will ordinarily take a few years, a staff of hundreds, and a pot of millions.

Conception may be painfully prolonged, a fact chronicled many times over by those who made classic musicals like *West Side Story* ("Some years passed . . . then more years passed . . . turned down by every producer in town") and *Gypsy* ("had other people on it for a year").

Along these lines, not much has changed. Schwartz tells us:

The producer, Alan Carr, wanted to do a musical of *La Cage aux Folles*. He went to France, got the rights, and then asked himself, "Who can I hire to write this for me?" [The selection took a few years.] Nothing unusual about that. . . . But in this case [*Rags*], Joe [Stein] had an idea, decided he would write it and then go to a producer or director.

What has changed, in Schwartz's opinion, is that nowadays "most shows are motivated by authors. I'm working on a thing I put together. It's my idea, I got the rights, I got the producer, I'll have a director."

Martin Charnin (and others) feel that

in those [old] days, I believe it was the producers mostly on Broadway who were optioning property. Since then it has gone in another direction. Now it's the authors, it's the composers and lyricists and the directors who are getting ideas and seeking out the producers.

The selection of worthy scripts by reading them, probably practiced even in ancient Greece, has not disappeared. The task of reading and choosing scripts by aspiring authors is certainly tedious and costly, but, like the quest for precious metals, it seems to be ineradicable. Producers never stop digging, convinced as they are that the diamond needle lies hidden

Joseph Stein, Charles Strouse, Stephen Schwartz at Rags *Rehearsal (1986)*

Stephen Schwartz *(right)* with the bookwriter Joe Stein *(left,* author of *Fiddler on the Roof)* and the composer Charles Strouse *(center,* composer for numerous shows*)* during a rehearsal of *Rags* (1986), a musical that did not work on Broadway. Authors like Schwartz get involved in the executive organizing of new shows from initiation of concept through the production process. On *Rags,* lyricist Schwartz even became the director for a brief period. (Photo credit: Martha Swope Associates/Carol Rosegg.)

somewhere in an enormous pile of haystacks. Perhaps one out of ten thousand scripts read is destined to be a smash hit. Organizations like Playwrights Horizons support "house authors" who generate scripts, but they also go on reading scripts. Schwartz refers to a serendipitous case: "What actually happened with *Working* was that I read a little squib about the book and I said to my wife, 'This is something for me.' We got the book and almost immediately I found a show in it."

Bennett's method was to initiate a deliberate search among congenial and professional acquaintances:

Most often what happens is that I sit down with a group of people I would enjoy working with and I say, "What story would we like to do?" We get teams together and having agreed upon an idea, discuss tone and a style within the many that exist. Then we're on our way.

Optimally, this group becomes the nucleus, the creative top executive team of collaborators.

Among onlookers, a new business, a new product, a new law, in short, any new project, commonly gives rise to skepticism expressed in a reflex, the response that "it'll never work." In the movie industry, maybe two out of ten films make their money back; in mom 'n' pop small businesses, six of ten may fail in five years, and we know that something like seven to eight of ten Broadway musicals flop. With such figures, doubters traverse the safe ground of averages and probabilities. They need not be called prophets to foresee that "it won't work."

The problem with this automatically negative response is that averages have no predictive value for single cases: they do not reveal how the dice will roll this one time. To be guided by a gut feeling is equally futile. Neither the laws of probability nor visceral sensations are reliable. Smashes do occur but they are unforeseeable—look at *Best Little Whorehouse in Texas*. That *West Side Story* was "turned down by every producer in town" is a tale told about many successes in every industry. In *Adventures in the Screen Trade*, William Goldman writes of other confident, if quixotic but creative and organized entertainment executives, the movie makers. They (the top executives) "just *don't know*" about the success of any single project (emphasis added).[10] This holds for Broadway musicals as well.

Foresight at the beginning, when executives are only selecting work, is difficult on Broadway, but then, turning musicals into films is doubly risky. Nichtern, whose office for Warner Brothers was created to exploit this transposition, admits, "The whole thing is chancy. . . . I don't know if there's a movie in any individual show." Neither does anyone else. Nevertheless, Nichtern, like others in her position, must commit funds to a project: "And you must be ready to contradict everything you said the day before. If somebody comes along with a play that I think is going to be a winner, I'll fight to get into it."

So, when Sam Cohn, theatrical agent, came in with a "package" (another source of Broadway musicals), Nichtern was delighted:

I said, "It's going to be a big hit." It *smelled* that way. I heard the music; I read and loved the story; I felt it could be updated very well. . . . Sam Cohn can make a package. He's brilliant at it. He gets the work. He finds the bookwriter, the music people, the director, the choreographer, the set designer, the theater and producer.

Woman of the Year was Cohn's package created for Lauren Bacall (a show that ran for two years, but did not recoup its investment). Thus, initially, executives design the outline for a project, starting with a theme for a show. Then come the roaring river, the waves of organization, the live show. Barnard tells us there is no secure way to create an effective team of executives. Or, as the saying goes: it's very hard to make predictions— especially about the future.

Stages of a Project: Cult to Sect to Church

But we can briefly portray the generic stages of most projects.

The first organizational stage of any project may be likened to that of a "cult" as envisaged by Max Weber.[11] The scheme of organizational development moves from *cult* to *sect* to *church*. (This phraseology is suggested by Ernst Troeltsch in his Weberian work on Christianity and its institutions.[12]) These stages roughly correspond to the evolution of a musical; however, only a successful musical moves into the church stage.

The *cult* exists while a Broadway project is still embryonic, still marked by a sense of limited resources, still challenged to produce a miracle. The vision of the show is shared by a primary creative team of executives ("I love the idea"). Then, high gusts of emotional energy swirl around this diffuse idea of the "show," eliciting strong initial efforts that money cannot buy. People work "on spec." Not unlike religious fervor, the feeling of high morale fuels and sustains group activity, with participants bent on a kind of crusade. A title and a story outline emerge with a few songs, and individual spirit and personal autonomy, real or illusory, fortify that crusade. A producer and other investors are called forth and an in-group develops. With everyone else part of the out-group, a cult thrives on its isolation. A director's charismatic energy suffuses and leads the onrush of ideas and plans. Often, even at this stage, conflict is endemic, but it is mostly overridden or creatively diffused by executive diplomacy. Sacrifice of energy, time, and money is expected and given; prodigious feats of ingenuity come spontaneously into being. Firings and hirings are endured by the group for its cause, paperwork proliferates, budgets are tested and overrun, the larger theater community is rife with rumors, expectations—and skepticism; media critics privately strive to remain publicly aloof.

All this goes on well before the public verdict of success or failure. It comes as no surprise, for one example, that until the penultimate moment Prince and his staff were convinced *A Doll's Life* (1982) would score. It lasted four days on Broadway. Practically all the staff of *Moose Murders* (1983) expected a flop, and got one. However, in each case, the cult psychology of organizational activity prevailed. It was enlivened by light or dark humor, and to that extent, probably desacralized. During *Moose Murders'* preliminary run, a plaintive cry was ascribed to one young actress, "Jesus, who do I sleep with to get out of this show?"

Sectarianism arises within the cult. It is nourished by a hierarchical corporate overlay, status striving, professional and technical division, the impersonal nexus ("I only work here"), along with greater resistance to change among higher and lesser staff. (Many ideas are called for and few are chosen.) The limits of a budget harden and reduce alternatives. The urge to routinize acts that were initially improvised, inventive, and spontaneous, and the settling in of a concrete power system, presage a condition in which the budget and artistic conviction becomes more resistant to experiment ("That third song is out!"). Factions crystallize in verbal and sometimes substantive combat. The choreographer and the bookwriter clash, musicians are isolated in the pit, stage hands and director wrangle as they negotiate terms, theater and house rules restrict designers. And additional firings leave a residue of negative emotions. Belief in the vision hardens ("It'll work. We'll make it work"). Critique ("Change the ending, get another actor") arouses more affect and is suppressed or delimited. In short, the project and its organization are ritualized, their motions expectable and coherent. Concrete arrangements develop to contain and form the artistic work itself. Readings and rehearsals help set fluid cultist ways and orderly sect processes into the relative rigidity of a partly formed product (even if the show keeps changing, creators always want one more day).

With luck, the merger of corporate routine and artistic form brings on a final phase, that of the *church*. Now, woe to innovators, anyone indisposed to obey, or plain skeptics who withdraw from group rituals. Last-minute

Rehearsal of Walking Happy *(1966)*

The initial organizing of the company often entails going over the script in jam-packed rooms with high-energy communication: the cult phase of musicals. Here the on-line producer Cy Feuer *(center)* is in charge, leading the flow of information among the company, making introductions, and taking the first big step toward the opening night of *Walking Happy*. Despite the high hopes, the show failed to recoup. (Photo credit: Billy Rose Theatre Collection, New York Public Library.)

crises involving money or the loss of personnel must be dealt with swiftly among top executives who risk the erosion of faith by staff, critics, and customers. Charnin agonizes over such a time:

Here's a mistake I'll never repeat. We needed five hundred thousand dollars to put the show on. I had it and figured that if I'd invest my own money as opposed to being one of these accountants who comes along and says, "Put my name up there," we'd be better off. At least I knew something about the business. So I put up five hundred thousand dollars, became a general partner and, all of a sudden, I was a producer. It would have been wiser to wait. [It flopped.]

Schwartz also portrays himself as being as much older and wiser as one can be in a dicey business:

Frankly, I'm sure that if after I've gone through this whole thing with *Rags* and we've done the workshop, when we're all ready to go and open in Boston where it's a catastrophe, I'll be packing my bags and they'll bring in Tommy Tune. But by then, *you're out of control.* All you can say is, "Write this off." The investors make what they can. And maybe you get a *Hello, Dolly!* out of such desperate situations. Then everybody pretends a year later that they liked it all along. But, no, those are mostly miseries. You just try to get the bucks.

Get the bucks and at last the show is ready or partly ready. Executives unwrap the hot product and plunge it into previews. Audience response swiftly tempers the hot work, bending a project either toward the cool routine of critical success or demolition and doom. A painstakingly constructed project can be deconstructed overnight to cut unnecessary losses. Failure is a very large part of all executive experience with musical projects.

But sometimes, as Barnard writes, failure trains executives how to treat a personal question impersonally. An author, after recounting "a horrible emotional experience" he had had (with Bob Fosse) before temporarily retiring from show biz, could calmly observe ten years later:

If a director wanted to change the ending, I don't think that would disturb me anymore. Now I would listen and say, "Why?" If the change sounded right, I'd make it. If not, I'd try to talk him out of it. There's training for collaboration. You have to learn how to do it.

Closing the Project: After the Fall

Much analysis is focused on durable, large-scale corporate entities. The failures, the precarious new start-up organizations, and the host of deteriorating firms that dot every part of our economy have received much less attention. As we have repeatedly noted, before being legally organized as an enterprise, a musical theater project has about a 75 to 80 percent chance of failing (if all attempts to get it staged are taken into account). Consequently, lack of attention to the demise of musical ventures and the executive ceremonies that attend a dignified and harmonious funeral are surprising. Even stable offices like those of such producers as Azenberg, Merrick, Cantor, Prince, and the Shubert Organization have a 40 to 50 percent failure rate. They survive in part by efficiently demolishing obvious failures.

Schoenfeld unsentimentally describes the termination and burial of a project:

> You have a computer. It shows you what you have in the bank. You generally know how business will be at any particular time of the year. You see what your costs are and how you can reduce them, how you can get waivers of royalties if you're able to do that. You see if your theater owner will reduce his rent. . . . But nobody can continue to run on losses. So you try to reduce your costs and if you foresee a few weeks of loss but you're approaching a strong part of the year, you absorb that loss, hoping to recoup it later on.

For marginal and occasional producers, the emotional accompaniment of this logical analysis is more vibrant than Schoenfeld's. Flaxman dwells upon the creative producer's personal, if hypothetical, experience of a flop:

> First, a certain amount of time would go to undamage my own soul which would be really crushed. . . . I'd think, "Well, there's evidently something wrong with my taste. I must face the facts. I believe in this work more than life itself and if nobody goes to see it—I'd better reevaluate whether I should be in the business."

Shows with mixed reviews and equivocal word-of-mouth require fast, hard executive action. Sometimes apparently unaccountable victory is snatched from the gaping jaws of defeat. This occurred when the backers of *The Fantasticks* (1959) made two decisions: (1) to put more money into publicity and operation and (2) not to move from Off-Broadway. After several decades, the profitable little show is still running. An example of snatching defeat from the jaws of victory occurred when Joseph Papp decided to move an artistically and commercially successful show, *The Human Comedy,* from the Off-Broadway Public Theater to Broadway, and to lavish publicity on it. This large-sized incarnation of the musical lasted one week.

Funny things happen on the way to the Broadway forum. The real distance between Not-Broadway and Broadway is several hundreds of thousands of dollars and a carload of glitz. Berman remembers that producing *Joseph and the Amazing Technicolor Dreamcoat* cost about $150,000 in Washington, D.C., about five hundred thousand dollars Off-Broadway, and

$1.2 million to open on Broadway. This "little show" almost got blown away by glitz on its journey to Broadway.

We had a little story from the Bible about a boy and his brothers and his father and the boy's growth. That's all. It's not *42nd Street*; it's not elaborate dance numbers; it's just a small story told in music. [The danger, seen at a production done at the Brooklyn Academy of Music (BAM)] is that they [BAM] glitzed this show up with lots of auxiliary things that did not help.

Only clear executive action, this time by neophyte coproducers, kept the director and designers from glitzing the show into oblivion (and the show succeeded on Broadway). Here we have a not uncommon technique for killing a live musical concept—a concept or vision murdered by an ambitious gang of top executives is the basis of many flops. The critics, then, only confirm its demise.

Producers: Top Executives and Control

No analyst has surpassed Barnard in his understanding of executive functions. Applied to the making of a musical, that understanding keeps *us* from developing tunnel vision. Removing the veils of sociologese, we can see that executive functions pervade an organization from top to bottom. Most acts are impersonal. Most of the system operates without specifics; if effective, any individual does more than his or her job description would suggest. This system is analogous to the central nervous system. "It [the brain] can hardly be said to manage the body, a large part of whose functions are independent of it [and] upon which it in turn depends."[13] Thus vital solutions may come from anyone in the project. Executive work is specialized, but, Barnard insists, it is an illusion that only executives manage the organization. The illusion is similar to that of Chanticleer, a rooster who believed his crowing made the sun come up.

Nevertheless, a subjective sense of power, derived from the illusion of total control, can be very satisfying to Broadway producers and directors. Michael Bennett's gratification, whether objectively justified or not, was clear and unlimited.

I am to a great degree a control freak. I enjoy creating a world that functions the way I think it should. You get a group of people together and create an atmosphere in which they feel comfortable, unthreatened, and able to create. I like that atmosphere for myself and I like to make it possible for other people.

And so what I became over a number of years was a director and a producer with control.

We have already heard Berman's phrase, "the producer's hand" that simultaneously touches everybody. It truly feels "heady" to have an exalted title that confers executive status on its recipient. Nichtern expresses the "rush of power" on her job: "I found *Crimes of the Heart.* I chose the director. I decided to let it be discovered at the Manhattan Theatre Club. The controls were all mine."

With or without illusions about control, producers and directors are executive leaders. Their functions intersect and overlap, yet each has a separable, recognizable area of actual expertise and control. Take producers. First, there is the theater owner, financial producer. Just what is it exactly that he largely does? Let Bernard Jacobs tell it in his own words:

I negotiate booking arrangements. Go over production budgets. As Gerald [Schoenfeld] and I do everything jointly, we decide which shows we will produce. Which shows we will present in our theaters. Which shows we will invest money in. Decide very often which artistic people we will employ for particular projects. Then there's the maintenance and operation of all these buildings. The supervision of the real estate. The placement of advertisements. How much money will be spent. What the advertising budget will be. The hiring of new press agents. Dealing with a host of people all the time. All the things an entrepreneur does in this business.

Not to mention dealing with taxes, Tony awards, etc., etc.

Another type of producer is called "on-line" (or creative), and enters the artistic process. Let us examine certain key functions of such producers.

Producers Who Create "On-Line"

While there are financial producers who invest their money and become general partners with unlimited liability, some of these overstep their bounds by trying for direct influence on the production itself. Putting them to one side for a moment, we will focus on line-producers, or creative producers. They carry an ultimate veto; thus they finally can control business, administrative, and artistic decisions, but in actuality they delegate these daily decision powers to company managers and directors. At one level, the full creative producer is, or had better be, a good collaborator with composers, lyricists, bookwriters, and choreographers—and at the project level, with business managers, designers, lawyers, accountants, public relations people, union reps, those in charge of group sales, and some other professionals. A recent prototype of a "creative producer" is Cameron Mackintosh. Nichtern, also a creative producer, gives us a good picture of the role:

Cameron Mackintosh, Producer (ca. 1990)

Cameron Mackintosh, producer, is based in London. His deep control over each of his shows represents the latest model of a highly successful "on-line" producer. He became quickly famous and wealthy in the 1980s and 1990s for *Cats, Les Misérables, The Phantom of the Opera,* and *Miss Saigon.* These book-song-spectacles now dominate the new image of Broadway. (Photo credit: Michael Le Poer Trench.)

I line-produced for the company *[Crimes of the Heart]*. I made all the decisions on production; I worked on marketing, casting, replacements, and organizing the road company. I had to help raise funds even though, strictly speaking, that wasn't my job. There were no stars. The author was an unknown. . . . Within ten weeks, the production began to show profits. I love the fact that I have to care for this show and that nobody else can say no to me.

But without "control," Nichtern feels thwarted. She experiences "role withdrawal." It has happened to her:

Q: You felt constrained?
A: I felt frustrated. I was not the line producer. I was not the general partner.
Q: What were you? The co-producer?
A: A producer/investor. Also consultant. But that element was a joke.

An author takes an insightful view of the producer:

His role is now very complicated and as important as that of the director or your partners in writing. Except who is he today? He used to be somebody like David Merrick. Neither the Shuberts nor the Nederlanders are qualified to utter one word about a musical. . . . What does a producer do? He hires. He fires. He lays out the road. He protects you and your client while you're busy. He makes quick decisions that are terribly important.

John Weidman, a younger Broadway bookwriter, places the same value on being a producer, that is, someone with a craft or skill "every bit as important as that of the other professionals who make a show work."

Howey, who wanted to land a successful show on Broadway, pinpoints the duality of business and art (as do Nichtern, Berman, and several others):

I never knew a producer until I was one. So it took me three or four years to figure out what I should be doing. At first I didn't want to do anything because I thought the director would want me out of the way. I still believe that but only if the director's fantastic. . . . The trick of a good producer, or, for that matter, a good director, is keeping one leg in the real world and one in the creative world.

The truth about this matter seems to be that in the "real" world, which is that of business, politics, and hard-line administration, one can be creative, and in the "creative" world, one can be "realistic" about business, and whoever masters this balance might become a good producer. But recall, as Nichtern does about musicals, that "unlike film and unlike television, there is nothing on the cutting room floor. You have eight performances a week; you live; it's a live thing."

And Masella: "If I'd just been a directing major in college, I would have had no idea about budget . . . about staff . . . or about how to motivate and direct an organization."

Getting the Option

The producer selects the idea or vision of a show she/he wants to work on. He or she must then first obtain an option to lease the copyrights from owners of basic works or from original owners of an adapted play (usually estates of the authors). Each such option presents its own administrative challenges. Many times the option to lease a copyright is unavailable either because the authors themselves or their estates will not permit it. Also, the cost of purchasing the option may simply be too high, or, "We'll let you do it, only Off-Broadway."

Charnin spent much time securing approval from the family to develop a musical about the opening of baseball to Jackie Robinson. Though generally thought to be well conceived, acted, and directed, it did not succeed on Broadway. Berman and her coproducer had difficulty persuading Tim Rice and Andrew Lloyd Webber, represented by the Stigwood Organization, to put *Joseph* on the Broadway boards. And Enid Futterman, an author, spent ten years trying to obtain an option to *The Diary of Anne Frank*. It took three more years and the powers of John Flaxman to persuade both the family estate and a number of creative people to sign contracts because of that prolonged struggle. Finally, Flaxman notes, you sign "the worst contract in the world," which you hope you can ultimately revise.

Getting into the Deep Pocket

It is fairly well known that producers—financial, creative, line, or collaborative—must have fundraising skills, not the least part of which may be attracting a "name" the movie industry would call "bankable." So for *Annie,* Charnin says that once he had persuaded Mike Nichols to come in, fundraising was less difficult.

Periodically, even the best go down, as Prince has learned:

Evita carried me, but not my [American] investors. . . . *Evita* was financed from England and so the biggest winner I ever had they're not party to. It would have taken care of *Merrily We Roll Along* and *A Doll's Life* [neither of which recouped] and so that's tragedy. . . . It's bad enough to feel awful about your own disappointments. The backers' money is one burden too many.

With the backing comes the start-up, and Oliver Smith, a master set designer, notes the pace of different producers. Some work slowly and carefully, others very rapidly, but their tempo or temper does not necessarily correlate with a plus or minus outcome.

Creating through Conflict Resolution

The techniques of settling disagreements also vary. Producers, like all of Barnard's efficient executives, must "synthesize. . . contradictory forces" and secure "essential efforts" to keep "communication" open. In theatrical lingo, they also need to retain a sense of the "whole show."

Nichtern, who loves control, knows the subtle uses of politics that are inextricably linked to her role: "You don't have to be democratic. You have to be *diplomatic.* You must listen and hear everyone in the room. Sometimes you discover they're not talking about what's there. Straighten it out tactfully and you'll do a lot better." When producers and directors truly collaborate, resolving artistic disputes is a joint function. Even though Masella maintains that it is a director's duty, he realizes a producer may join the effort. Conflicts over contracts, however, he leaves to the producer and lawyers and agents and authors.

For Berman, the collaboration between a line or creative producer and a director requires balance:

There is a built-in friction. I think it's healthy because it keeps everyone on their toes. . . . Though we're sitting there right on top of [the director] . . . a lot of times you have to acquiesce. . . . Obviously the director will see more than you do when you're handling 4,000 other things. [But] *we never had a deadlock.* It was give-and-take, this for that, him for her.

Like so many others, one respected theatrical agent feels that in the old days a producer such as Kermit Bloomgarden played the gentle father figure to his squabbling family of artists—distancing himself just enough to attain a measure of objectivity. Of course there were and are all kinds of father and mother figures. A few used their authority to promote conflict out of which creative ideas were expected to arise under deadline pressure. A standard ploy, traceable on the world stage to Machiavelli, this stratagem can never have been a mystery to power players.

The Hiring and Firing of Directors during Development

Unless otherwise constrained, the principle producer, rarely if ever defined in a group as such, with concurrence from the authors, selects a director judged to "fit" the "style" and "vision" of the show (unless a director is part of the writing team from the start). This is akin to the practice of large corporations hiring top executives from outside their own ranks. Sometimes the show goes on. Sometimes, perhaps after a workshop, a tryout, or the night before opening in a prime city—disaster strikes.

The Great Boston Massacre on the original version of *My One and Only* (1983) is history, but history with a happy ending. The muscle-producer (the one of eight with the most money involved) fired the director, the musical director, and the bookwriter before opening night. The choreographer became the director. Five million dollars and three consultant-doctors later, it was a hit show. In a little-known Buffalo massacre, the director was fired the night before the opening; the choreographer (whom we interviewed) also resigned; the lead actors left; the show (like many that never reach Broadway) died aborning (another unrecorded pre-Broadway flop).

In practically all projects, you get entangled in trouble with a show for a variety of reasons nearly always related to inescapable dilemmas. At these points, a priceless gift is that of being cool about hot material—being "objective."

Distance from the Show

Historians and survivors mark the twenties, thirties, and forties as an extended period in which old-time producers flourished as the top dogs of Broadway musicals. Burton Lane remembers a day in California when Alex Aarons reached him by phone. The year was 1939:

> Alex was best-known then for having produced the Gershwin shows. . . . "Burt, do you want to write a show?" I didn't even ask what the hell it was. He said Yip Harburg was going to do the lyrics. I said yes.
>
> In those days there were some producers like Aarons with a real sense of theater. Alex also had a sharp ear for music and could play the piano himself. He had real appreciation for quality in music.

Debuskey, extolling old line-producers, puts it another way:

> Once upon a time most producers had to have a long apprenticeship. . . . They knew the creative side of theater. If one of them had strong convictions about a particular property, he was capable of helping out in many ways, straight through to production.

Laurents reviews the past, then suggests that a good producer should keep a distance from the show to provide objectivity for the live artists:

There are so many really foolish notions about the theater. For example, authors shouldn't direct. Authors originally were the only ones who directed. Then producers directed, like David Belasco, like Arthur Hopkins, like Welles.

What I think the producer should do, he must get the money, of course; he should have taste, he should pick a play or a musical that he himself believes in and likes, try to get the best people and when they are working, he is the one, since he should retain objectivity, to say, "Look, this is what we're all going for and I think you're either off the track here and on the track there."

Schoenfeld, a prototype of the present-day theater owner and financial producer, is explicit about his role:

The involvement of a producer in the creative aspects of a show has become less and less pronounced because we are in a period of musicals which are very long and very intricate. Few producers have enough time or talent to devote to it.

Furthermore, those producers who have artistic sensibility run into the problem of sharing ideas with, or influencing, the strong director. Nichtern feels "passive" about not being a line-producer on one project; she is allowed to consult but feels that her advice is not taken seriously. Similarly, Prince's early experience with George Abbott was in some ways frustrating:

I was the producer in half a dozen shows or more that we did together. . . . I would make frequent suggestions. And maybe he accepted *one* in all those years. It was for *Fiorello.* Abbott said, "What a terrific idea! I'll do that tomorrow." And he did! It took me the longest time to realize that very likely 75 percent of the rest of my suggestions were very good.

Nichtern's conception of a line-producer includes much more presence:

Someone might say, "You can have artistic input, but you can't have financial input." There's no way to make that separation. If you don't have it *all,* you don't have anything.

We were told very plainly by Prince, Charnin, Laurents, Stone, Tune, and several others that they do not desire to be producers. Producers are usually unsung. As in any occupation, the majority are mediocre and can kill shows by obtrusive business (and artistic) decisions. (How many rock 'n' roll shows flopped after *Hair!*) So being a director is now a more sought-after role, if you want "control" of the show's artistic vision.

Directors Are a Different Breed

Directors, much more than producers, want to head up the "core artistic" work, to aim their talents and skills at pulling the whole show together. Charnin's analogy of a fleet is apposite:

The director is a visionary who ideally knows everything there is to know, for instance, about how to make orchestrations match costumes, dialogue, scenery and performance. A show is like an armada, a large fleet, with many ships. You bring them into port at different times because they arrive at different times. Once that fleet is docked, it's the show.

Charnin's figure of speech suits the situation. It captures the general complexity and the specific difficulty of communicating, as well as the maneuvering of forces, the need for exquisite timing, for coordination of "elements." Given the magnitude of a musical project, it is the overview that a director, in top executive form, must maintain.

Carol Hall adds to the imagery:

You've got all these crazies, each one howling like an Israelite in the desert. You need a Moses, and I guess that's what the director is.

Ed Kleban says that somebody's in a horrible car accident. You take him to the hospital. The eye surgeon and the brain surgeon operate, and the bone setter and the stomach specialist get busy and if the patient lives, it's a hit musical. That's a really good analogy. I think the director's important because he or she must lead these strong-minded experts.

Artistic Leader

The director must have a feel for the basic story, the vision of the show, and then go on to interpret it—else the role of artistic leader is abdicated. And there will be no show.

Tune sharply contrasts the director's work with the choreographer's:

Directing is interpretive. Choreographing is creative. Choreography doesn't exist in the script. The director is given the script. . . . A choreographer goes onto the stage and starts writing his script on the dances. They represent two different talents. But choreographers sometimes go off on their own tangents and take you very far away from the problem at hand, which is presenting the material. It's hard for me as a director to get them back to the librettist's interpretation. He wrote the words, and my job is to take it from there.

Whence the famous wars between bookwriters and directors and choreographers; and hence the reason other directors, such as Schwartz, make heroic collaborative efforts before all parts of the project start "to go forward together." But such efforts give way to personal or visceral reactions. Schwartz: "I'm a big one for getting together and saying 'All right, what's the show about, guys?' But I find that's often hard to say. At first I just go with my instincts." In a fascinating aside tossed off while recounting a sad saga about the vicissitudes of developing *The Baker's Wife,* Schwartz mentions that it took seven years to discover "what that show was about."

Tommy Tune and Twiggy in My One and Only *(1983)*

Not many directors are also choreographers and performers. Tommy Tune began his career as a dancer. Here he is shown dancing with Twiggy, his costar in *My One and Only* (1983), which Tune also directed. The show is a pastiche of Gershwin songs held together by a twenties-style musical comedy book. After a disastrous preview period in Boston, it was "reconstructed" and became a hit show on Broadway. (Photo credit: Kenn Duncan.)

The Directing Force

When organizations grow larger, executives must exert more power. As Broadway musicals got more costly, directorial power increased. In Broadway musicals of the eighties it was directors who had the last word on core artistic matters in general. Bennett's ruminations are indicative of certain psychological factors that may predispose some people to be directors.

Obviously, I was someone who at a very early age wanted to be a leader, not a follower. Otherwise, none of this would have happened to me. Directors are leaders of the group.

If a show is not working, that creates a great deal of tension and strain on all of the people who are responsible for that show, and it gets harder at that point for everyone to work well together. It's the leader who makes everything calm, gives everyone a sense of purpose and direction.

Likewise Prince:

I must have the final word. People have walked away from that over the past twenty-five years, which is their prerogative. Choreographers can leave or accept the finality of my word. There's no halfway house.

Charnin (as director) and Jules Fisher (as producer) and Laurents (as director) say very much the same thing.

Directors reach for control over all aspects of a show in order ultimately to "move an audience" (Bennett), to laughter, tears, tension, and resolution. We will discuss their vision and control of "staging the action" later in this book. Bennett pinpoints the aim:

From the moment a show starts, you want the audience to be with that show, not mind-tripping, not getting ahead of the plot, not reading their program, not getting bored. You don't want to lose them. You want to keep them right there and you want the show to have eruptions in the high points. You want your show stoppers. You want to provide the emotional experience that an audience expects and that is what is attached to what they consider a great live theatrical experience, that makes for something that makes them run out and say, "I want to see this again—I want to tell my friends about it."

A show, however entertaining, must also have a *soupçon* of intellectual content, a meaningful theme that also moves an audience.

By Moving Actors . . .

Those who directly affect the audience through dialogue and songs within the framework of a story are actors; the story is told by its principal actors.

For this reason a paramount function of the director must be casting the right actors and then moving them to move the audience. And moving actors remains a unique function of the director. In rehearsal, no other executive is supposed to address actors directly. The whole team may collaborate in selecting actors for key roles, but it is the director's task to move them to express the vision of the show. How this occurs is another story, but it partly resides in a director's style.

Masella analyzes the styles of directors:

There is a style of expression. This is the way a director expresses thoughts. Some people do it in a more naturalistic way, some in a more stylized way, just as a painter does. Some painters show their brush strokes. Some are more realistic. Some painters paint with their fingers, just to create different textures. Directors also can do that in the way they conceive the look and the motion of a production.

That, I think, comes first of all from within. From what excites you, what images, what rhythms interest you personally as a director. I like very bright stages . . . very smooth transitions . . . blackouts. . . . That comes from an aesthetic taste—for want of a better word. . . . You develop that and you figure out how to express it.

If you study directors, you notice that they have their different ways of making the production happen. Some yell and bark and carry on. Others are very cool.

And Growing . . .

But styles of expression, technical preferences, interpersonal skills, and themes should change over time, and Masella reflects on a period and personality he encountered at the start of his career:

George Abbott was in his heyday as great as he was because he was a man who developed. If you look at what he did over his life as a director, you get the sense that he started in this genre, then he moved on to that. He was *constantly changing.* As Hal has been. If you look at Hal's earlier shows like *Pajama Game* and look at *Evita,* you see a few years make a difference. That's good. I hope I have that kind of a career.

Bennett, then apparently in midcareer, had similar concerns:

I care that the theater goes on. I don't care that it goes on with any of the rules. I see older people try to keep things the same. I worry about the day when I start to want to keep things the same. It happens with age and it's going to happen to me. At the point where that happens, I hope I'm smart enough to retire.

We will have much more to say about directors' ways throughout the chapters of this book.

Bob Avian, James Kirkwood, Michael Bennett, Marvin Hamlisch, Nicholas Dante, Ed Kleban at the 3,389th Performance of A Chorus Line *(1983)*

Shown here are the cast and collaborative team of *A Chorus Line* at the 3,389th performance of one of the then-longest runs in Broadway history (1975–1990). Center stage is the director/conceiver Michael Bennett, backed by *(from left to right,* in tuxedos*)* Robert Avian (assistant director), James Kirkwood (coauthor), Marvin Hamlisch (composer), Nicholas Dante (coauthor), Ed Kleban (lyricist), and the company. While no longer on Broadway, the show continues to have a strong life here and abroad. (Photo credit: Martha Swope.)

Collaboration at the Top: Linking Project and Show

The executive set-up in a large-scale organization, Barnard wrote in 1938, is composed of positions, roles, and individuals, but he warned that no theory can equip us to forecast the effectiveness of a specific top-level team nor yet how to create a predictably effective executive system. This is also true in musical theater projects. But more than fifty years later, executives themselves still speculate about how they operate and about the pump that primes executive energy. Flaxman believes:

> What we have going is what I think everybody should have: "perfect coordination" between producer and director.
> A director should be a cockeyed optimist. He should believe that what he's doing is best and there's no question about it. If he doesn't feel confident, you're in trouble. The producer should be a little bit of a pessimist, someone who can cover any contingency. When you ask me about the budget, I've got to be concerned. The director shouldn't have to worry about that.

There are other organizational styles. David Merrick's is that of the strong, tough producer. But even in his case it is an illusion that any one man does a musical show. On *42nd Street,* Merrick may reap all the net profit, but Gower Champion, the director-choreographer, along with several others, had to have been more than competent for that long-running show to have worked.

Wearing his producer's hat, Bennett initiated the concept, selected the writers, assembled the creative team, and raised the money. He handed line-producing over to others and crowned himself the director, a man who enjoys full rein (or full reign). Prince also operates like this, except that his office people, who have a record of more than thirty years together, now do the work of producing. And a relative newcomer, Gail Berman, thinks out loud that maybe Merrick's mode is the "way to go"—even though her own organization at the top is what might be called "a community of unequals," or a "copartnership of line-producers."

In multimillion-dollar productions, there are almost always efforts by working coproducers to be in harmony with strong directors. How are producers and directors linked? Prince, in his book *Contradictions,* cites a number of mistakes in selecting top personnel, mistakes that when made again destroyed quality collaboration. What are the varying arrangements devised (and sworn by!) linking producers, directors, bookwriters, composers, and lyricists? Whatever the requirements for an effective executive system are, most teams stay together just long enough to close the flop. Each new project is undertaken by a new set of executives. The few stable producing offices (e.g., Prince, Shubert, Azenberg, Merrick) do manage to take their flops along with their hits. Barnard and Flaxman's search for "perfect coordination," Nichtern and Bennett's claim to "total control," Masella's commitment to "good communication," Schoenfeld's need to balance the "bottom line," Nichtern's idea of "creative organizing," and Charnin's grand metaphor of "docking a fleet"—each provides a piece of the puzzle. All portray executive efforts to construct and launch a musical project. There is much about themselves that remains unknown even to the collaborators themselves of Broadway musical projects.

Broadway Leadership

The strength of Broadway lies in its daring entrepreneurial flexibility. The invalid never dies, annual jeremiads notwithstanding. The stuff sells; the myths abound. In 1985, a new outfit called The Producers Group came into being, minus theater owners, mindful of the American Society of Composers, Authors, and Publishers (ASCAP) and the Songwriters Guild, the latter without publishers. The purpose of the new producers' group was to rejuvenate Broadway, in part with a refrain that is eternal: "To have a healthier industry we need more hits"—or fewer flops.

But, a flop on or Off-Broadway in New York City is, fortunately, not the last word. Schwartz reminds us:

In real life, speaking as a creative person and simply as a person who goes to see things, to me a show is ultimately a hit if it lives. It's a flop if it disappears, even if it's a big whatever—a nine day wonder and then disappears forever. If it doesn't have a life, then that's not what you meant it to do. But a show like *Working*, which was a flop on Broadway, didn't make money, ran three weeks, but now it's five years later and it's being done all over the place and it continues. That, to me, feels like a success.

A final note from Chester Barnard: "All purposeful social actions of individuals produce consequences not sought for"—as any top executive (and investor) must know before initiating a Broadway musical. [14]

4. Top Executives Score
the Action

F ew people know that Aristotle, in his great work *The Poetics,* circa
450 B.C., articulated principles of creating the "musical play" that
still provide us with profound insights into the modern American
Broadway renaissance of the twentieth century. Medieval mystery plays,
Shakespeare and Molière plays, Mozart, Verdi, and Wagner operas represent different Italian, English, French, and German/Viennese incarnations
of musical theater. In twentieth-century America, a new, popular, polyglot
form arose, combining an array of native and immigrant strains. Known
variously, and not always correctly, as the musical comedy, the Broadway
musical, the book musical, and, lately, the concept musical, or simply as
the musical play, both serious and comedic, it bears an ancient heritage.

Broadway musical plays in the twentieth century owe much to Aristotle's
teachings, as we shall see. But today, near the end of this century after the
great wave of Broadway vintage book musicals of the forties, fifties, and
sixties had spread their energy and receded, the infinite potential of high
technology and new musical sounds provides artists with fertile grounds for
movement in the musical art form.

Aristotle's view of poetry as the basis of musical plays provides us with
an arbitrary vantage point from which to consider the historically more
recent Broadway musical. In their ancient beginnings, the "poets" or "play-
makers" assumed that power lay in their vision, their theme, and, as we
would say today, their story line. Their continuity is real. Not so many
years ago, Oscar Hammerstein asserted that songs, score, and staging are
servants of the story. But the story must emerge with its theme intact.
How its beginning, middle, and end achieve closure or wholeness in the
experience of a live audience, in short, how a musical play is conceived and

executed—all this has undergone immeasurable change through the centuries.

Twentieth-century American musicals differ above all in one respect from musical theater of the past. While always a fusion of several art forms, earlier musical theater was not created through continuous collaboration or give and take among artists and artisans. In ancient Greece it was almost a one-man show. Much later, in European opera, a playwright would complete a libretto (dialogue and song lyrics), then a composer would set it; they would not work back and forth, but separately. Thus, in the past, a composer would literally "score the action" a playwright gave him, setting music to the text or story and lyrics to the music. Traditionally, composers of operas are given most of the credit for the work (who but cognoscenti know the names of Mozart's and Verdi's librettists?). "Scoring the action" in an American Broadway musical, on the other hand, has had a unique and ever-evolving history as a collaborative effort, a group skill still, as always, in transition and with many variations. Now, from the collaborative creation of several primary artists, each skilled in different crafts, emerges the first written draft of a musical (script and score) that is then transformed into live theater by being rehearsed many times on a stage before an audience. The fundamental method of collaboration among playwrights, lyricists, composers, and, now, directors has drastically changed. This process has served to change the craft, not to say the end product, of Broadway musicals.

As we write, the vintage book-musical is being replaced on Broadway with the book-song-spectacle. The size of the musical has grown and requires, as in one recent show, *Les Misérables,* the adaptation of a traditional realistic novel by the (publicly unknown) bookwriter and two (well-known) directors. Musicals with light books like *42nd Street* and *Cats* have emerged, requiring "construction" but not heavy-duty book or story. The small musical, struggling Off-Broadway and in regional theaters, re-emerges. It provides fallow ground for experiment, including musicals with no credited authors or with so many that they are all forgotten. The craft of bookwriter (also known as a musical playwright or librettist) is merged, when it is not submerged, in an historically new mode. The American musical is now created with many collaborators, and new visions materialize in the collective "poetry" of musical plays.

Action and Passion: Musical Drama

In Aristotle's time, and for at least a century before that, "poetry" was the generic term given to the work of "poets" (authors) who represented basic human action. The name "drama" was given to those poems (our plays) that imitated that action. According to Aristotle, wonderfully paraphrased by Francis Fergusson, well-made poems, preeminently those by an artist like Sophocles, encompass two contrasting but interrelated concepts: "action" and "passion" (or praxis and pathos).

Action is active: the psyche perceives something it wants, and (moves) toward it. Passion is passive: the psyche suffers something it cannot control or understand, and (is moved) thereby. In human experience, action and passion are always combined. . . . There is no movement of the psyche which is all passion totally devoid of purpose and understanding . . . [a]nd there is no human action without its . . . ill-defined feelings or emotions.[1]

In Aristotle's terms, action (praxis) does *not* simply signify deeds, events, or physical activity: the action that art tries to reproduce may be described metaphorically as a movement of the psyche toward what seems good to it at the moment—a "movement-of-spirit," Dante called it (or so Fergusson persuasively argues). When Aristotle says "action" in the *Poetics,* he means the working out of a psychic movement to its climax in success or failure.

Also, according to Aristotle, poetry expresses the universal moments of human action and pathos, and is therefore the opposite of historical writing, which in its language and purpose points to unrepeatable particulars. By universal, Aristotle meant "how a person of a certain type will on occasion speak or act, according to the law of probability or necessity."[2] However, "It is probable that many things should happen contrary to probability."[3] Thus universal moments can emerge for the audience either from rare or from ordinary events highlighted by a poet-playwright.

Drama was the Greek name given to those poems depicting "action in plays," through the device of "plots." For Aristotle, *"the poet or 'maker' should be the maker of plots* rather than of verses, since he is a poet because he imitates, and what he imitates are actions."[4]

Then, in Aristotle's formulation, the episodes of the plot unfold

in language embellished with each kind of artistic ornament . . . in the form of action, not of narrative. . . . By "language embellished," I mean language into which rhythm, "harmony," and song enter. . . some parts are rendered through the medium of verse alone, others again with the aid of song.[5] . . The Chorus too should be regarded as one of the actors; it should be an integral part of the whole, and share in the action.[6]

If song is integral to drama, to be most effective, the language of plays must be lyrical. Only through rhythm, and song with melody, harmony, and heightened lyrical images, can an audience empathize with the movement of the human spirit, or action, that the playwright is conveying. Aristotle also noted the main structural difficulty for [musical] playwrights to this day —namely, that authors may succeed in tying the knot of conflict in the first act, but fail to unravel it by the end:

[T]he plot, being an imitation of an action, must imitate one action and that a whole, the structural union of the parts being such that, if any one of them is displaced or removed, the whole thing will be disjointed and disturbed.[7]

The principle of "wholeness" in a play is largely achieved through a structure with a clear beginning and end to an action. Many creators of Broadway musicals with whom we spoke seemed to agree that basically there must first be an originating idea transformed into a story, and that this story must quickly seize the audience and then carry it to a closure, an ending, a consummation.

The action of a show is generated by a story idea or a *theme,* a basic generator of conflict and suspense, and *by a story line* (episodes) that moves the audience along. A story line has at least a beginning and an end. But the end must tie in with the beginning—and therein lies the mystery. The *theme,* the intent, hence the *raison d'être* or meaning, of a show is what makes it cohere, makes it coherent. Laurents:

The first question you have to resolve is what is it about. Once you have your theme, you put it in the back of your head. It will permeate everything you write.

I just said *Gypsy* was about the need for recognition. That is timeless. What you have to find is the universal.

Apropos *West Side Story,*

An idea clicked. It hit something in me. In this case, it was the combination of the social background and the idea that love is destroyed in a world of violence, and prejudice breeds violence.

Then what is it that makes a story? The issue is basic enough to quote from a variety of observers. First, a theme is not a story line, and without a story there is no drama. Howey: "If you have a passion to write this play, but you don't know how it ends, as far as I'm concerned, you really don't know why you wrote the play." A successful and especially astute agent, still very active in a career that began over thirty years ago, sounds the same note as Howey. She recalls Lillian Hellman, exclaiming: "What's wrong with the young playwrights? They know what they're against but they don't know what they're for."

Prince also affirms that the *raison d'être* of a work appears at the end of the story:

You hear about novelists, star novelists who don't know where novels are going to end? Well, there must be playwrights who do that, too. And there must be lousy musical books that have been written that way and have gone on to be very successful; but the truth is it's not a good rule. You really ought to know where you're going. Where you're going implies you had a reason to get there.

Laurents:

If you don't know where you will end, how can you know where to begin? I knew exactly what was going to happen at the end of *West Side Story*. The girl would not die as Juliet did, and she couldn't. She had too much strength. That's how I saw her character.

Stone:

You have an overall vision of the end, the middle, the beginning. . . . That *is* the scenario; that *is* the libretto.

Bennett:

A show is still basically a story and a story needs a good beginning, middle and end and it has to entice you gradually, get you involved. You have to root for characters and care about them.
   [A Chorus Line] was not the average book construction. [But] it still had a beginning, middle and an end. It breaks a lot of rules while it replaces the same values that the original rules were intended to do in the first place, so what it is is a different form of the same thing.

Laurents shows how the ending of *A Chorus Line* points up the theme: the metaphor of a "line" obliterates individuality:

These kids are told, "We are going to do a show. We want to know what each of you is and then we'll write the part just for you"—which is bull. How does the show end? They're *all* on the chorus line. Not one of them is special. The girl who is supposed to be is yanked out of the chorus line, falls on her ass and returns to the chorus line. She wasn't special. She still isn't.

A story, then, can be told in a few concise sentences and the universal idea or theme can be put into a few words. Developing these ideas into a show should technically proceed, as Aristotle, Laurents, and Stone (among many) tell us, from an *outline*. (More about this a little later.)

One of the many factors accounting for the high ratio of flops to hits on Broadway is that few shows start with a well-conceived theme and a story that goes from a beginning to an end. Thus, the producer Nichtern affirms that a show "has to start from a story" and "original ideas are very scarce.

Bookwriters for musicals are very, very hard to come by." It is her observation that too many shows are initiated by composer-lyricists who first create a score of songs and then try to "get" a story. The result is a "nonfit." Prince reiterates:

You've got to know the beginning and the end. You've got to know the trajectory. And if you know the trajectory, I think you are well on the way to having the spine for the show. The trouble with so many shows is that people don't know the trajectory.

Bennett:

I look for stories that I care about. The story comes first. I have to find a character I can relate to, one I can root for. I want to worry about what happens to people. The story must have a really nice beginning, a nice middle and a nice end.

Meaningful themes and their presence within a story line are very difficult to create, and are rare.

Plays without Song and Musical Plays

Few people today are aware that the creation of plays with little or no music and no song or dance began only in the 1700s. As a genre, "straight plays" proliferated perhaps in part because the musical dimension compounds a work's complexity, not to speak of practical difficulties in creating and producing it. Nevertheless, straight plays flop even more on Broadway than musicals: our figures indicate that 80 percent of all straight plays flopped on Broadway from 1940 to 1990 (see appendix 4.3). In the poor season of 1971–72, twenty-six of twenty-seven flopped and seventeen of twenty musicals also flopped. The inference is obvious (it has hardly gone unnoticed): large segments of the Broadway audience are not as attracted to straight plays as to musicals.

What is of import is that the interests and skills required for creating a straight play are different from those demanded of a musical play. Plays in which music and lyrics predominate are, in Tommy Tune's opinion, structured in ways different from straight plays.

It's a librettist's job in a musical to link all the higher moments together. He is not given high moments. If he writes a high moment, nine chances out of ten, the composer-lyricist is going to scoop that cherry off the top and tell it in music. He gets the job of leading up to and moving away from the plum and because the music, the song and the dance are higher energy expressions than the spoken word, I think regular dialogue pales.

Further ways in which musical plays are distinctively structured: scenes and monologues are replaced by songs or recitatives that take up stage time. Therefore, exposition in a musical play needs to be condensed. Music heightens the emotion of a play; it can take the place of or comment on words.

Thus, as Kurt Weill wrote, speech and words should fuse with the music and story:

A play must be conceived from the very beginning as a musical play, if the demands of musical theater are to be at all fulfilled; the form of the play must be created from the musical point of view; the action of the musical play must be more pliable than that of sheer drama. . . . The aim and meaning of the musical theater is the binding of speech and music, the most thoroughgoing fusion of the two. . . . Song is not a simple interruption of action. . . . It projects the actions of the play to a different and higher level. . . . It lifts the characters out of the frame of the play and makes them express, directly or indirectly, the philosophy of the author. The power of music makes it possible to extend the movement of a word and its operation so that the values of speech find their complement in the values of music.

One of the most difficult form problems of contemporary playwrights is the balancing of the opposed values of humor and tragedy without having one destroy the other. . . . In a musical play the author can mingle these elements with far greater freedom.[8]

In the last two centuries, most American playwrights have heard their dramatic vision in words alone—but a few feel they cannot fully express themselves in plays without songs. At times the rare composer, such as Kurt Weill, will lead strong playwrights into adapting stories for American musicals, e.g., Elmer Rice's *Street Scene* and Maxwell Anderson's *Lost in the Stars.*

The Universality of Song

Each theater song fits into a dramatic episode or scene, it is a whole, an entity, a cosmic, albeit a microcosmic, vignette. Great songs connect with one's soul, with each soul in an audience. They haunt you, they imprint, they last as long as we do. Carol Hall admits, "I'm not religious, but I learned you could be saved by a song." Songs heal. Songs arouse. They suit our moods. The reasons a song can be a powerful form of human communication were analyzed with unsurpassed wit by Yip Harburg:

It was eons before man began to invent language. Man could growl and grunt and groan, yodel and even sing. When he dragged his Neanderthal bride over the threshold of his cave his larynx was able to warble a lilting cadenza of joy long before he could say, "Baby, it's cold outside."

Kurt Weill, Elmer Rice, Langston Hughes Collaborating on Street Scene *(1947)*

One of the more innovative composers in Broadway history, Kurt Weill *(left)* wrote serious "musical dramas" with major American writers, whom he persuaded to collaborate on musicals. Here is Weill with the creative team of *Street Scene* (1947): Elmer Rice *(center)*, bookwriter, and Langston Hughes, lyricist. (Photo credit: courtesy Weill-Lenya Research Center, Kurt Weill Foundation for Music, New York.)

This perhaps explains why people today can hum a tune, but can't remember the words. Music, which is an extension of our emotions, comes naturally. It is the vested interest of the heart, a very ancient organ. The word must be worked at and memorized, for it is the vested interest of the frontal lobe, a rather recent development.

So man finally invented words. And words gave man his finest tool with which to confuse, conceal, obfuscate, and antagonize. And that's where the trouble began and where it's still at—no communication. You have only to read the Bible to know the mess that the ancient world and the Hebrew children were in. Always in danger of disappearing, like most of the ancient tribes . . . the song prevailed. And so did the Hebrew children, who now, after thousands of years of persecution and diaspora are still magnetized and brought together every year by the overwhelming magic of a hymn known as Kol Nidre.

But this kind of magic in song happens only when the words give destination and meaning to the music and the music gives wings to the words. Together, they go places.

Words make you think thoughts; music makes you feel a feeling. A song makes you feel a thought. To think a thought is an intellectual process; to feel a thought is an artistic process—that is getting to the heart of people. That's the great advantage. To feel the thought. You rarely feel a thought with just dialogue itself. And that's why song is the most powerful weapon there is. It's poignant and you can teach more through song and you can rouse more through song than all the prose in the world or all the poems.

You've got to bring that audience up to such an emotional pitch that they want to applaud. And this is what dialogue cannot do. Only song can do that, for the reason that I tried to explain, that song is the primitive, prime method, the tool for the human being to express the fullest emotions, the innermost quality of emotion—the tune plus the word.[9]

But within the arena of musical theater, within the story line, no song stands alone. The set of songs called a score must work together, integrated through a story line. Hence, the lyrical-musical craft of writing theater songs includes knowing how to create a full score. But each song must first be true to itself, then be true to the other songs, and most importantly, all of them must also be true to the story line.

Harvey Schmidt, one of the creators of a timeless work, *The Fantasticks,* put it in these words:

The songs that communicate the most directly have very strong profiles and usually appear on the first encounter [with each song] to be likeable, understandable and knowable. It is instantly clear . . . and you are free to respond accordingly. You quickly read its own special personality, characteristic, and color. It stands alone and is unlike any other song in the show.

If the *entire score* is successful, you end up with a whole family of such individual musical statements, each very personal and different, yet joining together to form an entire mountain range of strong profiles joined at the base in a common landscape of musical style.[10]

Unity and Wholeness

Because the story, song, dance, and staging in a musical exert a common demand, a great musical play weaves story, lyrical, and musical ideas toward that unity of action of which Fergusson reminds us:

"The unity of action," Coleridge wrote, "is not properly a rule, but in itself the great end, not only of drama . . . not only of poetry, but of poesy in general, as the proper generic term inclusive of all the fine arts as its species."[11]

And in the eighties, Frank Rich observed, "In a great musical, all the parts carry each other and the contributions should be roughly equal. They should become seamless. It should work like an organism." The power of theater songs, in one guise or another, reveals their presence in all cultures. But they must serve the play.

The American Musical on Broadway

In the Latest Beginning . . . While the names of composers in American musical theater are more or less well known, those of bookwriters (and lyricists)—like opera librettists—are often unknown. This situation has historical roots. The musical theater in America that emerged in the early 1900s on Broadway was woven eclectically from many sources, e.g., black minstrel shows, New York Yiddish theater, British music hall highjinks, vaudeville. In these genres discrete songs were performed by actors in skits and sketches, or simply in a solo song with a "bouncing ball" to let the audience participate.

In the early days of Broadway in this century, the "book" was rarely palpable. Producers did in fact borrow, transfer, and "interpolate" songs and speeches. Most versions of the newly developing American musical theater were revues, slapstick comedies, or vaudeville-burlesque. There was no need in any of them for a coherent book. They were spawned like flies (forty-eight new ones opened on Broadway in 1924) and had a fly's life span. The twenties Broadway musical comedy, to change a metaphor, grew like Topsy: it "never was born / never was born / [it] just grew like cabbage and corn."[12]

Yet within the plethora of flops and fly-by-night entertainments, a few sophisticated authors like Jerome Kern and his collaborators began to create American musicals with at least a faint line traceable from fifth-century Athens, but on Broadway at the Princess Theater. Kern wrote in

1917: "It is my opinion that the musical numbers should carry on the action of the play and should be representative of the personalities of the characters who sing them. Songs must be suited to the action and the mood of the play."[13]

The casual insertion of Tin Pan Alley singles or popular songs into a musical play was different from the paths tried by Kern and Hammerstein and the Gershwins, which demanded a new set of crafts, lyrics, and music, for theatrical songwriters.

When Kern and others set out to "carry on the action of the play" and suit the songs to characters who sang them, the role of a credited specialist, i.e., bookwriter, came into being. Most early bookwriters were ill trained and uninspired, but a few, like Guy Bolton and P. G. Wodehouse, were humorous and skillful. The early Gershwin books to Gershwin shows, while flimsy, began to have some "integrity." So much can be said for *Oh, Kay!* and *Lady, Be Good!*. The pioneer theatrical songwriters (as distinct from denizens of Tin Pan Alley) claimed they could not write without a book; they needed characters in a story to inspire them. Thus, throughout the twenties and thirties, given the humorous, continuous but weak story lines, the songs were much stronger than the vehicles; and some of these songs live now, whereas the shows do not.[14]

The Broadway musical comedy audience was predominantly composed of the new century American corporate professionals, the "tired businessmen" and their wives of the middle-upper class who could afford the price of a ticket. And the demand for a laugh, a song, romantic sensation, sexual innuendo, and, always, an upbeat ending shaped the newly emerging Broadway musical comedy, from the revues of Ziegfeld, Garrick, and George White to the more sophisticated play forms of Wodehouse, Field, and Bolton for the scores, among others, of Kern, Hammerstein, and the Gershwins.

Burton Lane, who started composing songs for Shubert revues when he was a sixteen-year-old boy in the late twenties, recalls:

Revues were like separate sketches, separate songs, like a glorified vaudeville show except you had new material. Rodgers and Hart started doing *The Garrick Gaieties*. Wonderful songs came out of it. George Gershwin wrote with Buddy DeSylva. They did *The George White Scandals,* or would interpolate songs. It was rare for one writer to do an entire revue. That happened later.

I recall the kind of musical shows we did as vehicles. I mean a show starring Fred Astaire, or Ethel Merman or Bert Lahr, a show starring Ed Wynn. Who in hell cared what the book was? You'd get professional writers, the kind of guys who would now do series on television, funny men, gag writers. They'd throw a book together when they were in rehearsal.

Guy Bolton, P.G. Wodehouse, Jerome Kern (ca. 1915)

The series of innovative musicals in the second decade of the 1900s, which played at the small Princess Theatre, broke new ground in the move toward the integrated vintage book musicals of the 1940s and 1950s. These small musicals were written by Guy Bolton, bookwriter *(left),* and Jerome Kern, composer *(right),* whose music was merged with the wit of P. G. Wodehouse, lyricist *(center),* an early collaborative team in the newly emerging American musical. (Photo credit: Theatre Collection, Museum of the City of New York.)

Harold Prince recalls:

The definition of what libretto writing is has changed totally. There are some guys who wrote great books in the forties and even in the thirties, but the run-of-the-mill musical comedy books when I was in college and starting in the theater were lightweight stuff. They were there to string together really terrific scores. Of course Bolton and Wodehouse did terrific stuff. They wrote five shows a year, you know.

(Compare with the eighties, when, for example *Les Misérables* took about ten-plus years from conception to production, *Annie* took six years, etc.)

The early development of American theater songs also called forth the credited lyricist. The names of Otto Harbach, Larry Hart, Ira Gershwin, Howard Dietz came first to be known as "secondary" artists to the composers, who all knew better than the public what the contribution of their word persons really entailed in the creation of a theater song. The great musical theater songwriters now sought for more serious content and stronger books. They began to "team up" with strong but straight playwrights, e.g., the Gershwins with George S. Kaufman. This "script-first-then-song" form of collaboration, modeled after W. S. Gilbert and Arthur Sullivan's method, continues even today.

One strategy for lyricists consisted of their becoming bookwriters as well (Hammerstein, Harburg, Lerner). Both "bookwriter" and "lyricist" developed as specialists. The bookwriter in musical theater remained least well known in these forms of collaboration, even though the best theater songwriters would all agree that the whole show derived from the theme and the story.

The great morning stars of the classic book musicals (yet to appear) were *Show Boat* (Kern-Hammerstein) in 1927, *Porgy and Bess* (the Gershwins and DuBose Heyward) in 1935, *Lady in the Dark* (Weill and Ira Gershwin and Moss Hart) in 1941 and *Oklahoma!* (Rodgers and Hammerstein) in 1943. They fused comedic humor and tragic drama into integrated, organic works of art (and commerce). Oscar Hammerstein's grandfather was an opera impresario and his father owned a vaudeville house. These two strains, of many, helped Hammerstein link his sense of tragedy, manifested in his recurrent themes of death and loss, and his sense of showmanship or sheer entertainment. Also a trained lawyer, he early on fused these strains into the aim of integrating book and song. His hallmarks were American operettas, or "musical operas," among them *Show Boat, Oklahoma!,* and *The King and I.* The Gershwins' and Heyward's work, *Porgy and Bess* (1935), further fused "Grand Opera" and "Broadway," to the consternation even today of the overspecialized opera and musical theater

Show Boat *(1927)*

The morning star of the later vintage era of American musicals was *Show Boat* (1927), with book and lyrics by Oscar Hammerstein II and music by Jerome Kern. Adapted from the acclaimed novel by Edna Ferber, the musical dealt with topics like racism, miscegenation, and broken families, and truly merged story and song, comedy and tragedy. Through revivals and two film versions, the show continues to attract audiences into the 1990s; its hit song, "Ol' Man River," became a classic. (Photo credit: Billy Rose Theatre Collection, New York Public Library.)

I'd Rather Be Right, *Director/Cobookwriter, George S. Kaufman; Lyricist, Lorenz Hart; Cobookwriter, Moss Hart; Composer, Richard Rodgers (1937)*

This early attempt at creating a strong integrated book and score in a musical play brought together the successful songwriting team of Richard Rodgers *(right)* and Larry Hart *(second from left)* with director George S. Kaufman *(left)* and Moss Hart, cobookwriters for the show *I'd Rather Be Right* (1937). This was a political satire that followed the successful Gershwin Brothers/Kaufman/Ryskind's Pulitzer Prize winner *Of Thee I Sing* (1931). (Photo credit: Billy Rose Theatre Collection, New York Public Library and the Alfredo Valente family.)

critics from academia and the press. The works of Brecht and Weill in Germany and Blitzstein in America also broke new ground, as did the Rodgers and Hart musicals—all preparing the way for the vintage years of the book-musical on Broadway—a musical art form that unknowingly followed Aristotle's ideas. For Aristotle's analysis of Greek plays revealed that *every* poet uses and "every play contains these elements": plot, character, diction, song, thought, and spectacle. Dance was not optional. And, as Fergusson paraphrases Aristotle: "The poet should endeavor, if possible, to combine all poetic elements: or, failing that, the greatest number and those the most important; the more so, in face of the cavilling criticism of the day."[15]

The Musical Theater Book-Song-Score

Creating a score of songs for a Broadway vintage musical play was only slightly similar to writing single popular songs for Tin Pan Alley. Many great popular songwriters—like Johnny Green and Johnny Mercer—never succeeded in Broadway musical theater. Others had to learn the craft of theater songwriting so that their careers could take off. Jule Styne, who made the transition, says:

The drama cannot be neglected in writing a musical play. That is the songwriter's [meaning lyric and tune writers] first obligation. . . . Songwriters found a subtler way to express the drama through words and music. The specific soliloquies have been replaced by a more general song making musical and lyrical entertainment by themselves and at the same time furthering the story.[16]

And Yip Harburg, a long-time writer of light verse, remembered:

It was clear to me from the start how much skill goes into writing [songs] for a whole show. Much more complicated than writing single songs for Tin Pan Alley, where a good titillating jingle does the trick. But in good musicals, each song is a whole scene; you need to soak yourself in character, motivation, mood, tempo. . . . You're advancing plot, you're extending dialogue, using music and lyrics to make the statement explosive and emotional. Each song has a different problem, or many problems. Each one has to be fitted, guided, placed.

That's why it's called act one and act two. You *act* things out. When you act things, you're dramatizing. To have drama, song gives you that extra dimension that plain conversation does not give you.[17]

Sheldon Harnick reminds us *de novo* that both lyric and musical ideas emerge from the plot:

I enjoy working to music because quite often music will suggest things that you hadn't thought of. Although it may be true that the emotions music suggests are general, they can, in my experience, suggest the specific lyric, especially if you're working in the context of a book, where your mind, consciously or unconsciously, is searching for a lyric idea.

Hammerstein wrote about this matter:

There are few things in life of which I am certain, but I am sure of this one thing: that the song is the servant of the play, that it is wrong to write first what you think is an attractive song and then try to wedge it into a story.[18]

Musical plays, then, are not "books" written by an author with songs later inserted by a composer and lyric writer. They are often written this way, but it is not a good way to write them and such plays seldom have a very long life.[19]

But Harnick gives an example of "piece-work collaboration" among composer, lyricist, and bookwriter who worked together for the first time and created an integrated musical:

One of the easiest [collaborations] to describe is *She Loves Me.* Joe Masteroff [the bookwriter] had never done a musical and Jerry Bock and I talked to him. He had said, "What do I do? How do I go about this?" We said, "Why don't you just write a script, only don't make it play length. Make it about 60 percent of what would constitute a full-length play. Leave room for us to do the music. Just write it and pay no attention to where the songs go. This is a very emotional story and along the way you're going to write emotional scenes and we will read what you write and we'll find music in those scenes."

He went off and wrote a book and Jerry and I combed through it looking for those moments which had a strong emotional base. It's where we thought the songs should be. That's not always the case. Sometimes a moment may strike you as ideal for a droll song or an unusual way to state through music and lyrics what the character is thinking.

Broadway Vintage Musical Plays

In the opinion of Peter Stone, a well-established Broadway bookwriter, taking a long look in the early 1980s,

The musical changed some forty years ago. It had been a collection of songs tied together by very loose words. It did not have a construction like a play.

From the Rodgers and Hammerstein era it really changed. The story suddenly became the most important part of the play. *Oklahoma!* would not have worked if the book had not worked. And through *Carousel*, again, a very strong book. *The King and I* may be the strongest book construction of all. [All three shows, book and lyrics by Oscar Hammerstein, music by Richard Rodgers.]

Gypsy's . . . real distinction is in the fact that at its heart it is a "serious" musical dealing with deep human drives and needs. And it manages to avoid the pitfalls that work against most attempts at "seriousness" in musicals: sentimentality and pretentiousness. [Book by Arthur Laurents, lyrics by Stephen Sondheim, music by Jule Styne.]

According to Jerry Herman, the musical play reached its peak in *Fiddler on the Roof* (1964):

In *Fiddler* you aren't especially aware of the songs, the ballets, the dialogue as such. You are captivated by all the arts blended into one piece of theater. You can remove a song, a ballet, a scene, or even a character from *Oklahoma!* and nothing much would happen to the rest of it. But you can't remove anything from *Fiddler*. It is this concept of a homogenized musical that is entirely new and is the result of a slow subtle progress over the years.[20] [Book by Joseph Stein; lyrics by Sheldon Harnick; music by Jerry Bock; direction and choreography by Jerome Robbins.]

These vintage musical plays must rely on total collaboration among producer, playwright, lyricist, composer, director, actor, and designers. Sheldon Harnick explains the creating of *Fiddler on the Roof:*

It was not a collaboration in the sense that it said on the program "Book by Joe Stein and Sheldon Harnick," or "Lyrics by Joe Stein and Sheldon Harnick." We all had our own roles to play, but it was a very close collaboration. . . . In all those production meetings we interacted very closely to dovetail our work. Joe offered suggestions to us; I offered suggestions to him. Jerry Bock offered suggestions to both of us and then Jerome Robbins [director] changed everything and made it better.

Prince was the producer who also made some suggestions. This is typical of other inspired collaborations resulting in the great vintage musicals like *My Fair Lady* (1956) and *West Side Story* (1957).

Some time ago the optimal collaborative condition for creating a musical play was set forth, as he saw it, by Oscar Hammerstein, who was a bookwriter and lyricist but not a composer:

It must be understood that the musician is just as much an author as the man who writes the words. He expresses the story in his medium just as the librettist expresses the story in his. Or, more accurately, they weld their crafts and kinds of talent into a single expression. This is the great secret of the well-integrated musical play.[21]

Blending book, lyric, and music through collaborative team work is extremely difficult, if not impossible, to understand, much less to teach. Training young musical artists is doubly difficult because so many of them tend to be aggressive, egoistic, or simply inexperienced. Outside the unique program for Musical Theater at New York University there has never been any formal university training in the collaborative arts of musical theater as art form. Hammerstein, Harburg, Kern, Berlin, the Gershwins, Hart, et

Director Joshua Logan (left), Costume Designer Elizabeth Montgomery, Bookwriter/ Lyricist Oscar Hammerstein II, Composer Richard Rodgers, Producer Leland Hayward at South Pacific *Rehearsal (1949)*

South Pacific (1949) is a classic American musical that addresses itself to the changes World War II made in American existence. It deals with such topics as interethnic and racial prejudices, large age differences between lovers, and wartime heroism. The score is vintage Rodgers and Hammerstein. The inspired collaborative team *(from right to left)* was Leland Hayward, producer; Richard Rodgers, composer; Oscar Hammerstein II *(standing)*, bookwriter/lyricist; and *(far left)* Joshua Logan, director. The woman is Elizabeth Montgomery (a.k.a. Motley), costume designer; and an undesignated assistant. (Photo credit: Billy Rose Theatre Collection, New York Public Library.)

Yul Brynner and Richard Rodgers on The King and I *Set (1951)*

This conversation between a leading actor (Yul Brynner) and a composer (Richard Rodgers) reflects in its quiet seriousness the intensity of the collaborative process among gifted artists who strive to share the vision of the whole show and its action. *The King and I* (1951) is another classic Broadway vintage musical, still playing on film and stages around the world. (Photo credit: Billy Rose Theatre Collection, New York Public Library; photographer: Bob Golby.)

al., learned, as did all others in the vintage years, by boldly synthesizing old traditions in a new way, above all by paying attention to the book and its centrality.

A landmark of an *original* musical story can be seen in *Finian's Rainbow* (1947). The book, lyrics, and music of Harburg, Saidy, and Lane typify the integratedness of the story and score, with dances by Michael Kidd. Stanley Green writes, "No other writer has appreciated the growing importance [of the integrated musical play] more than E. Y. Harburg"[22] (as he had demonstrated in the hit film musical *The Wizard of Oz*[23]). The story had four subplots and the hit songs carried the fantasy, the characters, and the politics of antiracism to a show that our bookwriter Peter Stone describes as "extraordinarily political."

Harnick learned about the story/book by being burned:

When we got to New Haven, the opening night went very badly and we had a meeting afterwards in a restaurant. George Abbott, who was a very candid man, just looked at us and said, "Gentlemen, I had a conception and it doesn't work. Anybody got any ideas?" I sat there thinking, "I have no ideas because I haven't been paying attention to the book." I assumed Papa George and Uncle Jerry [Robbins]—they'll do the work and we just fill in the songs. I didn't even know there were any problems. From that point on I made a point to study the book and to contribute as many ideas as I could to it, or at least to anticipate where problem areas might be. So that was my lesson.

Harnick learned from this experience that the lyricist must be involved with the development of the book because that is how to achieve "a closer wedding of lyrics to book." And music to lyrics. Such integration of crafts into a unified whole is and always was unusual.

So as Broadway musical plays fail much more frequently than they succeed, Harnick further candidly describes some earlier learning experiences in how not to do it. First, when the vision of the play was lacking, he asked himself:

What am I doing? I have taken this job for the wrong reasons, for money. And this was the early fifties. It was going to be a thousand dollars down and a thousand apiece for twelve songs. So I had the thousand, and it got to be an agony rousing myself every morning and working on that thing. We had written four or five songs, but one day the bookwriter called a meeting and he said, "I can't do this; I can't make this into a musical. I've come to hate it." I kept my mouth shut. We dropped it, and I was never so relieved.

However, even the attempt at intimate initial collaboration by true artists does not ensure the desired result. The mystery of collaboration on Broadway musicals is still an awesome matter. Martin Charnin, Harold Arlen,

Finian's Rainbow *("When the Idle Poor Become the Idle Rich") (1947)*

This scene from *Finian's Rainbow* (1947) shows the cast performing the satiric song, "When the Idle Poor Become the Idle Rich." This original fantasy from the imagination of Yip Harburg and Fred Saidy (bookwriters), with lyrics by Harburg and music by Burton Lane, was another inspired collaborative team effort. *Finian's* was the first Broadway show where black and white performers danced together and racism was addressed with satiric humor, outrage and compassion. Produced by L. Sabinson and W. R. Katzell. (Photo credit: Billy Rose Theatre Collection, New York Public Library.)

Hugh Wheeler, and the producer Saint Suber—all top-line Broadway musical executives—optioned a short story, and over forty-two songs were created. But the book never worked:

> It took two years. Saint Suber, Hugh [Wheeler], and Harold and I sat and we read it and we demonstrated it and we tried to lick the problems. . . . It was a strange idea for a musical—it took place in Japan in 1946, just after the American army of occupation begins to leave the country to the Japanese and it was a love story that we wrestled with. No matter how we would redo it, reexamine it, restructure it, rethink it, it always ended up being *Madame Butterfly* [which incidentally flopped on opening and was later successfully revived].

They felt that even a great score would not work with a weak book, and all forty-two songs went into Charnin's and Arlen's "trunks"—where they remain.

Story, Character, and Songs-in-Scenes

In musical theater, songs are sung by characters at the apex of an episode or scene. Songs are the climactic action; they derive their meaning from the flow of action. While the episodes of a story stem from the central story idea that generates action and pathos, the audience moves and is moved through "imitating" the "leading personae." As Laurents puts it: "There must be character. There must be emotion. There must be a drive to it." And therefore, the "dialogue has to have action which propels the play. Economy is the great thing." Thus the "lyrics should come from what the librettist has done," that is, the story.

Aristotle understood that "character is that which reveals moral purpose, showing what a man chooses or avoids. Speeches (songs, gestures), therefore, which do not make this manifest, or in which the speaker does not choose or avoid anything whatever, are not expressive of character." Character is expressed in the person(s) who carry the major action of the plot.[24]

Sondheim writes:

> Books are what musical theater is about . . . a book is not only the dialogue, it's the scheme of the show. The way the songs and the dialogue work together, the style of the show. . . . [It gives the director] an approach to the show; [it's] the seed from which a collaboration grows. . . . The important thing about the book is the characters, the essence of what dramatic song writing is about.[25]

The story-book-plot-libretto provides the action and context for lyricist and composers to create the song-within-the-scene. The character and his or her "movement of spirit" (praxis) are to be dramatically revealed, first through dialogue and then song—a "dramatic climax to the scene"—a "confrontation," creating pathos. But the musical theater song (a synergy of lyric and music) must communicate character, mood, and "a quality of the rest of the score."

Songs-in-scenes help establish character. But lyrics also shorten the spoken dialogue because, as Lerner points out, "You can accomplish more in four bars [of a song] than you can with ten pages of dialogue."[26] Jerry Herman cites Sondheim's "Some People" from *Gypsy:*

It's perfectly metered and rhymed, it's a lyric in the sense of a song lyric, and at the same time it is a piece of dramatic literature, poetry that defines the character of Madame Rose as clearly as three scenes of dialogue.[27]

Lerner, harking back to Aristotle by way of a Maxwell Anderson lecture at Princeton in the thirties, claims that the climax, "the high moment" in a story, is a "recognition scene" that *has* to be "captured in something musical":

Higgins singing "Accustomed to Her Face," for example; he had to recognize what the problem was for himself. It was the King in *Camelot,* thinking his life was over until he saw the little boy. And in the film, *Gigi,* the leading character, Gaston, suddenly has to face the fact that he was thinking of Gigi as a little girl and feeling about her as if she were a woman. That high moment had to be captured in something musical. We decided to write a piece in which she would actually grow up in his mind, unfold before him, so to speak.[28]

Or, so to sing.

Collaboration in Scoring the Action

The "Script First-Then Score" Method. Since the vintage years, as Peter Stone observed (in 1982), the books or the staging, not the scores (with or without stars), have carried the hits:

Not since Rodgers and Hammerstein—after Rodgers and Hammerstein—have the scores [alone] ever made a musical. Every hit musical was made either by a book or by staging. There has not been a score to make a musical since a section of *Hair.*

If you go back and look at the big hits from the sixties on, you see it's basically the books that work. Whether it was *Fiddler,* whether it was *Cabaret,* any of the big, long-running shows.

Spectacle shows, Stone remarks, like *42nd Street* or *Cats,* "are staged rather than written," but they require "construction" by a writer.

In the "script first-then score" collaboration, the bookwriter often has his strongest dialogue cut and replaced by songs. Lyricists often "raid the dialogue" openly and directly, something that, in Laurents's opinion, contributed to the integrity of *West Side Story*. Furthermore, the bookwriter receives little public credit, and, the most unkind cut of all, he only receives one-third (2 percent) of the 6 percent of royalties that go to the three (by now) so-called primary creators of the work. With this kind of "collaboration," the bookwriter loses a measure of control over his script. On this, there is much agreement from our respondents.

Jules Fisher, a lighting designer and occasional producer, makes these points about being a musical playwright:

If you're a quality writer, and you can write a novel, the whole thing is to your credit. If you're a quality writer and you write a book musical, you share your money and fame with a lyricist and a composer. Instantly all the monies are divided in three ways. You've got to give up two-thirds. *Two-thirds.* Not even half or a third. You have to give up a third for the lyricist and a third for the composer.

The chronic frustration is described by Ethan Mordden in his engaging book, *Broadway Babies: The People Who Made the American Musical,* in which he begins a chapter entitled "The Book" with an old but accurate chestnut:

When a musical makes a hit, who gets the credit? The songwriters, the performers, the director, the choreographer, the designer, the orchestrator, the stage manager, even the audience—for its good taste. When a musical bombs, who gets the blame? The author of the book.[29]

The "Full Three-Way" Collaboration. Gradually, with the success of vintage book-musicals, methods of writing a show through closer and more interactive association or actual merger of bookwriter and songwriting craftsmen arose. These methods are not far from those prescribed by Aristotle: "As for the story, whether the poet takes it ready made or constructs it for himself, he should first sketch its general outline, and then fill in the episodes and amplify in detail."[30] Which sounds much like the Oscar Hammerstein of 1960:

Dick [Rodgers] and I stay very close together while drawing up the blueprint of a play. Before we start to put words or notes on paper we have agreed on a very definite and complete outline, and we have decided how much of the story shall be told in dialogue and how much in song. We try to use music as much as we can.[31]

This process resembles that described by Laurents:

In my experience, someone gets an idea. Then the composer and the librettist, who may be one person, talk about it. And the librettist goes off to write an outline.

This doesn't have to be linear, but if you can't put it on paper and know where you are going, you're kidding yourself. Then, instead of talking theory and numbers all night long, you sit down with your outline for further discussion. It will change in the writing, but at least you have something to guide you.

Peter Stone continues:

You start breaking it [the idea in the outline] down in a number of ways. The more experience you have, the less detailed you are. But it's like being an abstract painter. He went through his realistic period. He knows how to draw. Now he doesn't have to any more. So our outline may be a little less formal than it might have been if we were just starting out.

We will have some notion of our climax, that is, when the break comes. We will know our characters. We will look for things along the way that are *more in the musical genre than in a straight play.*

It still won't be a play. It'll still be *an outline* written down on a yellow pad. And we'll get scenes. Finally we'll have an outline for, say, seven scenes in the first act, four in the second act—and a general concept of the score.

In a "full three-way" collaboration, however, the bookwriter integrates his ideas with those of lyricist and composer in such a way as to weave these ideas more evenly in a joint process of creation.

The Musical Playwright and the Choreographer

During the sixties and seventies, as the director's power increased and choreographer-directors were in the ascendant (with a concomitant loss of text), this hybrid type exerted more influence on the script and even on the score. Here indeed was the director or the director-choreographer as "auteur," organizing production values (sets, lighting, costume, technology, dance). Another factor leading away from strong book-musicals is critical to Walter Kerr:

Carousel was surely an operetta, you know, and maybe *The King and I* should be called an operetta, a very good one, but what happened was that this form [the Rodgers and Hammerstein model] became so exclusive it wiped out all the others, making them old-fashioned, out-of-date, you-can't-do-that-any-more. And so they started losing all the clowns, the stars of that time. They had a steady supply of perfectly good shows like *Bloomer Girl,* but eventually [this form] got pretty tedious.

The search for a new style emerged along with the new rock sound; the older operetta-based songwriters were swept aside along with the stars.

More and more, in the sixties, producers came to rely on the choreographer-directors, deadly antagonists to bookwriters like Stone ("I leave only Jerry Robbins out of this"). Lacking literary background, as Stone sees them, they are acutely uncomfortable in the presence of ideas and the words that express them: "I don't mean that they're dumb. They are like abstract painters except their forte is movement." They have no use for words "that can be directed but can't be *staged*." Robbins did value the book. He realized that it had to be dealt with and hired an assistant who helped take care of this. Robbins was "smart enough and talented enough" to do that.

Arthur Laurents suggests that until Rodgers and Hart there was no musical theater on Broadway. And hardly any composers. There were extraordinarily gifted songwriters who, however, by the Laurentian criteria, did not write theater music. And the libretto was insubstantial. Then it all changed, most markedly with a show like *On Your Toes* (1936), in which George Balanchine introduced ballet on Broadway as an integral part of unfolding the plot. Later, in Laurents's opinion, Agnes de Mille's contribution in *Oklahoma!* to what he regards as Oscar Hammerstein's sketchy book, was enormous. *Green Grow the Lilacs* became *Oklahoma!* and Hammerstein "left out the heroine's sexuality. Agnes restored it in the dance. That's what justified the whole relationship with Jud; you'd never know it from the book of the show, but she did it in her ballets."

Here we have a clear example where character is deepened by intelligent choreography. Yet even de Mille succumbed to convention with "everything up to date in Kansas City," cowboys tap dancing and similar silliness. Too often, as Laurents looks back on it, de Mille herself failed to search for a choreographic equivalent of the narrative (not supplied by Hammerstein). But like Balanchine, she exhibited the necessary intelligence that dictates that there should be a concept, a thesis, a librettist's theme by which the choreographer can be said to "probe character."

But alas for the art form, according to Stone. After Robbins, good choreographer-directors were hopelessly at odds with bookwriters. The best of them, Michael Kidd, Joe Layton, Gower Champion, and Bob Fosse, among those mentioned by Stone, were not content with a piece of the creative pie: "They wanted the whole thing." "At cross-purposes" is one of the milder terms for a relationship that this bookwriter characterizes as a little bizarre: "You want to preserve ideas through words and the choreographer's trying to get them out," to hide them, to muffle them, and, ultimately, to exclude them. For Stone, Gower Champion's transformation of *The Matchmaker,* a play by Thornton Wilder, into the musical *Hello, Dolly!* is a classic tip-off to the problem. As far as Stone is concerned, Wilder distilled the whole philosophy of his play in one scene that takes

Tamara Geva, George Church, Ray Bolger, Basil Galahoff in On Your Toes *(1936)*

On Your Toes (1936) was a breakthrough musical in that ballet and tap dance choreographed by George Balanchine were used to tell part of the story, with book by Richard Rodgers, Lorenz Hart, and George Abbott (also director), and a beautiful score by Rodgers (composer) and Hart (lyricist). Shown here are the leading dancers, Tamara Geva, George Church, Ray Bolger, and Basil Galahoff. The show ran successfully as a revival on Broadway in 1983— even with a mixed-negative review by the *New York Times* critic. (Photo credit: Billy Rose Theatre Collection, New York Public Library.)

place at a garden on 14th Street where key characters engage in their most revelatory discussion: "Gower put a curtain around the tables and staged a big splashy number, the waiters' dance. David Hartman was the head waiter. You could hardly miss him and the other dancers running around with trays. All you missed were matters of the utmost consequence—happening off-set behind a curtain."

The Art Form Changeth

The late sixties and seventies brought still more change in the musical book. Harold Prince had been the driving force toward the creation of *Cabaret* (1966). Led by the Prince-Sondheim approach, one quite distant from the late, more romantic but still vintage, shows, some of the artistic benchmarks were *Follies, Company, A Little Night Music, Pacific Overtures,* and *On the Twentieth Century* (score by Cy Coleman, Betty Comden, and Adolph Green). Three, however—*Follies, Overtures,* and *Twentieth Century*—commercially failed on Broadway.

While Sondheim's mentor had been Hammerstein, his works with Prince were a new departure in the musical play. Indeed, the Prince-Firth-Sondheim experiment in *Company* elicits Stone's observation that a rare mutant emerged:

Company (1970) is a strange example. Can a musical exist without its music? I would say no. I would say it shouldn't exist, but *Company*'s an odd example: a perfect show without its music, and a perfect show with its music. I can't think of any other case where it doesn't matter whether there's a score or not.

The Director as Auteur: The "Four-Way" Collaboration

When artistic control over the creation of a theme and a story outline and even the production process is at stake, there is a natural tension or antagonism between the musical bookwriter and the newly powerful director. Peter Stone, an established and accomplished bookwriter, views working with directors from the start as "exciting but unpleasant." Yet even Stone must submit to the potent Broadway trend of more imaginative and grandiose staging that such directors supply. In 1982, he described his cautious Apollonian approach to enlarging the full three-way collaboration to include this fourth talent: "The librettist, the lyricist, and the composer work together. After the initial stages, we will work together for two or three sessions and then in the fourth session the director will come in—after we have something."

Contrast this pattern with Bennett's method of "starting up." He called in his group of writers, he guided the ideas to a theme, they discussed the outline—the beginning, middle, and end—then he continued in the driver's seat throughout the development of the script, and ultimately, the production itself. Or here is Tommy Tune:

Hire talented and intelligent librettists who know their job, but still with enough writer's ego to keep giving it to you and giving it to you, no matter if it's just five lines of dialogue, it's condensed, and it is the strongest, the most powerful, the cleanest, the most direct, the most emotional.

Further, Tune (along with Prince and other directors) believes in "restructuring" the work and regards the outline as a very flexible tool: "Do an outline, but then you don't have to stick with it. You can do a whole lot of stuff on the way to change it any which way." And Harold Prince:

My needs as an artist require involvement at an early time. That can be exceedingly annoying to certain writers. . . . *Follies* was a perfect collaboration, and the most fun. Sure I liked being part author.

But the Dramatists Guild takes a dim view of such intrusive positions and a few years ago suspended Prince from membership in the guild for his role as an uncredited coauthor of the $6-million *Grind*. Prince, who ordinarily cares about plot, agonized over the problem of how to end *Grind*. That problem had to do with making sense or making money (probably a mucilaginous mixture of both). But Prince admits he made a mistake and decided on money. (It flopped quickly.) Prince, a rare person, whose candor in admitting error is only exceeded by his long list of successes—an astounding 60–40 hit-flop ratio—also admits to troubles with the ending of *Follies,* a show he loved.

The only problem we ever had was getting a number at the end that would make it run, and pretend to have an end. *Follies* ran twenty-one months, so I guess that's not exactly a flop, even though it didn't pay off. Nevertheless, the end, the final moment, that moment doesn't completely wash.

Neophyte bookwriters commonly defer to the maestro director. But older professionals must also submit themselves to the director. Even when a straight playwright or a bookwriter creates the theme and the story line, all based on a careful outline, the director who reinterprets may still take charge.

The Limitations of Writers: Staging the Action

In Prince's opinion, playwrights, lyricists, and composers cannot view a show as the director can. They don't ever see it from here [pointing away]. The director must see it from a distance, to see the whole arc of the show. Too few of them know or understand that at all. . . . I think the healthiest thing . . . is do it in concert with a director fairly early because you're working on a musical. You're not a [straight] playwright.

Sometimes material from the script is unilaterally removed from the show. But in Prince's experience, the Dramatists Guild has never stepped in at an author's request to recover it. Conversely, Bennett or Prince or Tune never actually do any writing (unlike Abbott or Feuer, who did it in the old days). Usually, in fact, Prince reports that authors are highly cooperative in cutting material if the show is too long.

I do, however, if I hit a knotty place in a show, ad lib my way through it with the actor and have the author come in later. I say, "Okay, fix this. You see we cannot get from A to C the way you did it, just can't." So I'm trying to show you how to help us get out of our problems.

It is not widely known that in *Oklahoma!*—a major landmark of American book musicals—the director, Rouben Mamoulian, strongly contributed to the full integration of the work. He was and is given little credit for his collaborative part in creating the "whole" of the show. Mamoulian had worked with Rodgers and Hart on the integrated musical film, *Love Me Tonight* (1932), in Hollywood. For the first time in a Hollywood musical, director, lyricist, and composer blended story, song, and dance into an integrated film musical. In 1935, Mamoulian directed the first-ever Broadway opera, *Porgy and Bess*. He is quoted in Aljean Harmetz's *The Making of the Wizard of Oz* as follows:

There is a kind of built-in resistance to new things with human beings. . . . For the last two weeks before we opened *Oklahoma!* on Broadway, no one even spoke to me. Rodgers thought I was destroying his music. He couldn't accept the singers having their backs to the audience. Everyone wanted me to restage it as an ordinary musical comedy. I refused, and they didn't even invite me to the opening night party. Besides, it's tremendously difficult to integrate a show. It's really easy to tell a story and toss in a song or dance here and there.[32]

In a collaborative art form like a musical play, top executives, those who contribute to the final product, also include the director—and not uncommonly the producer. But can anyone name the producer of *Oklahoma!*? What prevails is the notion that it was a "Rodgers and Hammerstein show."

Sometimes even directors and writers who usually understand each other do not completely grasp each other's intent. Prince's candor is once again refreshing and insightful, this time in remarks about *Sweeney Todd:* "For Steve it was about revenge. It was about [an individual's] revenge

Harold Prince (ca. 1974)

Harold Prince, a leading creator and innovator of Broadway musicals, who started as a producer and then became a director. He is the recipient of sixteen Tony awards. His lasting works as director include *Cabaret* (1966), *Company* (1970), *Evita* (1979–83), and *Phantom of the Opera* (1988). His book, *Contradictions* (1974), is rich in cogent observations about creating Broadway musicals. (Photo credit: Billy Rose Theatre Collection, New York Public Library; photographer: Jill Krementz.)

against society. It was about emotions he very strongly feels and that he wanted to express in musical form. I never understood [it exactly that way]."

The experienced director like Prince who reviews his career is less likely to say that in the beginning is the "word" than in the beginning is a "challenge."

Oscar Hammerstein said it, and he was right: "You've got to tell them in the first three minutes of the show what they have in store." That doesn't always mean who the main characters are. You've got to tell them what the theme, style, spirit, emotion, and mood of the piece will be. If not, you spend all that time on the road or in previews trying to get an opening number. So I work on the opening number *first:* I have worked on the opening number first for almost every show I've done.

As applied to the start of *Company,* Sondheim discusses how he and Prince went about working on it:

Looking back at the first page of notes I ever made about *Company,* I see that we sat around and talked about how to turn these one-act plays into a musical. We talked about the central character, and Hal Prince said it would be nice to have a number called "Company." Well, *company* is a word you can't rhyme—except Lorenz Hart rhymed it with "bump a knee," which is not my kind of rhyme—so it would be a little hard to do it as a title refrain. Then Hal said, "And also I would like it to introduce the various styles of the show, the way we are going to cut back and forth; also I would like it to introduce the main character and include all the other characters; also I would like it to use the set."[33]

Moreover, total collaboration is also required for the timing of a "whole" show. Bennett described it:

You have to imagine a show is like, well. . . . The composer gets this chunk, and the choreographer gets this piece and the writer gets this much in a scene and there's [the director] going, "Okay, you can have two minutes for this. You've got to cut this thing down from three pages to one page." And also sometimes the various artists working on a production will see that that dance number could have been a minute shorter and the original scene they wrote would have been all right.

In this cauldron, the playwright is only one of many creators who must guard the integrity of his design, but if it is a musical with a strong story line or book, his or her duty is to devise ways along with his fellow creators so that the "action" retains its "wholeness."

For in staging the action, making it live, a fourth dimension is created that only a company can generate. The "meanings" contained in the vision on the written page are recreated and reinterpreted into "stage imagery" different from their written language. It requires discovery as well as translation by a director and the company of artists such that the authors might be astonished (happy or angry) at what has been wrought in the passage from script and score into live production.

The New-Old Story Line: Dramaturge and Construction

Predictably, in an art form as wide open as American musical theater (in contrast to the museum rituals of European grand opera) one sees fairly rapid variations on the Aristotelian "playwright-plot-character" approach characteristic of the forties. It has been said, for example, that *Hair* broke ground into a "nonlinear" form of the musical. In this approach, "concepts" and "themes" become as important as character and plot. Prince contends that pre-Hitler Germany is the leading theme in *Cabaret* and the cabaret emcee its leading character. Further, *"Follies* certainly has no leading character. Does anybody who saw it think there's a leading character in it? I don't think so."

Not only did directors "restructure" a show; in the late seventies and eighties, producers such as Merrick and Shubert opted for more spectacle. Stone views with regret the disturbing trend towards pure staging or spectacles for their own sake, making shows that are "bookless." To him Fosse's *Dancin'* is not a musical; for Laurents, *Cats* has no book. *42nd Street* does not credit a bookwriter but lists "cross-overs" and "lead-ins". It's all "fun and games." *My One and Only* was described as a "pastiche of twenties musicals" with its score "stitched together from many shows" with a "silly book and innocuous plot and sets." Still, all these musical shows "work"; they achieve their "wholeness." Why? How? For every one of these hits, there are eight or more that don't succeed, e.g., *Merlin, Marilyn, The Tap Dance Kid, Jerry's Girls,* and on and on. For Stone (one of the play doctors who ministered to *My One and Only* in Boston) part of the answer is a playwright's sense of "construction," which involves more than the story. "It is where and how the show moves and sings and balances and programs"—even more than dialogue. From these skills and the development of craft, others are groping to find a more fluid but integrated musical that also carries serious themes and "wholeness."

Robert Brustein, a brilliant and perennial gadfly of American theater, stepped out of character to rhapsodize over a revival of an American opera (in his capacity as critic for *The New Republic*):

Eight years after its two performances at the Met in 1976, *Einstein on the Beach* was revived for one week in December as a climactic event of The Next Wave Festival at the Brooklyn Academy of Music. It confirmed a now legendary reputation as one of the masterpieces of modern opera and theater. Philip Glass, and the *conceiver*/director/designer, Robert Wilson, has *a spoken text devised by Christopher Knowles, Samuel M. Johnson, and Lucinda Childs* (who also did the choreography) [emphasis added].[34]

Where is the bookwriter? Does a shadow fall between the "conceiver" and three "text devisers?" Is this part of the Next Wave? Is conceiver a title henceforth to be institutionalized? Are those who devise a spoken text for a given opera to be as numerous as producers of a single Broadway musical?

On January 21, 1985, at Joseph Papp's Public Theater in Greenwich Village, *Tracers,* a new drama, with dance, song, and "sound," opened to hosannahs from Frank Rich. "At the beginning of *Tracers* . . . a snaking line of Vietnam veterans gyrates about the stage to a driving rock beat. It's an unexpectedly energizing sight. *Tracers* is a play about a grim war, *written and performed* [our emphasis] by men who were there, and yet this opening sequence provides the electric lift of the Jets' song in *West Side Story.*" Rich is unrestrained in his admiration for these men who use "kinetic body language and fraternal glances" to portray their "pride, fellowship and shared tribal codes," fusing them into a "palpable spiritual force." As to the Vietnam War, "We are on these veterans' side as soon as we meet them." And we stay there:

Those initial feelings compound steadily throughout the evening. There is, one could say, nothing new in *Tracers.* It's a blunt, free-flowing collage in which a platoon of all-American "grunts" once again stumbles ritualistically through the terrors of free-fire zones, trip-wires, body bags, subterranean rat-infested bunkers and search and destroy missions—only to return home, if they return at all, to a country that would rather forget. Even the accompanying period rock songs ("Sympathy for the Devil," "Higher," "Fixin' to Die Rag") are exactly the ones we would expect. But the piece is no less powerful for that.[35]

And so on, fortissimo with enthusiasm, doubtless deserved, and if Broadway is deemed ready for such potent stuff, we can dream of seeing it there (but that has yet to happen). Our interest, however, lies less in the evaluation than in the genesis of this show, which Rich explains: "*Tracers* . . . was devised [that word again] in 1980, in workshops at the Odyssey Theater in Los Angeles. Its authors are the eight veterans who initially appeared in it."[36] Indeed, the credits read:

Written by the original cast of Vincent Caristi, Richard Chaves, John DiFusco, Eric E. Emerson, Rick Galavan, Merlin Marston and Harry Stephens with Sheldon Lettich; conceived and directed by Mr. DiFusco; scenery by John Faisbella; costumes by David Navarro Velasques; lighting by Terry Wuhlrich; dramaturgy by David Berry; sound by Mr. DiFusco; production stage manager, Michael Chambers; associate producer, Jason Steven Cohen.[37]

Eight authors, a conceiver, and a dramaturge. Maybe this is another way to go, something fresh and new. Peter Neufeld is surely on the right track in declaring that "you never know when blades of grass pop up through the cement or how they'll grow. It's like that in the theater. Often, without any particularly good reason, people get ideas about something they want to do. Those ideas take them in a certain direction, and, if what they do is novel, many others will follow." But the blades of grass we have just been discussing popped up Off Broadway, and what was germinal Off Broadway might be terminal to Broadway audiences.

What seems clear is that these musical plays and many others contribute to the new and continuously developing art-form-cum-musical-show-business. The vintage musical plays are historic hallmarks of Broadway's all but global reputation. They seem to have become world classics that today have a cross-cultural life. But it is clear that a musical may take innumerable forms, and, cost and courage and imagination permitting, there are many yet to be invented. Furthermore, despite the hardships, and they are brutally real for an aspiring bookwriter, there is no dearth of talent in the next generation, Prince believes:

There are good playwrights. There are, happily enough, more good playwrights I know about now than I would have known about ten years ago, and that's because of the not-for-profit theater and because of institutions like the NYU Musical Theater writing program, giving people workshops, giving them performances and productions.

Meanwhile, on Broadway, artists like Prince continue to be the more articulate leaders, those who help define musical theater style, as do new directors like George C. Wolfe.

But style is also conserved and transmitted and changed by those who prepare or perform the theater songs and the show music for its audience —namely the designers, the arrangers or orchestrators, the conductors or directors, the sound mixers, the musicians, and the actors-who-sing or singers-who-act—and dance. New book-spectacles of the eighties conserve and develop the musical play, but in a grandiose, high-tech modern version of what Aristotle called "spectacle." Nowadays the production factors are an even more powerful part of the musical play—along, of course, with the story and score, seen, we dare to hope, in Matthew Arnold's phrase, "steadily and whole."

5. Producing the Musical Fabric: Unsung and Hidden Collaborators

In the Shape of the Music . . . and the Spectacle

Since Aristotle, the art of technical designers and craftsmen who help translate the dramatic action of a musical play from the script and score to a life on stage, has at various points in history been denigrated as peripheral, if not dangerous, to the true moral purpose of "high art." But Aristotle, ever the realist, defended these "additions" to the popular Periclean theater. The Greeks, of course, had a word for it, namely, *techne,* meaning "an art." An inspired technician is an artist. But the conventional values of the elite then (and now) dictate that an inspired technician is a "secondary" artist, therefore less valuable to a show than the "primary artist" (a category that these days includes certain actors, as well as composer, lyricist, bookwriter, and, lately, director). They were secondary persons in Athens because the essence of the "true" art of *epic* poetry lay in the *single* person of the poet who *privately recited* for the cultured wealthy rulers of the community. The *dramatic* form of poetry called "tragedy" or "comedy" presented at the Dionysia, an annual holy day, was for *masses;* these shows *required the technicians.* As an art form they were alleged by some aristocrats to be lowlier than the privately chanted epics by a poet before an elite group of aristos.

Aristotle took up the issue. Is the art of a dramatic poet, because it addresses "any and every one" who periodically attends the great Athenian theatrical festivals, a "lower," "uncultivated," more "vulgar" (demotic, popular) work than art that addresses a more restricted, "cultivated" (or wealthier) audience like that of the epic poet who sings or recites Homer and Hesiod?

144

Aristotle conceded that words originally sung in a sacred setting were so powerful at times that they did not wholly depend on a show, on "public performance and actors." Also, he realized that a sense of a tragedy could be experienced by reading it privately. But Aristotle defended the more popular art form over the "better public" that did not "need" live theater with music and spectacle to appreciate the glory of Homer's epic art. He argued that compared to the venerable epic recitations, tragedy was "the higher form of art," in part because it had all the essential elements of drama. Tragedy, he contended, has everything that the epic has, together with the considerable additions of "song" (a very real factor in the pleasure of the drama) and "Spectacle."[1]

All this, in its way, is background to the twentieth-century question: should musical theater on Broadway be called American opera? It is a question that speaks to what is the "higher," more appropriate form for the people of our own "city-state." It is no longer a question of theater versus recitation. Although we now have a large number of poets publicly reading their work, it is almost never epic or even narrative verse. Now the issue is musical theater, with modern American music, using English dialogue and lyrics, versus musical theater in another language, from another country and sometimes another century, called "grand opera." Class differences, as in Periclean Athens, at the upper rung and just below, enter into the matter. Broadway musical works are expensive, but grand opera is always subsidized by the rich and powerful. Money aside, the assumption is that a more "cultivated" audience goes to grand opera because the music and the type of vocal performance it employs are somehow "higher art." Nowadays, supertitles may be flashed above the heads of performers as if they were in a foreign movie or on television; however, this device only makes language as such a different kind of problem for the American audience.

For twentieth-century Broadway musical theater is more an American art form than its predecessor, European opera. The issue goes deep. "Any and every" American can understand and enjoy a musical. The music and lyrics sound American. The songs are wedded to American stories, and are brought to dramatic life in modern productions by modern-day inspired *techne:* directors, choreographers, and designers of today. The spirit of Dionysia survives. Throughout this century our musical theater forms have developed and changed. The first grand merger of European opera with the new American Broadway was *Porgy and Bess* (1935) and later *Sweeney Todd* (1979); from European operettas grew American incarnations, from *The Student Prince* (1924) to *My Fair Lady* (1956). The Broadway musical continues to evolve even as we write. We now know that the mysteries of American autonomous spirit and a newly developed collaborative art have succeeded in creating a genre of our own, the American musical, which has triumphed nationally and internationally in celebrating the American people in all our richness and diversity. The distinctively American sound, "in the shape of the music [and words] . . . and the spectacle," emanates from Broadway shows, which, when successful, reach audiences around the country and the world. Aristotle's defense of the popular musical theater as an art form has been tested and decided in America.

Thus, as in ancient Athens, before a musical reaches the public, the dyads and triads of top executives who started with a concept or a book and songs must first broaden into a company of artisans. Today, however, the finished look and sound of a large Broadway musical show has been constructed by well over a hundred artists, technicians, and workers. They form an ad hoc *Gemeinschaft* (roughly, a community), a company around one project, that must find its expression in a final melting pot of all their contributions. Paradoxically, every member of the company, although essential to the production, is considered expendable or replaceable—but only to save the project itself. For all this happens on the way to that other finality, the economic forum of "hit or flop," a judgment made ultimately by the audience.

The important creative functions of many members of this ad hoc community of technical artists in the making of a musical do not usually receive their due. Why? Perhaps because, as each project surges to completion, increasing strains heighten the tension of money versus art, of "primary" versus "secondary" artist. Conflicts rise to meet and confound the daily or hourly necessity of collaboration. Control of the show and the media becomes an overriding concern. The media act to hype the myths of the "primary" artists. But in the process of construction, everyone counts; some, however, who vary from show to show, count more than others. In reality, dependence and interdependence make almost everything a matter of ambivalent, though dedicated, collaboration among members of the primary creative team *and* a large corps of designers and technicians. *Techne* increase and subdivide as does their contribution to the whole musical show. A musical's fabric is woven by a myriad of artisans melding their talents. Looking closely at all their contributions would take another whole book. Here we will focus on arrangers and musicians, lighting designers, and actors, whose key collaboration we deem more invisible, or under-known and valued than, say, that of choreographers or set and costume designers. We conclude with the ultimate hidden collaborator—the audience.

Musical Arrangements: The Techne of Arranger and Orchestrator

From the first songs interpolated into bookless revues and follies early in this century, the Broadway musical (like European grand opera) has always needed an arranger and/or orchestrator (often the same person). An arranger weaves music and songs into a musical fabric that, if skillfully wrought, helps hold the action of the play seamlessly together. But with musical arrangements and then orchestrations comes the need for a conductor and musicians, separately unionized and salaried workers, essential to performing the score and bringing life to the songwriters' creations. One cannot do a show without them. The composer Burton Lane describes this compound form of collaboration and the social distance inherent in its hierarchy, from "I" to "we" to "them."

When I do a show, I sit with an arranger. Then I select the conductor, and he and the arranger and I will decide on the best instrumentation for the score and how many musicians we need in the pit. I don't select them. The conductor works with a contractor from the musicians union.

An arranger, chosen first, has considerable impact on the show. One of the best arrangers for Broadway shows defines the ambivalence of his professional function:

An arranger is a composer who is hired by another composer to finish an incomplete work. Completion can take virtually any form—it depends on how incomplete the work is. An arranger is, by my definition, a composer. You use the same skills; you hear and write music; you invent it and work with it.

What exactly does an arranger do? As John Glasel, the classically trained musician who has spent his working life in orchestra pits, explains it, even an old standard as familiar as "The Man I Love" will sound one way with a Shep Fields arrangement, another with one by Mantovani, yet another with a deep soul arrangement—or certainly with a "heavy metal" sound:

The whole feeling of the music is affected by the orchestration—even if the tempo is the same, even if the number of bars is the same. It's the sound: The orchestration—the instruments, the chords—gives it [a unique] sound.

The ability to create the "sound" that at once emanates from and enhances the script and the score is an art unto itself. In a broader sense, as the scholarly Francis Fergusson says, Aristotle's " 'harmony and rhythm' must refer, not only to music, but to the overall accords and correspondences that we enjoy in any beautifully formed work of art."[2]

The skill it takes to compose a song, to wed music with lyrics, is not the same as that required for writing inspired arrangements. The right sound for a show has to come from an understanding of instruments, including the voice, and what they can do. There is a sense of exclusivity based on this special knowledge. As our virtuoso arranger remarks:

There are very few people who know how to do it. . . . Virtually everybody I know in this field must take the time to study it. . . . That means playing in orchestras, conducting orchestras, living around orchestras and absorbing what they are all about. Composers [throughout time] have had their work orchestrated by other people, not beginning with but including Mozart, Berlioz, Bizet, Liszt, Debussy, Offenbach. I ran into Sergio Franchi the other day—he was going into a show that I orchestrated—and I was telling him how great an orchestrator I thought Puccini was. He told me Puccini had all his work orchestrated by another musician. His published correspondence is full of letters to an orchestrator!

The sound that an arranger orchestrates must come out of the pit and cross the footlights to communicate with actors on stage and, working with them, create a dramatic experience every night for a different, if similar, audience.

To arrange for the theater is a very specialized skill. You have to understand the dramatic demands and you have to be able to write for the acoustic orchestra. Flaws can be compensated for in a recording studio; they can't in the theater. . . . You have to write [or arrange] music that is wildly exciting [but] doesn't smother the lyrics.

Composers who work with lyricists feel responsible for and get paid to dream up musical ideas. For them, certain highly explosive moments of song define the whole show. They are also a prime source of royalties for a long time to come. But deciding and indicating what a particular instrument does is somebody else's job. Even if the primary composer has the skills to supervise the arranger, the crush of rehearsals and rewrites prevents him from doing more. Further, the composer "should be thinking of the total shape of the show. . . [not] writing a tuba part. . . . You have to find someone [an arranger] you trust absolutely . . . who understands you."

The dyadic issue of mutual understanding and trust, at the heart of songwriting collaboration, always laden with conflict, extends to every element of a show that affects the composer's and lyricist's work. The style of the *whole* show must be kept intact. The work that goes into maintaining solidarity between show and arrangements is largely unspoken, even unconscious. Thus Glasel: "Reviewers [almost] never review it, the people on stage are only marginally affected by it. Even the producers know from nothing 99 percent of the time."

It takes the specially sensitive and well-trained ear of a fellow composer to recognize and appreciate the arranger's ability to understand a song. When the sound is right, an orchestral subtext lies unobtrusively below the surface of a song. Deliberately difficult to perceive, such a subtext helps the song perform its theatrical function. Sondheim writes about the art of Jonathan Tunick:

Follies contains a lesson in sub-text, a song called "In Buddy's Eyes." It's a woman's song to her former lover, in which she says that everything is just wonderful and she's having a terrific time at home, she's so happily married. Nothing in the lyric, nothing, not a single word tells you that maybe it isn't true. Nothing in the music tells you. . . [except] something in the orchestration. . . . Jonathan Tunick, the orchestrator, understands. . . about sub-text because every phrase in that song which refers to Buddy, her husband, is dry, it's all woodwinds.[3]

For that you need a good arranger.

But the few are more artful than the many. And Glasel, as musician, reports that "a lot of shows come in with less than fine orchestration." In such circumstances, he himself has sometimes "fixed the arrangements" to sound better. Even when he has gone so far as to change voicings and chords, a less than fine arranger "couldn't tell the difference." Producers, wittingly or unwittingly, can further complicate the sound problem: "When they split it up among several orchestrators, you know there are economic factors at work." And then the musical fabric may be torn apart.

The primary composer's problem is to maintain as much of a say over the final sound as he can. For a strong example, Richard Rodgers wanted "no surprises." Most songwriting composers allow and expect much from their arrangers. But then they run some risks. Burton Lane says: "Trying to get somebody who will do a good job and be inspired is a problem." Our top arranger also feels the primacy of an inspirational side. For him, agreement on ideas is paramount in the production of any sound at all: "It's possible to arrange music with a composer when there is no personal rapport. But when you're seeking each other out in the first place, what you want to know is: 'Do we agree on basic things?' "

Maintaining the original links in a chain of collaboration matters so much because, once hired, the arranger, like the conductor, is involved in connecting the original and the evolving sound of the whole show to the work of all its other designers. For instance, the sound of the show, especially of the dance arrangements, is clearly crucial to the choreographer. But light-

Camelot *Rehearsal: Franz Allers, Conductor, Robert Goulet, Actor, Frederick Loewe,
Composer (1960)*

The orchestral sound made by highly trained musicians has been a major part of the American
musical since its early development in the 1900s. In the 1980s the live orchestra became more
visually hidden from the audience and its survival is threatened by computer technology. Here
is the orchestra rehearsing for the hit show *Camelot* (1960) with Robert Goulet (singing),
conductor Franz Allers, and composer Frederick Loewe *(rear)*. (Photo credit: Billy Rose
Theatre Collection, New York Public Library; photographer: Milton H. Greene.)

ing, as we are not likely to have suspected, may be important to the sound. Our orchestrator notes:

I work very closely, first hand, with the choreographer. But I also seek out the lighting designer. When I'm stuck on something, I often find that he can help me out. I ask him, "How are you going to light this?" Very often that gives me a good clue.

As a highly skilled designer, the arranger looks for clues from others that will solve his sound problems. "Somewhere along the line, you discuss the style of the show with the composer, the choreographer, the director. This does not always clarify things. . . . In that case, [you] look to others," above all, to the lyricist, for lyrics, although explicit, are also primary to the play's "action." The orchestration does more than succeed in not drowning out the words; the skilled arranger gives them Sondheim's subtext: "One orchestrates the lyrics as much as the music. The lyrics so often tell you exactly where to go. . . . I orchestrate the lyrics as much as the music." And the lyrics follow the story.

The Musical Director/Conductor

For the musical director, who trains the actors-who-sing the to-be-ar-ranged-and-orchestrated score, and the conductor (who may have both roles) the main nexus to an overriding vision of the show starts with the top executives. For Paul Gemignani, an experienced and artful freelance musical director-conductor, the show starts at various points.

Michael [Bennett] brought me in very early. [So did] Hal [Prince] and Steve [Sondheim]. I knew the score for *Sweeney Todd* before we went into pre-production. Other people call you up during rehearsal. It depends. Most of them get you involved as soon as you'd like to get involved. . . . So if I go to a composer's house to study a score I'm sure I'm going to do for a year or if I sit through auditions for three weeks and don't get any money for them, it's part of the same thing. . . part of your dedication, your belief in the product.

Actors are not the only ones mostly unemployed in show biz. ("They [the producers] are always worried about money." However, "they" get a percent of the gross.) Arrangers and musical directors are also hired hands who get a flat fee or a salary or a wage. And for them, there is no "killing," even with a smash hit. The incentive system of corporate enterprise is not different on Broadway. So those technicians who are for hire must work elsewhere on most occasions. Furthermore, even with a long-running show, a musical director-conductor dare not continue with it long after it opens, for fear of losing his "name."

Judy Holliday and Orchestra Listening to Playback of Bells Are Ringing *Recording (1956)*

The truth of the artist is tested each night before a live audience, but each performer must first collaborate with composer, lyricist, bookwriter, conductor, and musicians before the show—and afterward in the studio to make the cast album. Here is Judy Holliday, critically appraising her performance while the orchestra rests during a studio rehearsal. (Photo credit: Billy Rose Theatre Collection, New York Public Library.)

Collaboration with the composer is a prime link with the show as a whole. For Gemignani:

Some [relationships] are harder than others. The rapport ends up usually to be the same in the long run. It's harder because a lot of composers have been burned by guys that don't know what they're doing, so they don't trust you right away. Once they trust me I have no problem.

Unfortunately, the quality of available Broadway musical directors is not high, and of course this problem affects the show.

They'll take a piano player who's never conducted before and push him into the musical director's position [to train the actors to sing the score]. He doesn't know anything about voice. But nobody in his right mind is going to turn that job down, because it's a promotion. . . . There are things they miss. For example, diction in the chorus.

Further in the swirl of rehearsal, much work with the changing show requires close attention. Gemignani describes this:

I ask the director what he's going to do, and I ask him can I use everybody [in a given number] or is there anybody not going to be in the thing. And he says everybody's going to be in it or he says, "No, those four I have to have for a costume change." I don't use those four then. That's just a time-saving device. It doesn't mean anything. And then he comes in and hears it. And he'll say, "The soprano sound is too shrill," and I'll fix it, or he'll say, "That's great" or "Let's try something else because it's not working."

As we noted, a major aim is to hear the lyrics—the thoughts of the songs:

Fifty percent of the time when the lyrics cannot be understood, it has nothing to do with the sound department at all. It has to do with musical directors. It means they don't know how to make the score sung so that it can be understood. If you can't understand it with the mike off, you're not going to understand it with the mike on.

Conductors and the New Musical Plays. Further, the trend of musical theater will make matters even more demanding, Gemignani believes:

Shows are not getting easier—they're getting harder. They're more lyrical, more operatic. This show's wall-to-wall music [*Dreamgirls*]. *Sweeney Todd* had hardly any dialogue. *Evita* had little. That's a lot different than my mentor, Hal Hastings—who had two songs and then a four-minute book thing [without music]. Now the music is more sophisticated in the sense that there is more of it, and if you're not playing a song, you're playing underscoring. *You have to know how to aid dialogue.* If your conducting technique is not together, it's very difficult and ends up sloppy.

In any kind of musical show on Broadway, the flow of musical ideas emerges from many sources. The conductor and his orchestra are under

Paul Gemignani, at Rehearsal with Cast Members of Jerome Robbins' Broadway *(1989)*

Paul Gemignani, here as musical director of *Jerome Robbins' Broadway,* trains some of the cast to sing one of the many songs from different prior shows directed by Robbins. (Photo credit: Martha Swope.)

Jerome Robbins and Paul Gemignani at Rehearsal of Jerome Robbins' Broadway *(1989)*

Jerome Robbins, director, and Paul Gemignani, conductor and musical director, discuss adjustments to the musical sound to best fit the live action on stage for *Jerome Robbins' Broadway* (1989), produced by Emanuel Azenberg. (Photo credit: Martha Swope.)

constant pressure; requests, suggestions, angry negotiations are part of the job. Often another designer wants you to make changes in your work that will solve his or her problems. Gemignani sees it this way:

Very often requests are impossible. Somebody will come to you and say, "I want that big sweeping sound of a hundred violins." I say, "We've got six violins. For what you want to hear you've got to hire more people." That's a simplistic example, but a typical one. But more often I get things that are easy to do, not questions of aesthetic disagreement but really practical nuts-and-bolts things: "We need more music for the scene change or a certain effect there for the choreography or a big sweep here. We need the music to go up instead of down."

Much about the sound of the show is decided at these collaborative encounters. And those who cope with it are by tradition invisible.

The major problems of a conductor, however, are managerial, as Gemignani observes:

There are a lot of people who conduct. There are few, I think, who can handle a company, the musicians and the actors. When the director walks out of the building, the problems come to the stage manager and the [musical director] or the conductor, whether it's on paper or not, and you've got to be sensitive to the actor on stage all the time.

There are also only a few who "know what to do with an orchestra. . . . The level of conducting as an art form on Broadway could be raised." Glasel is more direct and specific:

Conductors, especially on Broadway, are not skilled masters either of their craft or of the art I really believe is the primary requisite of a conductor, which is managerial talent. When you're a conductor, you're in a position of getting a whole bunch of people to work together. You're in essence like a foreman in a factory. Nobody's going to be a successful manager if he has an abrasive personality, if he doesn't at least *exhibit* respect for his people . . . sympathy for them and understanding. A lot of these guys are completely cuckoo; they hate musicians. They're afraid of the people on the stage. [However,] some of them are very good, and there have been a few great conductors.

Miking the Sound—Accommodating a New Techne

The technique of miking, first executed for an Ethel Merman (!) show as early as 1939—amplifiers were placed in the footlights because the orchestra's brass section had been beefed up—has become what the Greeks meant by *techne:* an art. In addition to a primary composer, an arranger, a musical director, and everyone in the pit, amplified sound now requires its own designers. They work with the mikes, the amps, and the mixer.

Although such activity would seem to be a secondary function, composers and performers old enough to have worked without this technique do not see it that way. For Burton Lane, there is something wrong with amplification per se: "I want an orchestra to sound like an orchestra. I like pure sound." The reaction, predictably, is stronger in a singer and actress from the presixties whose feelings are unequivocal: "I hate amplification. It's like washing your hands with your gloves on. There is no direct communication. Everything seems aimed at further alienation." But one generation's alienation is another's need. Carol Hall reports:

I was doing the La Mama show and I had sent one of the girls up for an audition at the Winter Garden. "How did it go?" "You're not going to believe this! We had to go out on stage and just sing. I mean, we didn't have mikes or anything!" This child thought she'd really gotten the short end of the stick.

The new generation of sound in the sixties did indeed introduce amplification even unto the hallowed halls of Old Broadway. An arranger explains:

One of the things that created this problem [the need for sound designers] was the advent of rock instruments, specifically the electric bass and the drum set, because those are instruments designed for records where you have control over the volume. Just take the drums and put them on the side and you put the vocalist down the middle. In the theater you can't separate all those sounds and do your stereo mix and balance it just so. That's when amplification became a big problem.

New electronic instruments that came in with sixties rock were already amped. For Lonny Price, who describes himself as an actor-who-sings, gratitude was the keynote:

Body mikes aren't difficult. They're little things with tiny wires that go down over your pant leg. I was glad to be on the body mike in *Merrily We Roll Along* because, without it, when my voice got tired, I wouldn't have been able to sing. *Merrily* had four trumpets, two percussion instruments, electric guitar and electric piano. Now how would any merely human voice sing over all that?

This actor-singer wants the mike. Unlike our older actress-singer, he needs the gloves; they are working gloves.

From the point of view of sound designers, it is not the mikes but what one does with them that counts. The new technique must be, and sometimes is, transformed into an art. Gemignani:

Mikes were developed for performers like Glynis Johns. She's a magnificent actress but you can't hear her beyond the third row. What do you do? Get somebody who's not as good? You put a radio mike on her and if you have the taste of a Jack Mann, he was the sound designer for *Nine, A Little Night Music, Sweeney Todd;* he's tops in his business, that's great.

For Glasel, audible electronics could take the life out of music. A good designer must enhance the human voice, not kill "live theater":

I've been to too many shows where the sound was atrocious. It's the design of speakers in some theaters. They make a large cast of characters spread out across the stage. Everybody is equipped with one of these damned FM mikes, which sound as if they came from a single place. I loved the music in *Bubblin' Brown Sugar* but I couldn't tell where the sound was coming from. Whose mouth was moving? Same thing with the band. It had no depth. It was very flat. It's not live theater when you do that. It's TV.

Everyone, including sound designers, seems to agree that the art of sound design is in its infancy. But whatever the design of mikes and amps may be, in actual performance there is a secondary artist who handles the sound, just as a lighting technician handles the light; the "sound man" monitors, adjusts, and balances the total electronic input-output. More problems. Glasel describes one:

The sound man can destroy anything the conductor or the arranger does. A good conductor who is a strong personality working with a good sound man cannot control the situation because the sound man's in the back of the theater and the conductor has no ear phones. He can't hear what's going on. He can't hear what the sound man is doing. He's too close to the stage, too close to the orchestra. He can't hear what's coming out of those speakers.

Gemignani used to let his assistant conduct one show a week to allow himself to stay in the house and listen to the music. "Otherwise, I'd never have a chance to do that." Now he wears headphones also.

Sound technicians are not "designers" in the staff hierarchy because they must be members of the International Association of Theatrical Stage Employees (IATSE), the union that defends his job and his pay. This relatively new, and thus lower-status, hired hand in the community of artists may have a disproportionate effect on everyone else's work and on the whole question of Glasel's "live" sound.

There are a handful of really good sound men in IATSE, and I've worked with them. They're great. The composers love them. The arrangers and the conductors love them. So do I. But perhaps one tenth of one percent of the general population has the ears and the talent that it takes to become a sound man. Most of them don't want to do it anyway.

Still, the technology of amped sound is a challenge that many people are trying to meet. Their objective is not that of perfect sound which is unattainable anywhere. The aim for Broadway musical theater is to hear *meaningful sounds*—lyrics, underscoring, choral harmonies. In the eighties in certain houses for some large musicals such fidelity has already been attained. The arranger's words are hopeful: "I feel that a lot of improvement has been made in the last couple of years. . . . I have gone to some shows where the sound was absolutely marvelous."

Invisible Musicians "in the Pits" of Broadway

This weaving of sound to communicate both musical and lyrical feelings and thoughts requires intense collaborative linkage among the singers, the musical director-conductor, and the musicians. Actors may be low on the power structure, but musicians are literally lowest, down and maybe out; tapes, miked-in sound, and now computer disks are their future shock nightmare. "It's a free-lance peripatetic life" to John Glasel, a Broadway trumpet player for many years and then the president of his union. (He also has a degree from the Yale Conservatory of Music.)

It's a terrible life being a [pit] musician, a rough hard life. You've got to scuffle for jobs, play up to contractors because any one can have the power—virtually the power of life or death. . . . We're talking about it almost as if it were coolie labor. . . . [Musicians] are people with advanced degrees. They're highly sensitive and cultured people with good educations who have dedicated their lives to perfecting an art form and they're treated like indentured labor.

 The pits are much deeper than they used to be. In some cases, they're covered as in *A Chorus Line.* You don't even know there are musicians there. And they put mikes on them. It's just like TV or radio or a recording. Some people don't even know there are live musicians there. It's wrong.

As for the new sound:

I've lost hearing just from sitting in front of the drums; some of the rock and so-called electronic sounds are ear-shattering. Creative sounds are fine but some are so loud you can't hear yourself play. This is especially true in the pit where I've learned to carry ear plugs.

But the key to getting hired is still your ability as a trained musician. To do what? Not only to hear your own instrument but also to play it in relation to the distinctive sound style of a given show.

I was the first trumpet player in a lot of different Broadway shows, and I think the reason I kept getting called is not because I was any stronger or had higher notes or a more beautiful sound than any other trumpet player, but [because of] my own particular talent in understanding the different styles of music that are called for. When I hear a phrase or see it, when I hear how it's scored, I have enough experience to know what kind of sound is expected by the arranger or the conductor or the songwriter or whoever's in charge.

John Glasel, President, Local 802, American Federation of Musicians (1983–1992)

John Glasel, a Broadway "pit" musician for many years, was president of Local 802, American Federation of Musicians from 1983 to 1992. He trained at Yale University and wrote a book on relaxation techniques for musicians. (Photo credit: Courtesy Local 802, American Federation of Musicians.)

Once hired, the musician bears exactly those generalized skills that got him his job: "Most of us are trained to be extremely versatile . . . and to sight read music like crazy." But, unlike most actors, who are visible and may be applauded, musicians find the repetitive nightly performances an occupational hazard. Ennui is its name. Like all such problems, it resounds and clashes with the others. One man's boredom is another's prayer for consistency. For instance, a composer, Burton Lane, associates boredom with playing "a bad score," and sympathizes with musicians who have to play it over and over. He then shifts ground, puts on his composer hat, and finds fault:

A lot of musicians take nights off and put in substitutes. That's unfortunate. You get a trumpet player who's cracking all over the place and blowing your orchestrations because he's just been put in that night. The union permits a certain amount of this and it's a bad thing.

But Gemignani thinks substitution is "one of the best things the union has ever come up with." It gives a player some control over the havoc that can be wrought by boredom. "The unions don't word it this way, but orchestra members are in effect allowed to take 50 percent of their time off; they can play four shows and be off four shows." Interchangeability is the conductor's solution to controlling boredom insofar as it affects a musician's ability to play well while doing the same thing over and over.

In most cases, however, it is not the conductor but the producer's contractor who fills chairs in the pit. The failure of a musician to meet the composer's standards for his show then falls on the producer's "casting directors" (the contractors). To the musicians who must depend on them for jobs, producers' contractors can be serious trouble. He (for it almost certainly is he) does little more than fulfill union requirements. Gemignani does not regard it as a system conducive to maintaining a high-level orchestra. Where is the hitch or the glitch? "It has to do with how you pick personnel. Inconsistency is due to bad casting, the responsibility of a contractor in most cases." Although the selection of musicians is equally consequential to a composer, conductor, or arranger, the contract does not give any of them control. Except for a few artists who make sure to retain the final say. To one top arranger it looks like this:

I cast an orchestra the way you'd cast a show. I myself am in contact with so many of the musicians that I know who the better players are and I take particular interest in who, specifically, plays with my orchestras.

Gemignani, the conductor, also does his own casting.

Reducing the musician's invisibility would require deep changes in the relationship between art and commerce. Such changes might alter wage and hiring conventions that govern labor relations on Broadway. While wages have barely kept up with inflation since 1970, employment is always unsteady. But the musicians' role, meager as it is in monetary or artistic satisfactions, hazardous and dispiriting as it can be, speaks for much that gives life to the theater. On this we hear the authoritative Glasel, as eloquent as he is unpretentious:

What I feel devotion to doesn't necessarily pay good money. That's music. In most of these jobs, music is subservient to something else. Whether it is part of your religion or trying to help humanity or television or film or a dance or a Broadway show, 90 percent of the time music is an adjunct to some other form of social behavior. In this case it's a subsidiary adjunct to something called a musical.

Deeply disturbing to all theater musicians is the fact that, as of 1991, there exists in at least two nonunion dinner theaters a computer resource to eliminate the need for live musicians. The musical arrangement emerges from a single computer disk. Furthermore, the music can be managed manually at any point in the score to accompany a song rendition by singer or chorus. Equipment costs sixty thousand dollars, a sum that can be repaid within a few months of a running show. Just as they did not notice the addition of mikes, the live audience does not notice the absence of live musicians. Is this the coming wave in legitimate musical theater? No one knows yet.

Actors: Visible and Vulnerable

If competent arrangers, conductors, sound men, and musicians are in high demand, so are competent actors-who-sing (or vice versa). But the aspirants are many and, unlike sound men or musicians, they are hugely visible. All eyes are on the actors and actresses. However, today only few have the star status that gives them leverage. A trend away from the star vehicles once created for a Gertrude Lawrence, an Ethel Merman, or a Mary Martin from the twenties to the sixties is pronounced. The musical dramas of Prince and Sondheim in the seventies and shows generated in workshops, like *A Chorus Line* and *Godspell,* were consciously conceived not to be old-time star vehicles.

A star can still carry a show, but the fairly new *techne* of a casting director like John Lyons reflects an ever-widening pool of many-sided acting talent. Lyons maintains that each major acting part in a show could be carried by any one of three actors on his (computerized) files. Casting, like sound, has become a specialized secondary art that includes auditioning even for known and successful performers, to try to get the best fit for the show.

Auditioning may require weeks or months. Many (at times thousands) are called (literally on the phone) for a single role from the computer files of the casting director, but the army of unemployed actors is hardly touched. Usually directors have the final vote, but any of the top executives may participate in judging auditions. In cases of conflict, a skilled casting director will wait for the opportunity to sum up various candidates' strong and weak points vis-à-vis the role, and urge a specific choice on the divided group.

When there are no desirable or appropriate Broadway parts for the likes of Lonny Price in his role as a good actor who also sings, he must seek work on television or in films, the standard procedure of going where the money is. The actors' union is a problem to this actor-singer:

Equity is not very powerful. SAG [the Screen Actors' Guild] is a great strong union. . . . Producers are afraid of it. But they can twist Equity around their little fingers. Equity always says yes: "Can we cancel their day off?" "Yes." "Can they work extra hours?" "Sure." "Can we put them in a workshop for twelve weeks with no money?" "Of course you can!" I wish they'd merge with SAG and AFTRA [American Federation of Television and Radio Artists] and then we'd have one union for everybody.

But one union for everybody would not diminish the friction between the time an artist wants to spend rehearsing and a system of hourly bookkeeping designed for interchangeable hired hands.

But nothing, creative or not, guarantees the actor who did a workshop or out-of-town production of a show his role in the New York transfer. Price was asked to reaudition, to start from scratch in an Off-Broadway production in a play originally written for him, and was rejected. He had already played the role successfully, but only out of town. Such juggling prompts Sheldon Harnick to speculate: "It might not be wise to write for a specific performer. You may have written things that another performer cannot do as easily or as skillfully." But, if you have the performer in situ, on hand, already a known quantity and with proven talent, then both lyrics and music can be fitted to his or her voice and character. This is what the Gershwins did for Fred Astaire and Lerner and Loewe did for Rex Harrison. It is what Sondheim did for Lonny Price in *Merrily We Roll Along*. And while Price did not get his key song delivered to him until three days before the start of previews, through great team effort it was woven fully into the story with collaboration among the composer, lyricist, musical director, conductor, soundman, orchestra, actor, and director. And not least the lighting director.

Merrily We Roll Along *Recording Session (1981)*

Here is Lonny Price (with glasses, *second from left*), a leading self-styled "actor-who-sings," rehearsing with the cast for *Merrily We Roll Along* (1981). This show, with a score by Stephen Sondheim and directed by Hal Prince, was rejected by Broadway critics and audiences rather swiftly in its initial production, though the score is considered one of Sondheim's finest. Only 10–15 percent of the thirty-five thousand members of Actors Equity in New York are gainfully employed during a given year. Thus Price also became a director. (Photo credit: Henry Grossman.)

Technical Theater: The Musical Lighting
of Visual Gesture

In theory, everyone in a musical is equally involved and dedicated; actors and musicians struggle with the contradictions of their visible or invisible contributions as performing artists at the low end of a fairly elaborate hierarchy. Technical theater, machinery that maintains the constant flow of action on a stage, was Jules Fisher's minor area of studies at Carnegie Tech. His major was theater, but lighting design became his profession. He found it had few of the ambiguities inherent in performance. The work of doing set design, lighting, or costume begins and ends behind the scenes, in the magic of technical theater.

This kind of work requires "very, very little" basic scientific knowledge —no more than "a rudimentary knowledge of optics, physics, electricity, psychology . . . knowledge of human beings and of the world," and "you have to know electricity backwards, you really have to understand what it does and why."

Fisher, after much summer stock work, started a professional career during his last year of college.

Most of the shows I did in the beginning were Off-Broadway on shoestring budgets. . . . I made a lot of lights. If they couldn't afford to rent what I thought they needed I would buy soup cans or tomato cans and put light bulbs in them and make lighting fixtures. . . . I loved what I was doing, even though the size of the theater, as well as the budget, made it technically difficult. Once, I had to do a whole sunset at the Greenwich Mews Theater. The wall was five feet from the proscenium edge and there was no wing space, so I built a lighting instrument, a wall of lights. A stagehand kept pulling a large piece of colored gelatin scotch-taped together across these lights—and presto, the sunset.

But there is more—from improvisations or inventions to the imponderables of taste and talent—that cannot be taught.

Fisher's technical approach to his art is reflected in Lawrence Kramer's study of the deep interrelationship between music and poetry. Because both music and poetry "define their formal shape as a function of rhythmically integrated time," Kramer finds the "physical gesture" to be "a complex action so integrated that it is perceived as simple" (or not consciously perceived at all)—an appropriate metaphor for what is common in the movement of music and poetry. Thus, since all of the arts organize and characterize time, "The shapes of time evolved by the various arts may finally be more representational, more mimetic, than any pictorial, narrative, or programmatic content."[4] The lighting designer reshaping light-time

Jules Fisher (1992)

Jules Fisher, master lighting designer and producer, is an artist-magician who consciously integrates lighting with the rhythm of the music and dance and story-action to affect the audience subliminally. Mr. Fisher has worked on over 100 productions and received numerous awards. (Photo credit: courtesy Henry Grossman.)

is musician and poet and artist-magician manipulating our expectations of the natural order of things to help shape the overall theatrical gesture. A musical background is helpful to a lighting designer, not because one has to know music in order to light a musical but because all elements in the arts are generic, and lighting is one of them. Fisher elaborates:

Lighting itself has rhythm. It's a major factor in setting lighting cues: Pacing is as common to music as it is to lighting. In a two-hour play, the lighting moves just as the music does. It is constantly changing, literally breathing in the same way. It's subconscious, like your awareness of the complete cycle of lighting that changes with the sun every day of your life. Your mind is attuned to cycles and rhythms. If I change that rhythm and have the sun in the late afternoon start to back up again, you will be subconsciously affected.

Lighting design (unlike music but perhaps like electronically amplified sound) can be crucial in the presentation of a spectacle. Lighting, as Fisher reminds us, has become visible in its own right:

I came in on a wave of musicals that allowed for a greater expansion of light to be used in the form of fantasy—*Hair, Jesus Christ Superstar, Joseph and the Amazing Technicolor Dreamcoat,* the rock opera *Tommy.* All of them used lighting that was splashier, more gay, more wild, more vivid. In *Superstar,* in 1970 or 1971, I used ten very small lasers. It's hard not to notice something that had never been used before. That's why critics started to talk about lighting.

Spectacular lighting does more than make the stage visible. Its technological magic is surrounded by the aura of American success. The lighting architecture of *Dreamgirls* made it a landmark musical to critic Frank Rich. Fisher, an amateur magician in his youth, understands prestidigitation as the crux of his lighting job in a show: "As a magician I know how to get an audience to look or not look at a certain place"—in proper rhythm.

In a larger sense, "Lighting describes and marks the boundaries of space on the stage. I can make a very large space seem small with the lights; I control the space that will be seen. I mold it, very much like sculpture." Perhaps a combination of technical expertise and the lure of flexibility that goes with control of a theater's space induced Fisher the lighting designer to take on the producer's role. Probably his ability to make lighting seem central to the theater of technology also helped.

During the Creating and Staging. . .

The standard Broadway method of getting into production involves ten weeks of rehearsal time, i.e., technical creative time, rewrite, etc., as designated by Actor's Equity, plus additional time for integration of the technical artists' work. (Overtime pay involves substantial increases.)

Claire Nichtern, in her capacity as producer, describes the organized chaos that fills the air of every musical going into final rehearsal:

Everybody's there on the first day and it's very exciting because they read the play and the composer usually plays the music and then the dancers and the singers and the set [and other design] people split off into different rooms. Your hope is that you're going to come out of the rehearsal process with a tight script. But there's a certain intensity that comes from having to open on time in Boston, with a booking and all those subscribers at the other end.

Because there is so little time to work in lights, sets, costumes, and sound, the creators and producers of *Woman of the Year,* for example, Nichtern included, did not know the show had technical problems until it opened in Boston. (It was resurrected in New York.) Afterwards, Nichtern thought, "The visual concept was not clear. But you always say, 'We'll fix that after we open. We're going to work on it.' I now think the sets fought against the rest of the production."

This is the kind of initial pressure that Michael Bennett's "workshop" tried to ameliorate: "I needed to find another way to do shows that allowed me time to make mistakes, but not mistakes in Boston where I'd be dead." The regular Broadway production was the opposite in timing of Michael Bennett's workshop method. Supported by Joseph Papp and the Public Theater, Bennett took more than six months to build the script and the score around the cast and the idea of *A Chorus Line.* It then came to Broadway as a successful Off-Broadway production, much the way entire shows now come to Broadway from successful runs in London.

Gemignani believes that the failure of *Merrily We Roll Along* may have been a matter of difference in scale between sensing the show within a rehearsal space and a live theater space—technical matters. For designers who are called upon only at the point of production, interdependence of all the technical skills is crucial. To an arranger,

It's like baking a cake. You take the ingredients, put them in a bowl and mix them, pour the mixture in a pan and put it in the oven. Sometimes it just doesn't rise. A certain chemical reaction either does or does not take place.

This analogy points to two elements that shield technical theater artists from blame for the failure of a show: first, they think of their work as an invisible ingredient in the mix; and second, the chemical reaction that must take place among ingredients if the cake is to rise or the production to come alive is unpredictable. As long as their performance is adequate and inconspicuous, like that of the good Victorian child, it need not provoke comment.

Vision and Control of the Techne's Work: The Director's Unifying Role

In the sixties, seventies, and eighties, lyricists like Charnin, producers like Prince, actors like Price, composers like Schwartz, bookwriters like Laurents, choreographers like Robbins and Fosse-all moved to control the vision of the musical play through all its creative and technical elements by becoming directors. As such, they reached the locus of power and authority over all the *techne.*

The position of director entails one person through whom all the "visions" are supposed to pass. As Prince recalled one show:

[The producers thought they] didn't like it at all, but when we got the costumes and scenery and they heard the orchestration, *the whole thing came together.* So the [musical] theater is a collaboration and that collaboration includes scenery, costumes, orchestration, the lights [and so forth].

Is the director of a musical an *auteur,* as he (or occasionally she) is widely assumed to be in motion pictures? Is such a person the visionary who contributes most to a Broadway show's overall artistic and commercial success? That question, which in one guise or another keeps coming up, is as debatable for musicals as it is for films. We have seen that in recent history the director's importance and authority have increased considerably with the importance of dance, electronic sound, high-tech lighting effects, open staging, and so forth. The book, or megaspectacle, has more need of a director than the old revue that strung a show across an evening's entertainment. But the question bears repeating: how can one person's ideas control an essentially collaborative art form?

A director can see problems and monitor and revise them in the "mix," whether or not he is solely responsible for its "vision" or its "concept." For many, like Fisher, who grew up in the theater, the director is or should be "the sole power" in production: "You have to work with everybody, but I don't think you can please everybody else and not please the director." And the director must please the audience.

One reason he has real or illusory power is that everyone recognizes it as a genuine need. That includes a harassed producer like Nicholas Howey, who desperately declares: "If the director is strong, your problems are over. A good director can straighten out the choreographer, the actors, the costumes, everything." (And a chorus of voices, strophe-antistrophe, may ask, what if the show collapses even after everything is all straightened out?) In any event, a good director is paid to have all the pieces in mind. He is in charge of the fit and can arbitrate between ideas and execution, between the sound of words and music and the look of set and costume. When Carrie Robbins wants approval (it is never final until opening) on her costume designs she asks the director, "Are the words we said connected to this image [I have drawn]? Does it make any sense?" This felt need for the director makes Walter Kerr's explanation of that figure in developing a highly desirable communal spirit seem redundant. "The only way I [as a director] have ever found to bring people together on a project is to convince them—or to have them convinced by whatever means—that it is more important than they are."

Tommy Tune, choreographer, dancer, actor, frequently director, sounds another note of desire to control the vision: "It's very hard for a choreographer to work for a director. I guess that was part of my motivation to become a director. It meant one less pressure, one less person to collaborate with."

The directors' central role in unifying a given production, however, does not mean that any of them operates in the same style. Nor does it matter, according to Fisher, whose list of the greats includes choreographer-directors. "I've been terribly lucky. I've worked with most of the best directors: Mike Nichols, John Dexter, Bill Ball, Gower Champion, Michael Bennett, Jerry Robbins, Noel Coward, Lindsay Anderson, Bob Fosse. Each one is totally different from the others." But they were all charged with creating and preserving the integrity of the show.

According to Frank Rich (by way of Aristotle and Coleridge), all serious theater artists start with a vision (a once-exalted word in danger of being hopelessly trivialized by our eye-oriented world of images and messages and missions) of what the show should be and do. Sometimes "they stay with a vision and it is wrong"—*A Doll's Life* may have failed, he says, because its central vision of the heroine was at odds with a different understanding by the audience. Or, with *Barnum,* Rich notes,

It had a much longer book during the preview period in New York but the book was not communicating their vision so they jettisoned it and ended up with an entertaining show that probably communicated their vision better than the previous version.

Most of the flops, however, are "flopping like fish out of water" even before they come to Broadway. Rich recalls:

I saw legendary failures come to Washington and try to save themselves. The most interesting to me, in retrospect, was *Mr. President,* the last Irving Berlin musical

—an Irving Berlin, Russel Crouse, Howard Lindsay, Josh Logan musical—and that show, of course, had tremendous problems that were never solved. It was fascinating to watch very talented legendary figures fool around with it, throw out sets, throw out the second act, that kind of thing.

And even the shows that succeed are a turmoil of collaborative changes — presumably approved by a director, even if not initiated by him. Rich was intrigued:

I saw it happen with both of the two biggest hit musicals of Broadway in the 1960s —both tried out in Washington—*Hello, Dolly!* and *Fiddler on the Roof,* and those shows were in fairly good shape when they opened in Washington, but still underwent substantial changes on a day-by-day basis.

Broadway is rife with post-hoc analyses. Anything that was changed, like anything that was not changed, can be said retrospectively to account for failure or success. What audiences will actually do is unknowable. Then why keep changing and adjusting the production? Michael Bennett, exploding one more shibboleth, as he saw it (that choreographers do not know how to use words more realistically; some do, some do not), explains the interminable process of fixing a production. He seemed to see the audience as a very volatile but worthy adversary, constantly in motion, the ultimate challenge to a director's control in translating his vision of the show, as Bennett knew (and we repeat):

From the moment a show starts, you want that audience not to be mind-tripping, not soaring ahead of the plot, not reading the program, not getting bored. You don't want to lose them. So you want the show to have eruptions, a flow of high points. You want show-stoppers. You want to provide the emotion an audience expects, the feeling they attach to what they consider a great live theatrical experience. You want them to run out and say, "I have to see this again!" "I'll tell all my friends about it!" You want to move them.

The Ultimate Controller and Collaborator: The Live Audience

Schwartz: Ultimately, a show is a hit if it lives and a flop if it disappears.
Harnick: Technically, a flop is a show that loses all its money, and, more than that, has no future life. If you're lucky maybe a song or two will remain, but otherwise it's just a show that for all practical purposes is dead.

Opening out of town, Off or Off-Off-Broadway, going on the road or into workshop—these are methods by which to involve an audience in the production before a show meets the test of life or death on Broadway, and a possible afterlife in other settings. How an audience will respond is part of the project from its earliest beginnings. As the show gets further into production, closer to opening night, each artist, technician, and business-man has audience response in mind. While no one can be sure what will work, everyone knows that audiences provide the litmus test that demon-strates through plaudits and profits, whether their show is alive—or by their absence, that it is doomed.

How, when, and which audience response counts before the final proof of Broadway is no simple matter. Gail Berman insists that workshop or preview response should and, in her experience, did have an impact on the final production. Gut feeling is what defines the internalized other, the ability to know the minds and hearts and additional parts of our countrymen, of ourselves, the audience. An abiding mystery to professional theater people is that what they "know" to be funny, sad, romantic, dramatic, captivating, or devastating on stage ain't necessarily perceived as such by the audience. The "internalized other" that is externalized back into every occupied theater seat is forever unpredictable, baffling, unexpected. Years in the theater can instruct "the mind and heart" of a Burton Lane without overcoming his ever-alert consciousness of the audience as a delicate barometer recording the possible need for switches, tinkerings, turna-bouts. "If you're a wise, experienced, and sensitive creator, you're usually a step ahead of the audience. But you must allow them to teach you something. You must not close your mind to what they might convey to you."

The audience for Broadway musicals is not passive. Live theater is not by its nature passive. In Sophocles' Athens, poet-playwrights were praised or reviled, as they were under very different circumstances in Shake-speare's London. The tendency to react vociferously reached its apogee in Restoration theater, where boisterous cries from the stalls were matched by the roar of "critics" plying their invidious craft from seats *on the stage*. In the Yiddish theater of New York's famed Lower East Side, members of the audience might assail actors who displeased them, at least with catcalls and vegetables, while spouting Talmudic and philosophical—or plain popu-list—epithets. Our Black Baptist churches resound with the rhythms of exhortation and response. Counterculture theater of the sixties sought to break down the "fourth wall" that separated performers from their audi-ence, opening it up to sing along with them, forging their own sense of all-encompassing community wherein they promoted their several social and political causes.

For Broadway reflects and refracts a peculiarly American community with many of its subcultures celebrated in musical theater. World War II shows begot and nourished Americana in *Oklahoma!, Bloomer Girl,* and, in its Irish socialist way, *Finian's Rainbow.* This tradition continued to flourish in shows like *South Pacific* and *1776.* The ethnic or subcultural audience base of later (successful) shows expanded Broadway's audience, which had heretofore been altogether small and homogeneous; Hispanics turned out for *Evita,* Italians for *Nine,* Jews for *Fiddler on the Roof,* blacks for *The Tap Dance Kid,* gays for *La Cage aux Folles,* and southern country music fans for *Big River.* The smaller community is represented, its heritage and problems are portrayed with dignity, and their lives are given more pride as they, in turn, represent the large polyglot community of all Americans. Other less ethnic, cross-cultural, latent groups also emerge into an audience, such as cat lovers for *Cats.*

The good musical does even more. The music and movement (whether outright dancing or not) beats, pulses into their hearts and souls, makes them "feel thoughts" through song. Songs-in-scenes explode in them and they applaud and commune with their fellow theatergoers.

The audience has to work hard in a Broadway musical. Suspension of disbelief is not enough. One's senses, those of the participant observer, are enveloped in light and sound and movement. And on a sometimes superficial, sometimes unconscious level that should be of interest to depth psychologists, their folkways and thoughtways are ideally confronted by new questions. While every craft in musical theater is devoted to smoothing the flow of action from moment to moment, new ways of feeling and thinking are still out there, ready to be absorbed. The lyricist works hard, as Sondheim notes, "[not to set up] a conflict in the listener's ear. The lyric should match the music with a comma, a semi-colon, a period, or just the completion of a phrase."[5]

The audience is unlikely to be conscious of subtle lyric or musical interactions with orchestral arrangements, of background lighting, of set, or costume detail or of the director's fine integrating hand. But in a successful show, that audience "feels" the flow of "action."

Jeff Sweet, an Off-Off-Broadway composer, critic, author, and writer for *Dramatists Guild Quarterly,* summarizes much that is best in audience response on Broadway.

You take in the choreography, the lighting, the arrangements and the costumes. It's very easy to miss subtleties amid all that excitement. For instance, I didn't realize that "Side by Side" was a very sad number until I saw *Company* the second time. At the end when [we see a man who] doesn't have anybody to dance with, suddenly it's a sad number. You don't realize this the first time you see it because you are too busy trying to follow the words, and trying to make sense of the musical shape of the piece. There's so much to listen to and watch the first time you hear a number, I find it a miracle that people come out of a show understanding and recognizing as many tunes as they do.[6]

The contrast with audiences for European-originated grand opera is startling: that audience knows all the songs going in, as well as the story, and the characters. This older form of musical theater is meant to delight through the sheer beauty of hearing different, highly trained voices singing familiar music. But in an American, Broadway-based musical, the audience takes a journey into a new world. As Arthur Laurents remarks: "The musical takes you where nothing else will." And a multiple collaboration of artists, craftsmen, and technicians provides the creative means for any audience to take that journey. The recent book-song-spectacles, *Les Misérables* and *The Phantom of the Opera* (and more to come, maybe using American stories), were made possible by the coordination of *techne* and technology so effective in creating new shapes of music and lyrics and spectacle that they might even have impressed a contemporary, open-minded Aristotle.

The Public Forum

Yet for Jules Fisher and others, spectacular production values are inversely related to the listening and thinking of contemporary audiences. Megabucks break the web of artistic interdependence, dulling or deafening the audience's senses:

Commercial values on Broadway have given us the money to get anything we want —the best actors, the best scenery, the best lighting. If I need a lot of gold fabric I can afford it. On the other hand, we could make the same complaint that everyone makes of television: The audience is less demanding. With super-commercialism, less of the audience uses its brain. More and more, it's lulled into going to a musical just to see something very splashy and to be happy with nothing but glitz.

At the same time, there is no such thing as a "sure-fire hit" and taking chances is an existential necessity for Broadway producers. But with this tad of hyperbole in mind, what sayeth the theater owner? When Gerald Schoenfeld talks about the importance of not going into a Broadway production "thinly financed," he means that there should be some allowance for risk. In that way, successive audiences can gradually respond to a new show. But primary responsibility for making an audience want to buy tickets still lies with the show itself. Too often financial failure is made to spell artistic failure, community failure, the failure of life. Schoenfeld comes close to saying so.

Obviously there has to be some value that people can respond to. . . . You measure economically. If a show got marvelous reviews but still closed in three months, it would not be a success. The public wasn't buying.

Which brings us to the role of the critic. Representing standards of art in general, or musical theater in particular, and the prototypical response of an audience, this is the man or woman who is handed a free ticket to an orchestra seat, paid to listen, and tell the rest of us—the public—about it. Do critics affect the buying public and the success or failure of Broadway musicals?

6. The Critics and the Audiences

U nless one broadens the word too much, so that it also means censor and spectator, "the critic" does not seem to have existed until the seventeenth century. By 1670, John Dryden, in his epilogue to *The Conquest of Granada,* pays tribute to the influence of criticism more or less as we would recognize it today.[1] But Dryden's "critiques" (critics) provided vocal criticism throughout a play. They were "pit critics," "wits," "gallants" much given to on-the-spot derogation, perhaps because so many of them were rival or would-be playwrights. These men rented stools, sat onstage during a performance, and freely and stridently offered their reactions to the spectacle. This practice reached its height in Restoration theater when drama returned to London after the twenty-year silence imposed upon it by a Puritan commonwealth that would not tolerate secular public performances of any kind. During this hiatus, playwrights, actors, and their companies were stripped of royal patronage and came to be dependent on men of business known as theater managers. These men henceforth selected plays, hired actors, and supervised productions. With them came those pit critics who specialized in "the sport of maiming or killing a play at its first performance." So notes Elizabeth Burns.[2] Combining the historical literature on English drama and critics, Burns quotes from a treatise by D. F. Smith:

> Prologues and epilogues of the Restoration and eighteenth century give eloquent testimony of the presence and power of an army of critics in the London theaters which when occasion or faction or malice demanded could on opening night, launch an attack on a new play so fatal as at once to destroy all present or future chance of its success, and to leave the unfortunate author with reputation in ruins.[3]

Ben Jonson's reputation does not lie in ruins, but he felt himself to be ever the embattled playwright. High on his list of foes were the gallants who for two shillings became deadly critics, actually exchanging badinage onstage with the actors, thereby, as Burns says, offering performances of their own design to rival those of the playwright and his players. Jonson excoriated these spectator-critics as the ignorant, malicious, and destructive plague they were to him.[4]

Dekker could be even more venomous than Jonson. He is cited in *The Gull's Hornbook* of 1892 as having addressed the gallant who "by spreading your body on the stage, and by being a justice in examining of plays, you shall put yourself into such scenical authority that some poet shall not dare to present his muse rudely upon your eyes without having first unmasked her, rifled her, and discovered all her bare and most mystical parts before you at a tavern."[5]

For a while, especially as the eighteenth century waned, the most forceful criticism came from playwrights who skewered one another in pieces such as D'Avenant's *Playhouse to Be Lett,* "a pastiche of opera and tragedy."[6] This pastime reached its peak in Richard Brinsley Sheridan's *The Critic.* The English-language theater incubated and perpetuated written criticism and regular reviewing in the community through the "free press."[7]

Critics as Journalists

Throughout the eighteenth century a new profession, that of drama critic, was clearly in the making. By the 1770s, any new play might be reviewed in a dozen daily or weekly papers. Some carried more weight than others, but all seem to have been heavily didactic. As the critic developed his own niche within a traditional social setting, he not only taught himself but also instructed an audience that, despite its fondness for certain conventional categories, was eager to learn proper standards of taste and style. Burns gleans from playbills of the period that an evening's entertainment was "a careful arrangement of play, dancing, singing, and farce or harlequinade, during which the main actor appeared at the moment when the audience was expected to be most attentive." An account drawn in April 1772 from the *Town and Country Magazine* informs us that

the entertainment of the English theater consists of a prelude of music, a play, whether tragedy or comedy, with music and dancing between the acts and is concluded with a petit piece either farce or pantomime.[8]

Now and again the emphasis shifts, the mixture changes, but these components do not greatly differ from those by which a critic or a reviewer

of the 1990s is confronted. How honestly, skillfully, or thoroughly professional critics have performed their task, say from William Hazlitt through
George Bernard Shaw to Kenneth Tynan or Frank Rich, would make a
good doctoral dissertation, sure to reveal the same strains of continuity and
discontinuity that mark theatrical history and Western society over several
centuries.

Criticizing the Critics

As always, the contemporary picture is mixed. There are critics and critics.
Some evoke respect; many more do not. Those who speak for the musical
theater, for its prosperity and its quality, sound much like those who speak
for any of the arts. To most of them critics are a necessary evil whose
function is fuzzy. Gerald Schoenfeld doubts that there is "any agreement
among the critics about their own role," or that if there is, that the public
understands it. About this he raises a series of questions:

Are they giving us their own opinions? Or are they giving us their opinions about
what the public will like? And what is the public's notion of the difference? Is their
role on television different from their role in print? I've been told by a major network
that the critic is not a critic but a reviewer. I asked what the difference is or if
theatergoers know what the difference is? Nobody has clarified any of that.

The pervasiveness of a profession that came into being as an adjunct to
all of the arts is symptomatic of high culture and mass culture as well as of
the gray area in between them. Whether critics are viewed by people in
(and attached to) the creative arts or the performing arts, they are taken to
be necessary and evil, albeit unequally necessary and unequally evil. The
degree of their indispensability and their irresponsibility is correlative with
the power they are thought to wield, the power to make or break entrepreneurs, artists, careers, reputations. Complaints about drama criticism are
as old as the profession itself, and so in one way or another are the grounds
for those complaints.

Rating theatrical productions, particularly on a scale of one to ten, as TV
critics do, looks new, and it incenses a man like Schoenfeld. Numerical
rating is a "sickness" in our society; we are so "ten-oriented" that the
public is disinclined to see anything less than a ten, or number one becomes
Number One and no other number is worth our attention. The numerology
of TV critics prompts Schoenfeld to discharge another volley of questions:

What qualifies them to make judgments so imperiously? When they say something
is worth an eight, what does that eight mean? Does it cover sets, costumes,

lighting, direction, acting, content? Is each an eight? Are they statisticians who have factored it all out? Are they skilled? Do they have an idea of the difficulties that are part of designing a show? Of its logistics? Of any other problems connected with the show?

Evidently not. These critics should be exposed for what they are, and Schoenfeld has thought about how to do it. He would like to publish a book or write articles supplying a biography of every critic and providing "his box score over the years." Such documentation is classically available for literature and music in books like Henri Peyre's *Writers and Their Critics* and Nicholas Slonimsky's *Lexicon of Musical Invective.* [9] Contemporary critics invariably look bad. They inflate minor works, disparage masterpieces, and generally miss the boat. Or so it seems with every shift in public, aesthetic, or academic taste. With a further shift they may look good again. Rating critics of an earlier time makes their overall judgment look laughable; it is a game that discredits even the most eminent of them who too often praised nonentities while dismissing geniuses.

Still, we cannot entirely forbear a note, in passing, on the irony in Schoenfeld's position. He opposes rating *by* the critics and proposes rating *of* the critics. With his system of rating, it will be possible to conclude that "this guy is good or not so good or really not worth reading at all." Maybe. But what if that guy grows or atrophies, develops expertise or gets bored? Can his box score over the years help us to evaluate the criticism he writes today? As well ask, would we be helpfully guided to a four star restaurant of the sixties and seventies if it had gone to seed by the nineties? Such a rating system is inherently defective. It follows that when Schoenfeld rails against that system as such his point is better taken than when he espouses a form of the same system.

Concerning print reviews, Schoenfeld's objection goes shrewdly beyond them. It is his observation that the print media consistently justify the opinion of their critic: "They do that by running follow-up pieces and supplementary news. I seldom see a show that is panned receive additional treatment. There's nothing more about people in the cast or the director or the authors in those periodicals. Only if their critic likes the show, do you get cumulative material in support of his judgment."

But to Schoenfeld, critics, for all their shortcomings, are absolutely essential. "You need them," is his plaintive cry, plaintive because so few of them measure up to the job they are called upon to do. "Only in the performing arts, and most important in theater do you find the idea that almost anybody can be a critic." Fastidious publishers, assigning someone to review corporate balance sheets, make sure they have a person who knows his or her way around the business. Financial news is a big category, nearly as complicated in its subdivisions as economics per se, not to speak of economic history, econometrics, monetary theory, and the rest. Proper coverage of each area requires more than superficial grounding in it. So too in the creative arts: "They wouldn't think of sending just anyone to review an Egyptian art show at the Metropolitan Museum. Their critic would have to know a lot about Egyptian art . . . but they don't apply the same criteria to us."

Whatever the virtues of this argument, a rich folklore about the selection of critics, at least partly rooted in fact, does attest to its subjective validity. Thus everyone has heard of the sports reporter told to cover a concert at Carnegie Hall who wrote in his own patois: "Last night the orchestra played Beethoven. Beethoven lost." Or the classical pianist who playfully reported: "When I don't practice for one day, I know it. When I don't practice for two days, my audience knows it, and when I don't practice for three days, even the critics know it." These old anecdotes speak to a condition that has been bettered in some ways while being aggravated in others. Since the twenties, and slowly thereafter, the respectable press has hired better-educated journalists who moved their work to a possibly higher level of literacy than in prior times.

Critically speaking, there is nothing respectable about TV, the other medium through which Broadway shows, musical and otherwise, have come to be instantly evaluated. Although no one has a good word to say for the capsule TV review, many acknowledge its potency. Even those who at first curse the "almighty" *New York Times* occasionally admit on second thought that TV is gaining a deleterious ascendancy over some sectors of the theatrical audience.

Harvey Sabinson plumps for high standards and wants to universalize them: "I claim that if we demanded from the critics the same kind of excellence that they demand from us, most of them would be writing ship news." He is alluding to the best critics. About the worst he does not hesitate to use epithets like "awful," "unethical," "disgraceful," and "corrupt." Given his penchant for referring collectively to "the critics," a surprising number of them are or were, in Sabinson's estimation, good, honest, capable men and women. But, does it make any difference? Sabinson sits behind his office desk and recommends that we "look at today's *Variety*":

Let's see. *Merlin* got kicked around by the critics. It did $250,000 last week, a rise of $8,000 over the week before. Seems to be holding its own. [It ultimately flopped.] The revival of *On Your Toes* got unanimously great notices except from

The Times. They did a promising $218,000 last week, and they're racking up $50,000 a day. . . . A critic ought to ask: what are they trying to do on that stage and have they succeeded in doing it? Well, they're trying to revive *On Your Toes*. Did they do it well or did they do it poorly? I don't know if Rich asked himself that question. I think he simply hated *On Your Toes*. [A hit.] And that wasn't good enough for me.

Sabinson roots for *On Your Toes,* which, since it was a "success," will confirm his skepticism about the omnipotence of critics in general and those of the *Times* in particular: "Look at *Evita*. It opened in 1979 and will soon be four years old. A big money-maker. *Evita* got terrible notices." Terrible notices are compatible with success just as positive notices are compatible with failure. No notices are also compatible with success or failure. Individual producers have barred critics but so rarely that when they do it, their action is newsworthy: "Barring the critics was productive for David Merrick." How so? "It generated publicity."

Publicity versus Word of Mouth

Publicity helps, but does the absence of publicity hurt? Before the advent of television reviews, prolonged newspaper strikes provided a test. No publicity, no reviews, a few hits, many flops, and much vindication for those like Sabinson and Sheldon Harnick, who are convinced that word of mouth is decisive. On this issue they are unequivocal, until something causes them to swing from dismissing critics as demonstrably insignificant to magnifying them as all powerful. The same Harnick who bewails domination by one newspaper: "It's so frustrating, so deadly. The paper—you can't even say Frank Rich—you have to say the *New York Times*—has so much power," proves through his own experience that word of mouth has more power.

How was it with *Fiddler on the Roof?*

We opened in Detroit during a newspaper strike in '64. Next stop Washington where before we opened there were long lines at the box office—which led us to believe that people in Detroit were calling their friends in Washington and saying, "Hey, there's really something going on here." We began to feel optimistic. Then, in New York, the critics were split. There were about two smash reviews. But again, before we opened there were long lines at the box office. It began to look as though the show would not be dependent on critical response. The *Times* critic, whoever that was, as I remember it, started with a lamentation: "If only they'd had Ernest Bloch to write the music!" Failing that, Leonard Bernstein. Walter Kerr, in the *Trib* said, "Too bad, near miss, might have been good, wasn't." In the *Journal American* we read something like, "It could have been such a good show if they hadn't put that pogrom in at the end of the first act. It ruined everything." Only the *Daily News* gave us something close to a rave.

In 1964, New York still had many daily papers. In 1992, four remain, but one of them is thought to carry most weight with theatergoers. Suppose a *Times* man had been the only reviewer of *Fiddler on the Roof?* Harnick: "It wouldn't have mattered. The word was out." Today, "the *Times* has a monopoly" although, as we shall see, this worries its regular critic. Harnick shudders about a negative review in the *Times:* "It's hard to beat that rap especially when your show costs from four to six million dollars." Do television reviews reduce the monopoly? "Yes, they do." The musical *Nine* is offered in evidence. "If I recall correctly, he [Rich] didn't like the book but thought the score was wonderful and that Tommy Tune's work was brilliant. A split review. But almost all the television critics were ecstatic." It made little difference. *Nine* was destined to hit the jackpot. But by now TV criticism is less important than TV advertising: "My God, if it weren't, producers would not be investing $200,000 to make television commercials."

Harnick goes on. His theme is unfailingly yes-but. He expresses his confidence in TV advertising only, in the next breath, to cast doubt on it:

When I did *Rex* with Dick Rodgers back in 1976, we opened to bad notices. Much was wrong with the show, and I must say our producers gave us more than a fair shake. Their idea was to have us waive our royalties for six weeks. They'd spend whatever it cost to make a commercial and run it for those six weeks. We agreed. They tried but it didn't work.

Why not? Because after about a month, word of mouth—bad word of mouth—took its toll. Effective word of mouth, good or bad, requires about a month to work. Harnick feels so strongly about this length of time that, whenever possible, he would include enough money in the initial financing to keep a show going "just in case the reviews are bad." But—the inevitable but—"These days that might mean another million dollars in capitalization, and maybe it's just too much." Where are we? On a whirligig spun about by a talented and experienced man of the musical theater. Only the dogmatist that Harnick is not would freeze in a single posture on an issue that needs to be questioned at every turn.

Gail Berman tells of a successful show that had only one bad review, and she holds that review to have been tainted. The critic disliked her show in London and disliked it in Brooklyn. Opening on Broadway, she pleaded for another critic: "We just asked for a fair shake," a second opinion from someone whose mind was not already made up. The tabloid in question refused; the critic chose to come; and again he disliked it. Since all the other reviews were favorable, they appeared to be home free. But no: "If the *Times* had panned us, so everybody tells me, we would have had a very slim chance of getting by." At least Sabinson pluralizes the differential impact: "A minority of good reviews in the *right places* is much better than a majority of good reviews in the *wrong places.*" Not for Berman. Or not for the Berman who believes that New York's most prestigious paper has "the power of life or death" over musical and all other theater.

But there is a second Berman, who is alert to the rise of television and the decline of newspapers. Again it is more a matter of advertising than of criticism: "Since people watch TV more than they ever did before," Berman echoes Harnick, "you must include a place in your budget for television commercials." Ever since *Pippin* started this trend, "that's how you sell a show." There are exceptions: "You may for some reason have a two or three million dollar advance. Or you may have Elizabeth Taylor, and seats will be filled no matter what by people who just want to see how she looks."

Having said that, Berman reverts to the centrality of one critic who exercises tremendous power. Is there something wrong with that? "Probably, but when I wasn't producing I read the *New York Times* critic because I wanted to know his reaction." From the audience's side of the fence this habit is perfectly understandable. "If you have one night to go out and want somebody's opinion about how to spend your time and you respect the *New York Times,* then, it should have the power to affect your decision"—the very power that can make a *Times* critic tremble and about which Berman has heard producers wail: "Oh my God, the critics, the critics: they're killing our business." Berman is not so sure about this even from the producers' point of view, and from the patrons' point of view, "You need somebody to tell you where to spend fifty dollars for a ticket, more than a hundred dollars for the night." (Or a few hundred dollars-plus for suburbanites who travel, pay baby sitters, and dine out.)

Many theater people share Berman's double vision. They are patrons as well as producers and creators. Good guidance from a reviewer they "respect" (one whose taste has proved to be like their own) is essential lest they lose time and waste money on worthless fare. The rationality of relying on an institution like the *Times,* rather than on an individual, is something else. Why should an "all-powerful" *Times* man like Clive Barnes sink to insignificance when he switches to the *Post?* That he sinks signifies institutional power, such as it is, not individual power, such as *it* is. The Barnes who was admired for his good guidance or cursed for his insensitivity is the same Barnes who is currently dismissed or ignored. He did not lose his perspicacity overnight; he merely moved from "the world's best

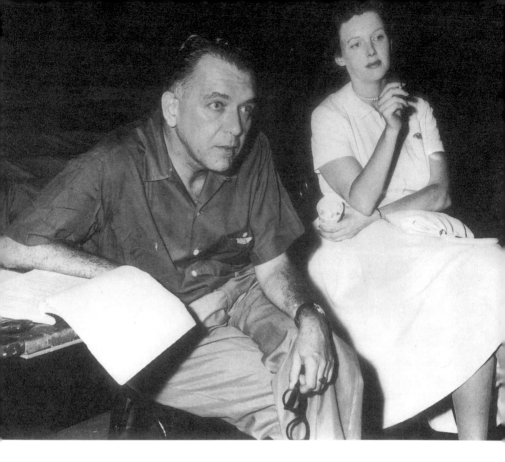

Walter and Jean Kerr in Rehearsal for Goldilocks *(1958)*

Walter Kerr, drama critic for the *New York Times* from 1966 to 1983, directed over ninety shows at Catholic University, and is author of several books and a few plays. Here he is at rehearsal of a Broadway show called *Goldilocks* (1958), book and some lyrics written by himself and *(at right)* his wife Jean Kerr; the show was not a success. (Photo credit: Billy Rose Theatre Collection, New York Public Library; photographer: Barry Hyams.)

newspaper" to one less prestigious. A change of venue made all the difference. The old venue retains its aura. We are in the land of emotions and hype.

Out of Town Reviews

"The road" or, as it is now called, "the tour," insofar as it has not been overwhelmed by the workshop or the pre-preview rumors, provides a drastically different venue. Critical response helps to set an index of audience expectation, which, however often confounded, is still taken to heart. Weidman, the then-inexperienced writer of *Pacific Overtures*, encircled by old hands in Boston, had every reason to believe that his show would open, get good reviews, and be such a big hit that "we would all live happily ever after." However, "Kevin Kelly [of the *Boston Globe*] hated the show." Although another, lesser critic also found fault with it, here and there his criticism might be construed as "useful." How so Weidman does not specify and may not remember. It is Kelly's review that sticks in his craw: "Kelly's criticism was so negative there was really nothing to be learned from it." Then why take that criticism to heart? "Because it showed that we did not have a success on our hands." People were not going "to shoot each other to enter the Colonial Theater where we were playing." Shock assailed all the principals, and not just Weidman, who was a newcomer: "They took it as hard as I did. That's one thing I observed at our opening night party. When the reviews came out and we read them in a Boston restaurant, I didn't notice any thick skins." (Prince was the director, Sondheim the composer-lyricist.)

Kelly's review left the company with an option: "Kill yourself or keep going." The show kept going. Audiences were no happier with it than the critics had been. What then? Frantic attempts to improve not so much the quality as the appeal of a show whose participants had originally evinced unshakable faith in it. Two and a half weeks of work went into the effort. Retrospectively, it seems to Weidman that the time was wasted: "The opening wasn't right. Steve rewrote it. Then we wound up with a shorter version of his original opening." Because of the poor critical reception, "Everybody looked at the show, trying to figure out what was wrong." Theoretically, there was time for correction: "We were going to Washington for a month." Same story there. This time, Kevin Kelly's review was prophetic. The show was going nowhere. Personally, Weidman, the bookwriter, salvaged a smidgen of consolation from Kelly's review. What made it possible to live through that review was its first paragraph, in which "he dismissed Steve's score as just junk. Then he started in on me. I was in good company!"

So it seemed and so, ambiguously, it was. *Pacific Overtures* opened on Broadway in January 1976. Weidman, who has the reviews "tucked away someplace," remembers that the show divided critics right down the middle. Clive Barnes, then of the *Times,* said in effect, "Well, there's much to be admired here, but I don't quite like this or that. The *News* hated it and the *Post* loved it." Any different with the weeklies? "No, *Newsweek* thought it was terrific and *Time* hated it. *New York Magazine* thought we were fabulous. The *New Yorker* could not stand us."

The show ran for six months, "but just by the skin of its teeth," a penultimate experience. For this saga has a happy little postscript. The musical, taken to California after its demise in New York, was a hit. With the critics and the public? "Exactly. That rounded it out in a pleasant way." Boston was one thing, New York another, Los Angeles and San Francisco yet another. What does all this say about out of town or, for that matter, in town critics? That generalizations about them, about their influence, confluence, and divergence, are as unsafe as most generalizations inside and outside the theatrical world.

We are reminded of an occasion when the late Paul Lazarsfeld was summoned before a congressional committee to testify on the causes of juvenile delinquency. A senator asked him, "Professor, do beer ads cause juvenile delinquency?" Lazarsfeld replied in his heavy Viennese accent: "Zumtimes zey do 'nd zumtimes zey don't." In that case, the senator, seeking substantiation of Dr. Frederick Werthem's wisdom, wished to know if crime comics caused juvenile delinquency. He received the same answer. Professor Lazarsfeld, a mathematical wizard, was never more accurate than in the testimony he gave on that memorable day in Washington, D.C. Do critics cause anything to happen in the musical theater? We follow Lazarsfeld (only in this respect and it is enough): "Sometimes they do and sometimes they don't."

Most likely Sabinson would agree with us but remain not entirely charitable to the newspaper critics of New York, past and present: "They start off tough, get good jobs and mellow. . . . Frank Rich is a bright young man" —no one ever gainsays his intelligence or his fluency—"who writes as if he had been around the theater for sixty years." Yet Sabinson numbers many critics around the country as personal friends. From his days as a press agent, Sabinson singles out Elliot Norton, Richard Coe, and Claudia

Cassidy for their taste and their incorruptibility. Over a period of decades, Cassidy was known as Chicago's cultural curmudgeon. Dropped by a Chicago radio station, she herself was news. A local paper referred to the end of her "Acid Reign". Sabinson admires her: "Cassidy didn't want third-rate companies coming into Chicago. She improved the standard of shows in that city." Whenever Sabinson brought a show into Washington or Boston he dined with Coe or Norton, and "I would not expect any favors: if they had given me any, I'd have had no respect for them."

Burton Lane retrieves the memory of a review in Boston that troubled but did not "throw" him. Instead he hurls invective at "a major critic" of *On a Clear Day,* whose Boston review brought bitter laughter to his mouth: "I thought this man must be deaf. He hadn't heard a thing." The critic found fault with the songs in *On a Clear Day,* generally for lacking melody—with one exception, and that exception was a patter song, "an interesting tune, but a patter song, like 'Why Can't the English?' in *My Fair Lady.* No melody. Even a beautiful melody would have been wrong there." Lane "knew" what he had in that show, and what he had was one good song after another. He mentions the title song, "a fantastic success," "Come Back to Me," "a big success," "What Do I Have That I Don't Have?" and "Melinda" —"there was a jazz waltz that jazz people play all over the world." Why was the major Boston critic deaf to all this? On account of his inadequacy? Of course. But such inadequacy is a constant.

Musically, this goes without saying for critics at large. Lane: "They don't have any real understanding." Or Glasel: "They're mostly unsophisticated." And they are not musicians. But musicians do not perform only for other musicians, they perform for audiences; critics mediate between them and those audiences. Nor is Glasel simply sneering when he asserts that musical theater differs from grand opera. Glasel is fully aware that each is a form of artistic expression based on aural sensibility, and that nonmusicians have something of value to tell musicians in either, or any, genre even if it is not what critics and reviewers think it is.

Most musical theater critics are not musicians, so they can hardly hear the "harmonic structure" anyway, is Glasel's belief:

The critic and the audience, the general public at large, are mostly unsophisticated about music. When you listen to a song as a nonmusician, hear the words, if you're lucky, you'll remember the melody. The harmony is unconscious to you, and when it comes to niceties about orchestration, that's completely subliminal to you. Now me, as a musician, I may not even hear the words. They'll go in one ear and out the other. I may not remember the melody. I'll be listening to the harmonic structure and the orchestration and the quality of the playing—a whole other way of looking at things.

Lane on critics: "I think they can tell when something is working." A kind word for the critics? No more kind than for the rest of us because, "Everybody can tell that. Everybody knows if it's working. You hear a song, and you feel good or you don't." The Boston critic failed to hear. Was the poor man deaf? Yes. But, why was he deaf? On account of the book, which made him a listener who could not hear. The fault lay not with him, but with the bookwriter, and his negative reaction to the songs, while it said nothing about them, said a great deal about the show.

Another musician—in this case an orchestrator, lambastes the critics, but only *en passant.* He embraces anonymity, prefers being ignored: "It's better than sticking your head in the lion's mouth" or being "raked over" by incompetents: "How does a critic know whether an orchestra is well conducted or not? It's such an esoteric skill. Why would any conductor want to be judged by such people one way or another," to be swallowed alive or licked and pampered by a wild animal? For recognition? "But at what risk?" The risk is that of "being ripped up" on the off-chance that something nice will be said about oneself. Who needs it?

Once again, however, the blame is deflected from critics, this time onto producers. The orchestrator finds it "amazing that for so long critics have been allowed to exercise commercial power." Allowed? By whom? "By the producers who take their quotes and use them. I really can't understand why they don't advertise their product the way everybody else does. You know, 'Buy our toothpaste. It gets your teeth cleaner than any other toothpaste.' All the producers need is, 'Come see our show. It's the funniest show in town.'" The lion's mouth would be harmless, its fangs removed, if producers circumvented the creature altogether. They should peddle their wares as sensibly as other businessmen who succeed whether or not *Consumers Union* gives them its seal of approval. And if the functional equivalent of *Consumers Union* is as untrustworthy as those critics who presume to judge a product they cannot understand, why "give them the power to destroy your product?" A turnabout is the idea: publicize the show, not persnickety critics of the show.

Out of Town Reviews and Early Repairs

Either way, Stephen Schwartz, and not he alone, is sometimes more grateful for out of town than for New York reviews:

Here's an example. We recently opened *The Baker's Wife* in Santa Barbara. It was a little amateur production reviewed by six or seven papers. Most of them were favorable. A couple were not. But a careful look told you that they all said the same thing. Those reviews led Joe and me to realize that we were still not there with the show, that we had to make more changes. . . . The positives and the negatives were just about identical. So we said to ourselves, "If these are our problems we've got to get over them." When you use out of town reviews that way they can be very helpful.

In New York "every single show" of Schwartz's has elicited a mixture of pans and raves, "real pans" and "real raves." By weighing their relative impact, he correlates the pans and raves with failure and success. "In three out of four cases, when we opened in New York," success stemmed from good reviews rather than failure from bad reviews because the good reviews appeared in "important papers." The fourth case was *Working,* which received good reviews on television and bad reviews in the *Times* and the *Post.* The show closed. Due to bad reviews in important papers? Schwartz almost leaves us with that impression, but not quite. He underscores the fact that *Working* was an expensive show, its pocket not long enough. There was no time to overcome two unfavorable notices. So cost and time intersect with critical reception (and other impalpable forces) that codetermine an unforeseeable outcome on Broadway or the world.

Theater people cling to their myths as they undermine them in midthought. We have emphasized one of those myths, that of the Times's omnipotence, which, if real, should have destroyed Schwartz's *Godspell.* For, "Only Clive Barnes, then of the *Times,* hated it. Everyone else's review was positive." What happened? "The television reviews were raves and we were able to run on those reviews for a week or two to overcome Barnes'. By the time all the magazines came in we were selling out. Word of mouth took over." Maybe it did. But what always takes over is a congeries of unknowns, immeasurables, interdependencies, imponderables —and an irresistible wish to rationalize each unrepeatable circumstance.

If out of town reviews prompt useful changes in a show (Charnin thanks Walter Kerr and his harsh criticism of *Annie* when it previewed at the Goodspeed Opera House in Connecticut), then in town reviews can save the Broadway flop and turn it into an out of town success. About *Working,* Schwartz, no enthusiast of the New York critics, feels compelled to defend them: "This show, which has been playing around the country so successfully isn't exactly what people saw on Broadway." Because of the panning it got in New York, changes were made and losses were recouped outside New York. *Because* the changes were made? Possibly. But Schwartz introduces another variable: *Working* opened in a very busy week on Broadway! "There were six or seven shows and *Working* was the fourth musical critics had to cover that week." An unenviable task, it deadened the senses. Schwartz wonders whether he could hear the score to *South Pacific* if he had to see three other musicals just before it. *Ain't Misbehavin'* came early in that crowded week. It was "a light revue" favored with great notices. "But *Runaways,* the show that followed ours, also got killed, and it was a show the same critics loved downtown [Off Broadway]. Suddenly, they hated it." Why? "They were sick of going to the theater and hearing music." We believe that Schwartz is on to something. Our own addendum would be that it also works the other way: there are dry spells when a critic's thirst for theater and music can too easily be slaked by poor fare. Taste has to be inconstant when much depends not only on what we get but also on how often it is served up to us. Critics would be less than human if they were not subject to cycles of hunger and satiety.

On or Off Broadway

But whatever their psychology, critics matter. And critics do not matter. Only one critic matters. And no critic matters. This is the *mélange,* laced with word of mouth, that comes to *us* over and over. After a few interviews we are prepared for a bill of fare that would be monotonous if it were not so ingeniously seasoned by clever and intelligent respondents. No one's digestive system is upset. What is more, an observer can take pleasure in the regularity of point, counterpoint, with each variation on a common theme.

So to Donald Farber: "I gotta tell you, two things are important in every production whether it's on Broadway or Off Broadway. One is reviews. Word of mouth is the other. You can hardly make it without both." *The Fantasticks* may have made it without either. This Off-Broadway musical that enriched its investors has been running for decades — with no end in sight. It was well received in the *Saturday Review.* As for the dailies' reviews, save for one, Farber recalls that "they were not good." The good one came from a critic "who was so drunk that we had to ask him to leave at the end of the first act. He gave us a rave review." He was not Brooks Atkinson of the *New York Times,* who "felt that it was a pretty nice little one-act play" (if so, the ejection of his colleague after act 1 may have been providential).

How did this miracle come about?

I'll tell you. First of all, there was a gal named Janis Marx whom I went to school with in Lincoln, Nebraska. She was a chantoozie, but a Method chantoozie who had a little club called The Baque Room, financed by three people from Actors Studio. I think Brando was one of them. Every night from eleven until three or four in the morning, she got hold of those songs [from *The Fantasticks*] and started singing them. Theater people would sit around after their shows and they'd listen. Harry Belafonte made a record of "Soon It's Going to Rain," and that didn't hurt. Lore Noto [producer] walked around town with *The Fantasticks* jacket album under his coat advertising it. . . . A lot of crazy things happened.

Most producers who start a musical Off Broadway aspire to making it big on Broadway. To have kept *The Fantasticks* Off Broadway may not have been such a crazy thing. Farber and others who backed the show look like wisemen for having stayed put. But who knows? *The Fantasticks* might have flourished on Broadway too. *Ain't Misbehavin'* made the move. It was critically acclaimed Off Broadway, and on Broadway, and will be remembered as a popular success in each milieu. "Crazy things" are the norm.

Farber would disagree. He wishes "people wouldn't rely on critics to the extent that they do." Then the qualifier: "I wish they wouldn't rely on the *Times* as much as they do." Had people relied on the *Times* after its tepid review of *The Fantasticks* they would not have been flocking all these decades to see that offbeat show. Farber's preferred alternative to one powerful critic is a committee of critics. Let us suppose that all the members of his hypothetical committee extolled *The Fantasticks*. It could hardly have done better by that show than haphazard hype and other "crazy things" did, provided Farber is right, for a show that could have expired as easily as most.

Put this argument to Farber, as we did, and notice how ready he is to demolish it with a saw we hear again and again: "For every rule there is an exception." In his experience that exception was *The Fantasticks*. Everyone else has a supply of exceptions. They are so abundant that we begin to suspect exceptions are the rule. Debuskey, not atypically, slides back and forth on the subject. Within a minute or two he earnestly claims as a veteran press agent that "there are very few occasions when publicity can overwhelm the reviews." Before we can give much thought to that authoritative view, it becomes, "There are very few shows that override Frank Rich's negative review." The operative phrase is "very few." Does Debuskey mean very few? No, he means exactly one: "If you try to enumerate critic-proof shows you come back to *Cats*. How many more can you name?" We name *Merlin*. Partial exception. Damned by the critics, *Merlin* ran a little longer than critics would have had it, though it still lost money. Word leaked out—part of the seepage came from negative reviews, among them

Frank Rich's—that this allegedly poor excuse for a musical was a good magic show. And there was an audience out there for that kind of show.

About this Debuskey waffles: "Unless you're privy to the economics of it, you don't know what the truth is." Is he any more privy to the economics of it than we are? Are the profits and losses calculated this year or next year or the year after? Are tax write-offs a consideration? Is there any limit to creative bookkeeping? Debuskey gives some credence to the rumor that Columbia Pictures "is losing a fortune" on *Merlin*—which without a deep pocket would have folded fast. The Hollywood connection surely provides a big, long pocket, but it also leads us into the land of financial prestidigitators where no explorer can find his way. Some years ago the redoubtable Mr. Michael Cimino directed a movie that reportedly cost $36 million. Knocked by three New York critics, it was "permanently" withdrawn. Was $36 million a fortune to the studio executives who decided to drop that sum? Are we privy to their Byzantine economics? Can anyone be?

Try Peter Stone on critics. Only one is of any consequence to him, and that one sits at the *New York Times*. Again, "It's the paper, not the critic, that's important. If Frank Rich left tomorrow, it would be somebody else." A weak notice from the *Times* "didn't used to be lethal. With many papers, a consensus in your favor could be reached." "Now [in 1983], the others don't mean a goddamned thing."

That leaves the incumbent reviewer of one paper as unchallenged master of Broadway. Yes, but. In the last ten years, the *News* (Howard Kissel) and *Newsday* (Linda Winer) have taken on importance. And for more than fifteen years the master's place has been shared by television critics, all of them "antagonistic, dangerous and destructive to the theater." They are another hurdle in the obstacle course to success. "And God knows we don't need another hurdle." As he warms to his subject, Stone tells us what these critics are. "They're oddballs. That's what they are." Networks and local stations are in a quandary about what to do with their oddballs. So they are converted into critics. They are untrained, devoid of background, not equipped to be critics: "I don't know who or what any of them are."

TV and the Theater

What Stone does know is that on any given night, television, in quest of the same audience, is an active competitor of the New York theater: "TV executives aren't delighted to make a hit out of anything" (which presupposes that they have the capacity to do so). "Basically, they want you to stay home at night watching television. Their prime time is our prime time.

Their unspoken antagonism is always there." This is a structural conflict of interest. And there is more. These TV critics, like TV meteorologists, have to be entertaining: "The station demands it, and they can't be entertaining with good reviews." Besides, "They are looking to advance themselves by running up a terrific score. How do they score? Not by being nice to shows. Every score is a knock including the word knock."

We have traveled some distance with Peter Stone from the *Times* critic, whoever he may be, to the oddballs of TV. A plague on all of them. Unless they turn out to be exceptions. For two years, Richard Eder, widely considered unsuitable for his position as theater critic of the *New York Times,* was an exception. In his case, it was the critic and not the institution. The institution could not carry a weightless critic, retained, some think, because to have dismissed him straightaway would have been a confession of poor judgment on the part of those who had hired him.

In the Eder era, God took a vacation. The power and the glory lay with others. Even then, with the *Times* impotent and irrelevant, its critic's voice stilled, true believers remained unshaken in their faith. Half the time, but only half the time, they tell you that one paper controls their fate. Since *Best Little Whorehouse* came along in the Eder era, that paper cut no ice. Carol Hall, its composer/lyricist, insists that "everybody" knew Eder was on his way out. So "nobody" paid attention to the *Times.* Eder disliked the show, but because "nobody" listened to him, it took off: "The *Times* didn't matter." Neither did it matter when, after Eder's departure, "Frank Rich loved the show and tried to say so many times while reviewing other things." Too late. Only one column matters—when it matters. The point, however, is to neutralize and circumvent all such columns: "You must try to create situations where they don't matter." With this admonition to herself and others, Hall interpolates a tribute to English criticism: "Open in London as we did with *Whorehouse,* and you can say to yourself, 'Well, eleven raves and eighteen pans. Good enough.' " It must have been like that, Hall assumes, "when New York had eight or nine papers."

In 1935, New York City had about ten daily papers, and in the 1934–35 Broadway season, of 120 shows, ninety-five were flops or *80 percent,* as reported by *Variety*[10] (about the same results as the 1933–34 season). *Variety* kept a batting average on the critics; the best predictors were John Mason Brown, with a .855 percent correct prediction of hits or flops; Gil Gabriel, second, with .854; John Anderson, third, with .836; and Brooks Atkinson, fourth, with .832.[11] When New York City still had about nine daily papers, *Variety* still kept a batting average on them. In 1944, for example, correct predictions of successes and flops ranged from 64 percent correct predictions to 91 percent, and averaged about 80 percent correct (for all Broadway shows).[12] Why the seeming continuity? Because we believe flops are quickly agreed on, but hits are *not*. Thus, if you say "It can't work" 100 percent of the time, you will be right 80 percent of the time about Broadway shows. Easy. But not so easy for 20 percent of the shows that the audience thought were good.

But England is England and in this country the old days are over. Now, says Carol Hall, there is Frank Rich, "who really cares for the theater but, like anyone else, has his prejudices: I know that Rich will love anything with Lauren Bacall in it," but he "wishes Elizabeth Swados's melodies were a little more singable. Liz doesn't write scenes. She's something different. I think you either go with Liz or you don't go with Liz. [So far] Rich doesn't go with her." If prejudice is unavoidable, then Hall's strategy is to "get away" from Rich and his colleagues: "You can start regionally and come in with a *Crimes of the Heart*. They keep hearing about it, and they're very susceptible to word of mouth. Or you can go downtown, unknown, without stars—no Gwen Verdon, no Robert Preston—but backed by a movie company."

Stevie Phillips [then working with Universal Pictures] is no dummy. Let's be honest. She knew it was no skin off the company's back if we just opened and closed. Martin Charnin said, "Stevie doesn't know what she's doing." Cheryl Crawford said, "It'll never work. Opening at the Entermedia is crazy. You'll lose ten thousand dollars a week down there." We did. The part nobody figured out was that ten thousand dollars is cab fare to Universal which had just acquired movie rights for three hundred thousand dollars.

Given audience approval, with relatively little loss, downtown soon paid off with a big profit uptown, and by the time *Whorehouse* got to Broadway, "we didn't invite a single reviewer." Word of mouth had worked its magic so that when critics eventually did come to bless or to damn the show, their feelings no longer counted.

There is practically no way to escape TV critics, "who are the worst because they don't know anything," says Hall. "They do have an influence with a certain group of theatergoers." If so, it is hard to discern in her examples: "They didn't know what to do with *Sweeney Todd*." But *Sweeney* had a decent run for over a year on Broadway. "All the TV reviewers loved *The First* which was a fast flop." From such examples one might believe that the segment of theatergoers influenced by TV critics is statistically insignificant.

Evasion of the critics is a tactic Claire Nichtern also favors. She means all of them, including TV critics, who are "very important." As Broadway previews and workshops supplant out-of-town tryouts, "You try to sneak in the way *Beatlemania* did." At the time, *Rock 'n' Roll: The First 5,000 Years* was "tentatively tiptoeing around the critics. You develop your own audience." (It flopped anyway.) How do you do that? "Just don't invite them." Won't they come uninvited? "No, critics don't review you unless you ask them to or until it gets to the point where they suspect you're trying not to be seen, but they'll give you time to postpone and postpone." Keep them away as long as you can, and if your show does not die, it might catch fire. Above all, keep Frank Rich away, despite, or because of, your conviction that "he's a brilliant guy." Would Nichtern or anyone else in the business always want to keep Rich away? We hardly think so, at least in the light of this obiter dictum: "If a play is done anywhere and Frank Rich gives it a rave review, the play will have a New York production, and you already feel that it's going to be a success." Sometimes. For it is with "sometimes" that Nichtern checks herself. We are hardly startled to learn that there are exceptions. *Grownups* is an exception that occurs to Nichtern as she modifies her dictum: "Sometimes it doesn't work out that way. No matter how much Frank Rich fought for *Grownups* you couldn't get that piece through to the audience. And he loved *Grownups*. It was one of his things."

Decline of the Critic?

Sometimes it is good to have the critics and sometimes it is bad to have them. Similarly, if you are a craftsman, it is sometimes good to be noticed by critics and sometimes it is not. To a lighting designer like Jules Fisher the fact that Brendan Gill of the *New Yorker* (and Edith Oliver, who succeeded him) unfailingly mention craftsmen in their short reviews is a mixed blessing. From "an ego standpoint" he is "probably pleased to be mentioned," but the attention violates his belief that "lighting should not be noticed." It should be so unobtrusive that neither audience nor critic is aware of effects that work only if they are inconspicuous.

Fisher guesses that the level of criticism has been declining for some time, surely "from the time I began and that's a pretty short period. I'm not so old. But during my time we've gone from Brooks Atkinson to types like Rex Reed." He will not even confidently vouch for Atkinson. Fisher's point is that "most critics are not versed in technical theater." He turns, for illustrative purposes, to another craft, that of the costume designer:

On the whole, they are impressed by pretty or showy things. Now, if you have a play that's set in a nunnery where everybody's wearing black habits, critics can't say whether the costumes are good or bad. Tony Awards almost invariably go to productions where everybody notices the costumes because they are showy. I've seen productions in which Ann Roth or Pat Zipprodt did absolutely gorgeous costumes that nobody noticed. People go for glitz.

Fisher taxes the critics for being dazzled by glitter, for failing to see the less spectacular but finer work of costume designers just as the same critics see too much of the lighting designers' technique. The reviewer unversed in that technique lacks all discernment. Such a critic, whether silent or strident, is reviled by every specialist in the musical theater.

We ask Paul Gemignani: how much understanding do critics have of your job as a conductor? "None. *Absolutely* none." Do they comment on it? "No," which is perhaps just as well. "Oh, once in a while they do. I got reviewed in *Sweeney Todd* because it was so overwhelmingly classical that the critics would have looked like fools if they hadn't said something." Is the something they occasionally have to say of any value? How could it be to a man who finds that "one of the most irksome things in this business is the critics' ignorance of what I do and what the orchestrator does." Not that ignorance is harmful. Or that sophistication is helpful. In "this business," no one factor like criticism tells the tale.

Peter Neufeld seems to be on target when he declares that "nothing is decisive for any particular project." What are plus and minus reviews? For one thing, they are less classifiable than producers think: "You can get favorable reviews that, for some reason, do not light a fire under people who go to the theater. You can also get less favorable reviews with something indefinable in them that captures the public imagination." Neufeld likens the undercurrent of passion in a moderate review to the gestural message some of us convey after seeing a show: our earnestness, the look in our eyes, the sound in our voices. Such a message transmitted in the media causes the reader to say, "I've got to drop all my other plans and get to that theater." In expounding this theory, Neufeld refuses to simplify word of mouth: it proceeds with or without various degrees of passion. So does a favorable review. Either can make the difference between a long run and a short run, but neither is isolable and prepotent. "Everything," time, place, material, a whole set of circumstances never precisely duplicated, is decisive.

Decline of the Musical?

Although the average number of musical productions appeared to be declining in 1982–83, no two seasons were or are quite alike. But the downward trend was so perceptible that Nichtern often felt as if musical theater was dying:

At Tony time for awhile you had to come up with five nominations. Now it's four, and there aren't four musicals worthy of nominating in an average year. But it's a large commercial business and the conferring of Tonys is televised all over the country. Anything that opens and breathes around that time is going to be nominated.

The paucity of worthy new productions will cause mediocre works to be inflated, publicized, and turned into a small string of hits. Tony Awards cannot be discounted. For the longevity of a show, Arthur Laurents thinks that Tonys matter more than reviews. His is a minority view, but no one in the majority thinks that they do not matter at all. Still, in individual cases they may matter very little. Laurents must have taken great satisfaction at Tony time in 1984, when *La Cage aux Folles,* which he directed, nearly swept the field. However, that profitable show, whatever its merits, needed no boost. It sold out from the beginning and promised to run on and on. In that sense, this musical proved to be both critic-proof and award-proof. Then there followed a few British musicals, show upon show, that proved to be just that, such as *Miss Saigon.*

Frank Rich, who feels the great weight of responsibility that falls on a *Times* critic ("In prior times a musical could get along without the *Times.* Today it's much more difficult"), also lightens that weight. Having seven or eight papers, with their possible diversity of opinion, gave shows that were not universally applauded the fighting chance they no longer have when obeisance is paid to only one paper. Even Rich momentarily shares the myth about Rich! Or about the *Times* and its puissance. He is grateful that at least on Sundays, a different voice, that of Walter Kerr, Benedict Nightingale, and now David Richards, emanates from the same institution, and the Sunday judgment may not coincide with Rich's. He alone, in all his fallibility, does not totally determine the success or failure of Broadway shows. Theatergoers also attended to Kerr, Nightingale, and Richards. Spreading internal responsibility around takes some of the heat off one person. But it leaves that responsibility ("the institution, not its mouthpiece") intact.

Then again, is the institution all that it is cracked up to be? Press Rich a little bit and he emits such a geyser of skepticism that the shriveled and desiccated myth, were it not indestructible, would be routed for good. Hear Rich on a big change since the early 1970s: smart producers have become sophisticated about merchandising, and it is only because some of them are

Frank Rich (ca. 1991)

Frank Rich became drama critic for the *New York Times* in 1980, when he was about thirty. Rich has wide knowledge, was a newspaper publisher briefly, and in his position as the leading critic for New York's major newspaper is both respected and feared by many musical theater executives and creators. His reviews of new shows influence a national audience. (Photo credit: courtesy The New York Times.)

not so smart that they rely on *the* critic. Those with the smarts, of whom there are more and more, understand

that you can advertise on television as well as the print media, and that you can go beyond them. They realize that, besides a star, there are things you can merchandise. You can sell an idea; you can sell a song. You have plenty of promotional techniques at your disposal.

It's hard to believe that as recently as fifteen years ago the only way you could buy tickets was by going with cash to the box office or to a broker. Now people who didn't normally go to the theater pick up a phone and reserve tickets without ever having to leave their homes.

Another big change is the targeting of specific audiences, kids, families, blacks, yuppies. Earlier, only theater-party tickets were sold en bloc. The addition of other groups "makes people feel they want to see a show regardless of what critics say about it." Hype directed at "specific audiences" is a technique "first developed by the movie business and initially used for Broadway shows like *Pippin* and *The Wiz.*" These musicals got "medium reviews." Merchandising made them hits. They were largely backed by movie studios to whose managers it occurred that they could transfer their own merchandising methods from one medium to another. Rich doubts that the Hollywood approach would work very well with a straight play, but he is impressed with its effectiveness in the promotion of "anything that has potentially broad appeal, like a musical."

Not that Rich leaves it at that. For merchandising, with techniques new or old, has its limits. So, he lays it down as a fact that "on Broadway, as in Hollywood, you cannot sell an audience something it just does not want to see." Apparently, there was no way to sell *A Doll's Life.* On Hollywood, "No amount of promotion could have sold Sidney Sheldon's *Bloodline.*" It got a huge amount of promotion. What happened? "Sidney Sheldon's *Bloodline* dropped dead on the day it opened." The book on which the film was based had been a best seller, meaning that it was blessed with a great deal of free publicity. That circumstance ought to have helped. Whoever remembers Lazarsfeld's lesson knows that "sometimes it does and sometimes it doesn't."

Since human endeavor is predictable up to a point and unpredictable beyond that point, none of us can live formulaically. If gimmickry will not sell a certain movie, it will (and did) sell *Grease,* first on Broadway and then in Hollywood. "Mediocre reviews" were irrelevant. *Grease* contained elements that "could conceivably appeal to a mass audience." To Frank Rich, who is fearful of his own power (when he is not busy denying it), these elements, exploited by smart producers "in conjunction with advertising agents," made *Grease* into a hit. And not only *Grease:*

I mean *Evita* was a smash hit. It got panned by Walter [Kerr] who reviewed it for the daily paper. Both *Pippin* and *The Wiz* got lousy reviews from Clive [Barnes] when he was the *Times* critic. *Cats* got a mixed review from me and from most critics.

Rich dwells upon the phenomenally successful *Cats,* a glitzy, spectacular, and plotless musical that had by 1989 broken all prior net profit records. What were its exploitable elements? Rich ticks them off: the great American obsession with cats; Andrew Lloyd Webber's popularity; the producers' shrewdness in getting Barbra Streisand to record a song from the show six months before it opened. And an ad campaign, without visuals from the show, "running day and night on television." Rich's small son loved that advertising, with "its air of mystery created by an inspired sell-line," namely, "Isn't the curiosity killing you?" Properly handled, these elements reduce the critical fraternity, including its avatar on the *New York Times,* to a state of irrelevance. Shows "can be sold like politicians" (an observation that makes us feel the weight of our years for we can remember when "Mad" Avenue first persuaded us that politicians could be sold like soap). But not always. Not regularly. No *naif,* Rich understands this: "Some producers try like hell to sell their product but they do it incompetently, or" —and here the circularity of Rich's reasoning is most transparent—"the thing is simply unsaleable."

About this anyone from Ad Alley would concur. The consumer of goods and candidates can be gulled over and over. This is a half truth, the other half being that the consumer is king. Because correlations are not chains of causation, you never know whether your campaign did what it was supposed to do. (A) You advertised, and (B) your product moved. Maybe A is related to B. Maybe not. You advertised and your product did not move. It could have been unsaleable. What hype—or criticism—really does is lost forever in the mist thrown up by a hundred intervening variables. "That's healthy. That's fine," is Rich's reaction. He would rather not take the credit or the blame for a responsibility so uncertainly connected with his function. At that juncture, he parts company with the advertising executive who is praised for success and, fairly or unfairly, blamed for failure.

The operation of chance, the randomness of time and place, an "intervening variable" here or there, will continue to hold sway over the musical theater, the straight theater, and the world theater we all inhabit. Most of the time, but not all of the time.

III

*Collaboration in
the Musical*

7. Conflict and Collaboration

Centripetal and centrifugal forces are as inherent in society as they are in the universe at large. Their omnipresence is demonstrable in every organization, in every group, and in each one of us. We are "balanced"—and the wonder is that we have not yet been torn apart—by attraction and repulsion, by action and reaction. So too with conflict and cohesion. Conflict is certainly different from cohesion; we may distinguish one from the other, but in action they are indivisible. In fact, wherever studious observers look and listen they find conflict-in-cohesion. It could scarcely be otherwise in Broadway musical theater—whether viewed as a business, a series of projects, or a group of collaborating artists working on a single show.

Contrariness prevails as much in musical theater as it does in any other human enterprise. Here too ambivalence or multivalence covers a broad spectrum of impulses, tendencies, temptations, and consummations. Even individual artists working in splendid solitude, as the exceptionally autonomous individuals they must be, experience their share of conflict. But for them the inner struggle is most intense. Contending with conscious and unconscious drives, they are prompted by "daimons" to create something that will move others to higher states of insight and understanding. Those who hear, see, or otherwise apprehend the creative artist's work at its best will somehow be transformed by it.

The task of such artists is to translate visions into objects, notes, words, pictures, and patterns; to order the chaos around them by one artistic device or another; to make the invisible visible, the inaudible audible. Men and women totally devoted to the creation of art, and hemmed in by it, are yet freer than most people. Ideally, they feel independent of other people. They use their own tools; they work at their own pace. Like a small number of free-floating intellectuals, these artists feel unattached to any organization. In their studies and studios, poets, painters, sculptors, and composers daily create a free and private space. As solitary craftsmen and cosmopolitan visionaries, however, they appear to be relics of a preindustrial past. By virtue of their precarious position in contemporary society, they are an endangered species, besieged on every side by the threat of cooptation. That so many still stand defiantly on their own two feet makes them an occupational marvel.

As the poet said, no one is an island. Away from their private sphere (an occasional reclusive genius like Emily Dickinson notwithstanding), they cannot escape from the society that surrounds them. Its institutions impinge on their lives, most obviously on their daily lives, but also and perhaps most importantly, on their professional lives. Rare are the artists who can be insulated from intermediaries. Agents, publicists, patrons, impresarios, dealers, editors, politicians, bureaucrats, critics, and curators stand between them and a fickle public that one must reach to achieve material success or even a *succès d'estime*. Much of their private world is real and all of it is essential to those who would avoid economic or political "contamination." There are such artists and, while we do not wish to exaggerate their plight, their romantic agony, their alienation from the pecuniary values that dominate our culture, these transformers of the commonplace (as the philosopher Arthur C. Danto has called them) still manage to hold their own —even if constantly besieged. In modern times the lone artist as visionary is above all an individualist who equates authenticity with autonomy.

The Collaborative Artist

If this little sketch of the "high" artist's social situation is approximately correct, then it is more tortuously true in musical theater. For the artist in musical theater is enmeshed in collective activity as much by preference as by the requirement of the art form, and remains so by being a standard bearer of collaboration. As Oscar Hammerstein once summed it up (we repeat), "Collaboration is the biggest word in the theater. It is the most important element in theatrical success."[1] And in its failures, which are the rule.

Of the poet-playwright who once conceived dramas that were only meant to be read hardly any are left. With a prototype like Seneca in ancient Rome (but not one in fifth-century B.C. Greece), the practitioner of this genre is a creature of the fourteenth century. In our time, such authors are read only as a footnote to Victorian literature. Even William Butler Yeats and T. S. Eliot, who wrote plays as a serious sideline, designed them for performance. Ours is not an era receptive to the closet drama, which we rightly associate with Shelley or Tennyson but not, say, with Auden, who, after failing as a playwright in the thirties, did collaborate successfully in the writing of librettos and some lyrics for the opera.

The modern musical theater, certainly the contemporary theater, is fashioned not for readers but for audiences. And those audiences for musical theater in the United States collectively are about forty to sixty million annually—including dinner theater, high school productions, and so forth. In this age of electronic entertainment, they constitute more than 20 percent of the American population of 250 million people.

The Art and Business of Musical Theater

Living theater is itself split into nonprofit and commercial spheres. If a single element decisively distinguishes one kind of theater from the other, Robert Brustein recently remarked, "it is the idea of a permanent collective organized for the purpose of refining theater art, as distinct from a temporary junta thrown together to create a hit."[2] No doubt the praise and the criticism implicit in this statement need to be modulated. One of Brustein's detractors tells us, with a touch of malice, that "Bob would like nothing better than to have a Broadway hit." Whether or not this is true of Professor Brustein, certainly nonprofit theater as a whole, with its constant quest for grants and subsidies, has yet to be disentangled from commercial constraints or the compromises they impose.

By the same token, commercial theater is full of artistic aspirations. Occasionally, those involved in it even claim artistic achievements—and sometimes, this is so. But in the main, that they are self-styled artists delivering important messages in their chosen medium who at the same time long for blockbusters is not the least of their conflicts. It may, however, be the greatest of them.

In show business, today more than ever, *l'art pour l'art* is unequally matched against *l'art pour l'argent.* Not that the first is entirely extinguished by the second. Box office matters, but so does self-expression. God or His surrogate—sometimes Science, in this case, Art—can still be heard by supersubtle listeners even when this God is routed and outshouted by Mammon. Therein lies the classic *conflictus Americanus.* It is epitomized in the commercial theater and compounded in Broadway musical theater. For our focus is on Broadway, a metaphor for an American cultural reality, and not just its historical geographic turf.

As we have seen, not only is Broadway musical theater dominated by the owners of about forty theaters but they in turn are also dominated by the dynamics of real estate demands: taxes, physical deterioration of plant, urban ecological changes (traffic patterns, sanitation, contiguous usage, e.g., porno houses, etc.). The other hard and ancient reality is the very short supply of well-conceived, well-written shows. This fact directly leads to the greatest stressor in musical theater as a business: most shows fail to recoup the original investment. Harsh business realities hang over all commercial collaboration at the project's inception and over the artistic collaboration in the show itself. They are like the sword of Damocles.

Then, within this risky, dynamic arena and directly or tangentially related to it come the "ego-smashing clashes" (Donald Farber) that are a deadly threat and a fruitful challenge to artistic collaboration. For along with a mythic ideal of "harmony" there is a *realpolitik,* as Sondheim notes, a "little abrasiveness" that seems to facilitate creative collaboration.

The Garden of Egos

The fusion of one talent with others, while indispensable for artistic collaboration, is also nearly indefinable and almost undecipherable. Why one personality will not mesh with another we are unlikely ever to understand in any depth, but it is clear that to yoke them unnaturally can spell disaster. Some simply "don't hit it off"; "one works mornings, the other nights." The bookwriter Peter Stone points out that Richard Rodgers and Alan Jay Lerner suffered from this kind of incompatibility. While in Stone's opinion Rodgers was the most talented composer and Lerner the most gifted lyricist, "they hated one another." These two men "could not get along." Habits and values and the mysteries of temperament may so deeply separate two such types as to preclude any collaboration. No producer or backer or director, however obtuse, can simply fling them together in an ad hoc junta. They will not coalesce. The "wrong" performer, the "wrong" composer, the "wrong" designer may be someone unsuited to others who are or are not equally "wrong." But at the end Rodgers did not "get along" with Hart either. Nor Gilbert with Sullivan. Yet "their products were successful." These cases are, however, in the minority. Besides the producer(s), "You must have an author, composer and lyricist who get along with the director who gets along with the star who gets along with the choreographer who gets along with the set designer" (and so forth). This is the lawyer Farber's limited—and casual—list of those who have to cooperate in a musical show.

The Legal Push and Pull

The same theatrical lawyer, Farber, who supplies a short catalogue of egos that clash by day and night, offers personal insight into the naturally adversarial area in which he operates. Without his kind of legal expertise no project gets off the ground, for shows are government-regulated businesses. And that area, as he perceives it, is filled with land mines planted through the ignorance of those who do not understand "this business," or the "entertainment industry" (terms universally applied to musical theater, and Farber uses them to the exclusion of all others, closely reflecting his own perspective). For one of *the* experts in his field, and Farber is that, "trouble," "frustration," "headaches," and "conflicts" rest squarely on a lawyer-to-lawyer and lawyer-to-agent basis:

> The first few times I'm willing to educate them. . . . They're not innately stupid, just dumb in this business. But when they start to fight with me about what I've been doing for more than twenty-five years, trying to convince me that we should or shouldn't do things in a certain way, I say, "Phooey," and let someone else deal with them.

Specifically, "When I represented the Chelsea Theater Off Broadway, one guy, a lawyer but not in the business, would get on the phone with me. In an hour and fifteen minutes, I'd explain the whole thing. Okay. I was willing to educate him. The first few times weren't so bad. But he kept calling, getting more and more contentious, moving farther and farther from reality. Finally I gave up." The same sort of confrontation occurs when Farber, representing a producer, must secure rights to a play or a "property" through an agent who represents an author. Also, "When I'm representing a producer who wants to hire a star, I've got to talk to the agent. Same thing if my client wants to hire a director."

As a knowledgeable lawyer, Farber is impatient with these middle men and women. For them and their likes, he has written a book, and frequently revised it.[3] Too many readers refuse to be edified, let alone guided through the legal labyrinth. Farber is more indulgent with Englishmen, "who do not understand the Broadway or the Off Broadway scene" until they are clued into it. Foreigners are educable, but years ago when an English or French agent "mentioned subsidiary rights, you'd blow the whole deal." Farber began duplicating pages of his book, mailing them to agents abroad, to inform the uninformed that "this is the way it's done here because Farber says that this is the way it's done here." In a humbler mood, the theatrical lawyer is ready to admit that "I don't know everything about what I'm doing." Just a great deal more than others. Hence, when people he has instructed oppose him—and oppose him they do—then at times his reaction is splenetic.

This abrasiveness appears in the *pre*-preliminary stages of a production. The potential for explosive exchanges in these stages should not be minimized. Disagreement over rights, clearances, regulations, and laws, all subject to overnight change, is omnipresent. When one adds ambiguity, hair splitting, and human perversity, it is easy to see why so many plans have, in the history of Broadway show biz, come to nothing—and how so many in the future will also fail to "get the rights," or get agreement on "artistic control."

Tommy Tune adds his own experience trying to delve into the deep pocket:

> . . . and they pulled a very immoral act by saying that they were interested and giving us some money to do the workshop, with the understanding that they would back the show, and then saying, "We decided we're not giving you the money," and leaving us stranded for a long time, but we won the race anyway.
> Q: Was there a contract with that?
> A: Yeah.
> Q: They broke the contract?
> A: No, they didn't break the contract. But there are many things in contracts that aren't cricket. We know that. Your morals enter into it.
> Q: Reinterpreted?
> A: Absolutely. You can get around anything. The point is, is that good faith? Is that helpful?

Plans also come to nothing, or at least to grief, on the road or in the development of a show. Testing, tinkering, altering, dropping, substituting, reconstructing: all this is par for the course. Each step in the process invites dissension. Everyone and every decision is at risk. When the degree of sophistication is deemed too high in Boston or New Haven or in previews, it must be adjusted—lowered to please an ostensibly "typical Broadway audience." If out-of-town critics are displeased, it is probably time to call in a doctor; if, after his recommendations have been implemented, the same critics continue to turn thumbs down, another and yet another doctor may be summoned. No one has counted those productions that died on the way to Broadway.

The Show Must Go On . . . and On

During our study, *My One and Only* (1983) provided a prime example of fractiousness. Before reaching New York, this musical, widely touted for its almost $5 million capitalization, was diagnosed, nursed, eviscerated, and rebuilt beyond recognition. The multiple producers, duly noting how poorly their product was received in Boston, sought advice from consultant after consultant. Directors came and went. So did songs from an inexhaustible supply of oldies by George and Ira Gershwin. So did story lines. Word spread that the turkey in Boston was too sick to survive. Boston's most influential reviewer even elaborated his objections in Boston to *My One and Only* in *New York Magazine* just prior to its Broadway opening. No matter. The bad word, passing through many channels, did not prevent this musical, by now in completely new shape, from becoming a Broadway hit. Such is the total unpredictability of box office success. To attain that success, with so much wear and tear, was surely no daily pleasure for any of the principals or their doctors. Intimations of civil war, of a little Hobbesian world, were clear to insiders and, more scandalously, to outsiders. The desired "retuning" was nevertheless achieved.

Nor is this a unique case. Consider that *Hello, Dolly!* (1964) had a last-minute save. But fractiousness of so pervasive a nature is obviously much more often fatal, e.g., *Carrie, Marilyn*. Great care, not to say timidity, thus becomes the watchword of producers and investors. They tend to stay on the safe side, exalting all the arts of diplomacy, seeking out those who will not step on tender toes or even more tender egos. With experience, they all learn that conflict persists, it sometimes helps, frequently hurts, but can never be banished. Merrick, the master, it is said, actually promoted conflict among the creators of *Gypsy* (1959) and other successes. He then "managed" the conflict to elicit creative ideas.

Is tension less extreme if the tryout occurs in a workshop? Not necessarily. Long after *The Best Little Whorehouse in Texas* (1978) had become a hit, Carol Hall, its composer-lyricist, felt bitter about a major change in personnel. A deep-dyed Texan, she and two old friends developed a musical that clicked on Broadway where, apparently, its long run might have been longer. The backers, in this instance, a film company, made *Whorehouse* into a profitable movie—which had been their intention all along. Neither on stage nor on the screen were there many critical kudos. But millions of viewers paid and applauded. Yet Hall and one of her collaborators —an old buddy, Larry King, who wrote the book with Peter Masterson— had a falling out. Their partnership appears to have been a one-shot affair. King then published a book airing all his grievances. Hall's are less well known. In any case, a many-sided collaboration worked well over the one-and-a-half-year period in a workshop where their brainchild was eventually formed, only to be deformed thereafter in the film (or so some contend).

Chatting with us, Hall makes it clear that a pre-Broadway shift in directors still troubles her:

It's just that I had to let go of a director I'd stuck with for so long and so determinedly because he did our workshop and because he was good. I was told by very powerful forces that we simply could not go with him.

Then she characteristically draws on her Texas background:

You know, Daryl Royal was a famous football coach at the University of Texas. One year he lost his star senior quarterback but made it to the Cotton Bowl via a very good sophomore. The senior recovered and was fit for the Cotton Bowl. He asked Daryl: "You gonna go with the sophomore who got you here or with the guy who's back in now?" Daryl's answer was: "I dance with the one that brings me." . . . I wanted to keep going with this very young director. I'd never drop anyone after six months, let alone a year, but after a year and a half, to be told, "Your trouble is he's unknown"—that's preposterous.

Yes, but it is not uncommon on Broadway.

Hall had other problems that, while seemingly peculiar to her (and of course they are not) all belong to a pattern of corporate control. About this and the tension that it induces there is much more to be said. For the tension is endemic. Everyone has problems.

When Frank Rich declares, "There's always conflict," we may take it as a truism based on his own involvement in that conflict. The daily reviewer of a powerful paper can scarcely escape antagonistic symbiosis with those he judges. The subjective element is no less present in his observations than in those of theater people who, as he notes, create a "kind of entertainment that requires large amounts of money to produce and therefore requires a large amount of money to survive." Still, being of the musical theater but not in it enables him to achieve some measure of objectivity. It cannot have taken Rich long to learn that although commerce and art "don't have to be antithetical," commerce too often does "shape" these shows. Despite his relative detachment, Rich grasps the situation as fully as those who are caught up in it. Therefore, "if you have a show that isn't working" in previews, "you're losing a lot of money. And you don't have all year to think about it."

A Shifting Hierarchy: Money and Status

If you are a lyricist, according to Martin Charnin, you have hardly any time to think about it. From his standpoint, the lyricist is low man on the "creative team." And it was no better, possibly worse, in the past. To explain this phenomenon, Charnin fires off a series of rhetorical questions:

Why was music always precious? And why were lyrics never precious? Why were you always expected to rewrite an entire song [lyric] overnight while no one rewrote the music to it? Why was it always my responsibility in Philadelphia to lock myself in a room just as the composer went off to dinner at Frankie Bradley's? What was the reason?

His answer is that it was "purely economic." The words "can always be thrown out" at practically no expense. "Oh, maybe the cost of a typewriter ribbon or xeroxing your new lyric."

Touch a piece of music, on the other hand, and "you start a chain reaction" that begins with the orchestrator, moves on to the conductor, and encompasses the whole orchestra.

You can do a new lyric without an orchestra call. You can't do a new song without an orchestra call. You can almost do a new lyric without a rehearsal. You can slip it under the door to Robert Preston at his hotel room.

Such was the attitude, a "most distressing one," as Charnin experienced it at the moment of triumph. It made him feel that his work was not taken seriously. Money talked. Lyrics could be altered on the cheap; tunes could not.

The lyricist enjoins us to ask, "How many times did Sheldon [Harnick] or Jerry [Bock] rewrite whatever it was?" He is confident of the reply:

I bet you right now that it'll always come out "I rewrote that song twenty-eight times." But was it twenty-eight times he rewrote the *song?* No, it was twenty-eight times I rewrote the lyric—or twenty-eight times that every one of us sat down and tried to fix the lyric.

Fixing lyrics costs less than fixing music, even with computers. Hence, in the preparation of a show, the lyricist is called upon to rewrite more than the composer and sometimes feels put upon. In a dyadic relationship—where only one composer and one lyricist are involved—their piece of the pie is equal. Other combinations, more than one composer, more than one wordsmith, or only one composer-lyricist working with one or more book-writers, greatly complicate both the financial and the psychological problem. The very short-lived *Marilyn* (1983) had fourteen teams of songwriters![4]

The economic thing ramifies in every direction. Consider how it affects a top lighting designer like Jules Fisher, who views general managers as his nemesis. "They try to get you for as little as possible." Their job is to hold costs down, to protect the investor or the producer. But the union minimum for a lighting designer was three thousand dollars (1983). Where money is the measure of all things, it is offensive to Fisher as a veteran designer that he should command a fee no greater than that of a beginner.

"Why shouldn't I be paid more than a neophyte? . . . I want to be paid for my experience and my taste." How much more? "I will demand another thousand dollars." Hardly pausing, however, Fisher escalates the sum to five or six thousand more dollars. Obviously, the calculation has less to do with dollars than with status. It is "experience and taste" that call for recognition. Such qualities are not uppermost in the minds of managers disinclined to reward anyone beyond a certain necessary point. That point is established by contractual obligations that already strike managers as onerous.

Taste, if not experience, comes into play once again when one lyricist replaces another, as we learn from Burton Lane's recollection of a show:

After two years of working on it there were five finished songs. It was a disaster. I came into it when Dick Rodgers resigned because he couldn't get along with Alan [Lerner]. Dick showed me a lot of the lyrics. I liked only one to which I wrote the music, and it became a big standard called "Come Back to Me." Otherwise, I took lyrics that I hated and set them to music just so the actors would have something to rehearse.

With Sheldon Harnick we go back to economics pure and simple. Unlike Fisher, our lighting designer, he does not castigate the producers, acknowledging that they are "in a terrible squeeze." For them "the cost of musicians, of stagehands, of materials, of actors keeps going up. But the bookwriter's contract has remained constant for I forget how many years," and now (1983) producers "would like us to take a smaller percentage so that they have a little more room to breathe. We understand that, but we're fighting it." Of this, too, *plus ça change, plus c'est la même chose.*

Change and Conflict

Peter Stone, in contemplating the bookless musical, points first to the economic factor—"Plays are growing more and more expensive; money's harder and harder to find"—and next to the predominance of producers "who are not basically interested in the theater." These coproducers, and nowadays there is a plurality of them, "go for safety in elements." Such elements are long established, well known, in a word—previously successful. Michael Bennett was a safe element: "Let's get him no matter what he does." The new breed of producer, heedless of content, "makes a total commitment to Michael Bennett. Michael Bennett makes a total commitment to no-words. And there you have the bookless musical!" (Naturally, Bennett disagreed with this assessment. Perhaps Fosse's *Dancin'* is a more telling example.)

Good book, bad book, or no book, safety is a curious aspect of the musical theater, where there is no safety. Danger, carrying its heavy weight of insecurity, lurks everywhere. Perhaps a key actor appears to be unsafe. If that "element" looks wrong at any point, even well into previews, out it goes. Such was the case in 1981 with *Merrily We Roll Along,* a notable flop of that season, praised everywhere for Stephen Sondheim's score and unanimously damned for its weak book. Lonny Price, one of the stars of the show, remembers, "We opened in New York for previews. There was so much changing all the time. . . . We were really in the process of trying to get it right." One principal actor "just didn't seem to work out in his role. The cast could tell that he wasn't terrific." So, his dismissal didn't come as "a complete shock to us. . . . But it was sad, it was very sad because you picture yourself in that position. You think, 'What would it be like if they let *me* go?' So you have a lot of empathy."

Turn the kaleidoscope a bit. Imagine a star who is not dropped belatedly but removes himself. This will cause all kinds of consternation. Look at it for a moment from an agent's point of view. To Merle Debuskey, each star has uniquely "exploitable" traits that should be emphasized in order to hype a show before its presentation on Broadway. Much work must be done, much time consumed. If the agent's efforts and the investor's money are lavished on actors who disappear, Debuskey is left in the lurch. Spadework, carefully programmed to highlight big names or familiarize the public with new names, must be launched. Pressures are intensified. Where to place the blame? Not on the actors who are signed to contracts from which they withdraw or on which they are judged to be incapable of delivering.

Take a show like *Amadeus.* You're scheduled to open in Boston next week. You learn on Monday morning that the costar is out of it. You're lucky if you don't get killed. Lots of people are angry. The whole thing is very discouraging. How are you going to exploit it? How do you know what to exploit next?

Conflict in the So-Called Creative Team

Crises of this sort may seem peripheral. They may be overcome (in *Amadeus* they were). Conflict in the creative team is more likely to be fatal because there the loss of a major "element" jeopardizes everything. Harnick recounts the story of an unsuccessful musical whose score was by Marc Blitzstein. The book, an adaptation of Sean O'Casey's *Juno and the Paycock,* was to have been written by Joe Stein and Will Glickman:

If I remember correctly, Will and Joe had an artistic falling out over how the show should be developed. Will wanted to make some changes that he thought were

Norman Wisdom, Cy Feuer in Rehearsal for Walking Happy *(1966)*

Photos of disagreements among the various groups of artists who collaborate within a company are rare and not easily available. Pictured here is an on-line producer, Cy Feuer, and an actor, Norman Wisdom, seeming to talk simultaneously during a rehearsal of the show *Walking Happy* (1966). Is this conflict semihumorous or semiserious? Both qualities must prevail among the creative team and among all small groups in the process of creating a musical show—even in the business office. (Photo credit: Billy Rose Theatre Collection, New York Public Library.)

necessary to bring it to Broadway. Joe wanted to keep it closer to the original O'Casey play. It was an impasse they could not resolve, and they ended their collaboration. So when we called Joe for *Fiddler on the Roof,* it was just Joe, no Will.

A nonnegotiable impasse was not overcome by creative compromise. And if it had been, would the patient have lived?

Yesterday's link that held so well will rust and crack on subsequent occasions. Lane, a composer who got along with one great lyricist, recalls that the same man later became "aggressively antagonistic" toward him. Where in the past they had worked "on an equal footing and nobody was boss," he later felt the lyricist's attitude was patronizing. Even in the old days when their relationship was at its best, Lane believed he was being slighted. Before their most memorable collaboration,

We played a couple of benefits and did some songs from the show. He would introduce me as his piano player, never as the composer. I told him after one of these things, "The next time you introduce me that way, you're going to be singing a capella."

This grievance, still rankling in Lane's breast, evidently did not interfere with the show that did come to fruition decades ago, with music, words, and plot that still evoke strong applause. Despite repeated efforts, these men were never able to regain enough rapport for further work in musical theater. If initial camaraderie contains the seeds of resentment between two Broadway creators, they may part company forever. The five geniuses who did *West Side Story* never again worked together as a group. "Couldn't." As for many other "one-shot" efforts of fly-by-night freelance Broadway teams, they are legion.

Who's in Charge of the Conflict?

Long ago, according to a legend about Lee Shubert, he addressed an entire crew in his theater as follows: "There's only one captain on this ship, and that's me and my brother J. J."[5] "Captain of the ship" is an incantation that reverberates through the discourse of theater people. Today, however, the captain is usually a director or a director-choreographer. The increasing number of director-choreographers strikes many as an obvious trend (or so they thought in the early eighties). In Tommy Tune, having come a long way from the chorus lad he once was, we behold the director-choreographer-performer. And yet, when these roles are split, with territoriality and authority at stake, Tune, the choreographer, defers to the director for whom he finds it inevitably "hard to work," adding that "directors deeply mistrust choreographers and I don't blame them." Therefore, yield to the director and eliminate the struggle. Or, better, be the director yourself.

Jules Fisher and many others claim that choreographers are less articulate than directors. In a war of words they stand little chance of winning: "Jerry Robbins is a perfect example. Robbins is probably one of the geniuses of our theater. But he has spent his life in the perfection of movement, not of speech." Arthur Laurents, a musical bookwriter of distinction, draws on his own experience to confirm Fisher's judgment:

> When we were out of town with *Gypsy* [1959], it became apparent that the show wasn't at all what Jerry Robbins thought it was going to be. He didn't see a word, he didn't hear a note till the thing was finished. Jerry thought it would be a great panorama of vaudeville with animal acts and jugglers. . . . Jerry wanted a whole burlesque show in it. I said, "Okay, you want it, I'll write it." But I told Jerry it wouldn't work. He wanted to know why not. "Because this will mean moving away from that woman (Gypsy Rose Lee's mother) and her kids for too long. The minute you leave those characters the show's going to sink," and that's what happened. I think the burlesque part lasted two nights in Philadelphia.

A triumph for the writer who nevertheless affirms that "the director must be captain of the ship." This captain can be overruled, not by anybody, but by "the strong." Fisher reports that he has been "on shows where the director threw the author out of the theater. I've seen that happen two or three times in major musicals." Or maybe a strong producer and the director bar the renowned authors from rehearsal, e.g., *Jamaica* (1957) and *1600 Pennsylvania Avenue* (1976). To be insubordinate in the theatrical hierarchy takes guts and knowledge, an awareness of rights and a willingness to cite the Dramatists Guild contract. Refusing to comply means that the captain's authority is undermined and lieutenants seize power that they themselves insist only the captain should exercise.

Who dares to say no? Laurents includes the bookwriter, the composer, and the lyricist. No doubt there are others. Still reminiscing about the original production of *Gypsy*, he discusses the fate of a ballad called "Little Lamb" that Robbins eliminated in favor of a big dance number that was to have featured jugglers and all the inhabitants of a theatrical boarding house. "Well, the dance didn't work and I'll never forget what happened after that." What happened was this: "Jule Styne, a dear man and funny and crazy," asserted himself. Styne let it be known that the song would have to go back. Captain Robbins's answer was that it would not go back. Deadlock. But not for long. At rehearsal

> Jule walked on the stage, carrying an attaché case and very nattily dressed. Jerry was in the audience. Jule said, "Mr. Robbins, I've just called the Dramatists Guild.

My lawyer's in New York. Unless that song is back in tonight, I'm withdrawing my score from the show." Yes, Jerry was captain of the ship but he went too far off course as far as Jule was concerned. "Little Lamb" stayed in, and nothing more was said about it.

In this instance the captain capitulated. On another occasion, he compromised. The writer, if he is Arthur Laurents, has enough clout to ensure give-and-take. Approximately this colloquy took place at another rehearsal:

Robbins: The show is forty-five minutes too long. Steve says that you have twenty-five minutes of cuts marked in the script.
Laurents: That's right.
Robbins: When are you going to make them?
Laurents: When you cut twenty minutes from those kiddies' numbers.

The proportion of song and dance to dialogue (if any) is a natural source of dispute. Who sings a song once it is seemingly accepted can also lead to recriminations. The complexity of an issue like this is multiplied severalfold when major tasks are divided in what Carol Hall calls "a real peculiar way." Not only was she the lyricist-composer for *Best Little Whorehouse,* with Pete Masterson and Larry King as the bookwriters, but Pete Masterson and Tommy Tune were codirectors. Two captains? Like Lee Shubert's one captain who turned out to be two producers, this extra weight cannot make for smooth sailing.

There was no quarrel over "Bus from Amarillo," a song that Hall envisaged as an answer to the ancient question, "What's a nice girl like you doing in a place like this?" In workshop, when the song was sung by X, people shouted "Bravo! Bravo!" With all the huzzahs, Y came to covet that song, and Pete, being closer to Y than to X, came to covet it for her. The result was "a lot of enmity. . . . It was our biggest and most terrible fight." Nobody won. Neither singer got the song because it was eliminated altogether. So Hall had to write another one, and, looking back on this experience, she sees it as the good part. "No regrets."

In fact, Hall, talking to us for two hours, punctuates her rehearsal of "ferocious" conflicts with exclamations of pleasure. "No regrets," "things worked out," and yet, as we proceed she professes to be fed up with Broadway, ready to abandon it after one more fling. This ambivalent attitude is so nearly paradigmatic that it is worth following in some detail.

I always got into arguments with directors. They're bossy. They're supposed to be bossy. They're directors because they like to move people around, tell them where to go, what to do. . . . They resemble surgeons who are bossy too. For good reason. They have no time to chat about whether or not to cut that artery. . . .

Some types are directors; other types are writers. *I'm always going to clash with directors, but I depend on them.* I'm a terrific lieutenant, but I need a captain of the ship. [Our emphasis.]

Even more graphically:

There are ways of wrestling each other to the floor. Tommy Tune used to bang his glass cane against the floor and say into a darkened theater, "They'll get you for that lyric, girl. They'll get you, Carol Hall." It didn't matter that I held my ground. I would skulk home and change it. The telegram I sent him on opening night read, "You were hard on me—and thank you."

Whether there would be an opening night at all became problematic for one anxious moment. A representative of Universal Pictures "wanted something out of the show that we didn't think ought to be out." Moreover, he insisted "that if it didn't go out, we wouldn't open." Hall found Masterson's response "interesting." It was simply, "Okay, don't open the show." What gave him the courage to be so defiant? "Pete's a good poker player. He understood the company had spent three hundred and fifty thousand dollars and of course they were going to open." The company men "kind of laughed." And then Larry, the other old buddy, pitched in, "Hell, man, you got five of your nine suggestions. Why don't you go back to L.A.?" The poker players knew how to handle their cards; their antagonist had gambled away too much, but basically they survived because "every night the audience was laughing." Besieged by her peers as well as those formally above and below her, Hall made it, but not without a bitter aftertaste. However, by the early nineties, this trio may work together again.

Playing through Conflict

Claire Nichtern, by contrast with Carol Hall, and from her very different vantage point as a producer, has been through innumerable fights, especially with bookwriters and composers. But she takes a chirpier view. "Somehow you get through the fights because you say they're worth it." Furthermore, "One can hope to learn from each such experience." Learn what? "How to be more clever, more aware of the problems up front so that you don't ever start rehearsals saying, 'Well, we'll work it out.' "

But can one learn? And if so, what does one learn? Martin Charnin asserts that at the beginning he was "too smart for his own good," and that translates into, "I called it as I saw it." What he "had to learn" was that "in the theater you don't always say what's on your mind." You discover that "there's a lot of smoothing over to be done." Knowing all that when he started out would have led to a "different kind of success much sooner." Charnin explains that he does not mean ordinary tact or intelligence or humanity. Something else galled him: "I'm talking about playing the game, which I never could do," evidently not even now, after much success, when the lesson has been learned. For he unconsciously changes tenses. Playing the game *today* is "terribly time-consuming," "wasteful beyond belief." It makes him "wildly impatient," a phrase that comes more than once to his lips: "When you know that to get from here to there all you have to do is walk this way, but the rule is that you go someone else's way, you become wildly impatient."

Someone else's way of walking or talking or dancing or singing is generally the director's way. Stephen Schwartz makes no bones about it: "Where I've had problems in my career, they've been with directors." In each case these problems arose after the show was written, the team assembled and ready to go, but still without a director (which, Schwartz maintains, is usually the case). Enter the director, with *his* concept and a great deal has to be changed: "If you don't really see eye-to-eye, it eventually becomes a real battle of egos." In part to avoid that battle, Schwartz was at first, but not later, his own director of *Rags* (1986).

His first and worst contretemps with a director occurred in *Pippin* (1972), a show that nonetheless worked out very well for the audiences and investors. Bob Fosse, like Tommy Tune a triple-threat choreographer-director-actor, directed *Pippin*. To Schwartz the composer-lyricist "Bob was a strong person who knew what he wanted." What Schwartz himself wanted had been germinating in his mind for six years: "Essentially it was what I had done at school with another kid." Nor was *Pippin* his debut. Schwartz was "coming off" *Godspell,* over which he "had a lot of control." So it shocked him that the director could throw out his ideas and "just do a whole other show." Schwartz puts the matter most colorfully in one sentence: "It seemed to me like those birds that take other birds' nests instead of building their own." He got very irritated by the process, but soon realized "that it *is* the process." When we asked, "So you accept dictation by the director or become the director? Is that it?" he answered,

Yes. Exactly. . . . What was so crushing about *Pippin* was to have finished a show and then have someone else tear it apart and put it together through his own vision.

Here two strong wills, one hierarchically empowered to be stronger than the other, were deeply at odds. The issue, in Schwartz's opinion, came down to a difference in "vision." As soon as that word is evoked, a deeper issue emerges, as we have seen throughout this book: can the collaborative art of musical theater contain a single creator's vision? The very concept of an autonomous artist's solitary vision is drawn from "high art." How far is it compatible with commodity-mindedness? Schwartz admits that Fosse had his own vision, which just happened to be at sixes and sevens with his and that of his bookwriter. That the show turned a good profit is not Schwartz's point. "It was no longer ours," is. Whether or not the director's vision was superior to theirs is irrelevant. What counts and grates on Schwartz's nerves is not money; it is that basically *Pippin* turned out to be Fosse's work: "He just put our names on it." And in this mindset not even credit matters.

Ambivalence and Metamorphosis

All this comes to the interlocutor as a heartfelt protest against the director's power. But, is it? Only if we stop with the *cri de coeur*. Schwartz does not. Indignation about the fate of *Pippin* is one thing. Admiration for the system that so upsets him is another. The aggrieved Schwartz soon becomes the appreciative Schwartz. The independent artist with a vision betrayed is transformed into the team man who wants help not only from directors but also from their acolytes: "Doing a full score is so difficult that you need little gadflies stinging you on to better work. . . . You need other eyes and other points of view and someone to say, 'I don't like that. Come up with something better.' " This is a love-hate relationship in full flower.

Schwartz, who needs to be his own man and needs to have other points of view, articulates the paradox of "collective art." That label is only sometimes an oxymoron. You can be your own man while cooperating with, but not belonging to others. Musical theater, in its devotion to a permeable authoritarian structure, does not differ from any other theater—or from any other organization. Authority formally bestowed on one person in a group is not synonymous with power informally wielded by those who may not, at first, realize that they have any power. The freedom to defy or comply or compromise is ever present in human affairs. The essence of collaborative art must be the generation of creative compromises or creative solutions in which collaborators are satisfied enough to keep going. Even Schwartz did not resign from *Pippin*.

So Who Has the Power—No One or Everyone?

To the casual observer producers have more power than directors. Captains are after all answerable to their superiors. The coproducer, Gail Berman, in discussing a musical, at first sounds like an admiral of the fleet:

We made it quite clear from the word go that we were involved in everything on this show, and our director was well aware of that before deciding to take the position. He knew that we would be sitting there right on top of them.

Who/whom—who does what to whom—is the old and still most pertinent question in power relationships. Since early in this century, when Max Weber formulated the concept for us, power in sociological terms has signified the capacity to make others do what one wants them to do whether or not they want to do it. Georg Simmel, more than any other sociologist, complicated this idea by demonstrating that the locus of power is not always where it seems to be, as we have seen in earlier chapters. "Sitting right there on top" of the crew is an assertion of naked power. In the unwritten table of organization, producers do exert more power than directors. That is to say, they are often vested with ultimate authority. But, alas for them, authority does not necessarily equal power. Any executive, including our chief executive in Washington, acts in accordance with this principle, or soon ceases to enjoy the authority conferred on him. Berman, when pressed, has to concede the point, and does so immediately after denying it: "A lot of times you must acquiesce to the director. You do hire him as an artistic person who can tell what goes on more thoroughly than you can. You have a thousand other things to do."

Rank order is one thing; reality is another. External deference may disguise subtle sabotage. The actor who allows himself to be moved about on stage may be stubborn off stage. Price is, in his own words, "a hindrance to producers because I know too much about their business." For this reason, they tend to get angry with him when financial matters are at issue: "They'll hand me a line, and if I know it's a lie, I say, 'What about that? Your break-even is such-and-such. Don't tell me you're not making money. You're taking in one hundred ten thousand dollars a week.' " Producers respond with mutterings like "Wait a minute. Hold it"; thus confronted, they capitulate. So also, the Shubert Organization rarely said no to Michael Bennett.

The Continuous Clash of Egos and Crafts

"Egos" and "temperaments" are the bane of a producer's life. Nicholas Howey, who has worked mostly in regional theater but has dealt with Broadway celebrities, contends that "people don't get into this business unless their egos are suffering. Their kickback is some kind of love. The more they are like that, the tougher it gets." And to some extent, they are all like that. What to do? He is sure that the problem is not unique to

musical theater: "It's just worse. The artists have an idea they don't want
to give up. It's theirs. And that gets in the way. They could be dead wrong,
and it takes an awful lot of time till they discover that they're dead wrong."
Howey contrasts magnetism or charisma with diplomacy. Either is a pre-
requisite for leadership. Equipped with one or the other, those in charge
are able to reduce destructive conflict, but "it's very difficult." Hard enough
outside New York, the trouble deepens on Broadway. Most of all Howey is
bothered by the "ego that everyone wears on his sleeve. . . . I've met
thirty or forty of these people in the last year—and oh, boy!" From top to
bottom they are all temperamental: "It's a very temperamental business.
I'm very temperamental." And then as an afterthought, either mistaking us
for men in the business or universalizing his perception of a certain subcultural phenomenon, he exclaims, "I suspect that the two of *you* are temperamental." (True.)

The Tony Awards

With inescapable conflict on every side and within every subdivision, one
annual event is calculated to draw the whole musical theater community
together. This, ironically, is a television event at which Tony Awards are
presented for the best work of a given season. It, too, is a show, this one
produced by the League of American Theaters and Producers. Few would
demur from Peter Stone's opinion that it is also a two-and-a-half-hour
commercial for the New York theater. Where self-congratulation is the
rule, Stone points out that "writers are the only group not allowed (in 1983)
to go up alone to collect their awards. . . . All the actors, all the directors,
all the choreographers, all the designers go up alone. For Best Play, the
writer and the producer go up together. Now there are eight producers.
So eight producers go up and the writer gets lost among them." This
appearance of the writer among multiple producers sometimes applied even
to straight plays. On occasion authors of musicals did not appear on camera
at all.

[One year] five Tonys [were] given off-stage: Best Sound, Best Lights, Best Set,
Best Book, and Best Score. Technicians and creators are put into one category,
and none of them was considered important enough to telecast.

The villains of this piece are producers, unfeeling about the problems of the
theater, "businessmen treating the talent like real estate." Stone and many
other writers idealize the old-fashioned producers who were businessmen,

too, but better and brighter in their line than the new breed. "They did not humiliate the talent."

The Tony Award ceremony, a symbolic ritual of unity within the industry, also produced divisiveness. A cooperative activity with competitive components led to discontent, even among winners if they happened to be authors. Stone as president of the Dramatists Guild voiced that discontent most publicly and most forcibly. He saw authors as gratuitously degraded once a year. And, much more seriously, he saw them as victims of injustice all year long. Stone was in the thick of an imbroglio that the *New York Times* referred to as "a bitter dispute on Broadway, dividing those who write plays and those who produce them."[6] The authors' unhappiness over Tony Awards, such as it is, or was, only affected their sense of self-esteem. The "bitter dispute" hit their pocketbooks.

When Conflict Goes to Court

As we saw, in 1982 the League of New York Theatres and Producers brought an antitrust suit against the Dramatists Guild to overturn a forty-one-year-old contract governing minimum royalties for playwrights, lyricists, composers, and bookwriters. But by October 1983, a *Times* writer could report that "as the case is waiting to be heard in United States District Court, the issue is being resolved in practice by the increasing use of waivers and royalties in dozens of plays." Bernard Jacobs, president of the Shubert Organization, which owns seventeen theaters and produces many of the plays for them, is quoted as saying, "I don't do any shows where I don't get some waiver or deferral agreement from the beginning. It's something I insist upon. I did it with *Dreamgirls* and even with *Cats*—and you couldn't have a hotter property than that."[7] In reaction to this practice, as recorded by the press, came Peter Stone's response, in substance identical with his private remarks. So was his ambivalence. Stone was quoted in the *Times* on the use of waivers and deferrals: "We are humiliated by it; we hate it and loathe it. But you can either have no money with a play open or have no money with a play closed. Which is more advantageous?"[8]

Samuel G. Freedman, author of the *Times* article, continues:

Hit musicals like *Nine* and *La Cage aux Folles* opened only after their royalty holders—the playwright, director, composer, lyricist and designers—had agreed to reduce their royalties until the show became profitable. Because *La Cage* must pay off a $5 million investment, the wait may last years. [Actually, it recouped in less than a year.]

"It's both distasteful and unavoidable," said Gilbert Parker, an agent of the William Morris Agency. . . . Martin Sherman, the author of *Bent,* lamented, "You spend two years writing a play and then the waiver is a fait accompli."[9]

Two days before *Bent* was to open on Broadway in 1979, Sherman's producers asked him to give up his royalties: "With a large cast, a mechanized set, a five-figure weekly theater rental, and a star to pay in Richard Gere, the producers said they needed the royalties due Mr. Sherman to pay for advertising—or the show might close." The show ran for seven months, but Martin Sherman informed the *Times* that he received full royalties for only one week.[10]

Why the inequity? Freedman recites the same litany we hear from all our respondents. The fixed cost factor is overwhelming. It includes theater rental, advertising, and wages to musicians, stage crews, and actors. All of the latter are unionized. Thus, royalties offer producers one of the few places for cutting the budget. "That cut, at the standard rate for play-wrights—ten percent of weekly box office receipts for a drama, six percent for a musical, scarcely seems out of line," but "the thousands of dollars in royalties can span the gap between red and black ink."[11]

On the other hand, agents and producers defend waivers or deferrals as indispensable. Without them, backers cannot be repaid as quickly as possible and might recoil from investing again. "As an example, many producers mention *Woman of the Year,*" a fact we can confirm from our own data. "In its two-year run," writes Freedman, "the musical paid off almost all of its royalties and only a pittance of its investment." With this anomaly in mind, a bookwriter offers us a witticism: *"Woman of the Year* is the scandal of the year."* There is no question that *Woman of the Year* provided ammunition for the League of New York Theatres and Producers in its lawsuit against the Dramatists Guild. The League's case, as encapsulated in the *Times,* was precisely that "investors must take precedence over royalty-holders in being paid or the financial foundations of Broadway may be jarred." May be jarred? In the crapshoot that underlies these financial foundations nobody claims to have found any sanity at all. Instability is already so great there can be little left to jar. Freedman himself concludes his piece with a pithy statement of the writer's dilemma. It is a quotation attributed to many. "You can make a killing on Broadway but you can't make a living."[12]

A highly experienced agent suggests one way to alleviate the writer's plight. She favors a union. Her model is the Writers Guild, which protects movie and television writers: "The Guild has been effective. And I deal with it a lot. Various of my clients belong to that union. I've worked very hard with them to set clearer and better standards." Since Broadway producers have begun to chip away at the old Dramatists Guild contract, such standards are more urgent than ever—and were in fact clarified in the new Dramatists Guild agreement of 1985, on which we have already dwelt.

Our agent refers to *Woman of the Year* not to show that investors were badly treated, although at first they were, but to show that writers are cooperative. They accepted what is now known as the *Woman of the Year* formula: "When the points for their people became too high, they renegotiated them." Further: "I've always found that when you struggle on getting a production into line, the writer is most cooperative. It's his work and his only time to get it on. He'll sacrifice more than anyone else. The stars and the directors are far less interested and far less cooperative."

Hands: Visible and Invisible

Yet, now and then the actors, the directors, the producers, the theater owners, even the much-maligned unions have also shown a certain aptitude for sacrifice. Cynics or realists might interpret short-range sacrifice as a technique by which to gain long-range preferment. When the sacrifice pays off everyone gains. The show goes on. Through the intervention of something like Adam Smith's marvelous invisible hand, selfish interest is said to produce a state of perfect competition that miraculously serves the common interest. Just so with social problems, including those that are set forth here. Given the commercial nature of a common enterprise, all relations in the musical theater are clothed in socioeconomic vestment. Selfishness is as rampant as Smith said it was in the early days of industrial capitalism. Business is still business and the business of America is still business. Why should musical theater be an exception to the rule?

On Broadway art matters; but when it does not simply become business, art matters less than business. Meanwhile, the striving to succeed continues. Dissonance, cognitive and otherwise, is its accompaniment.

Arthur Laurents, who takes pride in his craft, recognizes that readiness to cede precious dialogue is of paramount importance in the exercise of that craft. Such ceding defines the give and take of which we hear so much. It is generally regarded as the precondition for success. If give and take is not the precondition of success, it is the more familiar but not a sufficient condition. Compete, give and take boldly, slyly, by confrontation or indirection; be mindful, however, that you are involved in "antagonistic cooperation."

In this type of cooperation, deadlocks are the end of the game; an artist often can be replaced, but there are times when the project itself comes to a premature end.

Thus, along with conflict and antagonism, the free enterprise of competition must also generate its opposite, "self-sacrificing cooperation." Here the invisible hand of selfish competition must be submerged.

The Reduction of Conflict

Thus far our focus has been on what we observe as probably the normal conflict among specialists who create a musical—among lawyers, agents, bookwriters, directors, actors, composers, lyricists, and so forth—among and between all the various crafts and occupations called forth to create first the project and then the show. Conflict through business or artistic disagreement is inevitable and ubiquitous. There are shows, however, that the creators cite in which collaboration is wonderful and harmonious (in retrospect), such as Stephen Schwartz's *Godspell,* Jule Styne's *Gypsy,* Sheldon Harnick's *She Loves Me.* Each author may recall a "best." But even at these times there is conflict. The shows cited were ultimately successful, but the "harmony" of collaboration hardly correlates with flop or success. The normal experience is, as Peter Stone has put it, "exciting but unpleasant." Yet cooperation and collaboration proceed. No doubt Prince is right that "you have to be neurotic to be in musical theater."

How is conflict *limited* to antagonistic cooperation? Because, if not limited, the project is called off while trying to be conceived, or aborted before rehearsal or closed out of town. Who knows how many there are; such events are not systematically defined or recorded. A set designer who liked the score but not the book of a musical told us he quietly withdrew when "[the author] took a look at my designs and hated them." His judicious resignation stopped interminable conflict. He was replaced. (The show nevertheless flopped.)

But besides termination of the show or excision of dissenters, there is a stronger and more prevalent force that limits conflict. It is the old leadership appeal to the common touchstone, the whole show, the community, the group aim, everybody's shared integrity. There is too much invested—emotionally, creatively, financially; the show must not only go on, it must "hang together" at the core and in all its components.

Laurents is a champion of the show (as Aristotle was more than twenty-five centuries ago) in which every part is appropriate to the whole: "Steve Sondheim played, I guess, two-thirds of *Sweeney Todd* for me. It was supposed to be a small dark comedy." According to Laurents, the staging was inappropriate. A small black comedy did not call for an overwhelming set that suggested social comment: *"Sweeney Todd* is about revenge, and revenge is timeless." In the Broadway production—so goes this critique— it was pinned to a specific locale and embedded in the Industrial Revolution; it ceased to be a comedy. But for cable TV, "The musical was taped in close-ups without any enormous effects: It was much more successful" —the essence expressed more clearly.

Laurents obviously shares the general respect for Sondheim as a serious theater artist. But for Laurents, the idea that shows should be "all of a piece" also applies to *42nd Street,* a more lightweight but perfectly valid form of entertainment that may or may not be to the taste of high culture consumers but does what it sets out to do, in this instance by giving the audience an extravaganza. Though it is set in the 1930s, pseudoserious comment on the Great Depression would not work in a deliberately frivolous show.

Incongruous elements may spoil any show that unravels at precisely those points where seamlessness should be the objective. If the fabric is loose, "egos clash." These clashes are most pronounced in the musical theater, where story-lyric-music-costume-set-lighting-dance all must coalesce for success. The constant sense of attaining that wholeness in the mind of a strong producer or director is used to mediate conflict—but can never eliminate it.

Arthur Masella, a director so far devoted to only one craft, doubts that any tension point is more acute than others in a constellation made up of tension points. Director and choreographer do clash; so do director and designer, actor and composer. Masella observes conflict "in every department." From the responses and explanations reported in this chapter it would be hard to draw any other inference. Whether, as Masella insists, "The director must be the arbitrator because the buck stops with him" is arguable. More likely, the buck never stops till a consensus is achieved. Then the thing is done—unless it is redone or undone.

Gail Berman, the producer who does and does not believe that the buck stops with her, is no less aware of friction and its ubiquitous nature than Masella. The friction is there, but "it's healthy friction. It keeps everybody on his toes." When the outcome is positive, this formulation fits every musical. It reminds us that without friction there can be no movement. Artistic movement may develop through a flow of "healthy compromises" or "creative solutions," as one theater agent observes, but she adds that executives or artists in collaboration must avoid "lethal compromises" because then conflict may (or may not) recede but the "wholeness" and the "integrity" of the show gets killed. In conclusion, it is safe to say that without conflict, there is no cohesion, no wholeness, no sense of harmony. *The development of a musical must create and resolve conflicts in order to attain integrity.*

8. The Anatomy of Collaboration: Hierarchy, Critique, Consensus, and Creativity

If conflict is the ubiquitous feature of a collective art form like musical theater, then the dilemma of collaboration remains. How is order or cooperation maintained through conventional hierarchical authority that yet allows creative participation and even mutual inspiration to prevail? In large corporate arrangements, those who deviate from and carp about the party line—those gadflies, the individualists who form cabals are isolated, monitored, and dismantled or removed. They cannot "go too far." But in the collective hierarchy of a musical show, where a premium on original ideas is taken for granted, such ideas must be tied into other ideas or converted by intermediaries into serving the vision of a whole show. The brute force of authoritarian control would inhibit or preclude self-expression. Conversely, an anarchy of individualists would let loose an intolerable divisiveness, hatch artistic factions, and lead to economic disaster.

Our unit of study, the Broadway musical, provides a miniature version of the Hobbesian question: how do we maintain any order at all? Writ large among superpowers or other nation-states, it is writ small but just as significantly on that fraction of a community we have sought to understand in this book. Every human group, including the group of two, lives precariously. We subsist on the edge of chaos. Humankind, in possession of culture, is providentially intractable, notoriously unpredictable, filled with impulses that are ungovernable. This is the backdrop of our condition. But the Hobbesian answer (in effect), that we must maintain order "by Draconian means, with an iron fist," has proved to be as impractical as it is offensive to the moral sense. Quarrelsome, irrational, aggressive, ever-

229

larger and more numerous groups of the species have so far managed to maintain a tolerable existence.

An ageless struggle by artists for freedom of personal expression provides every society with a spiritual vanguard that abhors tyrants. For the most part, American musical theater arose as a form of entertainment, by sons and daughters of immigrants, to uplift that spirit. It has become a castle of hopeful fantasy on the edge of the desert of despair. Neither sweet reason nor brute force can create such a castle. Cooperation, coordination, collaboration do. Whether the brief affections among members of a team are sincere or simulated hardly matters. One such attitude can seldom be separated from the other. But the ceaseless tension between forces of freedom by artists and forces of authority by the director or producer who controls and channels self-expression creates constant turmoil in the collaborative structure of each Broadway musical.

The formal hierarchy of authority moves from producer to director to primary creators, secondary designers and interpreters (including actors and musicians), managers and "hired hands." The designers and interpreters must adjust to the demands of the primary creators as they in turn adjust to the director who must deal with the demands of the producers. But these accommodations are for the most part instruments of "diplomatic control." Ultimately, we have been arguing, collaboration emerges from an underlying population that is anything but powerless. Peter Stone says: "These are your partners, your life's partners, the show being your life. This is a [collective] marriage you're going to have to work at." There is a community of collaborators; there is a "company."

In the company hierarchy, when all goes well, personal rights and duties having been allotted, there must arise a larger unity experienced as teamwork. Within each set of teams, individual artists submit to a partial submergence of self but also feel a margin of freedom to create, to be heard, respected, considered—to offer suggestions that may even be accepted by their group leaders. In turn, they accept the reality that their performances are subject to relentless daily scrutiny and evaluation around which they adjust or negotiate and without which there can be no new consensus. It is within this arena of give and take that collective art generates a product, the musical, that no artist could do alone.

Authority: The Boss or the Bosses?

Who then is the boss in a theoretically "democratic family," or community where every member sees himself as a collaborator contractually bound to all the others? The lawyer Farber's spontaneous answer to this question is categorical: "The producer is the boss. Why? Because he hires and fires. Only the producer can run the show." Not the director? "But the producer hires the director." No paradox about this. Still, hardly missing a beat, Farber lays out the paradox: "I've sat up all night with managers and directors. Each one tries to tell me his is the most important role in the show. That's bullshit. They're *all* the most important." To a prime legal counsel the producer's ascendancy is clear until it is challenged by the director. Each one maintains his is the most important role, and they are both wrong. In no time at all, Farber's picture gets cloudy. *They,* not just the would-be bosses, but designers, writers, and actors are most important. Farber's not atypical reasoning simply oscillates: "The only reason the producer's more important is that he can fire them all." Very well. "But, if he's got any brains, he won't fire them all. His job is, number one, getting money, and number two, hiring the right people." A tough job, tougher than a lawyer's:

The legal problems are solvable. We either can get the rights or we can't get the rights or we can get them with certain qualifications. When you're dealing with people, problems aren't always solvable in the same way.

They are even less solvable when we take Farber's Orwellian dictum into account: "Let me say this. All people are created equal. It's just that some are created more equal than others."

Who truly is most important and consequently has the "final say" in a pervasively collaborative effort? There can be no more plausible answer than that of Walter Kerr, a critic and author, who spent ten years of his life directing some ninety plays in Washington, D.C.: "It changes from show to show." As formal authority is somewhat fixed by title and contract, the moving element is power. This abstract quality is spread through the hierarchy, and whosoever has the most power is "the muscle." People with the least power are usually ignored in decision making, but there are exceptions. And these exceptions become a rule in themselves. Let us take an extreme example.

The Power of the Powerless

On the face of it, actors are powerless. They do not create; they interpret in accordance with the wishes of those who do create. Does it really work that way? Berman, the producer, is sure that "actors have no voice," until she unself-consciously amends her statement, *"Contractually,* they have no voice." So speaks the producer, tacitly admitting that there are extracontractual considerations. Carrie Robbins, costume designer, insists that actors have no say: "Good costume designers don't listen to an actor. I know one who says, 'If you don't wear that hat, we'll get another actor.' " So the actor, apart from a possibly electrifying performance onstage, is, as Lonny Price says, "at the bottom of the totem pole." (This spot is shared by musicians in the pits, who, however, sometimes rearrange the music on their own.) So much for them. But what about someone like Katharine Hepburn? "Oh, Katharine Hepburn is Katharine Hepburn. Everyone listens to her." Is it worth deferring to her if she is adamant about something? "In many cases, yes." So an actor is an actor. But a star is a star, a celebrity is a celebrity, and they are high on the totem pole. This is so if for no other reason than that large sums of money may be riding on their names.

They lack "muscle" only if their names are as unfamiliar to the public as those of most producers and directors. On the other hand, totally unknown names, those of "the producer's wife, the director's girlfriend, or the casting director's friends" may flex muscle enough: "You talk to them." Formal affiliation intersects with informal power. Why not? Cultivating those just outside an allegedly small group is a facet of "the psychological method," as Jules Fisher, and others who allude to the subject more circumspectly, understand it. Fisher deplores this violation of the rules, which, he assures us, is nonetheless a real factor. And, "That's not what theater is about. It's like graft. It's not the clean way. But it's there. You can't deny that."

With some actors, benign solicitude of the kind Dr. Spock would prescribe is simulated. With others it is genuine. If for many, Hepburn is Hepburn, for Walter Kerr, "Merman was Merman. She never had one flop in her whole long career." Hepburn and Merman are first among equals in a democratic family setting. Or they were. For it strikes Kerr that today we are in a nonstar period. Even so, it is still necessary for authority figures to butter up ordinary actors, some of whom by Equity union rules are "principal actors" and have strong contractual rights. Let the producer, director, and other executives be wary about how they treat the "lowly" actor. Creative ideas or disruptive conduct can emerge from any source properly or even improperly channeled.

Diplomatic Control: A Case Study of the Cast Album

The daily balance of authority and artistic expression, however, must always tilt to conserving authority in the "normal" run of affairs. The inmates must never be allowed to run the asylum, but in musicals, the divisive antics of top executives (producers, director, and primary creators) too often provide evidence for never allowing them full authority. When the show has been put together and lo! it works, it runs, then, the special "theater of the cast album" offers us a view of this balance of power in a tight little collaborative world away from the packed house, yet playing to a wider audience.

Tom Shepard is widely known for his excellent, theatrically true original cast recordings. Over a period of years he made RCA and then MCA cast albums and now makes them freelance. He works very closely with composers, lyricists, bookwriters, conductors, and orchestrators. He makes no mention of producers (or agents and lawyers) until we wonder if teamwork at this level is difficult: "Only if you deal with somebody like David Merrick, who's impossible." It turns out that the old-style single producer may be a presence *and* a nuisance even in something so ancillary to the show as a cast album. Only this seemingly omnicompetent type interferes with "the very good working relationship" that Shepard generally enjoys.

And then this flat statement needs to be modified. If what Shepard wants on the album is different from what his collaborators are used to, "it's either gratefully received—'Oh, what a wonderful idea! Let's try that'—or 'What the hell do you think you're doing with my baby?' " And then? "You may cut the baby in half. Or someone just makes an end run" (presumably with the whole baby). Neither solution reflects the wisdom of Solomon. Then again, how many rulers can be expected to display such wisdom? Most rulers, when they are not simply manipulated by their courtiers, lay down the law. It is their prerogative, and with it they achieve good working relationships. Resentful of one patriarchal ruler, Shepard, within his turf, soon echoes all top executives in musical theater: "I don't feel comfortable making a cast album unless I know that I in fact have the final say about what goes into it."

But a moment later we hear in slightly more conciliatory tones: "I do require consensus by contract about what gets recorded. The creators have to participate in the selection of which material goes on the record. I mean, if they're extremely eager to have a certain number, and I hate that number, chances are they will prevail." How far will they prevail? "I'm not so sure. At least we'll do the recording which I may or may not issue." For the moment, they are appeased. The number is recorded, but whether or not it will be issued is out of their hands.

Shepard's domain is mostly terra incognita to the makers of a musical, and he rightly sees record making as an art form in itself:

Mandy Patinkin, Bernadette Peters, Thomas Z. Shepard, James Lapine, Stephen Sondheim at Sunday in the Park with George *Recording Session (1984)*

Pictured here at the recording session for Stephen Sondheim and James Lapine's Broadway musical *Sunday in the Park with George* are, *left to right,* Mandy Patinkin (who played George), Bernadette Peters (who played Dot), Thomas Z. Shepard (the album's producer and then RCA Red Seal Division vice president), James Lapine (bookwriter/director), and Stephen Sondheim (composer/lyricist). The digital recording sessions took place in RCA's Studio A in New York on May 27 and 28, 1984. (Photo credit: Billy Rose Theatre Collection, New York Public Library.)

I think there are some very bad show albums because people didn't pay attention. For instance, *Coco* is not a good album. I think the *Woman of the Year* album could have been better. They don't sound right. The performances don't quite deliver. There are things on them that you can't understand unless you study the liner notes because they make contextual references. . . . There's no attention paid to ambience, to perspective, and so it sounds bad; it sounds just like a collection of numbers. It doesn't have a theatrical feeling to it.

When a cast album is made, it needs yet another kind of guided collaboration:

Remember, the theatrical job is done. They've already put a ribbon on their work, and now they're in a fairly alien atmosphere. No sets, no lighting, no costumes. To a degree, they're secure: they know what they've got. *And* they're insecure: they don't quite know how a studio operates. That makes for a very good working relationship.

By and large they work very well: "I must say that though the sessions are hard work, there's usually not much flaring of ego." Insecurity in an atmosphere alien to them but familiar to him subdues the kind of squabbling that might go on if everyone felt at home. Shepard, as producer-director, has the key role—a role he plays unobtrusively and therefore all the more effectively. The cast album is his baby, to be cut or not as he sees fit.

In this context, composers, lyricists, bookwriters, conductors, orchestrators, and sound engineers recede a bit and actors come to the fore. On them he bestows his warmest accolades: "They are wonderful to work with. They'll risk a lot. They'll take chances for you. They'll try anything." The record producer skillfully works with the actors; he is delighted with their malleability: "This is hard work but lots of fun." Since the material is human, he is collaborating as a choreographer collaborates with a dancer or a painter with a model. A gulf separates these collaborators if only because on his home ground he is far less replaceable than they are. The boss presides diplomatically and the others gracefully comply.

Authority and Consensus

While making a cast album is certainly another collaborative art form in which we can sense the flow of control and its outcome, this enterprise lacks the open-ended, myriad small-group opportunities for conflict, and dissension that mark the creation of the original show. Arthur Laurents "always found a threesome more complicated than a twosome"; he also knows that in musical theater, creation of a show cannot be limited in numbers. In contrast to any other art form, "the *whole thing* winds up being a collaboration—whether you like it or not." On balance, he likes it. But he also knows it is based on "give and take," critique, conflict and inspired discussion leading to consensus.

How do authority and conflict and consensus work? Here is how one ˙ tough-minded director responded with an illustration:

I felt the work [a song] was not good enough—was not achieving what it set out to do. The composer, lyricist, and librettist felt it did and I said, "Well, in that case, I'm wrong. For you. If you believe in this, then get someone else." I don't think it's a director's function to insist on his ideas. You insist up to a point and then you say, "Well, if you don't see it that way, okay, I'm the wrong director," because in the theater, when you get right down to it, somebody has to be captain of the ship. . . . There is no way when the collaborative team is at odds for the thing to work. Somebody has to give and somebody has to take responsibility. And I think the other way to do it is, I said to the author, "Well, convince me that it's right."

So there are (at least) two sides of a "captain": the "order giver" and the "consensus maker."

Authority, the Small Group, and Collaborative Work

Most of the ideas that transform a written script and piano score into a living work emerge from a multitude of two-, three-, or four-person craft groups carrying out the dictates and suggestions of the director. In this analysis, we will assume that small groups are basic units within which there are a "superior" and "subordinates," that is, any small group within a hierarchy of authority—composer, arranger, conductor, or composer and lighting designer. Take the director, who has the authority in many different small-group configurations.

Lonny Price describes some functions of a director, the key artistic authority. First, control over the production: "When you're working on a Hal Prince show, you know who's running the show. You know who the top man is. The shoes don't get on stage without Hal Prince saying, 'I like those shoes.'" Next, organizational efficiency or morale: "When you're working for him, it's a lot like doing it for the old Gipper. It's his team and you're all on it together. He has an enormous amount of enthusiasm. It's terribly exciting." Then, control of the vision of the *whole* show by being the only one who knows every idea that has flowed to him from all others, and the one who decides which ideas to direct back to them. Price again:

Steve [Sondheim] worked a lot with us on *Merrily,* explaining the numbers and the moments, but mostly what we got done was with Hal. If you're trying to please everybody you're in a lot of trouble. I think that's why there is a director. He's one man to talk to. He has meetings with Steve and George Furth [the bookwriter] and all the others. They say, "God, I wish Lonny would stop doing that," and then have him give me the note. If I had everybody coming to me and saying, "Do this," I'd go crazy.

But as we have seen, every specialist must develop his or her own work and merge it with the craft of several others. Conflicts are built into this process, the more so under severe time pressure and daily, hourly critique. The constant testing of ideas occurs in a cauldron called the rehearsal period when a *written* script and score must become *live*.

Research on the operation of small groups is voluminous. Many experiments simulate organizational situations, but others are carried out in natural settings—in factories, offices, military camps, at political events, in classrooms. In this context, we are particularly interested in industrial social psychology focused on "conflict resolution" such as that of Chris Argyris's "expressive learning"[1] or Norman Maier's work on "problem solving."[2] These general ideas are directly applicable to collaboration in small groups creating a musical. They fit Masella's perception:

When you get disasters, real flops, not just shows the critics don't like, but those that fall apart, that have no rhyme or reason to them—at the bottom of all that, you're likely to find lack of communication or mutual understanding.

It depends on "whether or not our people talk and get through to each other." Talk includes "screaming and yelling." In the course of every production, "people get angry at other people" and let them know it. To Masella these outbursts are "mix-ups" that do no harm. Often they are useful. So-and-so openly vents his anger by informing an associate that "I hate what you did." The associate replies, "Well, I hate what you did." In that way, "what we don't like" becomes clear, and the group, having aired its differences, can reach "some sort of resolution." The dissensus is a means by which to achieve a new consensus, perhaps a better artistic solution.

We should remember that constant critique is at the cutting edge of every encounter. When the "leader" (superior or boss) is too harsh, too swift to reject, too scornful or sarcastic, conflict ensues over and above the merits of an idea. Most supervisors and artists (and critics) are untrained in the art of informed critique. This art carries at least two major and implicit injunctions: (1) learn what the others are trying to do, and (2) adjust your comments to concrete matters that either now deter or might later enhance their effort. Simple enough but violated by the insensitive or unsophisticated evaluator who usually wants to go for different goals and by other means, and whose aggression is provocative. "That's awful." The conflict commences. Or, "Why do it that way? This way is better." Or, "It's too fast and won't work."

Some few research results on major factors that generate creative solutions in small groups can be briefly stated. Within a small group (two to six) where there is a conflict over ideas and the leader (ordinarily one in authority) is "open," not "closed" to ideas, the subordinates are "assertive" as opposed to passive, and the group has a "mixed" as opposed to a homogeneous background (occupation, age, gender, etc.) and all are committed to the goals of a larger project—these factors measurably increase the possibility of finding creative solutions. Otherwise, the outcome is (1) imposed by the leader and/or (2) things are done the conventional way, or (3) they are done in an ill-fitting manner. On average, consensus on a creative solution that arises out of interaction by group discussion induces greater individual satisfaction than solutions that are imposed or mechanically repeated.[3]

Through the hierarchy of networks, new solutions are passed along formal and informal lines of communication. Barnard's description, already quoted, deserves to be requoted: "Back and forth, up and down, the communications pass, reporting obstacles, difficulties, impossibilities, accomplishments; redefining, modifying purposes level after level."[4] This is not so different from Masella's important point (which we requote):

> The assistant [director] helps [the director to] put it all together, keeps the channels of communication open and makes sure people know what's going on. . . . Everybody's all over the place. Someone or a small group has to be sure where everybody else is, what the others are doing and thinking.

At the top of a hierarchy is the director with his small group of primary creators and their shifting but constant conflict and consensus. "Give us, oh director, our daily critique." "Give me, my team, your best effort, your best ideas."

By critique and new solutions, jointly inspired, new ideas flow daily to the top executives, the primary team, including, at crisis times, the producer(s), and especially the director. They seize and weave and then "order" cuts or new actions—all intuitively calculated to integrate the show, inform its emotional arc, transforming the basic "script-score" into a live, complete musical theater work. Interpersonal collaboration, played out in a myriad of small groups, is transformed into the larger structure of collaboration across these groups. Finally a whole show emerges at the dress rehearsal. Sometimes. And sometimes not.

Selection and Critique among Primary Artists

Most of the time, Harold Prince told us, he fluctuates between liking the collaborative way and loving it (like the famous gamut from A to B). "If you know what you're getting into when you go in there, you might as well face the fact that you get angry once in a while, but you get something in return. You get Jerry Robbins; it's worth the trouble." He recognizes himself as a gregarious man, facile, "very verbal," requiring company and reveling in it. With all these traits, he "gets to know people real fast." No trouble there, but after thirty years at it, perhaps a bit of calculation: "I'm not a secret keeper. I tell them right off what's wrong with me. Maybe that's more of a ploy than I'm willing to admit. I let them know my misgivings about myself and about their material." Still, "I am nervous. I worry." But now Prince does not have to admit to any anxiety; when he thinks he is wrong, he just says so. "It's unnecessary for me to say that I don't know something or that *I*'m scared." Success has liberated him enough to announce: "Everything we did yesterday was sheer trash. Forget it. Let's start from scratch." The ultimate self-criticism.

Problems arise only when his coworkers get "too defensive." Prince welcomes anyone who "criticizes a scene or a song and is articulate about it" as a real collaborator who, however, had better have an alternative in mind: "I suspect the defensive person who resists going back and doing it again." That person is a spurious collaborator.

Prince's *beau ideal* of a real collaborator is Stephen Sondheim. Their relationship worked without having to be worked at, uncomplicatedly, perdurably, in prosperity and in adversity. Why did this director and this composer-lyricist get on so well? For starters, from Prince's point of view, because in all their years together, "Sondheim never resisted for one second." And in turn, now and then, when Prince was unhappy about a song, Sondheim told him, "You'll love it," and Prince came to find that he would. But more often,

Sondheim said, "Okay," went and wrote another one, and it was better. That is one of the ways we worked. He'd play a song and I immediately criticize it and he'd say, "Right." To this day, I think, when he plays a song for me, he's worried, and to this day, I will tell you, when I show him a scene [on stage], I'm worried. So, it's fair.

How rare is the empathy between these two men! Compare it with the way Prince feels about would-be collaborators who resist and are screened out:

Periodically they come in and play their material. If I don't like it at all, there's no point in going on. I say, "Thank you very much. I appreciate your playing for me."

But if I do like it, if it interests me, *I criticize it.* And if that leads nowhere I back away because it's never going to work. *Not between us.*

It may work between others. Perhaps the purveyors of material that did not engage Prince might go on to be successful. They have to find appropriate partners. The crux of the matter is not the material, often at least potentially first-rate, but the trust and empathy that, if it fails, will likely make a second-rate partnership. Which is statistically normal—and the result is usually, but not always, a second-rate show. Also normal.

Selecting the Right Directors

As we saw, the rise to power of the post-sixties director in the musical theater hierarchy created a scramble for that role by lyricists, lighting designers, actors, playwrights, choreographers, producers. Even some composers stepped up for a transient try. Some neophytes, still heady from the sixties, even believe they can create the whole show, write the book, the lyrics, the music, and also direct. Reality does not deter these "pushing young particles." In the history of Broadway musicals, only a single show ever succeeded in which one person actually created an original book (unadapted from another source) *and* the lyrics *and* the music: Marc Blitzstein in *The Cradle Will Rock* (1937). But delusions remain. For this reason, as several informants suggest, the Peter Principle is very active among primary musical theater creators who, according to Stone, "don't want to do what they know how to do," or more charitably, "want to do something they haven't done before," and will probably botch the job. To master one role in the theater takes some doing. There are nuances, niceties, mutual expectations, and other supersubtleties to be learned. They are unlearned in new rites of passage, in gradual resocialization. Insofar as personality is socially constructed, it makes chameleons of us all.

With due regard to the few directors who can be good leaders and even *auteurs,* the producer may err by picking a director who is totally unsuitable to a specific musical project. Like all professionals, a director must fit into the vision and action required by a given show. Examples of errors are legion. Charnin, for an old example, is still convinced that such a director was responsible for a pre-Broadway *débacle* called *Mata Hari.* How could this come to pass?

It happens when G [a powerful producer of the old school] produces a musical I write with Jerry Coopersmith and Eddie Thomas. I'm the lyricist. It's my idea. I want to get it on because I haven't done a show in four years. So I go to G because he makes things happen. G doesn't have backers' auditions. We never did them for *Mata Hari*. G hires Vincente Minnelli as the director. . . . Why does he pick Minnelli? To this day it is a mystery. We beg him not to hire Minnelli, but G has what Liv Ullmann calls "the muscle" and he uses it. We get Minnelli, and from the moment he says "Action" at rehearsal [thereby betraying his long and, we must note, successful career in Hollywood movies] it's clear that we have the wrong man for this musical.

Flops are instructive. Charnin learned from them, as in the private little drama synopsized above, that "the director is the key guy." Accordingly, Charnin experienced a familiar epiphany: "I resolved to become a director." And so he did. Along with Laurents, Schwartz, Tune, Prince, Kerr, Price, among those we interviewed who came from other roles into the new role, with or without training as apprentices in the craft. (Even Jules Fisher tried his hand at directing.) In life as in Broadway musical theater, any training on the job for new roles is governed by chance.

The Informal Apprentice

Indeed, there is no royal road to learning new roles in show biz or learning how to collaborate with several partners. For the small group of two or three creators who meet and click, scores and scores meet and are poorly fitted. For them there is no love at first sight; others are deprived of it at second sight. Mr. or Ms. Right may never come along. On the other hand, a foursome, however complicated, may work—even if the show is not a commercial success. For John Weidman, at the time a comparatively young bookwriter, *Pacific Overtures,* on which he collaborated with Prince, Sondheim, and Hugh Wheeler, was a turning point. It provided on-the-job training in collaboration among primary creators. A young writer emerged from that experience with the insight and confidence that were to serve him well then and thereafter.

At the time he was "half-apprentice and half-professional." Such a role is ambiguous, poorly defined, consequently difficult and troublesome, and Weidman lightly flails himself for not having been outspoken enough. From subsequent collaborations it is clear to Weidman that he "should never have been unable to look at the show independently," to offer suggestions on his own, rather than "wait for Hal to make it all better." As a full professional Weidman has learned how vital it is for collaborators "to stand up on their hind legs and holler about whatever they think, to argue and negotiate. That seems to me to be the life blood of any collaboration."

The project began with a straight play Weidman had written that Prince proposed to musicalize: "It was the end of the spring. Hal said, 'I'm going to Spain this summer and Steve [Sondheim]'s coming over for two weeks. I want him to do it.' " Hal had to be persuasive because at first "Steve was reluctant to do it," but after a while he too evinced enthusiasm for the project:

In the fall, when Hal came back to town, he and Steve and I started to meet once a week to talk about how the show might be turned into a musical. . . . I will frankly admit I was sitting there wide-eyed in the presence of these guys waiting to see what would happen.

Awestruck, Weidman, after completing the first act, was more observer than participant. "At that point, most of the conversations and decisions about what would be musicalized were taking place between Hal and Steve." Had Weidman been more experienced, "It would have been more of a three-way thing," but, with a rehearsal set for September 1975, Weidman finished the script that spring. "Hal was happy with it, but not *real* happy."

Therefore, with the addition of Hugh Wheeler, a playwright, it became a four-way relationship. Feeling frustrated, Weidman welcomed Wheeler as a consultant: "I was a big fan of Hugh's. I admired his musicals." All the better that "he became another member of the collaborative team." Weidman and Wheeler "wound up working together quite closely. To begin with, we completely rewrote the second act." That *Pacific Overtures* subsequently failed to recoup on Broadway (it got split reviews) does not detract from Weidman's recollection of a job well done. Furthermore, "Since then I've been in a couple of abortive theater projects. The show I'm doing now is almost finished, and I'm very happy with it. There's no doubt that working with Hal and Steve and Hugh served me in good stead." The latter show never made it to Broadway; we sense again that neither being well apprenticed nor being "happy" about the collaborative work has any direct relationship to the fate of a Broadway musical (though Weidman's *next* show, *Anything Goes* (1987), was a big hit).

Visions of Harmonious and Conflictful Collaborations

Working with Joe Stein (bookwriter), Jerry Bock (composer), and Jerome Robbins (director) was extremely gratifying to Sheldon Harnick. For, as he sees it, this quartet (and Hal Prince, the producer), playing harmoniously, brought *Fiddler on the Roof* into being. "It was a collaboration in the real sense. We all had our own roles to play, and they dovetailed at every production meeting." Of course, the collaboration could not have been a completely frictionless relationship. In any case, we can only report the recalled subjective responses to an interaction that either satisfies or disappoints those for whom it counts most heavily. With *Fiddler,* in the beginning and "for a change," no producer or director or agent was involved. The initial configuration was triangular. It consisted of Stein, Harnick, and Bock plus a star: "His name was Sholem Aleichem." The compatibility of these men, all possessed by an idea, boded well for their future agreement about a producer and a director who would help them "blend and balance" their way to success.

Hence it comes as no surprise that a lyricist like Harnick should exalt "real team feeling," which signifies that "all of us contribute, including me." Harnick first savored this feeling in *She Loves Me,* a musical that, despite the ascendancy of "a very strong director," diminished no one. (It failed to recoup on Broadway but hit ever after.) A foretaste of this pleasure came to him in *Fiorello,* a musical directed by George Abbott, who may have been Broadway's strongest director. Harnick again collaborated with Bock (the composer), Abbott (the director and cobookwriter), and Jerome Weidman, Sr. (the librettist): "Hal Hastings, our orchestra conductor, said he didn't remember ever having worked on a show in which there were so few problems." Problems did crop up on the road but they were easily resolved: "The show came in and it was a hit." Just so. Not bumpy or lumpy. This smoothness Harnick attributes to Abbott's guiding hand. The legendary director, after "generations and generations of experience, was still in his prime." Between his notion of how to put a musical together and Weidman [Sr.'s] literary abilities, "things went swimmingly." What about Sheldon and Jerry? "We were good, too." The show was a big hit and won the Pulitzer Prize.

Yet such harmonious collaboration with a hit show is rare. Stephen Schwartz asserts that

no one expects it all to be joy. . . . Personally, I had to overcome the *Godspell* syndrome. It took me about ten years to get over expecting that every experience could be like doing *Godspell,* with the kids saying, "Oh, let's get together in the barn and do the show." Since that was my first experience, I kept looking for it again. Finally, I have learned that *I'm not going to find it.* That's okay. There are other experiences of dealing with good, solid successful, creative people that can be inspiring.

Other recollections we heard conjured up tension, conflict, and doubts. A major bookwriter finds that a collaborator's mistrust is less troublesome to him than being accused of incomprehension.

George Abbott, Jerome Weidman, Sr., Robert E. Griffith, Harold Prince, Sheldon Harnick, Jerry Bock, Executive Team for Fiorello! *(1959)*

The top executive team of the hit show *Fiorello!* (1959) was a harmonious and successful collaboration: (left to right) George Abbott, director and coauthor; Jerome Weidman, Sr., bookwriter; Robert E. Griffith and Harold Prince, coproducers; Sheldon Harnick, lyricist; and Jerry Bock, composer. Conflict within this team was handled openly, directly, with mediation, and usually with creative solutions. (Photo credit: Billy Rose Theatre Collection, New York Public Library.)

Tom Bosley and Cast in Fiorello! *(1959)*

The hit show *Fiorello!* ran 796 performances at the Broadhurst Theatre and became another Broadway vintage musical play in the heritage of the Gershwin/Kaufman/Ryskind political satires in the late 1920s and early 1930s, starting with *Strike Up the Band* (1927). (Photo credit: Billy Rose Theatre Collection, New York Public Library.)

After all, an author isn't able to sit down and play the piano. That opens him to a certain amount of blackmail. I wonder why the composer can't rewrite a song. He tells me I don't understand. He can throw in a new song, but he can't rewrite that one. I trust him to be honest, but I don't know what he means. I go back and rewrite a scene ten or twenty times. Why can't he rewrite a song? There's no explanation. That's just the way it is.

Dealing with choreographers can also be trying, and about this problem the bookwriter is less baffled. It is more difficult because he and they "are talking different languages. You use words; they are abstract." In point of fact, "They don't like talk very much at all. Choreographers do not like words." They express ideas in movement and gestures; for them words "are too real, too direct," and their use points up a discomfiting fact about choreographers: choreographer-directors, using body language, are at odds with bookwriters, using words. "They'll try to remove as many words as they can, and a bookwriter makes his living out of words." This bookwriter would never try to dissuade junior members of his profession from working with these men ("God knows, they have a successful record. I wanted Michael Bennett to direct my shows"), but he warns them that they "will not be gratified by the relationship." Similarly, directors and choreographers also at times relate as antagonists. However, whether the collaboration is "harmonious" or "antagonistic," the pertinent action is that which results in generating new creative solutions to technical artistic problems. Then the collaboration is working (the quality of a given solution would be the subject of another treatise).

The Small Group with No One in Authority: Conflict and Consensus in the Songwriting Collaboration

Nowhere is the collaborative process seen more clearly than in writing songs for the theater, with the story as a starting point. Like the show, the song is a product larger than the collaborators; it comes about through incremental construction, the result of a multitude of agreements and disagreements, the product of a small group. But the songwriting group, the composer and lyricist, unlike a "company," usually has no hierarchy: one person is not given formal power *vis-à-vis* the other. (And we are of course talking about the cases where composer and lyricist are not the same person.) Here is a small group in which only a democratic *consensus* will do, even when there may be an informal leader. This is parallel to the situation not uncommon among top executives in musical theater and in some large corporations. It was the rule at the Constitutional Convention in

1776—also among the five Iroquois tribes who constituted a confederacy. It is still the rule at the United Nations, among representatives of the top world powers (as of 1946). The rule of consensus even holds ideally in American marriage, an arrangement often used by a clichéd analogy to characterize a songwriting team.

Maybe the awesome task of creating a family of songs (a score) explains why the goal of "perfect collaboration" is so often compared to another fiction, that of the "perfect marriage." In creating musical theater, good marriages may be relatively long-term (the Gershwin brothers, Lerner and Loewe) or short-term (the creators of *West Side Story* wrote only that one show together) or even serial (Harburg and Lane). More accurately, the songwriting partnership is most like a good business partnership. After all, one does not have to like a collaborator to produce great songs in great shows (W. S. Gilbert and Arthur Sullivan didn't get along for years), though good feeling provides a more congenial working environment.

Richard Rodgers, who had two long-term collaborators, Lorenz Hart and Oscar Hammerstein, felt that

in many ways a song-writing partnership is like a marriage. Apart from just liking each other, a lyricist and a composer should be able to spend long periods of time together—around the clock if need be—without getting on each other's nerves. Their goals, outlooks, and basic philosophies should be similar. They should have strong convictions, but no man should ever insist that his way alone is the right way. A member of a team should even be so in tune with his partner's work habits that he must be almost able to anticipate the other's next move. In short, the men should work together in such close harmony that the song they create is accepted as a spontaneous emotional expression emanating from a single source, with both words and music mutually dependent in achieving the desired effect.[5]

While "liking each other," "not getting on each other's nerves," "sharing outlooks and basic philosophies," and "being in tune with his partner's work habits," sound like guidelines for the ideal collaboration, in fact, Rodgers's long-time "marriage" to Lorenz Hart, which yielded a cornucopia of wonderful theater songs, was described by Rodgers himself as follows:

He [Hart] hated doing it [writing lyrics] and loved it when it was done. There was the never-ceasing routine of trying to find him, locking him up in a room, and hoping to fire his imagination so that actual words would get down on paper. It wasn't wise to leave him alone for a moment because he would simply disappear and have to be found all over again. His pencil would fly over the paper and soon the most difficult part of all would begin: the material had to be edited and he loathed changing any word once it was written down. When the immovable object of his unwillingness to change came up against the irresistible force of my own drive for perfection, the noise could be heard all over the city. Our fights over words were furious, blasphe-

George and Ira Gershwin at Work in Beverly Hills (1937)

The Gershwin brothers working in their Beverly Hills home in 1937—Ira writing; George at piano. Before becoming almost exclusive collaborators, each wrote over seventy songs with others, though only a few became hits. After teaming up in 1924, the brothers began to write a consistent stream of great theater songs that have outlasted the shows they came from, as well as cultural changes through the decades. Read *Fascinating Rhythm: The Collaboration of George and Ira Gershwin* by Deena Rosenberg. (Photo credit: courtesy Mrs. Ira Gershwin.)

Alan Jay Lerner and Frederick Loewe (ca. 1960)

Lyricist Alan Jay Lerner *(left)* and composer Frederick Loewe became a team later in their careers than the Gershwins, and then turned out a series of hit shows, including the vintage masterpiece *My Fair Lady* (1956). Loewe wrote almost exclusively with Lerner, but Lerner collaborated with others. They "split up" for over a year after their first hit. Rodgers and Hammerstein also suffered a year-long split, rarely reported; the vintage plays on Broadway with their great collaborative songwriting/story teams ended with the rock revolution. (Photo credit: Globe Photos.)

mous, and frequent, but even in their hottest moments we both knew that we were arguing academically and not personally. I think I am quite safe in saying that Larry and I never had a single personal argument with each other.[6]

Yes, a good business partnership. No paradoxical intimacies every day like those in a real marriage over many years in the same house. Maybe the ideal of a "life-long collaborator" is only an absurd myth. Maybe "serial teams" lasting only for several shows are more productive in creating new visions for the Broadway musical. Maybe, as in Sondheim's song, the dream of collaborators should be, "Marry me a little."

Arguments in a good collaboration are about technical matters, and as Rodgers says, they are not "personal," not ad hominem. Thus, this from Ira Gershwin, as told to Isaac Goldberg in his book *George Gershwin,* about the writing of "Fascinating Rhythm":

[George's tune had] a tricky rhythm . . . and it took me several days to decide on the rhyme scheme. . . . The rhyme scheme is a,b,a,c, —a,b,a,c. When I got to the eighth line I showed the lyric to George. His comment was that the fourth and eighth lines should have a double (or two-syllable) rhyme where I had rhymed them with single syllables. *I protested* and, by singing, showed him that the last note in both lines had the same strength as the note preceding. . . . But this George couldn't see, and so, on and off, *we argued for days.* Finally I had to capitulate and write the lines as they are today:

4th line: I'm all a-*qui*ver
8th line: —Just like a *fliv*ver,

after George proved to me that I had better use the double rhyme; because, whereas in singing, the notes might be considered even, in conducting the music, the downbeat came on the penultimate note.[7]

Ira's "capitulation" was the last note in a consensus over one of many conflicts that go into the construction of a song. But perhaps more frequently, profound conflicts in critique lead to dissolution of the partnership.

When Conflict Does Not Lead to Consensus

Sheldon Harnick recounts this experience with a potential collaborator on an idea Harnick initiated:

We had a very, very awkward scene, and finally I said, "I'm going to do this show myself because I don't think this is the right approach and I've begun to feel I'm going to make any composer I work with uncomfortable by breathing down his back." He was very upset by this. He even said, "You're a very capable composer; why don't we make this a collaboration? You do the music and I'll do the lyric." I said, "Can you do that?" He said, "I think so."

But it turned out he couldn't. Because, for the same reasons, I would bring in something I thought was right and he'd say, "That's wrong. Can't you hear it? That's wrong for this show." I'd say, "I think it's right." So, *we couldn't collaborate. We parted company.*

Collaboration is seldom as idyllic or professionally complete as it appears to have been for Rodgers and Hammerstein. Sometimes collaboration is done "piecework" style. In these cases the bookwriter and/or the composer and/or the lyricist are "loners" who work separately. Their solo work is ultimately pieced together. This method practically ensures malintegration, anything but the whole show that Aristotle and, in their own way, Laurents, Hammerstein, and Schwartz, among many others, so strongly endorse. Burton Lane reflects on the dangers of specialization. "You have book writers who don't know how to collaborate. They cannot sit in a room with other people. . . . You can work up to a point by yourself. But beyond that, it's very tough." Piecework collaboration is full of pitfalls. Sometimes the writers do not even have time to assemble in the same room: they have other piecework to do. They lead a freelance life, overloaded with commitments, and the quality of work usually suffers. The freelance life means coming and going, living a peripatetic life: "Show me a [lyricist, composer, bookwriter, director, or producer] and I'll show you someone whose bags are packed." The following "impossible collaboration," which Harnick now recalls, is widespread, even among professionals who "should know better":

We began to work, which would be difficult enough for somebody who was just a composer. But M. is also a performer and an orchestrator and either he was on tour in Canada or he was in California scoring a film, or he was in Paris with his family, or occasionally he was in New York. . . . It proved to be an impossible collaboration. Who could do it by tape and long distance? So we missed our deadline. The show was canceled.

The Click: When Creative Consensus Optimizes Solutions

But every funny now and random then, the right lyricist meets the right composer; there is a "click" and the magic of full collaboration generates moments of truth. The right note meets the right thought after numerous attempts and minor failures. So Harnick tells of his work with Bock:

He did not expect me to accept each of [his] musical themes as a thing in itself. I felt free to ask him, is it possible to give it a different release? Is it possible at this point in the song to go somewhere else? And he was very flexible. Yes, or no, for whatever reason . . . Jerry would many times suggest lines. Sometimes they would just occur to him while we were rehearsing songs, or he would sing and I would burst out laughing and say, "Wonderful."

Here, from the past, is an ideal collaborative paradigm: Ira Gershwin and Harold Arlen had been old friends since the thirties; each was a gentle, brilliant person and a serious artist who had years of collaborative experience with others and a bit with each other. An astute observer of the actual process of collaboration between Ira Gershwin and Harold Arlen for the score of the film *A Star Is Born* (written with Moss Hart) reports that first the outline of the story suggested seven scenes for songs to be sung by Judy Garland. One scene was for a "dive" (barroom) song in a situation that paralleled Judy's personal life. Both men knew Garland over many years.

Arlen played an eight-bar theme (which later became "the night is bitter / the stars have lost their glitter") and Gershwin responded with a title, "The Man That Got Away." Ira believed that the title is over half the work in writing a song. The subsequent musical and lyrical work between these two men was *"so close that each made suggestions on the music and lyrics; one ceased being merely a lyricist and the other a composer."* The song was a true wedding of their crafts; the working relation was full of mutual respect, sensitivity, and even love, for each other and for Judy Garland. The song became a classic.[8]

Perfect collaboration. Each person worked in his own craft, and worked in the other's, and was worked with even as he worked. Each understood himself, the other, and was understood even as he understood himself. When this happens, the ego is in the service of professional discipline: one listens with respect and criticizes with thought informed by the other's intent. As these men simultaneously exchanged feelings and thoughts, they created the ideas, and shared the incremental construction of their song— a new product for millions of others to experience. The same process of joint weaving of music and lyric and story also occurs on Broadway and, at times, among other small groups: arranger, set designer, costume designer; actor, director, lyricist, conductor; composer, conductor, dancers; and so on. When all the artistic work is woven together, then the fabric of a whole show may emerge. At times.

Secrets of Song Collaboration: Informed Critique and Consensus

These realities of a good working team of lyricist and composer are details in the process of creating a song that is accepted as "a spontaneous emotional expression from a single source." Critique is informed and constructive, easily given and readily accepted. Burton Lane refers to his work with Yip Harburg:

When I'd say to Yip, "That line's not clear," or "It doesn't seem right," he never argued; he would change the line. He respected my judgment and he would change it and there was no problem. I never worked with a more flexible lyricist. I think one reason Yip liked working with me is that I never objected if by accident he added notes that shouldn't have been there. But to me the lyric was more important than the tune because you had to say it right. The music was subjective. [The audience] would get that later.[9]

Frequently, mutual respect and creative consensus that allow good songs to emerge are only a one-time event or a growing, learning "how-to-give-and-take-critique," an intense encounter with your partner. Full collaboration can be learned, not from handbooks, but by practice. Harnick reveals some difficulties:

At first, even though we [Jerry Bock and I] did hit it off and became good friends as well as collaborators, it was always very hard to take criticism professionally and not personally. Both of us were thin-skinned. I've watched Jerry invite his wife down to hear something we've just done. We would ask her, "Give us your honest opinion," and she would say, "Gee, you've done better." And he would say, "What do you know?" So it's very, very difficult to accept criticism on an "objective" level.

Whether there is a fast "click" or a protracted learning time, a good collaboration does indeed have certain qualities of a good affair. But a good affair usually doesn't last. Thus Lane adds: "I loved writing songs with Yip. He was the best, the best. And worth the pain of other things just to sit in a room and write songs with him, *but* Yip and I were not talking after *Finian*."[10]

The Breakup

It is called breaking up. And it happens with some frequency among these writers of song (and writers of musicals). Even with a fairly extended relationship there comes "the end of a beautiful friendship," as the Arlen/Harburg song goes (unpublished, 1976, *marcato* and not too fast):

Here's to the end of a beautiful friendship
Here's to the stardust we promised to share,
Here's to our beautiful illusions,
May . . . they . . . still . . . be . . . there
For my . . .
Next affair.[11]

Burton Lane and Yip Harburg (1970s)

The lyricist E. Y. (Yip) Harburg wrote great songs with many composers: "Brother, Can You Spare a Dime?" with Jay Gorney; "April in Paris" with Vernon Duke; "Over the Rainbow" with Harold Arlen. The masterwork *Finian's Rainbow* was written with composer Burton Lane, whose musical imagination truly fitted the story's lyrics. Later, composer Lane teamed with lyricist Lerner for the cult show (and song) *On a Clear Day You Can See Forever* (1965). Maybe "serial collaborations" lasting only for several shows are most productive in creating new visions for Broadway musicals. Maybe the dream of collaborations should be like Sondheim's song title, "Marry Me a Little." (Photo credit: Mr. and Mrs. Burton Lane.)

Sheldon Harnick ruefully recalls:

I made a dreadful mistake. Jerry was very angry about something, very upset, and tended to be rigid on the subject, and instead of confronting him as I should have done and saying, "Look we have a problem and we'd better work it out . . ." I knew I should do that. (I'm not even sure of the reasons now.) I told myself, if I bring this up there will be such a fight that the whole project may go down the drain. That turned out to be a terrible mistake, because by holding my peace the problem only got greater. Eventually, although the show was done, it contributed to splitting us up. I don't know if Jerry has ever quite gotten over it. I think I did, but I was never able to get him to commit to another collaboration.

As one of our interviewees recalled, Hart's behavior became too much even for Richard Rodgers:

It got to the point with his drinking and general neurotic problems that they couldn't even collaborate unless Hart was in the same room with him. He had to be at the piano while Hart was there, and then Hart would write very quickly, but otherwise he was just irresponsible.

Even Rodgers and Hammerstein had a small split-up that lasted about a year; Lerner and Loewe had a major split after their first hit. Both teams did get back together. Harold Arlen and Yip Harburg broke up because of the "politics" of what was to become *Finian's Rainbow:* Harold did not like what he called "propaganda" and Yip called "education."

But for too many talented artists, the single life is not happy:

I don't have a lyric writer I'm teamed with; I don't have a bookwriter. I'm anxious. Anxious is a weak word. I am desperate to be involved in the theater and I have to try to get something rolling.

Not unusually, therefore, the disintegration of the partnership occurs visibly or *sotto voce* during the creation and production of the show—whether it succeeds or not.

The Designers: Authority and Creativity

In musical theater, where the director is the muscle most of the time, even he must merge his craft with that of many others, including so-called secondary artists. Why secondary? Although scenic, lighting, sound, dance, and costume designers, or conductors, musical directors, and orchestrators are important, they are conventionally classified in Broadway musical theater as secondary collaborators. They are to be treated respectfully, but not even the best of them are commonly heeded by primary artists. "I just had a designer, as big as there is, suggest that I change the location of one scene because it didn't fit in with his scheme for the show. Since he's very bright and very sensible, I considered it—for a moment." Sometimes, though, designers have crucial suggestions for directors and writers, as set designer Robin Wagner, lighting designer Jules Fisher, and costume designer Toni-Leslie James had for George C. Wolfe on *Jelly's Last Jam* (1992).

And yet—as always—the "bosses" must be diplomatic in judging the designers. Gail Berman, who has had experience on and off Broadway as a coproducer working with only one other producer, found that after exposure at an early meeting to the set of a show, she was most displeased with it. Riding in a taxi:

Susan and I looked at each other and said, "What the heck was that? What happened to the pyramids and everything else we wanted?" We didn't know how our director felt about it. There wasn't much intimate discussion at the meeting.

That night they called Tony, the director, who was as dismayed as they were. In fact, "It turned out that *nobody* liked what Karl had shown us." They minced no words and, "Tony told us, 'I'm so happy to hear that.' . . . He went to see Karl, who by the following afternoon had redone the whole thing."

The procedure was circuitous. The producers talked to the director who talked to the set designer. Would a set designer be so compliant if he had been challenged in the presence of others? Berman thinks not: "You don't tell him that his set isn't what you want in front of the costume designer and the lighting designer. You also don't ask your director what he thinks in front of those people." If someone is not humiliated before his peers he ungrudgingly tries to give them what they want. Karl, or anyone else in his position, might have balked if he had been put on the spot. Subtle social relations are at play. Hierarchical roles, formal and informal, call for a network of communication that must be used to keep or restore the peace.

Conversely, designers must be diplomatic with their "bosses." Jules Fisher is presented with a lighting problem: to make the dagger in an actor's hand visually salient. The director tells him to "raise the lights." This specialist knows his business. He does not quarrel with his superior, but simply orders his subordinate, the electrician, "not to change a thing but to take down the lights [on one side of the stage only]." Later, the director—seeing the dagger and sensing the drama—believing his orders have been fulfilled, says, "Gee, that's wonderful. I can see perfectly." Sure. "All right, I tell a fib, but as long as he's happy, why rock the boat?" As a man of experience, Fisher is able to overrule those who know less without offending them: "It's a little psychological game, and I have to win." The silent victory comes to him in an atmosphere of agreement whose upshot is, "I am pleased, the director is pleased, and the audience is pleased." A technical solution is achieved through creative diplomacy, and with no loss of integrity, serious conflict has been averted.

Gemignani, the musical director-conductor, also has much to say about good and bad collaboration. The director of a show will sometimes lean on him, which is okay since "that's his right. It's part of collaboration." And collaboration is a two-way street: "If I don't like a scene on stage, *I* have a perfect right to tell the director. . . . I wouldn't work a show where I had to shut up and just do music. It's boring." From where he stands, all of the company ought to participate in decision making. Even "actors should open their mouths":

The thing that made *Dreamgirls* work is that every single person in the room had an opinion, and had something to do with the lines and something to say about musical phrases. That includes all of the actors.

Gemignani cannot remember ever having suffered from the misfortunes of shows that did not hit. In *Merrily We Roll Along,* esprit de corps was high partly because "we used to sit downstairs and talk. I would give [nonmusical] suggestions and they listened to me." Such internal together-ness could not save the short-lived musical, all of whose participants were reportedly euphoric about its probable reception before opening night. When we spoke to Gemignani, he was just as happy about the good collaboration in a musical that must have seemed much chancier at its outset, but turned into a hit: "In this show *[Dreamgirls],* if something goes wrong, I say to Michael [Bennett], 'You've got to fix that entrance; it's too long; it's not working.' " The director either agrees and fixes or disagrees and declines to fix it. In either case the conductor's opinion is taken seriously, which makes him "listened to." A decent respect for the opinion of every contributor makes for a pleasant experience. The cash flow that accompanies a commercial success (as in this instance) makes it even better. That success, however, cannot be attributed solely to the benefits of real or illusory egalitarianism. In the maze of independent variables that makes for commercial success or failure, good collaboration, with its aura of equality, is no more reliable than difficult collaboration. To have loved one and hated the other makes a personal difference, but any emotion— trust or distrust, like or dislike—appears compatible with any commercial outcome.

A Focus on Costumes and Collaboration

If you are not one of "the key guys," your collaborative behavior is no less complex. This, for example, is the perception of a highly regarded costume designer like Carrie Robbins, who is impressed by the sheer number of "artistic people collaborating in a musical." In nonmusicals there is just the script to study—which implies interaction with the playwright, the director, and other designers. In musicals, there are all these plus a choreographer, and, "You might have to deal with the entire musical department." Sometimes the arranger "comes up with a whole chunk of music that's nowhere in the script. It's all plotted out, though not written in the text, and you have to dress people moving around the stage to a passage of music," frequently without lyrics that might clarify the passage. This situation is mercurial; reading it correctly will require rereading every time it changes; the commotion overtaxes Robbins's intuitive powers. "Finally, you must talk to these musical people and find out what's going on in their heads," and translate their tentative plans into visual ideas that are first put down on paper and then fitted to a number of human beings so that they adequately represent other human beings and aid the story.

Apparel is no small part of impersonation, but how does the costume designer dress her characters when "in any new musical, there's a shift a minute?" Let the composer or the lyricist introduce a new theme on the road, and there will also have to be a new set: "You think you've got a set, and then they turn it upside down. The end of the second act becomes the bottom of the third act." Who can doubt Robbins when she says that "the logistics are really something"? Nor are they limited to song shifts. The book itself may be in continuous flux. On *The First,* which she did with Martin Charnin and Joel Siegel, there were "maybe thirty previews" in New York:

During all those performances, Martin was busy pulling out scenes, literally giving actors new pages of script. Joel Siegel was rewriting on a daily basis. I discovered that unless I was there with the actors I might not get the pages.

Not getting the pages could precipitate crises. Likewise, since "Martin was in charge of the show," he had to be pursued with questions. "Joel did the writing," and Carrie went to him with still more questions. *The First,* which, for the usual unknowable reasons, failed on Broadway, was a serious musical based on breaking the color bar in major league baseball. Robbins, in her own quest for "esoteric realism," had to know where the baseball games were: if the players were inappropriately "suited up," verisimilitude

Billie Allen, Carrie Robbins on Women in Theatre Network Panel (ca. 1985)

Here Carrie Robbins *(at right)*, costume designer, is on a panel with Billie Allen, director/actress, at a Women in Theater Network conference ca. 1985 in a panel entitled "Dare to Use It: Realizing the Potential of Women in Theater." With exceptions, Broadway musical theater top creators have been white males; in the 1980s, women began entering the executive ranks; for instance, the composer, lyricist, bookwriter, director, and some of the major producers of the hit musical *The Secret Garden* (1991) were all women. (Photo credit: Billy Rose Theatre Collection, New York Public Library; photographer: Lauren Radack.)

would be sacrificed and credibility lost among sports fans for whom such matters were anything but esoteric.

More importantly, the story revolved around Jackie Robinson, a hero, but not the only hero. How much credit should be given to the Brooklyn Dodgers' owner? To the villains who originally opposed integration and soon saw the error of their ways? To Carrie, Charnin at work was a hero who did "some incredibly daring things." When she first heard a lyric offstage, it seemed to her to be too daring, but rehearsing it onstage, "I thought it was fabulous." Thirty days later the song was eliminated. Much backing and filling. Choices, choices. "I wasn't making those choices. I was just adjusting the clothes." Or readjusting them. Doing that turns out to be as arduous a task as any other.

Friendship Won't Make It So

Is familiarity, intimacy, or long association what it takes? Yes and no. The Robbins who postulates these qualities also dismisses them. She was the costume designer for *Grease,* which stood as Broadway's longest-running musical until its record was broken by *A Chorus Line* in 1983. Although Robbins was not enamored of rock music or nostalgic about the fifties, she felt close to the writers of *Grease* because it originated in "their yearbook which was my yearbook and the two producers' yearbook." The same high school, a group of contemporaries reliving and dramatizing their adolescence in that high school: what could be more propitious? And the director? He was Tom Moore, who "not only did *Grease,* but did *Over Here,* the Andrews Sisters show, and most recently, *'Night, Mother.* Tom's wonderful. We've worked together for a long time." Did that make it easier? Not at all:

Sometimes I'd draw and draw for Tom, thinking I understood him so well I would know exactly what he wanted, and he'd say "What are you doing? That's all wrong. Throw it out!" I have a pile of Tom rejects.

After Tom or any other director reacts that way, "I return to my drawing board. And then I try to find an assistant to be my legs, go out on the street and get the cloth so we can begin to put it together with my pictures."

Back and forth, bit by bit, meticulous work once cast aside ("Throw it out!"), later accepted ("Right on!"), all this replicated at every level, and once in a great while you unaccountably get a *Grease,* which fattens everyone's bankroll. Robbins: "I had no idea it would run for eight years." Who did? It is no easier to explain the blockbuster except by a redundancy ("The collaboration worked") than it is to explain a flop ("The collaboration failed").

Collaboration and Inspired Work

It is obvious that the creation of a musical play requires a "fusion of speech and music."[12] The words by a bookwriter, by a lyricist, and the music by a composer must emerge from collaboration among the primary artists and then must be staged by a director, a choreographer, and a team of designers and performers. The social, psychological, and technical skills in such collaboration are taken for granted by experienced professionals. But to teach newcomers these matters is difficult, largely because the training must be from "doing" and the principles are mostly left unarticulated by practitioners. We have lightly touched on a few parameters of collaboration, but in fact there is much to discover for the few who teach and analyze the intricacies of working in this art form.

Yet one more concept must be part of this book. Let us call it "inspired collaboration." Quite apart from critical reaction and box office receipts, the synergy of ordinary collaborative work is always mysterious. The mystery of inspired collaboration is even more awesome, and is usually a one-time affair in the history of Broadway musicals. The exceptions are not the point here. Yes, there were the Gershwin brothers, Rodgers and Hart, Rodgers and Hammerstein, Prince and Sondheim. And let us recall that the five brilliant primary executives and their designers who were collaborators on *West Side Story* never worked together again. Lerner and Loewe, as successful as their collaboration was in *My Fair Lady* (which was optioned as *Pygmalion* by dozens of aspiring producers and writers who could not make it a musical), stopped writing together after their next show, another commercial hit, *Camelot.* Thus, the Gershwins also had their hits followed by flops, from *Of Thee I Sing* (1931) to *Let 'Em Eat Cake* (1933), as did Rodgers and Hammerstein, from *The King and I* (1951) to *Pipe Dream* (1955), and so did all the rest of the few teams that lasted for more than one show.

The elusive process of collaboration is at times an "inspired" synergy. When this occurs, the power of collective energy and shared artistry becomes a potent factor that provides more than individual efforts. When this magic occurs, it is not accurate to say that any one person in the primary or creative team worked as an individual. For instance, a composer may not have written what ultimately became a brilliant score without the

Stephen Sondheim, Arthur Laurents, Harold Prince, Robert E. Griffith, Leonard Bernstein, Jerome Robbins Rehearsing West Side Story *(1957)*

The hit musical *West Side Story* (1957) took five to eight years to come to life, was turned down by "every producer in New York City," and finally emerged with a creative executive team whose one-time collaboration was brilliant though not free of conflict. *From left to right:* Stephen Sondheim, lyricist; Arthur Laurents, bookwriter; Harold Prince and Robert Griffith, coproducers; Leonard Bernstein, composer; and Jerome Robbins, director/choreographer. This musical is another Broadway vintage classic whose score continues to inspire generations around the world; but the collaborative team never worked together again. (Photo credit: Theatre Collection, Museum of the City of New York.)

stimulus of the story, the characters, and his collaborators. Thus, Bernstein is not solely responsible for the music in *West Side Story,* even if he is given public and program credit (and a certain percent of the royalties) for composing the music. Rodgers wrote beautiful melodies, first in one style with Hart, and then in another style with Hammerstein. But he was unable to find another long-term collaborator after Hammerstein's death, could not himself write lyrics well enough, and never again created lasting, inspired songs. For better and worse, whom he collaborated with appears to have affected the quality of the music. There are no words in the English language (or in scientific discourse) for this phenomenon.

West Side Story was the result of "individuals-creating-together," in a group that acted to produce an extraordinary success collaboratively and simultaneously woven by each contributor into an "inspired work." The factor of collectivity, a sociopsychological mesh, is only intuitively credited or even noticed. Conventional language in the street and on the media may credit a team (in group sports) but American, or more accurately, Euro-American, culture searches for the hero, the individual, *numero uno,* the premier creator—when in fact the major force may be located *between and among* members of the group or the team. The most creative or productive groups know how to blend individual talent with a shared group consciousness of a common vision. These collective forces then may *reciprocally* act on the "leaders" (the quarterback, the bookwriter, lyricist, and the composer, the director, choreographer, and the designer) to generate an inspired work. Such a work is often more enduring and exerts a greater influence on the community or the nation than individual effort. A creative group at the time and place of maximum collaboration is itself, like the work, a unique artistic achievement. Its next effort will be *de novo:* no one steps into the same river or the same theater twice. In the work of Broadway musical theater, artists hang together or the audience and critics hang them separately.

Epilogue

Chance, Skill, and the Broadway Musical

Experience with Broadway musicals tells us (if we may say this yet again) that about 80 percent of the time, critics and audiences proclaim, "The show doesn't work." Furthermore, no one knows beforehand if a musical, a play, a little domestic drama or a world-historical movement, a war, or a revolution will succeed. Afterward, those behind and those in front of the curtains will analyze the outcome. Some insist on its inevitability; others will fix blame or distribute credit here and there. But no explanation, no rationalization, is empirically acceptable. We like to believe that one explanation makes more sense than another. Indeed, the historian's logic may be impeccable. But logic is no substitute for verifiability, and for musicals there is no more verifiability after the fact than there is predictability before the fact.

This truism applies no less to success and failure than to the interaction, the communication, and the collaboration that underlie them. Early in his career, Robert Merton formulated a sociological maxim centered around the "unanticipated consequences of purposive social action." He understood these consequences to be positive or "functional." Somewhat later Merton reformulated the maxim so that it incorporated negative or "dysfunctional" consequences.[1] In plain English, Merton's point is that although we set out to do something, it is impossible to foresee what the result will be, let alone whether that result will be good or bad. Ergo, the success of any individual show is unknowable before the fact.

Harold Prince admits:

I can't know the answers, and I also don't know even why certain things work and certain things don't. I reluctantly take off for London to do this thing about Eva Perón with a clause in the contract that says without my permission they cannot do that play in America. And I say to them the day we go into rehearsal, "I think it's going to be fun; we're going to have a wonderful time, but of course it's never going to travel anywhere." [Actually, it ran on Broadway, 1979–1983.] You just never know. And yet with *A Doll's Life,* on the night it opened, I was sure it would be running for the next three years. I was sure of it, and I was sure the audience was sure of it too, and I was not alone in that feeling. [It ended in days.]

Elizabeth McCann, writing in *USA Today,* said, "Every hit is a surprise."[2] In short, a hit is a single event.

But opposed to this line of logic another set of facts forces its own logic and counterdicta upon us. The facts concerning successful producers of Broadway musicals are clear: Prince, Merrick, Shubert, Azenberg, Cantor, and a few others attain an average success of *about* 55–60 percent. These odds are not only more compelling to gamblers but they certainly differ from the usual average Broadway success rate of 20–25 percent, and are greater than an average chance level of fifty-fifty or five out of ten. If the outcome of each musical is "unknowable," then these producer-director teams operate on other ways of knowing and beating the odds. This interpretation rests on the idea that chance events can be generated, discarded, or seized upon, and turned to one's artistic advantage by skill, craft, courage, and, as Pasteur said, "a prepared mind." This skilled use of chance events is one aspect of something called serendipity. The dictum is that strong design can generate or optimize serendipity. And design, Buckminster Fuller once told us, is infinite. How does this work for musicals?

Bernheim commented on the Broadway scene in 1931:

Not infrequently do we hear it said that the professional theater is nothing but a vast gambling enterprise in which the few winners make fortunes and the majority lose their stakes. This is not so. The results of a theatrical venture depend upon judgment, skill and general economic trends. What we call luck is a factor in every venture. Perhaps it is a larger factor in the theater than in most businesses. But luck alone will no more make a successful producer than it will make a successful grocer or stock trader. And what we call luck is, more often than not, vision and foresight and *the ability to take advantage of the situation.*

The theater is a business fraught with a very high degree of risk—but that is by no means the same as saying that it is a gambling enterprise. Those who are skilled succeed in reducing the percentage of risk against them; those who are unskilled augment the natural hazards.[3]

This is the "nonrandom" scenario.

The producer selects the design (a show) that he assumes has a greater-than-chance potential to attract the variety of Broadway audiences who, over time, will buy the most tickets. The director's job is to take the untried show and stage it in a high-pressure situation—like fighting an old-fashioned war or marketing products under deadline or doing "musical rehearsals." An alert, skilled, daring leader can "learn while doing" by seizing on chance ideas. He can guide the actors, the creative team, and the designers into performance action they never thought of, and they can respond with ideas never thought of by him, seizing on newly creative solutions generated by conflict and tension in small groups. With the whole company, he can create a "live show" that beats the odds of failure. In a high-risk speculative business-and-artistic venture like musical theater, the deep-pocket investors can absorb several losses for one smash hit. Accordingly, they continue to gamble on the next Broadway project, hiring those directors and creative teams with the best track records. "Luck," Branch Ricky is alleged to have said, "is the residue of design." A strong design is a producer's dream, and a strong creative team is a director's fantasy, but will the collaboration be inspiring or will the conflict produce disarray? The answer to that question remains as elusive as ever.

In the early eighties, after a run of flops directed by Harold Prince, a story was heard around Broadway: Harold Prince dies and goes to heaven. He's met at the pearly gates by St. Peter, who is delighted to see him.

"Hal!" exclaims St. Peter. "Great to see you! We've been waiting for you to get here! God's got an idea for a new musical . . ."

"Oh no," says Prince, "I'm through with all that. I'm finally going to get a rest. And besides . . ."

"Hal," says Peter, "music by Mozart."

"Mozart? You're kidding! But, no, my answer is still no."

"Hal, book and lyrics by Shakespeare."

"Shakespeare??! The book and lyrics? Wow! . . . But, no, no, I came up here to get away from all that."

"Hal, scenery and costumes by DaVinci."

"*Leonardo* DaVinci??! Oh man! Mozart, Shakespeare, DaVinci—and God, the producer—I'll never get a chance like this again. All right! All right! This is too good to pass up. I'll probably regret it, but I'll do it! I'll do it!"

"Great!" says Peter. "We start tomorrow."

As Prince is about to walk away, St. Peter stops him, puts an arm around his shoulders and says, "Oh, Hal? One more thing. God's got this girlfriend . . ."

Appendix 1: Brief Bios of Persons Interviewed

MICHAEL BENNETT—Director/Choreographer

Director, choreographer, producer, and dancer, the late Mr. Bennett began his career performing in such Broadway musicals as *Subways Are for Sleeping*. His choreographic contributions to *How Now, Dow Jones, Your Own Thing,* and *By Jupiter* were uncredited. His choreography for *A Joyful Noise, Henry, Sweet Henry, Promises, Promises, Coco,* and *Company* earned him Tony Award nominations. He received seven Tony Awards for his choreographic work on *Follies* (also as codirector with Hal Prince), *Seesaw, Ballroom, Dreamgirls* (with Michael Peters), and the Pulitzer Prize-winning *A Chorus Line* (with Bob Avian as codirector). He directed and produced George Furth's play *Twigs* and Neil Simon's play *God's Favorite*. In 1986, he was elected to the Theater Hall of Fame.

GAIL BERMAN—Producer

As part of the producing company Estrin, Rose, Berman (with Melvyn J. Estrin and Susan R. Rose), Ms. Berman coproduced *The Nerd,* the Broadway and touring companies of *Joseph and the Amazing Technicolor Dreamcoat,* which was nominated for seven Tonys in 1982, *Hurlyburly,* which received four Tony nominations in 1984, and *The Blood Knot,* Tony nominee for Best Play in 1986. Off Broadway, the company presented *Tent Meeting* in 1987. They are currently developing TV projects for Highgate Pictures/New World Television.

ROBERT A. BUCKLEY—General Manager

Mr. Buckley has served as producer and general manager in both professional theater and opera. He coproduced *Beethoven's Tenth* and *Today I Am a Fountain Pen* and was executive producer and general manager of *Show Boat*, starring Donald O'Connor. He has also been associated with *Black and Blue, Treemonisha, Porgy and Bess* (1976 Tony Award), *Hello, Dolly!, Whodunit, A Woman of Independent Means*, and the Off-Broadway hit *How I Got That Story*. Other positions include associate director/producer, Houston Grand Opera; vice president, Radio City Music Hall; executive vice president, Boston's Wang Center for the Performing Arts; and assistant general manager, Minnesota Opera Company. He was also managing director of Circle-in-the-Square Theater.

MARTIN CHARNIN—Director/Lyricist

Mr. Charnin began his career as a member of the original cast of *West Side Story*. He conceived, directed, and wrote lyrics for *Annie*, for which he received the 1977 Tony Award. He has also conceived, directed, and written songs for numerous revues and *The First*, for which he received two Tony nominations in 1981 as Best Director and Best Librettist (with Joel Siegel). He wrote the lyrics for such shows as *I Remember Mama*, with music by Richard Rodgers. For his work in television and recordings, he has received numerous awards, including three Emmys, several Grammys, and has several gold and platinum records. He is also the author of two books.

MERLE DEBUSKEY—Press Representative

Mr. Debuskey has represented over 350 shows on and Off Broadway, including *The Rose Tattoo, Flahooley, Paint Your Wagon, The Crucible, A View from the Bridge, A Raisin in the Sun, Walking Happy, Hallelujah, Baby!, Purlie, No, No, Nanette, The House of Blue Leaves, Jesus Christ Superstar, Two Gentlemen of Verona, Man of La Mancha, Dreamgirls, Dancin', Inherit the Wind, Amadeus, Little Me, Sarafina, Six Degrees of Separation*, and the Pulitzer Prize-winners *The Diary of Anne Frank, How to Succeed in Business without Really Trying, Look Homeward, Angel, No Place to Be Somebody, That Championship Season*, and *A Chorus Line*; and seventeen Drama Critics and twelve Tony Award winners. He has also represented productions of the New York Shakespeare Festival from 1958 to 1985, Circle-in-the-Square, and Lincoln Center Theater. He has been president of the Association of Theatrical Press Agents and Managers since 1967.

DONALD FARBER — *Theatrical Lawyer*

Specializing in entertainment law, Mr. Farber has lectured and taught extensively on the subject at schools such as New York University, Toronto, Hofstra University School of Law, Hunter College, and the New School for Social Research. His books include *From Option to Opening: A Guide for the Off-Broadway Producer, Producing Theater: A Comprehensive Legal and Business Guide,* and *Actors' Guide: What You Should Know about the Contracts You Sign.* He was coauthor (with Paul A. Baumgarten) of *Producing, Financing, and Distributing Film,* and he served as general editor of *Entertainment Industry Contracts: Negotiating and Drafting Guide,* published by Matthew Bender.

CY FEUER — *Producer*

In partnership with Ernest H. Martin, Mr. Feuer produced such shows as *Where's Charley?, Guys and Dolls, Can-Can, The Boy Friend, Silk Stockings, Whoop-Up* (of which he was also coauthor), *Skyscraper* (also directed), *Walking Happy* (also directed), *The Goodbye People,* and *The Act.* He also produced the film version of *Cabaret* and the film *Piaf.* In 1975, with Ernest Martin, he became co-managing director of the Los Angeles and San Francisco Light Opera Association. He is currently president of the League of American Theatres and Producers.

JULES FISHER — *Producer/Lighting Designer*

Mr. Fisher has produced the musicals *Dancin', Rock 'n' Roll: The First 5,000 Years, The Rink,* as well as the play *Lenny.* As lighting designer, he has worked on over a hundred Broadway and Off Broadway productions, including *La Cage aux Folles, Chicago, Beatlemania, Hair, High Spirits, No, No, Nanette, Jesus Christ, Superstar, Lenny, Frankenstein,* and *Butterflies Are Free.* His lighting designs for *Grand Hotel, Dancin', Pippin,* and *Ulysses in Nighttown* earned him Tony Awards.

JOHN FLAXMAN—Producer

A partner of Harold Prince since 1968, Mr. Flaxman began his career at Columbia Pictures where he worked on the *Profiles in Courage* TV series. He also headed Universal Pictures' literary department, and as literary agent at William Morris he developed the screenplays for *The Thomas Crown Affair, Bullitt,* and *Love Story.* He produced *Something for Everyone* (the first film directed by Harold Prince) with Angela Lansbury and Michael York. His production of *The Caine Mutiny Court Martial* was seen on CBS TV.

PAUL GEMIGNANI—Musical Director/Conductor

Mr. Gemignani has served as musical director for more than twenty Broadway productions, including *Follies, Pacific Overtures, A Little Night Music, Sweeney Todd, Evita, Dreamgirls, Merrily We Roll Along,* the Pulitzer Prize-winning *Sunday in the Park with George, Into the Woods,* and *Jerome Robbins' Broadway.* He has also been conductor for numerous original cast albums and is a regular guest conductor with world-renowned symphony orchestras, including the Royal Philharmonic. In 1989, he received a special Drama Desk Award for Consistently Outstanding Musical Direction.

JOHN GLASEL—Musician

From 1983 to 1992, Mr Glasel was president of Local 802, American Federation of Musicians. As a professional trumpeter, he worked on numerous Broadway and television shows and was a member of the New York Brass Quintet (1954–1961). He is the composer of *Saints Alive!* and is the author of the book *Relaxation Techniques.* He edited *Musician's Voice* and has taught trumpet at Columbia University Teachers College.

CAROL HALL—Composer/Lyricist

Ms. Hall's work has been seen on, Off, and Off-Off-Broadway in musicals such as *The Best Little Whorehouse in Texas, To Whom It May Concern, Good Sports,* and *Wonderful Beast.* She has composed for films and television, including the Emmy Award-winning special, *Free to Be You and Me.* Her songs have been recorded by such artists as Barbra Streisand, Mabel Mercer, Harry Belafonte, Neil Diamond, and Barbara Cook. She is also a published author of children's books.

SHELDON HARNICK—*Lyricist/Composer*

Mr. Harnick's works include *New Faces of 1952, Two's Company, The Shoestring Revue, The Littlest Revue, Horatio, John Murray Anderson's Almanac, Portofino, The Body Beautiful, Tenderloin, She Loves Me, Baker Street, The Apple Tree, The Rothschilds, Rex,* the Pulitzer Prize-winning *Fiorello!,* and *Fiddler on the Roof,* garnering Tony Awards for the last two shows. He is also a composer. He has served as an officer of the Dramatists Guild, ASCAP, and as a Trustee of the National Institute for Music Theater.

GEOFFREY HOLDER—*Choreographer*

Choreographer, director, designer, and performer, Mr. Holder began his career as a dancer, appearing with numerous companies, including his own, at such festivals as Jacob's Pillow, Spoleto Festival of Two Worlds, Harkness Dance Festival, and at the Metropolitan Opera. He made his Broadway debut in *House of Flowers* and appeared as Lucky in *Waiting for Godot* in 1957. He directed and designed costumes for the original production and revival of *The Wiz,* for which he received two Tony Awards in 1975. He was director, choreographer, and costume designer for *Timbuktu!,* earning a Tony nomination in the latter capacity. He has also appeared in a number of films, among them *Annie,* and has had numerous books (including a cookbook) and articles published nationally.

NICHOLAS HOWEY—*Producer/Director*

Mr. Howey received a Ph.D. in theater from Wayne State University in Detroit. He has taught theater at American University in Washington, D.C. In 1972, he cofounded the Harlequin Theater in Washington, D.C. He cofounded a production company that has produced national touring productions of *Gigi,* with Louis Jourdan and Betsy Palmer, *Oliver!, Seven Brides for Seven Brothers, Singin' in the Rain, Brigadoon, The King and I, The Mystery of Edwin Drood, My One and Only, West Side Story,* and *Me and My Girl.* Their recent production of *Can-Can,* starring Chita Rivera and the Radio City Music Hall Rockettes, toured Japan in the fall of 1989.

WALTER KERR—*Critic*

Mr. Kerr was drama critic for the *New York Times* from 1966 to 1983, the *New York Herald Tribune* from 1951 to 1966, and *Commonweal* from 1950 to 1952. From 1938 to 1949 he was on the faculty of Catholic University, where he directed numerous shows. He is also the author of numerous books, including *How Not to Write a Play, The Silent Clowns,* and *Journey to the Center of the Theater,* as well as the plays *Touch and Go* and *King of Hearts.* In 1978 he received the Pulitzer Prize for criticism and was inducted into the National Institute of Arts and Letters. In 1982 he was elected to the Theater Hall of Fame.

BURTON LANE—Composer

Mr. Lane's music has been heard in such Broadway musicals as *Three's a Crowd, The Third Little Show,* the ninth edition of *Earl Carroll's Follies, Singin' the Blues,* and *Americana.* He composed the score for *Hold on to Your Hats* and *Finian's Rainbow* with lyrics by E. Y. Harburg. He also collaborated with Al Dubin on lyrics and composed music for *Laffing Room Only.* In collaboration with Alan Jay Lerner, he wrote the score for *On a Clear Day You Can See Forever.* His work in film includes songs for *Dancing Lady, Babes on Broadway* (Academy Award), *Royal Wedding* (Academy Award nomination), *Give a Girl a Break,* and the film version of *Finian's Rainbow.* He has received numerous awards, including the Grammy. He has been president of both ASCAP and AGAC and was the recipient of ASCAP's first Sigmund Romberg Award.

ARTHUR LAURENTS—Bookwriter/Playwright/Director

Author and director, Mr. Laurents has written numerous works for stage and screen, including the plays *Home of the Brave, The Bird Cage, Time of the Cuckoo, A Clearing in the Woods, Invitation to a March, The Enclave, Scream,* and *Running Time.* He is also the author of the books for the musicals *West Side Story, Gypsy, Anyone Can Whistle, Do I Hear a Waltz?, Hallelujah, Baby!,* and *Nick and Nora* (which he also directed).

His screenwriting credits include *The Way We Were, The Turning Point, The Snake Pit, Anna Lucasta,* and *Anastasia.* In addition to his own works, he has also directed such productions as *I Can Get It for You Wholesale, The Madwoman of Central Park West, Birds of Paradise,* and *La Cage aux Folles.* He is the recipient of numerous awards, including the Tony, Golden Globe, Screenwriters Guild, and Drama Desk, among others. He was elected to the Theater Hall of Fame and is a member of the Dramatists Guild Council, Motion Picture Academy, Screen Writers Guild, and PEN.

JOHN LYONS—*Casting Director*

Mr. Lyons was casting director of Playwrights Horizons from 1979 until 1985. During that period, he cast such musicals as *March of the Falsettos, Sunday in the Park with George,* and the original production of *Into the Woods.* Since that time, he has continued to cast for theater, television, and film.

ARTHUR MASELLA—*Director*

Mr. Masella has worked on Broadway, Off Broadway, and in opera compa- nies throughout the United States. He staged Harold Prince's production of *The Phantom of the Opera* in Stockholm, Hamburg, Berlin, and Australia. He has directed *The Music Man, Cavalleria Rusticana, Of Mice and Men, I Pagliacci, La Cenerentola, Clementina's Cactus, La Bohème, Amahl and the Night Visitors, Rappaccini's Daughter,* for the New York City Opera, Minnesota Opera, Brooklyn Academy of Music, Houston Grand Opera, John F. Kennedy Center, and many others. He directed *Yours, Anne* Off- Broadway. He received his early training with Harold Prince, working on a dozen productions, including *Pacific Overtures, Candide, Sweeney Todd,* and *Merrily We Roll Along.* He is special consultant to the Musical Theater Program at New York University's Tisch School of the Arts.

PETER NEUFELD—*General Manager*

Mr. Neufeld has been managing theater and dance productions since 1963. In partnership with R. Tyler Gatchell for more than twenty years, he was general manager for numerous shows on and Off Broadway, as well as road companies including *No, No, Nanette, Jesus Christ Superstar, Don't Bother Me, I Can't Cope, Annie, Working, Evita, March of the Falsettos, The First, Cats, Oliver!, Timbuktu!, Lettice and Lovage, Aspects of Love,* and *Crazy for You.* He was also executive producer of *Evita* and *Cats.*

CLAIRE NICHTERN—*Producer*

Ms. Nichtern has produced such works as *The Banker's Daughter, The Typist and the Tiger, Luv, Jimmy Shine, The Trial of Abraham Lincoln, I Got a Song, The House of Blue Leaves, Absent Friends,* and *Cold Storage.* She was also associate director and producer-in-residence at Circle-in-the- Square, where she produced *Waltz of the Toreadors.* In 1979, she became president of Warner Theater Productions, for which she produced the Pulitzer Prize-winning *Crimes of the Heart, Beyond Therapy, Woman of the Year, Mass Appeal, Foxfire, The Fifth of July, The Dresser, The American Clock, Grown Ups,* and *March of the Falsettos.*

LONNY PRICE—Actor/Director

Mr. Price has performed on Broadway in productions including *Burn This, Broadway, Rags, Master Harold . . . and the Boys, Merrily We Roll Along, The Survivor,* and starred in the pre-Broadway tryout of *Durante.* He has also appeared in Off-Broadway productions such as *A Quiet End,* at Theater Off Park, and *The Immigrant,* for which he won an Obie Award. He has also directed the American Jewish Theater's revival of *The Rothschilds* and *The Education of Hyman Kaplan,* and *Juno and the Paycock* at the Vineyard Theatre.

HAROLD PRINCE—Director/Producer

Mr. Prince has produced and directed numerous works for the New York and London stages, among them *The Pajama Game, Damn Yankees, New Girl in Town, West Side Story,* the Pulitzer Prize-winning *Fiorello, A Funny Thing Happened on the Way to the Forum, She Loves Me, Fiddler on the Roof, Cabaret, Zorba, Follies* (codirector with Michael Bennett), *Company, A Little Night Music, Candide, Pacific Overtures, On the Twentieth Century, Evita, Sweeney Todd, Merrily We Roll Along, Phantom of the Opera,* and *Kiss of the Spider Woman.* He has also directed numerous operas for leading opera companies, including the Metropolitan Opera, the New York City Opera, the Vienna Staatsoper, the Lyric Opera of Chicago, and the Houston Grand Opera. He is the recipient of sixteen Tony Awards.

FRANK RICH—Critic

Mr. Rich has been theater critic of the *New York Times* since 1980. While at Harvard, he was drama critic of the *Crimson.* Previously, he had been a film and television critic, as well as an associate editor for *Time* magazine. He was also film critic for the *New York Post* from 1975 to 1977, and film critic and senior editor of *New Times* magazine.

CARRIE ROBBINS—Costume Designer

Ms. Robbins has designed costumes for more than twenty Broadway shows, including *The Boys of Winter, The Octette Bridge Club, Raggedy Ann, Agnes of God* (Tony nominee), *Grease* (Tony nominee), *Over Here!, The Beggar's Opera, The Iceman Cometh, The First, Happy End, Yentl, The Secret Affairs of Mildred Wild,* and George Abbott's *Broadway.* She has also designed for the New York Shakespeare Festival and for theaters and opera companies across the country and internationally. Ms. Robbins is a member of the design department at New York University's Tisch School of the Arts.

HARVEY SABINSON—Administrator

Mr. Sabinson was appointed executive director of the League of American Theatres and Producers in 1981, where he had been director of special projects since 1976. From 1946 to 1973, he was press agent for over 250 productions on and Off Broadway, countless films, and entertainers. He has also served as an officer and board member of the Association of Theatrical Press Agents and Managers and the American Academy of Dramatic Arts. He was also visiting professor of theater administration at Yale University, adjunct associate professor of speech and drama at Queensborough Community College, and has been a consultant to prominent theaters and universities across the country. He is also the author of the book *Darling, You Were Wonderful.*

GERALD SCHOENFELD—Theater Owner/Producer

Mr. Schoenfeld has been chairman of the Shubert Organization since 1972. A leading theatrical attorney, he represented the Shubert office from 1957 to 1972. With Bernard Jacobs, president, the Shubert Organization has been associated with such distinguished productions as *Jerome Robbins' Broadway, Cats, Les Liaisons Dangereuses, City of Angels, A Few Good Men, The Circle, Tru, Lettice and Lovage, The Grapes of Wrath, Chess, Dreamgirls, Dancin',* and the Pulitzer Prize-winning *The Heidi Chronicles, Sunday in the Park with George, The Gin Game,* and *Glengarry Glen Ross.* Mr. Schoenfeld is third vice president of the League of American Theatres and Producers.

STEPHEN SCHWARTZ—*Composer/Lyricist*

Mr. Schwartz's music and lyrics have been heard in musicals on and Off Broadway, including the Tony Award-winning *Pippin, Godspell, The Magic Show, The Baker's Wife, Working, Rags,* and *Personals.* He also wrote lyrics for Leonard Bernstein's *Mass. Children of Eden,* his latest musical, was recently produced in London and recorded.

THOMAS Z. SHEPARD—*Cast Album Producer*

Mr. Shepard has produced original cast recordings of numerous major Broadway musicals, including *Company, Sweeney Todd, La Cage aux Folles,* the 1976 Houston Grand Opera *Porgy and Bess,* the concert version of *Follies,* and *Jelly's Last Jam.* The winner of many Grammys, he worked with Goddard Lieberson at CBS Records, and he was with RCA Red Seal for twelve years. He has also produced recordings of major symphony orchestras. A composer and classically trained pianist, he has composed music for the soundtrack of the film *Such Good Friends* and an opera based on André Schwartz-Bart's novel *The Last of the Just.*

OLIVER SMITH—*Set Designer*

Set designer, producer, and painter, Mr. Smith has worked in theater, film, ballet, and opera. On Broadway, he has designed numerous productions, including *Rosalinda, The New Moon, On the Town* (which he also coproduced), *No Exit, Brigadoon, High Button Shoes, Gentlemen Prefer Blondes* (also coproducer), *Paint Your Wagon, Pal Joey, On Your Toes, My Fair Lady, Auntie Mame, Candide, West Side Story, The Sound of Music, Camelot, Becket, Hello, Dolly!,* and *Baker Street.* In 1945 he became codirector of American Ballet Theater, with Lucia Chase, and he designed sets for many of the company's ballets. His work has been seen in such films as *Guys and Dolls, The Band Wagon, Oklahoma!,* and *Porgy and Bess.* He is the recipient of numerous awards, including seven Tonys, and is a master teacher in scene design at New York University's Tisch School of the Arts.

PETER STONE—*Bookwriter/Playwright*

Mr. Stone has written the books for numerous Broadway musicals, including *Kean, Skyscraper, 1776* (for which he received a Tony Award), *Two by Two, Sugar, Woman of the Year* (Tony), *My One and Only* (with Timothy

S. Mayer, 1983 Tony nomination), and *The Will Rogers Follies* (Tony). He was a contributor to *Grand Hotel* during its tryout. He has worked on such films as *Charade, Father Goose* (Academy Award), *Sweet Charity, 1776, Arabesque, The Taking of Pelham 1–2–3,* and *Who Is Killing the Great Chefs of Europe?* Since 1981 he has been president of the Dramatists Guild.

TOMMY TUNE —Director/Choreographer/Dancer

As director, choreographer, and performer, Mr. Tune's work has been seen on Broadway in such musicals as *Grand Hotel* (two Tony Awards, Director and Choreographer), *My One and Only* (two Tony Awards, Best Actor and Choreographer, with Thommie Walsh), *Nine* (Tony, as director), *A Day in Hollywood / A Night in the Ukraine* (Tony, as choreographer, with Thommie Walsh), *The Best Little Whorehouse in Texas,* and *Seesaw* (Tony, Best Supporting Actor). He has also directed *The Club* and *Cloud 9* Off-Broadway.

JOHN WEIDMAN —Bookwriter

With Timothy Crouse, Mr. Weidman coauthored the book for the Tony Award-winning revival of *Anything Goes.* He also wrote the book for *Pacific Overtures* (for which he received a Tony nomination) and for *Assassins.* He is also the coauthor (with Robert Waldman and Alfred Uhry) of the musical *America's Sweetheart.* Mr. Weidman is a former editor of *The National Lampoon* and has written for PBS's *Sesame Street.*

Appendix 2: Alphabetical Listing of Broadway Musicals Mentioned in Text

Dates indicate year show opened on Broadway

Ain't Misbehavin' (1978)
Annie (1977)
Annie Get Your Gun (1946)

The Baker's Wife (pre-Broadway opening and closing 1976)
The Best Little Whorehouse in Texas (1978)
Big River (1985)
Black and Blue (1989)
Bloomer Girl (1944)
Bubblin' Brown Sugar (1976)

Cabaret (1966)
Camelot (1960)
Candide (1956)
Candide [revival] (1974)
Carousel (1945)
Carrie (1988)
Cats (1982)
Chaplin (pre-Broadway opening and closing 1983)
A Chorus Line (1975)
Company (1970)
The Cradle Will Rock (1938)
Cyrano (1973)

Damn Yankees (1955)
Dancin' (1978)
A Doll's Life (1982)
Don't Bother Me, I Can't Cope (1972)
Dreamgirls (1981)

Einstein on the Beach (1976)
Evita (1979)

The Fantasticks [Off-Broadway] (1960)
Fiddler on the Roof (1964)
Finian's Rainbow (1947)
Fiorello! (1959)
The First (1981)
Follies (1971)
42nd Street (1980)
Funny Girl (1964)

Gigi (1973)
Godspell (1976)
Grease (1972)
Grind (1985)
Guys and Dolls (1950)
Gypsy (1959)

Hair (1968)
Hallelujah, Baby (1967)
Hello, Dolly! (1964)
Hellzapoppin' (1938)
Hot Spot (1963)
How to Succeed in Business without Really Trying (1961)
The Human Comedy (1984)

Jamaica (1957)
Jerome Robbins' Broadway (1989)
Jerry's Girls (1985)
Jesus Christ Superstar (1971)
Joseph and the Amazing Technicolor Dreamcoat (1982)

The King and I (1951)
Kiss Me, Kate (1948)

La Cage aux Folles (1983)
Lady, Be Good! (1924)
Legs Diamond (1988)
Les Misérables (1987)
Let 'Em Eat Cake (1933)
A Little Night Music (1973)

The Magic Show (1974)
Mame (1966)
Man of La Mancha (1965)
Marilyn (1983)
Mata Hari (pre-Broadway opening and closing 1967)
Me and My Girl (1986)
Merlin (1983)
Merrily We Roll Along (1981)
Miss Saigon (1991)
Mr. President (1962)
Mummenschanz (1974)
The Music Man (1957)
My Fair Lady (1956)
My One and Only (1983)

Nick and Nora (1991)
Nine (1982)
No, No, Nanette [revival] (1971)

Oh, Calcutta! (1969)
Oh, Kay! (1926)
Oklahoma! (1943)
On a Clear Day You Can See Forever (1965)
On the Twentieth Century (1978)
On Your Toes (1936)
On Your Toes [revival] (1983)
Over Here (1974)

Pacific Overtures (1976)
The Pajama Game (1954)

The Phantom of the Opera (1988)
Pins and Needles (1937)
Pipe Dream (1955)
Pippin (1972)
Porgy and Bess (1935)
Promises, Promises (1968)

Rags (1986)
Raisin (1973)
Rock 'n' Roll: The First 5,000 Years (1982)
Roza (1987)
Runaways (1978)

1776 (1969)
She Loves Me (1963)
Shenandoah (1975)
Show Boat (1927)
The Sound of Music (1959)
South Pacific (1949)
Starlight Express (1987)
Sugar Babies (1979)
Sunday in the Park with George (1984)
Sweeney Todd (1979)

The Tap Dance Kid (1983)
They're Playing our Song (1979)

Very Good Eddie [revival] (1975)

West Side Story (1957)
Whoopee! (1979)
The Wiz (1975)
Woman of the Year (1981)
Working (1978)

Appendix 3: Broadway Theaters (1991)
by Camille Croce Dee

Included in this list of legitimate Broadway houses are both those theaters still extant (as of March 1991) and any that have been demolished since 1945 but were in use as legitimate houses until their demise. A list of the 42nd Street theaters to be renovated for potential use as Broadway houses follows.

The names of the theaters have been culled from *The City and the Theatre* by Mary C. Henderson, *Variety, Notable Names in the American Theatre,* the League of American Theatres and Producers, the 42nd Street Development Project, and various files of material on individual theaters at the Billy Rose Theatre Collection, New York Public Library. Former names of theaters are indicated in parentheses. (An asterisk denotes theaters protected by landmark designation granted by the New York City Landmarks Preservation Commission.)

Current Name	*Opening Date*
1. Ambassador* 215 W. 49th St.	02/11/21
2. Belasco* (Stuyvesant) 111 W. 44th St.	10/16/07
3. Bijou 222 W. 45th St.	04/12/17; demolished 1982
4. Biltmore* 261 W. 47th St.	12/07/25

5. Booth*   10/16/13
    222 W. 44th St.
6. Broadhurst*   09/27/17
    235 W. 44th St.
7. Broadway   12/08/30 (as legitimate theater)
    (B. S. Moss's Colony, Universal
    Colony, B. S. Moss's Broadway,
    Earl Carroll's Broadway, Cine
    Roma)
    1681 Broadway
8. Brooks Atkinson*   02/15/26
    (Mansfield, Lew Field's Mansfield)
    256 W. 47th St.
9. Century   10/06/21; demolished 1962
    (Jolson's, Shakespeare, Venice,
    Yiddish Art, Molly Picon) 7th Ave.
    bet. 58th & 59th Sts.
10. Circle-in the-Square   11/15/72
    1633 Broadway
11. Cort*   10/20/12
    148 W. 48th St.
12. Criterion Center   10/03/88
    Broadway bet. 44th & 45th Sts.
13. Edison   03/05/70 (as Edison)
    (Arena)
    240 W. 47th St.
14. Ethel Barrymore*   12/20/28
    243 W. 47th St.
15. Eugene O'Neill*   11/24/25
    (Coronet, Forrest)
    230 W. 49th St.
16. George Abbott   12/24/28; demolished 11/14/65
    (Craig, Adelphi, Fifty-Fourth St.)
    152 W. 54th St.
17. Gershwin   11/19/72
    (Uris)
    1633 Broadway
18. Helen Hayes   10/20/11 (as legitimate theater)
    (Folies Bergere, Fulton)   demolished 1983
    210 W. 46th St.
19. Helen Hayes*   03/12/12
    (Little, Anne Nichols Little, Win-
    throp Ames, CBS Radio Playhouse,
    NY Times Hall, ABC-TV Studio)
    238 W. 44th St.
20. Henry Miller's*   04/01/18
    124 W. 43rd St.

21. Imperial*   12/25/23
    249 W. 45th St.
22. International   01/21/03; demolished 1954
    (Majestic, Park, Park Music Hall,
    Cosmopolitan, Columbus Circle)
    5 Columbus Circle
23. Jack Lawrence   04/15/11
    (Playhouse)
    137 W. 48th St.
24. John Golden*   02/24/27
    (Theatre Masque)
    252. W. 45th St.
25. Longacre*   05/01/13
    220 W. 48th St.
26. Lunt-Fontanne*   01/10/10
    (Globe)
    205 W. 46th St.
27. Lyceum*   11/02/03
    (New Lyceum)
    149 W. 45th St.
28. Majestic*   03/28/27
    245 W. 44th St.
29. Mark Hellinger*   12/13/34 (as legitimate theater)
    (Hollywood, Fifty-First St.,
    Warner Bros.)
    237 W. 51st St.
30. Marquis   08/10/86
    1535 Broadway
31. Martin Beck*   11/11/24
    302 W. 45th St.
32. Minskoff   03/13/73
    200 W. 45th St.
33. Morosco   02/05/17; demolished 1982
    217 W. 45th St.
34. Music Box*   09/22/21
    239 W. 45th St.
35. Nederlander*   09/01/21
    (National, Billy Rose,
    Trafalgar)
    208 W. 41st St.
36. Neil Simon*   11/22/27
    (Alvin)
    250 W. 52nd St.
37. Palace*   03/24/13
    1564 Broadway
38. Plymouth*   10/10/17
    236 W. 45th St.

39. Princess   03/06/80; demolished 1990
    (22 Steps, Latin Quarter, Cotton
    Club)
    200 W. 48th St.
40. Rialto   1935
    (Victoria, Rialto)
    NW cor. 7th Ave. & 42nd St.
41. Richard Rodgers*   12/24/24
    (Forty-Sixth St., Chanin's,
    Forty-Sixth St.)
    226 W. 46th St.
42. Royale*   01/11/27
    (Golden, CBS Radio Playhouse)
    242 W. 45th St.
43. St. James   09/26/27
    (Erlanger)
    246 W. 44th St.
44. Sam S. Shubert*   09/29/13
    225 W. 44th St.
45. Virginia   04/13/25
    (ANTA, Guild)
    245 W. 52nd St.
46. Vivian Beaumont   12/12/65
    65th St. & Amsterdam Ave.
47. Walter Kerr   03/21/21
    (Ritz, CBS Radio Playhouse, NBC
    Radio Studio, ABC Radio Studio,
    ABC-TV Studio)
    223 W. 48th St.
48. Winter Garden*   03/20/11
    1634 Broadway
49. Ziegfeld   02/02/27; demolished 1967
    (Loew's Ziegfeld)
    Ave. of Americas & 54th St.

42nd Street Theaters to be Renovated (1990s)

1. Apollo   11/18/20 (as legitimate theater)
   (Academy, Bryant)
   221 W. 42nd St.
2. Harris   08/19/14 (as legitimate theater)
   (Candler, Cohan and Harris, Sam
   H. Harris)
   226 W. 42nd St.
3. Liberty   10/10/04
   234 W. 42nd St.
4. Lyric   10/12/03
   213 W. 42nd St.

5. New Amsterdam*   11/02/03
   214 W. 42nd St.
6. Selwyn   10/03/18
   229 W. 42nd St.
7. Times Square   09/30/20
   217 W. 42nd St.
8. Victory   09/27/1900
   (Theater Republic, Belasco, Republic)
   207 W. 42nd St.

Appendix 4: Summary Lists and Charts

1. Number of Productions of New Musicals
Opening on Broadway in Three-Year Averages (1900–1990)

Year[a]	New Musicals	3–Year Average	Year[b]	New Musicals	3–Year Average
1899	14	14			
1900	26		1945	16	
1901	21		1946	13	
1902	27	25	1947	12	14
1903	30		1948	14	
1904	29		1949	16	
1905	32	30	1950	12	14
1906	34		1951	8	
1907	37		1952	9	
1908	33	35	1953	8	8
1909	36		1954	12	
1910	34		1955	7	
1911	39	36	1956	9	9
1912	36		1957	11	
1913	37		1958	12	
1914	24	32	1959	14	12
1915	26		1960	15	
1916	25		1961	17	
1917	38	30	1962	11	14
1918	32		1963	16	
1919	43		1964	16	
1920	51	42	1965	14	15
1921	37		1966	11	
1922	41		1967	11	
1923	41	40	1968	14	12
1924	46		1969	14	
1925	48		1970	13	

1. (continued)

Year[a]	New Musicals	3–Year Average	Year[b]	New Musicals	3–Year Average
1926	49	48	1971	16	14
1927	53		1972	17	
1928	43		1973	10	
1929	35	44	1974	11	13
1930	29		1975	14	
1931	27		1976	11	
1932	27	28	1977	11	12
1933	15		1978	13	
1934	19		1979	16	
1935	14	16	1980	18	16
1936	11		1981	10	
1937	16		1982	11	
1938	18	15	1983	10	10
1939	18		1984	6	
1940	14		1985	10	
1941	16	16	1986	10	9
1942	18		1987	13	
1943	19		1988	6	
1944	19	19	1989	8	9
			1990	7	

[a] *Source: Variety,* 6/6/90
[b] *Source:* From our lists of Broadway musicals.

2. Percentage of Hits/ Flops of Broadway Musicals per Year, 1945 to 1989–90

Year	Hits	Flops	Total Number	Percent Flops
1945	6	16	22	73
1946	3	14	17	82
1947	6	10	16	63
1948	5	11	16	69
1949	2	14	16	88
1950	3	14	17	82
1951	3	12	15	80
1952	4	5	9	56
1953	3	6	9	67

Year	Hits	Flops	Total Number	Percent Flops
1954	7	6	13	46
1955	2	9	11	82
1956	3	6	9	67
1957	3	9	12	75
1958	5	8	13	62
1959	4	13	17	77
1960	5	11	16	69
1961	4	16	20	80
1962	3	10	13	77
1963	3	14	17	82
1964	5	15	20	75
1965	5	11	16	69
1966	3	10	13	77
1967	1	11	12	92
1968	2	13	15	87
1969	4	12	16	75
1970	4	13	17	77
1971	4	16	20	80
1972	4	17	21	81
1973	2	13	15	87
1974	2	12	14	86
1975	5	14	19	74
1976	10	11	21	52
1977	5	14	19	74
1978	2	15	17	88
1979	5	18	23	78
1980	5	20	25	80
1981	4	15	19	79
1982	3	11	14	79
1983	2	14	16	88
1984	2	7	9	78
1985	1	13	14	93
1986	2	11	13	85

2. (*continued*)

Year	Hits	Flops	Total Number	Percent Flops
1987	3	14	17	82
1988	1	7	8	88
1989	3	10	13	77
		Total Average:		76%

3. Percentage of Hits/Flops of Straight Plays on Broadway per Year, 1945–46 to 1989–90

Year	Hits	Flops	Total Number	Percent Flops
45–46	7	38	45	84
46–47	8	39	47	83
47–48	9	33	42	79
48–49	9	37	46	80
49–50	4	28	32	88
50–51	7	34	41	83
51–52	6	40	46	87
52–53	11	26	37	70
53–54	10	26	36	72
54–55	9	24	33	73
55–56	11	25	36	69
56–57	6	31	37	84
57–58	8	30	38	79
58–59	10	26	36	72
59–60	9	31	40	78
60–61	6	25	31	81
61–62	6	27	33	82
62–63	4	33	37	89
63–64	7	30	37	81
64–65	4	23	27	85
65–66	8	26	34	76
66–67	7	20	27	74
67–68	11	29	40	73
68–69	7	21	28	75
69–70	5	18	23	78
70–71	4	17	21	81
71–72	1	26	27	96
72–73	4	20	24	83

Year	Hits	Flops	Total Number	Percent Flops
73–74	2	14	16	88
74–75	6	18	24	75
75–76	3	15	18	83
76–77	9	15	24	63
77–78	6	17	23	74
78–79	4	17	21	81
79–80	4	31	35	89
80–81	2	21	23	91
81–82	6	20	26	77
82–83	5	24	29	83
83–84	6	13	19	68
84–85	3	14	17	82
85–86	5	12	17	71
86–87	5	15	20	75
87–88	4	9	13	69
88–89	2	12	14	86
89–90	3	7	10	70
				Total Average: 80%

Total shows less than actual number due to unavailable data; excludes pre-Broadway flops.

Chart 4.1 Prime City Box Office Totals

Cities	1981–82			1986–87			1988–89		
	Playing Weeks	Shows Played	Total B.O. Receipts	Playing Weeks	Shows Played	Total B.O. Receipts	Playing Weeks	Shows Played	Total B.O. Receipts
Washington	189	36	$ 20,802,127	126	28	$ 21,881,536	118	22	$ 28,081,388
Los Angeles	185	26	$ 46,463,667	161	24	$ 34,033,658	156	19	$ 48,004,593
San Francisco	140	19	$ 19,465,349	115	12	$ 24,826,142	112	15	$ 15,250,970
Toronto	108	12	$ 24,536,102	96	16	$ 18,649,357	50	9	$ 13,358,162
Chicago	82	11	$ 27,755,714	32	9	$ 7,845,724	33	6	$ 10,603,422
Baltimore	33	9	$ 6,436,223	33	10	$ 8,274,340	3	9	$ 6,931,741
Philadelphia	31	11	$ 9,553,874	30	11	$ 7,607,368	37	6	$ 13,196,049
Boston	25	7	$ 3,022,620	34	12	$ 7,768,437	39	12	$ 13,059,534
Dallas	13	8	$ 4,560,387	17	9	$ 6,173,414	8	5	$ 2,080,282
Miami Beach	12	6	$ 3,941,944	14	6	$ 6,570,025	13	5	$ 6,895,951
Denver	12	7	$ 3,261,084	14	7	$ 5,585,795	6	4	$ 1,404,881
St. Louis	11	10	$ 2,541,240	11	10	$ 3,163,392	6	6	$ 3,107,313
Atlanta	8	6	$ 2,927,104	6	5	$ 3,622,718	10	8	$ 4,442,958
Cleveland	8	4	$ 1,586,277	24	4	$ 9,722,427	13	9	$ 1,936,286
Detroit	8	4	$ 1,586,277	24	4	$ 9,722,427	22	10	$ 6,681,323
Houston	7	4	$ 2,031,825	7	5	$ 2,855,042	6	6	$ 1,699,939
Fort Lauderdale	7	2	$ 1,756,959	17	6	$ 3,573,299	6	6	$ 3,734,078
Pittsburgh	6	6	$ 2,350,923	3	3	$ 1,217,174	16	14	$ 6,592,369
Buffalo	6	6	$ 2,314,073	5	4	$ 2,042,442	4	5	$ 1,117,605
Louisville	5	4	$ 1,522,791	7	6	$ 2,138,501	7	7	$ 2,490,518
Hartford, CT	3	3	$ 1,234,380	6	6	$ 2,988,070	5	5	$ 2,045,206

City									
San Diego				7	6	$ 2,138,624	3	3	$ 1,168,706
Wilmington				7	7	$ 1,446,671	6	6	$ 1,715,647
Schenectady				3	3	$ 1,115,597			
New Haven							11	7	$ 3,507,610
Palm Beach							11	6	$ 2,065,327
Seattle							8	5	$ 2,754,192
New Orleans							7	7	$ 2,375,452
Kansas City							6	5	$ 2,622,317
Tampa							6	5	$ 2,611,148
Nashville							6	6	$ 1,784,599
Orlando							5	5	$ 2,165,401
Columbus, OH							5	5	$ 1,922,478
St. Petersburg							5	5	$ 1,485,961
Portland							5	4	$ 1,346,475
Costa Mesa, CA							4	4	$ 2,759,101
Rochester, NY							4	5	$ 1,419,193
Vancouver							4	4	$ 1,349,018
Grand Rapids							4	4	$ 1,199,354
Minneapolis							3	3	$ 1,833,664
Cincinnati							3	3	$ 1,263,857
Hershey, PA							3	3	$ 1,169,623
Total:	899	201	$189,650,940	799	213	$194,962,180	792	283	$231,233,691

Note: The above figures apply only to so-called Grand Rights productions, not bus-and-truck, one-night scheduled shows or regional, resident, or stock operations. Also, cities having less than $1 million total box receipts during the season have been omitted.

Source: Variety 6/8/88, 6/14–20/89.

Chart 4.2 Top Road Grossers (1988–1989)

The following are the thirty-five top-grossing "touring or local" productions of the 1988–1989 season. The list includes all shows grossing a total of $1 million or more during the thirty-two week season. Parenthetical designations are for Musicals, Plays, Solo Shows, and Revivals *(Variety,* 6/14–20/89).

1.	*Les Misérables* (2 companies) (M)	$ 77,735,722
2.	*Cats* (2 companies) (M)	30,168,516
3.	*Me and My Girl* (M)	14,379,639
4.	*Cabaret* (M) (R)	11,090,334
5.	*Can-Can* (M) (R)	10,014,214
6.	*South Pacific* (M)(R)	9,804,746
7.	*Search for Signs of Intelligent Life* (So)	8,933,701
8.	*Into the Woods* (M)	8,584,304
9.	*Driving Miss Daisy* (P)	7,461,314
10.	*Penn & Teller*	5,698,769
11.	*Elvis* (M)	5,109,560
12.	*Oba-Oba* (M)	4,765,324
13.	*Anything Goes* (M) (R)	3,738,941
14.	*Broadway Bound* (P)	3,637,295
15.	*Steel Magnolias* (P)	3,487,117
16.	*Born Yesterday* (P)	3,152,655
17.	*Nunsense* (M)	3,143,426
18.	*Les Liaisons Dangereuses* (P)	2,264,605
19.	*Canciones de mi Padre* (M)	1,917,119
20.	*Michael Feinstein* (M)	1,808,847
21.	*Ain't Misbehavin'* (M)(R)	1,774,388
22.	*Sleuth* (P)	1,662,436
23.	*Damn Yankees* (M)(R)	1,617,480
24.	*Annie Get Your Gun* (M)(R)	1,538,094
25.	*Mystery of Edwin Drood* (M)	1,460,679
26.	*Hapgood* (P)	1,364,671
27.	*Odd Couple* (P)	1,251,730
28.	*Sophisticated Ladies* (M)(R)	1,178,785
29.	*Gypsy* (M)(R)	1,171,303
30.	*The Nerd* (P)	1,162,512
31.	*Clarence Darrow* (So)	1,142,137
32.	*Dreamgirls* (M)(R)	1,109,695
33.	*The Business of Murder* (P)	1,093,808
34.	*American Jukebox* (M)	1,027,975
35.	*Phantom of the Opera* (M)(Ken Hill version)	1,027,489
	Total	$236,479,330[a]

[a]Twenty-two, or 63% percent, are musicals, which generate 82 percent of the total.

Chart 4.3 Broadway Musical Shows Playing Over One Thousand Performances

1920–29	None

1930–39
1. *Pins and Needles* (1937–1938)
2. *Hellzapoppin* (1938–1939)

1940–49
1. *Oklahoma!* (1942–1943)
2. *Annie Get Your Gun* (1945–1946)
3. *Kiss Me, Kate* (1948–1949)
4. *South Pacific* (1948–1949)

1950–59
1. *Guys and Dolls* (1950–1951)
2. *The King and I* (1950–1951)
3. *The Pajama Game* (1953–1954)
4. *Damn Yankees* (1954–1955)
5. *My Fair Lady* (1955–1956)
6. *The Music Man* (1957–1958)
7. *The Sound of Music* (1959–1960)

1960–69
1. *How to Succeed in Business without Really Trying* (1961–1962)
2. *Hello, Dolly!* (1963–1964)
3. *Funny Girl* (1963–1964)
4. *Fiddler on the Roof* (1964–1965)
5. *Man of La Mancha* (1965–1966)
6. *Mame* (1965–1966)
7. *Cabaret* (1966–1967)
8. *Hair* (1967–1968)
9. *Promises, Promises* (1968–1969)
10. *1776* (1968–1969)
11. *Oh, Calcutta!* (1969–1970)

1970–79
1. *Oh, Calcutta!* (1970–1971)
2. *Don't Bother Me. I Can't Cope* (1971–1972)
3. *Grease* (1972–1973)
4. *Pippin* (1972–1973)
5. *The Magic Show* (1973–1974)
6. *The Wiz* (1974–1975)
7. *Shenandoah* (1974–1975)
8. *A Chorus Line* (1975–1976)
9. *Oh, Calcutta!* (Revival) (1976–1977)
10. *Annie* (1976–1977)
11. *Ain't Misbehavin'* (1977–1978)
12. *Dancin'* (1977–1978)
13. *They're Playing Our Song* (1978–1979)
14. *The Best Little Whorehouse in Texas* (1978–1979)

Chater 4.3 Broadway Musical Shows Playing Over One Thousand Performances *(cont.)*

	15. *Evita* (1979–1980)
	16. *Sugar Babies* (1979–1980)
1980–89	1. *42nd Street* (1980–1981)
	2. *Dreamgirls* (1981–1982)
	3. *Cats* (1982–1983)*
	4. *La Cage aux Folles* (1983–1984)
	5. *Big River* (1984–1985)
	6. *Les Misérables* (1986–1987)*
	7. *Me and My Girl* (1986–1987)
	8. *The Phantom of the Opera* (1987–1988)*
	9. *Grand Hotel* (1989–1990)

*Still playing in 1991.
Source: *Variety*, 6/6/90.

Appendix 5: The Phantom of the Opera Staff (1989-on Broadway)

1. Producer — Cameron Mackintosh
2. Managing Director — Martin McCallum
3. Executive Director — Richard Jay-Alexander
4. Production Administrator — Mitchell Lemsky
5. Production Associate — Cherrie Sciro
6. Production Associate — Barbara Hourigan
7. Chairman, Shubert Organization — Gerald Schoenfeld
8. President, Shubert Organization — Bernard B. Jacobs
9. Director — Harold Prince
10. Composer — Andrew Lloyd Webber
11. Lyricist — Charles Hart
12. Additional Lyrics — Richard Stilgoe
13. Bookwriter — Richard Stilgoe
14. Production Designer — Maria Bjornson
15. Lighting — Andrew Bridge
16. Sound — Martin Levan
17. Musical Supervision and Direction — David Caddick
18. Orchestrator — David Cullen
19. Musical Staging and Choreography — Gillian Lynne
20. General Manager — Alan Wasser
21. General Press Representative: — Merle Frimark
    The Fred Nathan Co.
22. Director's Assistant — Ruth Mitchell
23. Associate General Manager — Allan Williams
24. Technical Production Manager — John H. Paul III
25. Company Manager — Michael Gill
26. Production Stage Manager — Mitchell Lemsky
27. Stage Manager — Fred Hanson
28. Stage Manager — Bethe Ward

Cast[a]

29. The Phantom of the Opera	Timothy Nolen
30. Christine Daae	Patti Cohenour
31. Christine Daae (at certain performances)	Dale Kristien
32. Raoul, Vicomte de Chagny	Steve Barton
33. Carlotta Giudicelli	Judy Kaye
34. Monsieur André	Chris Groenendaal
35. Monsieur Firmin	Nicholas Wyman
36. Madame Giry	Leila Martin
37. Ubaldo Piangi	David Romano
38. Meg Giry	Elisa Heinsohn
39. Monsieur Reyer	Peter Kevoian
40. Auctioneer	Richard Warren Pugh
41. Porter/Marksman	Jeff Keller
42. Monsieur Lefevre	Kenneth Waller
43. Joseph Buquet	Philip Steele
44. Don Attilio ("Il Muto")/Passarino	George Lee Andrews
45. Slave Master ("Hannibal")	David Loring
46. Flunky/Stagehand	Barry McNabb
47. Policeman	Charles Rule
48. Page ("Don Juan Triumphant")	Olga Talyn
49. Porter/Fireman	William, Scott Brown
50. Page ("Don Juan Triumphant")	Candace Rogers-Adler
51. Wardrobe Mistress/Confidante ("Il Muto")	Mary Leigh Stahl
52. Princess ("Hannibal")	Rebecca Luker
53. Madame Firmin	Beth McVey
54. Innkeeper's Wife ("Don Juan Triumphant")	Jan Horvath
55. The Ballet Chorus of the Opéra Populaire	Nicole Fosse
56.	Charles Gehm
57.	Lisa Lockwood
58.	Lori MacPherson
59.	Dodie Pettit
60.	Catherine Ulissey
61. Ballet Swing	Denny Berry
62. Swings	Keith Butterbaugh
63.	Frank Mastrone
64.	Suzanne Ishe

U. S. Design Staff

65.	Associate Scenic Designer	Dana Kenn
66.	Associate Costume Designer	Cynthia Hamilton
67.	Associate Lighting Director	Debra Dumas
68.	Assistant Sound Designer	Larry Spurgeon
69.	Assistant to Scenic Designer	Paul Kelly
70.	Assistant to Scenic Designer	Paul Weimer
71.	Assistant to Scenic Designer	Steven Sakland
72.	Assistant to Costume Designer	David Robinson
73.	Assistant to Costume Designer	Marcy Froelich
74.	Assistant to Lighting Designer	Vivien Leone
75.	Assistant to Lighting Designer	Wendy Bodzin
76.	Assistant to Sound Designer	Jonathan Westin
77.	Assistant to Sound Designer	James M. Bay
78.	Assistant to Sound Designer	Joan Curcio

U. K. Design Staff

79.	Production Technical Consultant	Martyn Hayes Associates
80.	Associate Scenic Designer	Jonathan Allen
81.	Associate Costume Designer	Sue Willmington
82.	Associate Lighting Designer	Howard Eaton
83.	Automation Consultant	Michael Barnet
84.	Draperies Consultant	Peter Everett
85.	Sculptures Consultant	Stephen Pyle
86.	Sound Consultant	Ralph Collin
87.	Assistant to Gillian Lynne	Naomi Sorkin
88.	Associate Technical Production Manager	Marie Berrett
89.	Associate Technical Production Manager	Jake Bell
90.	Associate Manager	Thom Mitchell
91.	Dance Captain	Denny Berry
92.	Casting Associate	Tara Jayne Rubin
93.	Production Carpenter	Joseph Patria
94.	Production Electrician	Robert Fehribach
95.	Production Propertyman	Timothy Abel
96.	Production Sound Operator	Steve Kennedy
97.	Production Wardrobe Supervisor	Adelaide Laurino
98.	Production Wig Supervisor	Wayne Herndon
99.	Head Carpenter	Elbert Kuhn
100.	Automation Carpenter	Michael Wyatt
101.	Automation Carpenter	James Harris
102.	Assistant Carpenter	John Cennamo
103.	Flyman	Dick Miller
104.	Head Electrician	Alan Lampel

105. Assistant Electrician	J. R. Beket
106. Assistant Propertyman	Michael Bernstein
107. Assistant Propertyman	Victor Amerling
108. Assistant Propertyman	Alfred Ricci
109. Sound Operator	Scott Marcellus
110. Assistant Wardrobe Supervisor	Alan Eskolasky
111. Hairdresser	Jean Migdal
112. Hairdresser	James Post
113. Hairdresser	Manuel Rodriguez
114. Hairdresser	Carl Wilson
115. Associate Conductor	Jeffrey Huard
116. Associate Conductor	Paul Schwartz
117. Orchestra Contractor	Mel Rodnon Music Management, Inc.
118. Musical Preparation Supervisor	Mathilde Pincus
119. Musical Preparation Supervisor	Victor Jarowey
120. Synthesizer Consultant	Andrew Barrett
121. Rehearsal Pianist	Kristen Blodgette
122. Rehearsal Pianist	David Lai
123. Assistant to General Manager	Fred Bimbler
124. Assistant to General Manager	Lizz Cone
125. Assistant to General Manager	Harriet Kittner
126. Assistant to General Manager	Jane Klein
127. Assistant to General Manager	Larry Reitzer
128. Assistant to General Manger	Peter Royston
129. Press Assistant	Bert Fink
130. Press Associate	Scott Taylor
131. Press Associate	Marc Thibodeau
132. Press Assistant	Fifi Schuettich
133. Public Relations for Andrew Lloyd Webber	Brown & Powers
134. Assistant to Technical Production Manager	Rhys Williams
135. Assistant to Technical Production Manager	Judy Barrett
136. Assistant to Technical Production Manager	Laura Eichholz
137. Production Assistant	Rachel Abroms
138. Mr. Nolen's Personal Dresser	Mary Jestice
139. Mr. Nolen's Makeup Artist	Thelma Pollard
140. Legal Counsel	Paul S. Woerner
141. Legal Counsel	S. Jean Ward
142. Legal Advisor to the Really Useful Co.	Paul, Weiss, Rifkind, Wharton & Garrison
143. Accounting	Bernard Rosenberg [no relation to the coauthor]
144. Merchandising	DeWynters Advertising Ltd.
145. Merchandising Concessionaire	Loring & Mathews Merchandising, Inc.

146. Advertising and Logo Design	DeWynters, Ltd.
147. Advertising	Serino, Coyne & Nappi
148. Insurance (U. S.)	Robert A. Boyar
149. Insurance (U. K.)	Richard Walton
150. Banking	Noreen Tobin (Morgan Guaranty)
151. Banking	Barbara von Borstel (Morgan)
152. Travel Agent	Gloria & Associates Travel
153. Customs Broker (U. S.)	PTL Customs House
154. Customs Broker (U. K.)	Theatours, Ltd.
155. Payroll Service	Handly Walker, Inc.
156. Production Photographer	Clive Barda
157. Associate Photographer	Bob Marshak
158. Additional Photography	Peter Cunningham
159. House Manager	Spofford Beadle
160. Makeup Creator and Designer (for Nolen)	Christopher Tucker

The Really Useful Theatre Company, Inc.

161. Director	Brian Brolly
162. Director	Bridget Heyward
163. New York Office Manager	Judy Insel

Orchestra

164. Conductor	David Caddick
165. Associate Conductor	Jeffrey Huard
166. Associate Conductor	Paul Schwartz
167. Violin	Louann Montesi
168. Violin	Fred Buldrini
169. Violin	Alvin E. Rogers
170. Violin	Gayle Dixon
171. Violin	David Davis
172. Violin	Abraham Appleman
173. Violin	Leonard Rivlin
174. Violin	Jan Mullen
175. Viola	Stephanie Fricker
176. Viola	Veronica Salas
177. Cello	Bonnie Hartman
178. Cello	Jeanne LeBlanc
179. Bass	John Beal
180. Harp	Henry Fanelli
181. Flute	Sheryl Henze
182. Flute/Clarinet	Ralph Olsen
183. Oboe	Robert Botti
184. Clarinet	Matthew Goodman
185. Bassoon	Atsuko Sato
186. Trumpet	Lowell Hershey

187. Trumpet	Francis Bonny
188. Bass Trombone	Garfield Fobbs
189. French Horn	Gary Johnson
190. French Horn	R. Allen Spanjer
191. French Horn	Peter Reit
192. Percussion	Eric Cohen
193. Percussion	Jan Hagiwara
194. Keyboard	Jeffrey Huard
195. Keyboard	Kristen Blodgette

Total: 195 Members of the Project

aNot the original cast

Appendix 6: Lists of Broadway Musicals (1945–1991)

The following lists include musical productions that (1) played at legitimate Broadway houses under first-class production contracts and (2) were listed in the Broadway sections of the two main theater annuals, *Theatre World* and the *Burns Mantle Theater Yearbook: Best Plays* series. In dubious instances, inclusion on or omission from *Variety's* annual list of Broadway Hits and Flops was used as the final arbiter. The following types of productions were not included: limited engagements, ice shows, puppet theater, shows in repertory, dance recitals, folk theater, and productions of national tours appearing on Broadway.

For shows that closed and opened either in translation or within the same season, the show was counted as one in the arithmetical computation of hits and flops, e.g., *Party with Comden and Green, Sing, Israel, Sing.* Also, pre-Broadway flops have been added into the final total of shows for each season. They should be *subtracted* from the total for the actual number of musicals produced on Broadway in a given season. When the sources disagreed on the pre-Broadway flops in a season, the number given represents only titles they list in common.

Variety does not specify tryout flops as musicals until the 1948–49 season. *Burns Mantle* began reprinting hits/flops, etc., as per *Variety* in 1952–53 through 1960–61. It began its own listing of plays that closed out of town in the 1961–62 volume. *Theatre World* stopped listing pre-Broadway closings in the 1980–81 volume. *Variety's* last list that included them was for the 1981–82 season.

The Sources

The primary source of information for this report was the annual series, *Theatre World*. Missing information was culled from the annual series *The Burns Mantle Theater Yearbook: The Best Plays*. The hit/flop classifications were found in the weekly paper *Variety*. Note: The terms "hit" and "flop" are only used to indicate whether or not a musical recouped its investment as of its Broadway closing.

The Productions

New musicals are designated by an *N* in the production column; *R* indicates revivals.

The Performances

Performance numbers come from the two main sources; when at times conflicting accounts within one source were given, the higher number was chosen. These numbers should not include previews, although this may not always be true. For shows still running at the end of the 1989–90 season, performance numbers are given through the 1989–90 season, with the exception of *The Phantom of the Opera*. For this production, the performance number is given as 1,000 + to indicate its having passed this milestone.

The Theaters

Only shows appearing in *legitimate* Broadway theaters were listed. See appendix 3.

Compiled by Camille Croce Dee.

Broadway Musicals, 1945–1946

Title	Prod.	Theater	Open	Close	No. Perf.	E⟩ Res
Marinka	N	Winter Garden	07/18/45	12/08/45	165	Fl⟩
Mr. Strauss Goes to Boston	N	Century	09/06/45	09/16/45	12	Fl⟩
Carib Song	N	Adelphi	09/27/45	10/27/45	36	Fl⟩
Polonaise	N	Alvin	10/06/45	01/12/46	113	Fl⟩
The Red Mill	R	Ziegfeld	10/16/45	01/18/47	531	Hi⟩

Title	Prod.	Theater	Open	Close	No. Perf.	End Result
Girl from Nantucket	N	Adelphi	11/08/45	11/17/45	12	Flop
You with It?	N	Century	11/10/45	06/29/46	264	Hit
Day before Spring	N	National	11/22/45	04/14/46	167	Flop
on Dollar Baby	N	Alvin	12/21/45	06/29/46	219	Flop
w Boat	R	Ziegfeld	01/05/46	01/04/47	417	Hit
Would-Be Gentleman	N	Booth	01/09/46	03/16/46	77	Flop
lie Bly	N	Adelphi	01/21/46	02/02/46	16	Flop
e Song	N	Plymouth	02/06/46	06/08/46	142	Flop
Duchess Misbehaves	N	Adelphi	02/13/46	02/16/46	5	Flop
ee to Make Ready	N	Adelphi	03/07/46	12/14/46	323	Hit
Louis Woman	N	Martin Beck	03/30/46	07/06/46	113	Flop
Me Mister	N	National	04/18/46	01/10/48	734	Hit
nie Get Your Gun	N	Imperial	05/16/46	02/12/49	1147	Hit

nber of New Hits	=	4
nber of New Flops	=	12
nber of Revival Hits	=	2
nber of Revival Flops	=	0
TAL NEW SHOWS	=	16
TAL REVIVALS	=	2
-Broadway Flops	=	4
al Shows	=	22
cent Flops	=	73%

-Broadway Flops:
Theater World: Spring in Brazil, The Passing Show, Love in the Snow, Shootin' Star, Windy City
Variety: Love in the Snow, Shootin' Star, Spring in Brazil, Windy City

roadway Musicals, 1946–1947

Title	Prod.	Theater	Open	Close	No. Perf.	End Result
dbits of 1946	N	Plymouth	07/08/46	07/13/46	8	Flop
urs Is My Heart	N	Shubert	09/05/46	10/05/46	36	Flop
ypsy Lady	N	Century	09/17/46	11/23/46	79	Flop
rk Avenue	N	Shubert	11/04/46	01/04/47	72	Flop
l Nègre	N	Belasco	11/07/46	12/22/46	54	Flop
the Shoe Fits	N	Century	09/17/46	12/21/46	20	Flop
plitzky of Notre Dame	N	Century	12/26/46	02/15/47	60	Flop
eggar's Holiday	N	Broadway	12/26/46	03/29/47	111	Flop
reet Scene	N	Adelphi	01/09/47	05/17/47	148	Flop
nian's Rainbow	N	46th St.	01/10/47	10/02/48	725	Hit
veethearts	R	Shubert	01/21/47	09/27/47	288	Hit
he Chocolate Soldier	R	Century	03/12/47	05/10/47	69	Flop
rigadoon	N	Ziegfeld	03/13/47	07/31/48	581	Hit

Broadway Musicals, 1945–1946 (*cont.*)

Title	Prod.	Theater	Open	Close	No. Perf.	End Result
Barefoot Boy with Cheek	N	Martin Beck	04/03/47	07/05/47	108	Flop
The Medium and The Telephone	N	Barrymore	05/01/47	11/01/47	211	Flop

Number of New Hits   = 2
Number of New Flops   = 11
Number of Revival Hits   = 1
Number of Revival Flops   = 1
TOTAL NEW SHOWS   = 13
TOTAL REVIVALS   = 2
Pre-Broadway Flops   = 2
Total Shows   = 17
Percent Flops   = 82%
Pre-Broadway Flops:
Per *Theater World* and *Variety:* Sweet Bye and Bye, In Gay New Orleans

Broadway Musicals, 1947–1948

Title	Prod.	Theater	Open	Close	No. Perf.	End Result
Louisiana Lady	N	Century	06/02/47	06/04/47	4	Flop
Music in My Heart	N	Adelphi	10/02/47	01/24/48	124	Flop
Under the Counter	N	Shubert	10/03/47	10/25/47	27	Flop
High Button Shoes	N	Century	10/09/47	07/02/49	727	Hit
Allegro	N	Majestic	10/10/47	07/10/48	315	Flop[a]
Caribbean Carnival	N	International	12/05/47	12/13/47	11	Flop
Angel in the Wings	N	Coronet	12/11/47	09/04/48	308	Hit
The Cradle Will Rock	R	Mansfield	12/26/47	02/07/48	34	Flop
Make Mine Manhattan	N	Broadhurst	01/15/48	01/08/49	429	Hit
Look Ma, I'm Dancin'	N	Adelphi	01/29/48	07/10/48	188	Hit
Inside USA	N	Century	04/30/48	02/19/49	339	Hit
Hold It!	N	National	05/05/48	06/12/48	46	Flop
Sally	R	Martin Beck	05/06/48	06/05/48	36	Flop
Ballet Ballads	N	Music Box	05/18/48	07/10/48	62	Flop

Number of New Hits   = 5
Number of New Flops   = 7
Number of Revival Hits   = 0
Number of Revival Flops   = 2
TOTAL NEW SHOWS   = 12
TOTAL REVIVALS   = 2
Pre-Broadway Flops   = 2
Total Shows   = 16
Percent Flops   = 69%
Pre-Broadway Flops:
Per *Theater World:* Paris Sings Again, Bonanza Bound, My Romance
Per *Variety:* Paris Sings Again, Bonanza Bound
[a] *Variety* listed *Allegro* as a "hit," but several sources indicate that it closed without recouping its investment.

Broadway Musicals, 1948–1949

Title	Prod.	Theater	Open	Close	No. Perf.	End Result
Sleepy Hollow	N	St. James	06/03/48	06/12/48	12	Flop
Hilarities (of 1949)	N	Adelphi	09/09/48	09/18/48	14	Flop
Small Wonder	N	Coronet	09/15/48	01/08/49	134	Flop
Heaven on Earth	N	Century	09/16/48	09/25/48	12	Flop
Magdalena	N	Ziegfeld	09/20/48	12/04/48	88	Flop
Love Life	N	46th St.	10/11/48	05/14/49	252	Flop
Where's Charley?	N	St. James	10/11/48	09/09/50	792	Hit
My Romance	N	Shubert	10/19/48	01/08/49	95	Flop
As the Girls Go	N	Winter Garden	11/13/48	01/14/50	420	Hit
Lend an Ear	N	National	12/16/48	01/21/50	460	Hit
The Rape of Lucretia	R	Ziegfeld	12/29/48	01/16/49	23	Flop
Kiss Me, Kate	N	New Century	12/30/48	07/28/51	1077	Hit
Along Fifth Avenue	N	Broadhurst	01/13/49	06/18/49	180	Flop
All for Love	N	Mark Hellinger	01/22/49	05/07/49	121	Flop
South Pacific	N	Majestic	04/07/49	01/16/54	1925	Hit

Number of New Hits   = 5
Number of New Flops   = 9
Number of Revival Hits   = 0
Number of Revival Flops   = 1
TOTAL NEW SHOWS   = 14
TOTAL REVIVALS   = 1
Pre-Broadway Flops   = 1
Total Shows   = 16
Percent Flops   = 69%
Pre-Broadway Flops:
Per *Theater World:* That's the Ticket, Raze the Roof (Musical Revue), Ed Wynn's Laugh Carnival (Musical Variety Revue)
Per *Variety:* That's the Ticket

Broadway Musicals, 1949–1950

Title	Prod.	Theater	Open	Close	No. Perf.	End Result
Cabalgata ("A Night in Spain")	N	Broadway	07/07/49	09/10/49	76	Flop
Miss Liberty	N	Imperial	07/15/49	04/08/50	308	Flop
Touch and Go	N	Broadhurst	10/13/49	03/18/50	176	Flop
Lost in the Stars	N	Music Box	10/30/49	07/01/50	281	Flop
Regina	N	46th St.	10/31/49	12/17/49	56	Flop
Texas, Li'l Darlin'	N	Mark Hellinger	11/25/49	09/09/50	293	Flop
Gentlemen Prefer Blondes	N	Ziegfeld	12/08/49	09/15/51	740	Hit
Happy as Larry	N	Coronet	01/06/50	01/07/50	3	Flop
Alive and Kicking	N	Winter Garden	01/17/50	02/25/50	46	Flop
Dance Me a Song	N	Royale	01/20/50	02/18/50	35	Flop
Arms and the Girl	N	46th St.	02/02/50	05/27/50	134	Flop
The Consul	N	Barrymore	03/15/50	11/04/50	269	Hit

Broadway Musicals, 1949–1950

Title	Prod.	Theater	Open	Close	No. Perf.	End Result
Great to Be Alive	N	Winter Garden	03/23/50	05/06/50	52	Flop
Peter Pan	N	Imperial	04/24/50	01/27/51	320	Flop
Tickets, Please	N	Coronet	04/27/50	11/25/50	245	Flop
The Liar	N	Broadhurst	05/18/50	05/27/50	12	Flop

Number of New Hits   = 2
Number of New Flops   = 14
Number of Revival Hits   = 0
Number of Revival Flops   = 0
TOTAL NEW SHOWS   = 16
TOTAL REVIVALS   = 0
Pre-Broadway Flops   = 0
Total Shows   = 16
Percent Flops   = 88%

Broadway Musicals, 1950–1951

Title	Prod.	Theater	Open	Close	No. Perf.	End Result
Michael Todd's Peep Show	N	Winter Garden	06/28/50	02/25/51	278	Flop
Pardon Our French	N	Broadway	10/05/50	01/06/51	100	Flop
Call Me Madam	N	Imperial	10/12/50	05/03/52	644	Hit
The Barrier	N	Broadhurst	11/02/50	11/04/50	4	Flop
Guys and Dolls	N	46th St.	11/24/50	11/25/53	1200	Hit
Let's Make an Opera	N	John Golden	12/13/50	12/16/50	5	Flop
Bless You All	N	Mark Hellinger	12/14/50	02/24/51	84	Flop
Out of This World	N	New Century	12/21/50	05/05/51	157	Flop
Where's Charley?	R	Broadway	01/29/51	03/10/51	56	Flop
The King and I	N	St. James	03/29/51	03/20/54	1246	Hit
Make a Wish	N	Winter Garden	04/18/51	07/14/51	102	Flop
A Tree Grows in Brooklyn	N	Alvin	04/19/51	12/08/51	267	Flop
Flahooley	N	Broadhurst	05/14/51	06/17/51	40	Flop

Number of New Hits   = 3
Number of New Flops   = 9
Number of Revival Hits   = 0
Number of Revival Flops   = 1
TOTAL NEW SHOWS   = 12
TOTAL REVIVALS   = 1
Pre-Broadway Flops   = 4
Total Shows   = 17
Percent Flops   = 82%
Pre-Broadway Flops:
Per *Theater World* and *Variety:* If You Please, Lady from Paris, Little Boy Blue, Red, White, and Blue

Broadway Musicals, 1951–1952

Title	Prod.	Theater	Open	Close	No. Perf.	End Result
Courtin' Time	N	National	06/14/51	07/14/51	37	Flop
Seventeen	N	Broadhurst	06/21/51	11/24/51	180	Flop
Two on the Aisle	N	Mark Hellinger	07/19/51	03/15/52	276	Flop
Borscht Capades	N	Royale	09/17/51	12/02/51	90	Flop
Music in the Air	R	Ziegfeld	10/08/51	11/24/51	56	Flop
Top Banana	N	Winter Garden	11/01/51	10/04/52	356	Hit
Paint Your Wagon	N	Shubert	11/12/51	07/19/52	289	Flop
Pal Joey	R	Broadhurst	01/02/52	04/18/53	542	Hit
Three Wishes for Jamie	N	Mark Hellinger	03/21/52	06/07/52	94	Flop
Four Saints in Three Acts	R	Broadway	04/16/52	04/27/52	15	Flop
Of Thee I Sing	R	Ziegfeld	05/05/52	07/05/52	72	Flop
Shuffle Along	R	Broadway	05/08/52	05/10/52	4	Flop
New Faces of 1952	N	Royale	05/16/52	03/28/53	365	Hit

Number of New Hits   = 2
Number of New Flops   = 6
Number of Revival Hits   = 1
Number of Revival Flops = 4
TOTAL NEW SHOWS   = 8
TOTAL REVIVALS   = 5
Pre-Broadway Flops   = 2
Total Shows   = 15
Percent Flops   = 80%
Pre-Broadway Flops:
Per *Theater World* and *Variety:* A Month of Sundays, Curtain Going Up

Broadway Musicals, 1952–1953

Title	Prod.	Theater	Open	Close	No. Perf.	End Result
Wish You Were Here	N	Imperial	06/25/52	11/28/53	597	Hit
Buttrio Square	N	New Century	10/14/52	10/18/52	7	Flop
My Darlin' Aida	N	Winter Garden	10/27/52	01/10/53	89	Flop
Two's Company	N	Alvin	12/15/52	03/08/53	90	Flop
Hazel Flagg	N	Mark Hellinger	02/11/53	09/19/53	190	Flop
Maggie	N	National	02/18/53	02/21/53	5	Flop
Wonderful Town	N	Winter Garden	02/25/53	07/03/54	559	Hit
Can-Can	N	Shubert	05/07/53	06/25/55	892	Hit
Me and Juliet	N	Majestic	05/28/53	04/03/54	358	Hit

Number of New Hits   = 4   TOTAL REVIVALS   = 0
Number of New Flops   = 5   Pre-Broadway Flops   = 0
Number of Revival Hits   = 0   Total Shows   = 9
Number of Revival Flops = 0   Percent Flops   = 56%
TOTAL NEW SHOWS   = 9

Broadway Musicals, 1953–1954

Title	Prod.	Theater	Open	Close	No. Perf.	End Result
Carnival in Flanders	N	New Century	09/08/53	09/12/53	6	Flop
Comedy in Music (Victor Borge)	N	John Golden	10/02/53	01/21/56	849	Hit
Kismet	N	Ziegfeld	12/03/53	04/23/55	583	Hit
John Murray Anderson's Almanac	N	Imperial	12/10/53	06/24/54	229	Flop
The Girl in Pink Tights	N	Mark Hellinger	03/05/54	06/12/54	115	Flop
By the Beautiful Sea	N	Majestic	04/08/54	11/27/54	270	Flop
The Golden Apple	N	Alvin	04/20/54	08/07/54	125	Flop
The Pajama Game	N	St. James	05/13/54	11/24/56	1063	Hit

Number of New Hits   = 3
Number of New Flops   = 5
Number of Revival Hits = 0
Number of Revival Flops = 0
TOTAL NEW SHOWS   = 8
TOTAL REVIVALS   = 0
Pre-Broadway Flops   = 1
Total Shows   = 9
Percent Flops   = 67%
Pre-Broadway Flops:
Per *Theater World, Variety,* and *Burns Mantle:* Little Jesse James

Broadway Musicals, 1954–1955

Title	Prod.	Theater	Open	Close	No. Perf.	End Result
The Boy Friend	N	Royale	09/30/54	11/26/55	483	Hit
On Your Toes	R	46th St.	10/11/54	12/04/54	64	Flop
Peter Pan	N	Winter Garden	10/20/54	02/26/55	149	Hit
Fanny	N	Majestic	11/04/54	12/16/56	888	Hit
Hit the Trail	N	Mark Hellinger	12/02/54	12/04/54	4	Flop
The Saint of Bleecker Street	N	Broadway	12/27/54	04/20/55	92	Flop
House of Flowers	N	Alvin	12/30/54	05/21/55	165	Flop
Plain and Fancy	N	Mark Hellinger	01/27/55	04/14/56	476	Hit
Silk Stockings	N	Imperial	02/24/55	04/03/56	461	Hit
3 for Tonight	N	Plymouth	04/06/55	06/18/55	85	Hit
Ankles Aweigh	N	Mark Hellinger	04/18/55	09/17/55	176	Flop
Damn Yankees	N	46th St.	05/05/55	10/19/57	1022	Hit
Seventh Heaven	N	ANTA	05/26/55	07/02/55	44	Flop

Number of New Hits   = 7
Number of New Flops   = 5
Number of Revival Hits = 0
Number of Revival Flops = 1
TOTAL NEW SHOWS   = 12

TOTAL REVIVALS   = 1
Pre-Broadway Flops   = 0
Total Shows   = 13
Percent Flops   = 46%

Broadway Musicals, 1955–1956

Title	Prod.	Theater	Open	Close	No. Perf.	End Result
Almost Crazy	N	Longacre	06/20/55	07/02/55	16	Flop
Catch a Star	N	Plymouth	09/06/55	09/24/55	23	Flop
The Vamp	N	Winter Garden	11/10/55	12/31/55	60	Flop
Pipe Dream	N	Shubert	11/30/55	06/30/56	245	Flop
My Fair Lady	N	Mark Hellinger	03/15/56	09/29/62	2715	Hit
Mr. Wonderful	N	Broadway	03/22/56	02/23/57	383	Flop
The Most Happy Fella	N	Imperial	05/03/56	12/14/57	678	Hit

Number of New Hits   = 2
Number of New Flops   = 5
Number of Revival Hits = 0
Number of Revival Flops = 0
TOTAL NEW SHOWS   = 7
TOTAL REVIVALS   = 0
Pre-Broadway Flops   = 4
Total Shows   =11
Percent Flops   =82%
Pre-Broadway Flops:
Per *Theater World, Variety,* and *Burns Mantle:* Reuben, Reuben, The Amazing Adele, Strip for Action, Ziegfeld Follies

Broadway Musicals, 1956–1957

Title	Prod.	Theater	Open	Close	No. Perf.	End Result
Shangri-La	N	Winter Garden	06/13/56	06/30/56	21	Flop
New Faces of 1956	N	Barrymore	06/14/56	12/22/56	221	Flop
Li'l Abner	N	St. James	11/15/56	07/12/58	693	Hit
Bells Are Ringing	N	Shubert	11/29/56	03/07/59	925	Hit
Candide	N	Martin Beck	12/01/56	02/02/57	73	Flop
Happy Hunting	N	Majestic	12/06/56	11/30/57	413	Flop
Ziegfeld Follies (of 1957)	N	Winter Garden	03/01/57	06/15/57	123	Flop
Shinbone Alley	N	Broadway	04/13/57	05/25/57	49	Flop
New Girl in Town	N	46th St.	05/14/57	05/24/58	432	Hit

Number of New Hits   = 3
Number of New Flops   = 6
Number of Revival Hits = 0
Number of Revival Flops = 0
TOTAL NEW SHOWS   = 9
TOTAL REVIVALS   = 0
Pre-Broadway Flops   = 0
Total Shows   = 9
Percent Flops   =67%

Broadway Musicals, 1957–1958

Title	Prod.	Theater	Open	Close	No. Perf.	End Result
Simply Heavenly	N	Playhouse	08/20/57	10/12/57	62	Flop
Mask and Gown	N	John Golden	09/10/57	10/12/57	39	Flop
West Side Story	N	Winter Garden	09/26/57	06/27/59	734	Hit
Copper and Brass	N	Martin Beck	10/17/57	11/16/57	36	Flop
Jamaica	N	Imperial	10/31/57	04/11/59	558	Hit
Rumple	N	Alvin	11/06/57	12/14/57	45	Flop
The Music Man	N	Majestic	12/19/57	04/15/61	1375	Hit
The Body Beautiful	N	Broadway	01/23/58	03/15/58	60	Flop
Oh, Captain!	N	Alvin	02/04/58	07/19/58	192	Flop
Portofino	N	Adelphi	02/21/58	02/22/58	3	Flop
Say, Darling	N	ANTA	04/03/58	01/17/59	332	Flop

Number of New Hits	= 3	TOTAL REVIVALS	= 0
Number of New Flops	= 8	Pre-Broadway Flops	= 1
Number of Revival Hits	= 0	Total Shows	= 12
Number of Revival Flops	= 0	Percent Flops	= 75%
TOTAL NEW SHOWS	= 11		

Pre-Broadway Flops:
Per *Theater World, Variety,* and *Burns Mantle:* The Carefree Heart

Broadway Musicals, 1958–1959

Title	Prod.	Theater	Open	Close	No. Perf.	End Result
Goldilocks	N	Lunt-Fontanne	10/11/58	02/28/59	161	Flop
Maria Golovin	N	Martin Beck	11/05/58	11/08/58	5	Flop
La Plume de Ma Tante	N	Royale	11/11/58	12/17/60	835	Hit
Flower Drum Song	N	St. James	12/01/58	05/07/60	602	Hit
Whoop-Up	N	Shubert	12/22/58	02/07/59	56	Flop
Party with Comden and Green	N	John Golden	12/23/58	01/24/59	38	Hit
Redhead	N	46th St.	02/05/59	03/19/60	455	Hit
Juno	N	Winter Garden	03/09/59	03/21/59	16	Flop
First Impressions	N	Alvin	03/19/59	05/30/59	84	Flop
Party with Comden and Green	N	John Golden	04/16/59	05/23/59	44	Hit
Destry Rides Again	N	Imperial	04/23/59	06/18/60	472	Flop
Nervous Set	N	Henry Miller's	05/12/59	05/30/59	23	Flop
Gypsy	N	Broadway	05/21/59	03/25/61	702	Hit

Number of New Hits	= 5	TOTAL REVIVALS	= 0
Number of New Flops	= 7	Pre-Broadway Flops	= 1
Number of Revival Hits	= 0	Total Shows	= 13
Number of Revival Flops	= 0	Percent Flops	= 62%
TOTAL NEW SHOWS	= 12		

Pre-Broadway Flops:
Per *Theater World, Variety,* and *Burns Mantle:* At the Grand

Broadway Musicals, 1959–1960

Title	Prod.	Theater	Open	Close	No. Perf.	End Result
Billy Barnes Revue	N	John Golden	08/04/59	10/17/59	87	Flop
Happy Town	N	54th St.	10/07/59	10/10/59	5	Flop
At the Drop of a Hat	N	John Golden	10/08/59	05/14/60	216	Flop
Take Me Along	N	Shubert	10/22/59	12/17/60	448	Flop
The Girls against the Boys	N	Alvin	11/02/59	11/14/59	16	Flop
The Sound of Music	N	Lunt-Fontanne	11/16/59	06/15/63	1443	Hit
Fiorello!	N	Broadhurst	11/23/59	10/28/61	796	Hit
Once upon a Mattress	N	Alvin	11/25/59	07/02/60	460	Hit
Saratoga	N	Winter Garden	12/07/59	02/13/60	80	Flop
Beg, Borrow or Steal	N	Martin Beck	02/10/60	02/13/60	5	Flop
Greenwillow	N	Alvin	03/08/60	05/28/60	95	Flop
Bye Bye Birdie	N	Martin Beck	04/14/60	10/07/61	607	Hit
From A to Z	N	Plymouth	04/20/60	05/07/60	21	Flop
Christine	N	46th St.	04/28/60	05/07/60	12	Flop
Finian's Rainbow	R	46th St.	05/23/60	06/01/60	12	Flop

Number of New Hits   = 4
Number of New Flops   = 10
Number of Revival Hits   = 0
Number of Revival Flops = 1
TOTAL NEW SHOWS   = 14
TOTAL REVIVALS   = 1
Pre-Broadway Flops   = 2
Total Shows   = 17
Percent Flops   = 77%
Pre-Broadway Flops:
Per *Theater World:* The Pink Jungle, Lock Up Your Daughters
Per *Variety* (and *Burns Mantle,* which reproduced *Variety's* list at this time): The Pink Jungle, Lock Up Your Daughters, Free and Easy

Broadway Musicals, 1960–1961

Title	Prod.	Theater	Open	Close	No. Perf.	End Result
Vintage '60	N	Brooks Atkinson	09/12/60	09/17/60	8	Flop
Irma La Douce	N	Plymouth	09/29/60	12/31/61	527	Hit
Laughs & Other Events	N	Barrymore	10/10/60	10/15/60	8	Flop
Tenderloin	N	46th St.	10/17/60	04/23/61	216	Flop
The Unsinkable Molly Brown	N	Winter Garden	11/03/60	02/10/60	532	Hit
Camelot	N	Majestic	12/03/60	01/05/63	873	Hit
Wildcat	N	Alvin	12/16/60	06/03/61	172	Flop
Do Re Mi	N	St. James	12/26/60	01/13/62	400	Flop
Show Girl	N	Eugene O'Neill	01/12/61	04/08/61	100	Hit
The Conquering Hero	N	ANTA	01/16/61	01/21/61	8	Flop
13 Daughters	N	54th St.	03/02/61	03/25/61	28	Flop
The Happiest Girl in the World	N	Martin Beck	04/03/61	06/24/61	97	Flop

Broadway Musicals, 1960–1961 *(cont.)*

Title	Prod.	Theater	Open	Close	No. Perf.	End Result
Carnival!	N	Imperial	04/13/61	01/05/63	719	Hit
Young Abe Lincoln	N	Eugene O'Neill	04/25/61	05/07/61	27	Flop
Donnybrook!	N	46th St.	05/18/61	07/15/61	68	Flop

Number of New Hits   = 5
Number of New Flops   = 10
Number of Revival Hits = 0
Number of Revival Flops = 0
TOTAL NEW SHOWS   = 15
TOTAL REVIVALS   = 0
Pre-Broadway Flops   = 1
Total Shows   = 16
Percent Flops   = 69%
Pre-Broadway Flops:
Per *Theater World:* None
Per *Variety* and *Burns Mantle:* Aloha, Hawaii

Broadway Musicals, 1961–1962

Title	Prod.	Theater	Open	Close	No. Perf.	End Result
The Billy Barnes People	N	Royale	06/13/61	06/17/61	8	Flop
From the Second City	N	Royale	09/26/61	12/09/61	87	Flop
Sail Away	N	Broadhurst	10/03/61	02/24/62	167	Flop
Milk and Honey	N	Martin Beck	10/10/61	01/26/63	543	Flop
Let It Ride	N	Eugene O'Neill	10/12/61	12/09/61	68	Flop
How to Succeed in Business . . .	N	46th St.	10/14/61	03/06/65	1415	Hit
Kwamina	N	54th St.	10/23/61	11/18/61	32	Flop
An Evening with Yves Montand	R	John Golden	10/24/61	12/16/61	55	Hit
Kean	N	Broadway	11/02/61	01/20/62	92	Flop
The Gay Life	N	Shubert	11/18/61	02/04/62	113	Flop
Subways Are for Sleeping	N	St. James	12/27/61	06/23/62	205	Flop
A Family Affair	N	Billy Rose	01/27/62	03/25/62	65	Flop
New Faces of '62	N	Alvin	02/01/62	02/24/62	28	Flop
No Strings	N	54th St.	03/15/62	08/03/63	580	Hit
All American	N	Winter Garden	03/19/62	05/26/62	80	Flop
I Can Get It for You Wholesale	N	Shubert	03/22/62	12/08/62	300	Flop
A Funny Thing Happened . . .	N	Alvin	05/08/62	08/29/64	965	Hit
Bravo, Giovanni	N	Broadhurst	05/19/62	09/15/62	76	Flop

Number of New Hits   = 3   TOTAL REVIVALS   = 1
Number of New Flops   = 14   Pre-Broadway Flops = 2
Number of Revival Hits = 1   Total Shows   = 20
Number of Revival Flops = 0   Percent Flops   = 80%
TOTAL NEW SHOWS   = 17
Pre-Broadway Flops:
Per *Theater World:* Kicks & Co., We Take the Town
Per *Variety* and *Burns Mantle:* Kicks & Co., We Take the Town, Lena Horne Show

Broadway Musicals, 1962–1963

Title	Prod.	Theater	Open	Close	No. Perf.	End Result
Stop the World, I Want . . .	Off N	Shubert	10/03/62	02/01/64	556	Hit
Mr. President	N	St. James	10/20/62	06/08/63	265	Flop
Beyond the Fringe	N	John Golden	10/27/62	05/30/64	673	Hit
Nowhere to Go but Up	N	Winter Garden	11/10/62	11/17/62	9	Flop
Little Me	N	Lunt-Fontanne	11/17/62	06/29/63	257	Flop
Oliver!	N	Imperial	01/06/63	11/14/64	774	Hit
Tovarich	N	Broadway	03/18/63	11/09/63	264	Flop
Sophie	N	Winter Garden	04/15/63	04/20/63	8	Flop
Hot Spot	N	Majestic	04/19/63	05/25/63	43	Flop
She Loves Me	N	Eugene O'Neill	04/23/63	01/11/64	302	Flop
The Beast in Me	N	Plymouth	05/16/63	05/18/63	4	Flop

Number of New Hits   = 3
Number of New Flops   = 8
Number of Revival Hits = 0
Number of Revival Flops = 0
TOTAL NEW SHOWS   = 11
TOTAL REVIVALS   = 0
Pre-Broadway Flops   = 2
Total Shows   = 13
Percent Flops   = 77%
Pre-Broadway Flops:
Per *Theater World* and *Variety:* La Belle, Get on Board-The Jazz Train (Revue)
Per *Burns Mantle:* Foxy, La Belle

Broadway Musicals, 1963–1964

Title	Prod.	Theater	Open	Close	No. Perf.	End Result
Student Gypsy	N	54th St.	09/30/63	10/12/63	16	Flop
Here's Love	N	Shubert	10/03/63	07/25/64	338	Flop
Jennie	N	Majestic	10/17/63	12/28/63	82	Flop
110 in the Shade	N	Broadhurst	10/24/63	08/08/64	330	Hit
Tambourines to Glory	N	Little	11/02/63	11/23/63	24	Flop
The Girl Who Came to Supper	N	Broadway	12/08/63	03/14/64	112	Flop
Double Dublin	N	Little	12/26/63	12/28/63	4	Flop
Hello, Dolly!	N	St. James	01/16/64	12/27/70	2844	Hit
Rugantino	N	Mark Hellinger	02/06/64	02/29/64	28	Flop
Foxy	N	Ziegfeld	02/16/64	04/18/64	72	Flop
What Makes Sammy Run?	N	54th St.	02/27/64	06/12/65	540	Flop
Funny Girl	N	Winter Garden	03/26/64	07/01/67	1348	Hit
Anyone Can Whistle	N	Majestic	04/04/64	04/11/64	9	Flop
High Spirits	N	Alvin	04/17/64	02/27/65	375	Flop

Broadway Musicals, 1963–1964 *(cont.)*

Title	Prod.	Theater	Open	Close	No. Perf.	End Result
Cafe Crown	N	Martin Beck	04/17/64	04/18/64	3	Flop
Fade Out-Fade In	N	Mark Hellinger	05/26/64	11/14/64	199	Flop

Number of New Hits   = 3
Number of New Flops   = 13
Number of Revival Hits = 0
Number of Revival Flops = 0
TOTAL NEW SHOWS   = 16
TOTAL REVIVALS   = 0
Pre-Broadway Flops   = 1
Total Shows   = 17
Percent Flops   = 82%
Pre-Broadway Flops:
Per *Theater World:* Zenda, Three Cheers for the Tired Businessman (Revue)
Per *Variety:* Prisoner of Zenda [*sic*]
Per *Burns Mantle:* Zenda, Cool Off!

Broadway Musicals, 1964–1965

Title	Prod.	Theater	Open	Close	No. Perf.	End Result
Follies Bergere	N	Broadway	06/02/64	11/14/64	191	Flop
Fiddler on the Roof	N	Imperial	09/22/64	07/02/72	3242	Hit
Oh What a Lovely War	N	Broadhurst	09/30/64	01/16/65	125	Flop
Cambridge Circus	N	Plymouth	10/06/64	10/24/64	23	Flop
Golden Boy	N	Majestic	10/20/64	03/05/66	569	Flop
Ben Franklin in Paris	N	Lunt Fontanne	10/27/64	05/01/65	215	Flop
Comedy in Music-Opus 2	R	John Golden	11/09/64	04/24/65	192	Flop
Something More!	N	Eugene O'Neill	11/10/64	11/21/64	15	Flop
Zizi	N	Broadway	11/21/64	01/02/65	49	Hit
Bajour	N	Shubert	11/23/64	06/12/65	232	Flop
I Had a Ball	N	Martin Beck	12/15/64	06/12/65	199	Flop
Kelly	N	Broadhurst	02/06/65	02/06/65	1	Flop
Fade Out-Fade In	R	Mark Hellinger	02/15/65	04/17/65	72	Flop
Baker Street	N	Broadway	02/16/65	11/14/65	313	Flop
Do I Hear a Waltz?	N	46th St.	03/18/65	09/25/65	220	Flop
Half a Sixpence	N	Broadhurst	04/25/65	07/16/66	512	Hit
Flora, the Red Menace	N	Alvin	05/11/65	07/24/65	87	Flop
The Roar of the Greasepaint . . .	N	Shubert	05/16/65	12/04/65	232	Hit

Number of New Hits   = 4   TOTAL REVIVALS   = 2
Number of New Flops   = 12   Pre-Broadway Flops = 2
Number of Revival Hits = 1   Total Shows   = 20
Number of Revival Flops = 1   Percent Flops   = 75%
TOTAL NEW SHOWS   = 16
Pre-Broadway Flops:
Per *Theater World:* Royal Flush, Pleasures and Palaces
Per *Variety* and *Burns Mantle:* Royal Flush, Pleasures and Palaces, Awf'lly Nice (Musical Revue)

Broadway Musicals, 1965–1966

Title	Prod.	Theater	Open	Close	No. Perf.	End Result
Pickwick	N	46th St.	10/04/65	11/20/65	56	Flop
Drat! The Cat!	N	Martin Beck	10/10/65	10/16/65	8	Flop
On a Clear Day You Can See . . .	N	Mark Hellinger	10/17/65	06/11/66	280	Flop
Skyscraper	N	Lunt-Fontanne	11/13/65	06/11/66	248	Flop
Man of La Mancha	N	ANTA Wash. Sq.	11/22/65	06/26/71	2329	Hit
Anya	N	Ziegfeld	11/29/65	12/11/65	16	Flop
The Yearling	N	Alvin	12/10/65	12/11/65	3	Flop
La Grosse Valise	N	54th St.	12/14/65	12/18/65	7	Flop
Sweet Charity	N	Palace	01/29/66	07/15/67	608	Hit
Wait a Minim!	N	John Golden	03/07/66	04/15/67	457	Hit
Pousse-Cafe	N	46th St.	03/18/66	03/19/66	3	Flop
It's a Bird . . . It's Superman	N	Alvin	03/29/66	07/17/66	129	Flop
A Time for Singing	N	Broadway	05/21/66	06/26/66	41	Flop
Mame	N	Winter Garden	05/24/66	01/03/70	1508	Hit

Number of New Hits   = 5
Number of New Flops   = 9
Number of Revival Hits = 0
Number of Revival Flops = 0
TOTAL NEW SHOWS   = 14
TOTAL REVIVALS   = 0
Pre-Broadway Flops   = 2
Total Shows   = 16
Percent Flops   = 69%
Pre-Broadway Flops:
Per *Theater World* and *Variety:* Hot September, Love Is a Ball (Musical Revue)
Per *Burns Mantle:* Hot September

Broadway Musicals, 1966–1967

Title	Prod.	Theater	Open	Close	No. Perf.	End Result
The Apple Tree	N	Shubert	10/18/66	11/25/67	463	Flop
Let's Sing Yiddish	N	Brooks Atkinson	11/09/66	01/29/67	107	Flop
Cabaret	N	Broadhurst	11/20/66	09/06/69	1166	Hit
Walking Happy	N	Lunt Fontanne	11/26/66	04/16/67	161	Flop
I Do! I Do!	N	46th St.	12/05/66	06/15/68	561	Hit
A Joyful Noise	N	Mark Hellinger	12/15/66	12/24/66	12	Flop
At the Drop of Another Hat	N	Booth	12/27/66	04/09/67	105	Hit
Sherry!	N	Alvin	03/28/67	05/27/67	65	Flop
Illya Darling	N	Mark Hellinger	04/11/67	01/13/68	320	Flop

Broadway Musicals, 1966–1967 *(cont.)*

Title	Prod.	Theater	Open	Close	No. Perf.	End Result
Hallelujah, Baby!	N	Martin Beck	04/26/67	01/13/68	293	Flop
Sing, Israel Sing	N	Brooks Atkinson	05/11/67	05/21/67	14	Flop

Number of New Hits	=	3
Number of New Flops	=	8
Number of Revival Hits	=	0
Number of Revival Flops	=	0
TOTAL NEW SHOWS	=	11
TOTAL REVIVALS	=	0
Pre-Broadway Flops	=	2
Total Shows	=	13
Percent Flops	=	77%

Pre-Broadway Flops:
Per *Theater World, Variety,* and *Burns Mantle:* Breakfast at Tiffany's, Chu Chem

Broadway Musicals, 1967–1968

Title	Prod.	Theater	Open	Close	No. Perf.	End Result
Henry, Sweet Henry	N	Palace	10/23/67	12/31/67	80	Flop
How Now, Dow Jones	N	Lunt-Fontanne	12/07/67	06/15/68	220	Flop
The Happy Time	N	Broadway	01/18/68	09/28/68	286	Flop
Darling of the Day	N	George Abbott	01/27/68	02/24/68	31	Flop
Golden Rainbow	N	Shubert	02/04/68	01/12/69	385	Flop
Here's Where I Belong	N	Billy Rose	03/03/68	03/03/68	1	Flop
The Education of Hyman Kaplan	N	Alvin	04/04/68	04/27/68	28	Flop
George M!	N	Palace	04/10/68	04/26/69	435	Flop
I'm Solomon	N	Mark Hellinger	04/23/68	04/27/68	7	Flop
Hair	N	Biltmore	04/29/68	07/01/72	1750	Hit
New Faces of 1968	N	Booth	05/02/68	06/15/68	52	Flop

Number of New Hits	=	1
Number of New Flops	=	10
Number of Revival Hits	=	0
Number of Revival Flops	=	0
TOTAL NEW SHOWS	=	11
TOTAL REVIVALS	=	0
Pre-Broadway Flops	=	1
Total Shows	=	12
Percent Flops	=	92%

Pre-Broadway Flops:
Per *Theater World, Variety,* and *Burns Mantle:* Mata Hari

Broadway Musicals, 1968–1969

Title	Prod.	Theater	Open	Close	No. Perf.	End Result
Noel Coward's Sweet Potato	N	Barrymore	09/28/68	10/12/68	17	Flop
Her First Roman	N	Lunt-Fontanne	10/20/68	11/02/68	17	Flop
Maggie Flynn	N	ANTA	10/23/68	01/05/69	82	Flop
Noel Coward's Sweet Potato	N	Booth	11/01/68	11/23/68	36	Flop
Zorba	N	Imperial	11/17/68	08/09/69	305	Flop
Promises Promises	N	Shubert	12/01/68	01/01/72	1281	Hit
The Fig Leaves Are Falling	N	Broadhurst	01/02/69	01/04/69	4	Flop
Celebration	N	Ambassador	01/22/69	04/26/69	110	Flop
Red, White, and Maddox	N	Cort	01/26/69	03/01/69	41	Flop
Canterbury Tales	N	Eugene O'Neill	02/03/69	05/18/69	122	Flop
Dear World	N	Mark Hellinger	02/06/69	05/31/69	132	Flop
1776	N	46th St.	03/16/69	02/13/72	1217	Hit
Come Summer	N	Lunt-Fontanne	03/18/69	03/22/69	7	Flop
Billy	N	Billy Rose	03/22/69	03/22/69	1	Flop
Trumpets of the Lord	N	Brooks Atkinson	04/29/69	05/03/69	7	Flop

```
Number of New Hits      =  2
Number of New Flops     = 12
Number of Revival Hits  =  0
Number of Revival Flops =  0
TOTAL NEW SHOWS         = 14
TOTAL REVIVALS          =  0
Pre-Broadway Flops      =  1
Total Shows             = 15
Percent Flops           = 87%
```
Pre-Broadway Flops:
Per *Theater World:* A Mother's Kisses
Per *Burns Mantle:* A Mother's Kisses, Love Match

Broadway Musicals, 1969–1970

Title	Prod.	Theater	Open	Close	No. Perf.	End Result
Jimmy	N	Winter Garden	10/23/69	01/03/70	84	Flop
Buck White	N	George Abbott	12/02/69	12/06/69	7	Flop
La Strada	N	Lunt-Fontanne	12/14/69	12/14/69	1	Flop
Coco	N	Mark Hellinger	12/18/69	10/03/70	333	Hit
Charles Aznavour	R	Music Box	02/04/70	02/22/70	23	Hit
Gantry	N	George Abbott	02/04/70	02/14/70	1	Flop
Georgy	N	Winter Garden	02/26/70	02/28/70	4	Flop
Purlie	N	Broadway	03/15/70	11/07/70	689	Flop
Blood Red Roses	N	John Golden	03/22/70	03/22/70	1	Flop
Minnie's Boys	N	Imperial	03/26/70	05/30/70	80	Flop
Look to the Lilies	N	Lunt-Fontanne	03/29/70	04/19/70	25	Flop
Applause	N	Palace	03/30/70	05/27/72	900	Hit
Cry for Us All	N	Broadhurst	04/08/70	04/15/70	8	Flop

Broadway Musicals, 1969–1970 *(cont.)*

Title	Prod.	Theater	Open	Close	No. Perf.	End Result
The Boy Friend	R	Ambassador	04/14/70	07/18/70	119	Flop
Park	N	John Golden	04/22/70	04/25/70	5	Flop
Company	N	Alvin	04/26/70	01/01/72	690	Hit

Number of New Hits	= 3
Number of New Flops	= 11
Number of Revival Hits	= 1
Number of Revival Flops	= 1
TOTAL NEW SHOWS	= 14
TOTAL REVIVALS	= 2
Pre-Broadway Flops	= 0
Total Shows	= 16
Percent Flops	= 75%

Broadway Musicals, 1970–1971

Title	Prod.	Theater	Open	Close	No. Perf.	End Result
The Rothschilds	N	Lunt-Fontanne	10/19/70	01/02/72	505	Flop
Light, Lively and Yiddish	N	Belasco	10/27/70	01/10/71	87	Flop
The President's Daughter	N	Billy Rose	11/03/70	01/03/71	72	Flop
Two by Two	N	Imperial	11/10/70	09/11/71	343	Hit
The Me Nobody Knows	N	Helen Hayes	12/18/70	11/28/71	587	Hit
Lovely Ladies, Kind Gentlemen	N	Majestic	12/28/70	01/09/71	19	Flop
Soon	N	Ritz	01/12/71	01/13/71	3	Flop
Ari	N	Mark Hellinger	01/15/71	01/30/71	19	Flop
No, No Nanette	R	46th St.	01/19/71	02/04/73	861	Hit
Oh! Calcutta!	R	Belasco	02/25/71	08/12/72	1316	Hit
Follies	N	Winter Garden	04/04/71	07/01/72	524	Flop
Johnny Johnson	N	Edison	04/11/71	04/11/71	1	Flop
70, Girls, 70	N	Broadhurst	04/15/71	05/15/71	35	Flop
Frank Merriwell	N	Longacre	04/24/71	04/24/71	1	Flop
Earl of Ruston	N	Billy Rose	05/05/71	05/08/71	5	Flop

Number of New Hits	= 3
Number of New Flops	= 10
Number of Revival Hits	= 1
Number of Revival Flops	= 1
TOTAL NEW SHOWS	= 13
TOTAL REVIVALS	= 2
Pre-Broadway Flops	= 2
Total Shows	= 17
Percent Flops	= 77%

Pre-Broadway Flops:
Per *Theater World, Variety,* and *Burns Mantle:* Prettybelle, Lolita, My Love

Broadway Musicals, 1971–1972

Title	Prod.	Theater	Open	Close	No. Perf.	End Result
You're a Good Man Charlie Brown	R	John Golden	06/01/71	06/27/71	31	Flop
Jesus Christ Superstar	N	Mark Hellinger	10/12/71	07/01/73	711	Hit
Ain't Supposed to Die . . . Death	N	Barrymore	10/20/71	07/30/72	325	Flop
To Live Another Summer . . .	N	Helen Hayes	10/21/71	03/19/72	173	Flop
On the Town	R	Imperial	10/31/71	01/01/72	65	Flop
The Grass Harp	N	Martin Beck	11/02/71	11/06/71	7	Flop
Only Fools Are Sad	N	Edison	11/22/71	03/26/72	144	Flop
Two Gentlemen of Verona	N	St. James	12/01/71	05/20/73	613	Hit
Wild and Wonderful	N	Lyceum	12/07/71	12/07/71	1	Flop
Inner City	N	Barrymore	12/19/71	03/11/72	97	Flop
The Selling of the President	N	Shubert	03/22/72	03/25/72	5	Flop
A Funny Thing Happened . . .	R	Lunt-Fontanne	03/30/72	08/12/72	156	Flop
Sugar	N	Majestic	04/09/72	06/23/73	506	Hit
That's Entertainment	N	Edison	04/14/72	04/16/72	4	Flop
Lost in the Stars	R	Imperial	04/18/72	05/21/72	39	Flop
Don't Bother Me, I Can't Cope	N	Playhouse	04/19/72	10/17/74	1065	Hit
Different Times	N	ANTA	05/01/72	05/20/72	24	Flop
Hard Job Being God	N	Edison	05/15/72	05/20/72	6	Flop
Don't Play Us Cheap	N	Barrymore	05/16/72	10/01/72	164	Flop
Heathen!	N	Billy Rose	05/21/72	05/21/72	1	Flop

Number of New Hits	= 4
Number of New Flops	= 12
Number of Revival Hits	= 0
Number of Revival Flops	= 4
TOTAL NEW SHOWS	= 16
TOTAL REVIVALS	= 4
Pre-Broadway Flops	= 0
Total Shows	= 20
Percent Flops	= 80%

Broadway Musicals, 1972–1973

Title	Prod.	Theater	Open	Close	No. Perf.	End Result
Grease	N	Broadhurst	06/07/72	04/13/80	3388	Hit
Man of La Mancha	R	Beaumont	06/22/72	10/21/72	140	Hit
From Israel with Love	N	Palace	10/02/72	10/08/72	8	Flop
Dude	N	Broadway	10/09/72	10/21/72	16	Flop
Hurry, Harry	N	Ritz	10/12/72	10/13/72	2	Flop
Pacific Paradise	N	Palace	10/16/72	10/21/72	5	Flop
Mother Earth	N	Belasco	10/19/72	10/28/72	12	Flop
Pippin	N	Imperial	10/23/72	06/12/77	1944	Hit
Dear Oscar	N	Playhouse	11/16/72	11/19/72	5	Flop
Ambassador	N	Lunt-Fontanne	11/19/72	11/25/72	9	Flop

Broadway Musicals, 1972–1973 *(cont.)*

Title	Prod.	Theater	Open	Close	No. Perf.	End Result
Via Galactica	N	Uris	11/28/72	12/02/72	7	Flop
Purlie	R	Billy Rose	12/27/72	01/07/73	14	Flop
Tricks	N	Alvin	01/08/73	01/13/73	8	Flop
Shelter	N	John Golden	02/06/73	03/03/73	31	Flop
A Little Night Music	N	Shubert	02/25/73	08/03/74	601	Hit
Irene	R	Minskoff	03/13/73	09/07/74	605	Flop
Seesaw	N	Uris	03/18/73	12/08/73	296	Flop
Cyrano	N	Palace	05/13/73	06/23/73	49	Flop
Nash at Nine	N	Helen Hayes	05/17/73	06/02/73	21	Flop
Smith	N	Eden	05/19/73	06/03/73	17	Flop

Number of New Hits	= 3	Pre-Broadway Flops	= 1
Number of New Flops	= 14	Total Shows	= 21
Number of Revival Hits	= 1	Percent Flops	= 81%
Number of Revival Flops	= 2	Pre-Broadway Flops:	
TOTAL NEW SHOWS	= 17	Per *Theater World:* Comedy	
TOTAL REVIVALS	= 3	Per *Burns Mantle:* Comedy, Halloween	

Broadway Musicals, 1973–1974

Title	Prod.	Theater	Open	Close	No. Perf.	End Result
The Desert Song	R	Uris	09/05/73	09/16/73	15	Flop
Raisin	N	46th St.	10/18/73	12/08/75	847	Flop
Molly	N	Alvin	11/01/73	12/19/73	68	Flop
Gigi	N	Uris	11/13/73	02/10/74	03	Flop
Good Evening	N	Plymouth	11/14/73	11/30/74	438	Hit
The Pajama Game	R	Lunt-Fontanne	12/09/73	02/03/74	65	Flop
Lorelei	N	Palace	01/27/74	11/03/74	320	Flop
Rainbow Jones	N	Music Box	02/13/74	02/13/74	1	Flop
Sextet	N	Bijou	03/03/74	03/10/74	9	Flop
Candide	R	Broadway	03/05/74	01/04/76	740	Flop
Over Here	N	Shubert	03/06/74	01/04/75	341	Flop
Words and Music	N	John Golden	04/16/74	08/03/74	127	Flop
The Magic Show	N	Cort	05/28/74	12/31/78	1859	Hit

Number of New Hits	= 2	TOTAL REVIVALS	= 3
Number of New Flops	= 8	Total Shows	= 15
Number of Revival Hits	= 0	Percent Flops	= 87%
Number of Revival Flops	= 3	Pre-Broadway Flops	= 2

Per *Theater World:* Gone with the Wind, Rachael Lily Rosenbloom and Don't You Ever Forget It
Per *Variety:* Brainchild, Rachael Lily Rosenbloom . . .
Per *Burns Mantle:* The Student Prince, Brainchild, Rachael Lily Rosenbloom . . .

Broadway Musicals, 1974–1975

Title	Prod.	Theater	Open	Close	No. Perf.	End Result
Gypsy	R	Winter Garden	09/23/74	01/04/75	120	Hit
Mack and Mabel	N	Majestic	10/06/74	11/30/74	66	Flop
Good News	R	St. James	12/23/74	01/04/75	16	Flop
The Wiz	N	Majestic	01/05/75	01/28/79	1672	Hit
Shenandoah	N	Alvin	01/07/75	08/07/77	1050	Hit*
Man on the Moon	N	Little	01/29/75	02/01/75	5	Flop
The Night . . . Made America Famous	N	Barrymore	02/26/75	04/06/75	75	Flop
Goodtime Charley	N	Palace	03/03/75	05/31/75	104	Flop
The Lieutenant	N	Lyceum	03/09/75	03/16/75	9	Flop
The Rocky Horror Show	N	Belasco	03/10/75	04/06/75	45	Flop
Doctor Jazz	N	Winter Garden	03/19/75	03/22/75	5	Flop
A Letter for Queen Victoria	N	ANTA	03/22/75	04/05/75	18	Flop
Rodgers and Hart	N	Helen Hayes	05/13/75	08/16/75	108	Flop

```
Number of New Hits      = 2
Number of New Flops     = 9
Number of Revival Hits  = 1
Number of Revival Flops = 1
TOTAL NEW SHOWS         =11
TOTAL REVIVALS          = 2
Pre-Broadway Flops      = 1
Total Shows             =14
Percent Flops           =79%
```
Pre-Broadway Flops:
Per *Theater World* and *Variety:* Miss Moffat
Per *Burns Mantle:* Miss Moffat, I Got a Song
Variety listed *Shenandoah* as a "flop" but the League records indicate it was a "hit."

Broadway Musicals, 1975–1976

Title	Prod.	Theater	Open	Close	No. Perf.	End Result
Chicago	N	46th St.	06/01/75	08/27/77	947	Hit
A Chorus Line	N	Shubert	10/19/75	04/28/90	6137	Hit
Treemonisha	N	Uris	10/21/75	12/14/75	64	Flop
Me and Bessie	N	Ambassador	10/22/75	12/05/75	453	Hit
Hello, Dolly!	R	Minskoff	11/06/75	12/21/75	51	Flop
A Musical Jubilee	N	St. James	11/13/75	01/01/76	92	Flop
Boccaccio	N	Edison	11/24/75	12/30/75	7	Flop
Very Good Eddie	R	Booth	12/21/75	09/05/76	307	Hit
Home Sweet Homer	N	Palace	01/04/76	01/04/76	1	Flop
Pacific Overtures	N	Winter Garden	01/11/76	06/27/76	193	Flop
Rockabye Hamlet	N	Minskoff	02/17/76	02/21/76	7	Flop
Bubbling Brown Sugar	N	ANTA	03/02/76	12/31/77	766	Hit
My Fair Lady	R	St. James	03/25/76	02/20/77	384	Flop
Rex	N	Lunt-Fontanne	04/25/76	09/05/76	48	Flop

Broadway Musicals, 1975–1976 *(cont.)*

Title	Prod.	Theater	Open	Close	No. Perf.	End Result
So Long, 174th St.	N	Harkness	04/27/76	05/09/76	16	Flop
1600 Pennsylvania Avenue	N	Mark Hellinger	05/04/76	05/08/76	7	Flop
Something's Afoot	N	Lyceum	05/27/76	07/18/76	61	Flop

Number of New Hits	= 4		TOTAL REVIVALS	= 3
Number of New Flops	= 10		Pre-Broadway Flops	= 2
Number of Revival Hits	= 1		Total Shows	= 19
Number of Revival Flops	= 2		Percent Flops	= 74%
TOTAL NEW SHOWS	= 14			

Pre-Broadway Flops:
Per *Theater World:* Truckload
Per *Variety:* Truckload, Salute to Broadway
Per *Burns Mantle:* Truckload, Salute to Broadway, An Evening with Romberg

Broadway Musicals, 1976–1977

Title	Prod.	Theater	Open	Close	No. Perf.	End Result
Godspell	N	Broadhurst	06/22/76	09/04/77	527	Hit
Guys and Dolls	R	Broadway	07/21/76	02/13/77	239	Flop
Let My People Come	N	Morosco	07/22/76	10/02/76	106	Flop
Going Up	R	John Golden	09/19/76	10/30/76	49	Flop
Oh! Calcutta!	R	Edison	09/24/76	08/06/89	5959	Hit
Porgy and Bess	R	Uris	09/25/76	01/09/77	122	Hit
The Robber Bridegroom	R	Biltmore	10/09/76	02/13/77	145	Flop
Don't Step on My Olive Branch	N	Playhouse	11/01/76	11/14/76	16	Flop
Music Is	N	St. James	12/20/76	12/26/76	8	Flop
Your Arm's Too Short . . . God	N	Lyceum	12/22/76	01/01/78	429	Hit
Fiddler on the Roof	R	Winter Garden	12/28/76	05/21/77	167	Hit
Ipi-Tombi	N	Harkness	01/12/77	02/13/77	39	Flop
Party with Comden and Green	R	Morosco	02/10/77	04/30/77	92	Flop
I Love My Wife	N	Barrymore	04/17/77	05/20/79	864	Hit
Side by Side by Sondheim	N	Music Box	04/18/77	03/19/77	390	Hit
Annie	N	Alvin	04/21/77	01/02/83	2377	Hit
The King and I	R	Uris	05/02/77	12/30/78	719	Hit
Happy End	N	Martin Beck	05/07/77	07/10/77	75	Flop
Beatlemania	N	Winter Garden	05/31/77	10/17/79	920	Hit

Number of New Hits	= 6		TOTAL REVIVALS	= 8
Number of New Flops	= 5		Pre-Broadway Flops	= 2
Number of Revival Hits	= 4		Total Shows	= 21
Number of Revival Flops	= 4		Percent Flops	= 52%
TOTAL NEW SHOWS	= 11			

Pre-Broadway Flops:
Per *Theater World* and *Burns Mantle:* The Baker's Wife, Hellzapoppin
Per *Variety:* The Baker's Wife, Hellzapoppin, Selma, The Golden Apple

Broadway Musicals, 1977–1978

Title	Prod.	Theater	Open	Close	No. Perf.	End Result
Man of La Mancha	R	Palace	09/15/77	12/31/77	124	Hit
Estrada	N	Majestic	09/20/77	09/24/77	7	Flop
Comedy with Music (Victor Borge)	N	Imperial	10/03/77	11/27/77	66	Hit
Hair	R	Biltmore	10/05/77	11/06/77	43	Flop
The Act	N	Majestic	10/29/77	07/01/78	233	Hit
Jesus Christ Superstar	R	Longacre	11/23/77	02/12/78	96	Flop
Elvis: The Legend Lives!	N	Palace	01/31/78	04/30/78	101	Flop
On the Twentieth Century	N	St. James	02/19/78	03/18/79	460	Flop
Timbuktu!	N	Mark Hellinger	03/01/78	09/10/78	243	Flop
Hello, Dolly!	R	Lunt-Fontanne	03/05/78	07/09/78	152	Flop
Dancin'	N	Broadhurst	03/27/78	06/27/82	1774	Hit
A History of the American Film	N	ANTA	03/30/78	04/16/78	21	Flop
Ain't Misbehavin'	N	Longacre	05/09/78	02/21/82	1604	Hit
Angel	N	Minskoff	05/10/78	05/13/78	5	Flop
Runaways	N	Plymouth	05/13/78	12/31/78	199	Flop
Working	N	46th St.	05/14/78	06/04/76	25	Flop

```
Number of New Hits      =  3
Number of New Flops     =  8
Number of Revival Hits  =  2
Number of Revival Flops =  3
TOTAL NEW SHOWS         = 11
TOTAL REVIVALS          =  5
Pre-Broadway Flops      =  3
Total Shows             = 19
Percent Flops           = 74%
```
Pre-Broadway Flops:
Per *Theater World:* Alice, The Last Minstrel Show, The Prince of Grand Street, Spotlight
Per *Variety:* The Last Minstrel Show, The Prince of Grand Street, Spotlight, Barbary Coast, In De Beginnin', Mice and Men, Nefertiti, The Utter Glory of Morrissey Hall
Per *Burns Mantle:* The Last Minstrel Show, The Prince of Grand Street, Spotlight, Nefertiti, The London Music Hall

Broadway Musicals, 1978–1979

Title	Prod.	Theater	Open	Close	No. Perf.	End Result
Best Little Whorehouse . . .	N	46th St.	06/19/78	03/27/82	1577	Hit
Eubie!	N	Ambassador	09/20/78	10/07/79	439	Flop
King of Hearts	N	Minskoff	10/22/78	12/03/78	48	Flop
Platinum	N	Mark Hellinger	11/12/78	12/10/78	33	Flop
Ballroom	N	Majestic	12/14/78	03/24/79	116	Flop
A Broadway Musical	N	Lunt-Fontanne	12/21/78	12/21/78	1	Flop
The Grand Tour	N	Palace	01/11/79	03/04/79	61	Flop
They're Playing Our Song	N	Imperial	02/11/79	09/06/81	1082	Hit
Whoopee!	R	ANTA	02/14/79	08/12/79	204	Flop

Broadway Musicals, 1978–1979 *(cont.)*

Title	Prod.	Theater	Open	Close	No. Perf.	End Result
Sarava	N	Mark Hellinger	02/23/79	06/17/79	140	Flop
Sweeney Todd	N	Uris	03/01/79	06/29/80	557	Flop
Carmelina	N	St. James	04/08/79	04/21/79	17	Flop
The Utter Glory . . . Morrissey Hall	N	Mark Hellinger	05/13/79	05/13/79	1	Flop
I Remember Mama	N	Majestic	05/31/79	09/02/79	108	Flop

Number of New Hits   = 2
Number of New Flops   = 11
Number of Revival Hits = 0
Number of Revival Flops = 1
TOTAL NEW SHOWS   = 13
TOTAL REVIVALS   = 1
Pre-Broadway Flops   = 3
Total Shows   = 17
Percent Flops   = 88%
Pre-Broadway Flops:
Per *Theater World:* Home Again, Home Again, Oh, Kay!, Back Country, Joley
Per *Variety:* Home Again [*sic*], Oh, Kay!, Back Country, Alice, Doin' It, Seven Brides for Seven Brothers
Per *Burns Mantle:* Home Again [sic], Back Country, Oh, Kay!, Alice

Broadway Musicals, 1979–1980

Title	Prod.	Theater	Open	Close	No. Perf.	End Result
The Madwoman of Central Park West	N	22 Steps	06/13/79	08/25/79	86	Flop
Got Tu Go Disco	N	Minskoff	06/25/79	06/30/79	8	Flop
Broadway Opry '79	N	St. James	07/27/79	08/02/79	6	Flop
But Never Jam Today	N	Longacre	07/31/79	08/05/79	7	Flop
Peter Pan	R	Lunt-Fontanne	09/06/79	01/04/81	578	Hit
Evita	N	Broadway	09/25/79	06/25/83	1568	Hit
The 1940's Radio Hour	N	St. James	10/07/79	01/06/80	105	Flop
Sugar Babies	N	Mark Hellinger	10/08/79	08/28/82	1208	Hit
The Most Happy Fella	R	Majestic	10/11/79	11/25/79	53	Flop
King of Schnorrers	N	Playhouse	11/28/79	01/13/80	63	Flop
Oklahoma!	R	Palace	12/13/79	08/31/80	301	Flop
Comin' Uptown	N	Winter Garden	12/20/79	01/27/80	45	Flop
Canterbury Tales	R	Rialto	02/12/80	02/24/80	16	Flop
West Side Story	R	Minskoff	02/14/80	11/30/80	341	Flop
Reggae	N	Biltmore	03/27/80	04/13/80	21	Flop
Happy New Year	N	Morosco	04/27/80	05/10/80	17	Flop
Barnum	N	St. James	04/30/80	05/16/82	854	Hit
A Day in Hollywood/A Night . . .	N	John Golden	05/01/80	09/27/81	588	Hit
Musical Chairs	N	Rialto	05/14/80	05/25/80	15	Flop

Broadway Musicals, 1979–1980 *(cont.)*

Title	Prod.	Theater	Open	Close	No. Perf.	End Result
Blackstone	N	Majestic	05/19/80	08/17/80	104	Flop
Billy Bishop Goes to War	N	Morosco	05/29/80	06/07/80	12	Flop

Number of New Hits   = 4
Number of New Flops   = 12
Number of Revival Hits   = 1
Number of Revival Flops = 4
TOTAL NEW SHOWS   = 16
TOTAL REVIVALS   = 5
Pre-Broadway Flops   = 2
Total Shows   = 23
Percent Flops   = 78%
Pre-Broadway Flops:
Per *Theater World* and *Burns Mantle:* Daddy Goodness, Swing
Per *Variety:* Daddy Goodness, Swing, Day by Day

Broadway Musicals, 1980–1981 *(cont.)*

Title	Prod.	Theater	Open	Close	No. Perf.	End Result
Your Arm's Too Short . . . God	R	Ambassador	06/02/80	10/12/80	149	Flop
It's So Nice to Be Civilized	N	Martin Beck	06/03/80	06/08/80	8	Flop
Fearless Frank	N	Princess	06/15/80	06/25/80	12	Flop
42nd Street	N	Winter Garden	08/25/80	01/08/89	3486	Hit
Charlie and Algernon	N	Helen Hayes	09/14/80	09/28/80	17	Flop
Brigadoon	R	Majestic	10/16/80	02/08/81	133	Flop
Banjo Dancing	N	Century	10/21/80	11/30/80	38	Flop
Tintypes	N	John Golden	10/23/80	01/11/81	93	Flop
Perfectly Frank	N	Helen Hayes	11/30/80	12/13/80	16	Flop
Onward Victoria	N	Martin Beck	12/14/80	12/14/80	1	Flop
The Pirates of Penzance	R	Uris	01/08/81	11/28/82	772	Hit
Shakespeare's Cabaret	N	Bijou	01/21/81	03/08/81	54	Flop
The Five O'Clock Girl	N	Helen Hayes	01/28/81	02/08/81	12	Flop
Piaf	N	Plymouth	02/05/81	06/28/81	165	Flop
Sophisticated Ladies	N	Lunt-Fontanne	03/01/81	01/02/83	767	Hit
Bring Back Birdie	N	Martin Beck	03/05/81	03/07/81	4	Flop
Broadway Follies	N	Nederlander	03/15/81	03/15/81	1	Flop
Woman of the Year	N	Palace	03/29/81	03/13/83	770	Flop[a]
Copperfield	N	ANTA	04/16/81	04/26/81	13	Flop
Can-Can	R	Minskoff	04/30/81	05/03/81	5	Flop
The Moony Shapiro Songbook	N	Morosco	05/03/81	05/03/81	1	Flop

Broadway Musicals, 1980–1981 *(cont.)*

Title	Prod.	Theater	Open	Close	No. Perf.	End Result
Inacent Black	N	Biltmore	05/06/81	05/17/81	14	Flop
Lena Horne: The Lady . . . Music	N	Nederlander	05/12/81	06/30/82	333	Hit

Number of New Hits   = 3
Number of New Flops   = 15
Number of Revival Hits = 1
Number of Revival Flops = 4
TOTAL NEW SHOWS   = 18
TOTAL REVIVALS   = 5
Pre-Broadway Flops   = 2
Total Shows   = 25
Percent Flops   = 84%
Pre-Broadway Flops:
Per *Theater World* and *Burns Mantle:* One Night Stand, A Reel American Hero
Per *Variety:* A Reel American Hero, Steps in Time, Turn to the Right
[a]*Variety* did not list final information on this show. The producer's office confirmed the show did not recoup as of its Broadway closing.

Broadway Musicals, 1981–1982

Title	Prod.	Theater	Open	Close	No. Perf.	End Result
This Was Burlesque	R	Princess	06/23/81	07/17/81	28	Flop
My Fair Lady	R	Uris	08/18/81	11/29/81	119	Flop
Marlowe	N	Rialto	10/12/81	11/22/81	48	Flop
Oh, Brother!	N	ANTA	11/10/81	11/11/81	3	Flop
Camelot	R	Winter Garden	11/15/81	01/02/82	48	Flop
Merrily We Roll Along	N	Alvin	11/16/81	11/28/81	16	Flop
The First	N	Martin Beck	11/17/81	12/12/81	37	Flop
Dreamgirls	N	Imperial	12/20/81	08/04/85	1522	Hit
Little Me	R	Eugene O'Neill	01/21/82	02/21/82	36	Flop
Joseph and the . . . Dreamcoat	R	Royale	01/27/82	09/04/83	747	Hit
Pump Boys and Dinettes	N	Princess	02/04/82	06/18/83	573	Hit
Little Johnny Jones	R	Alvin	03/21/82	03/21/82	1	Flop
Is There Life . . . High School?	N	Barrymore	05/07/82	05/16/82	12	Flop
Nine	N	46th St.	05/09/82	02/04/84	739	Hit
Do Black Patent Leather Shoes . . .	N	Alvin	05/27/82	05/30/82	5	Flop
The Best Little Whorehouse . . .	R	Eugene O'Neill	05/31/82	07/24/82	63	Flop

Number of New Hits   = 4   TOTAL REVIVALS   = 6
Number of New Flops   = 6   Pre-Broadway Flops   = 3
Number of Revival Hits = 0   Total Shows   = 19
Number of Revival Flops = 6   Percent Flops   = 79%
TOTAL NEW SHOWS   = 10
Pre-Broadway Flops:
Per *Variety:* Colette, The Little Prince and the Aviator, Say Hello to Harvey, Christmas Carol
Per *Burns Mantle:* Colette, The Little Prince and the Aviator, Say Hello to Harvey

Broadway Musicals, 1982–1983

Title	Prod.	Theater	Open	Close	No. Perf.	End Result
Blues in the Night	N	Rialto	06/02/82	07/18/82	53	Flop
Cleavage	N	Playhouse	06/23/82	06/23/82	1	Flop
Play Me a Country Song	N	Virginia	06/27/82	06/27/82	1	Flop
Seven Brides . . . Seven Brothers	N	Alvin	07/08/82	07/11/82	5	Flop
Your Arm's Too Short . . . God	R	Alvin	09/09/82	11/07/82	69	Flop
A Doll's Life	N	Mark Hellinger	09/23/82	09/26/82	5	Flop
Cats	N	Winter Garden	10/07/82		3193+	Hit
Rock 'n Roll!: The First . . .	N	St. James	10/24/82	10/31/82	9	Flop
Herman Van Veen: All of Him	N	Ambassador	12/08/82	12/12/82	6	Flop
Merlin	N	Mark Hellinger	02/13/83	08/07/83	199	Flop
On Your Toes	R	Virginia	03/06/83	05/20/84	505	Hit
Show Boat	R	Uris	04/24/83	06/26/83	73	Flop
My One and Only	N	St. James	05/01/83	03/03/85	767	Hit
Dance a Little Closer	N	Minskoff	05/11/83	05/11/83	1	Flop

Number of New Hits	= 2
Number of New Flops	= 9
Number of Revival Hits	= 1
Number of Revival Flops	= 2
TOTAL NEW SHOWS	= 11
TOTAL REVIVALS	= 3
Pre-Broadway Flops	= 0
Total Shows	= 14
Percent Flops	= 79%

Broadway Musicals, 1983–1984

Title	Prod.	Theater	Open	Close	No. Perf.	End Result
Mame	R	Gershwin	07/24/83	08/28/83	41	Flop
La Cage aux Folles	N	Palace	08/21/83	11/14/87	1761	Hit
Zorba	R	Broadway	10/16/83	09/02/84	362	Hit
Amen Corner	N	Nederlander	11/10/83	12/04/83	83	Flop
La Tragedie de Carmen	R	Beaumont	11/17/83	04/28/84	187	Flop
Marilyn: An American Fable	N	Minskoff	11/20/83	12/03/83	16	Flop
Doonesbury	N	Biltmore	11/21/83	02/19/84	104	Flop
Baby	N	Barrymore	12/04/83	07/01/84	241	Flop
Peg	N	Lunt-Fontanne	12/14/83	12/17/83	5	Flop
The Tap Dance Kid	N	Broadhurst	12/21/83	08/11/85	669	Flop
The Rink	N	Martin Beck	02/09/84	08/08/84	204	Flop
The Human Comedy	N	Royale	04/05/84	04/15/84	13	Flop
Oliver!	R	Mark Hellinger	04/29/84	05/13/84	17	Flop

Broadway Musicals, 1983–1984 *(cont.)*

Title	Prod.	Theater	Open	Close	No. Perf.	End Result
Sunday in the Park with George	N	Booth	05/02/84	10/13/85	604	Flop
The Wiz	R	Lunt-Fontanne	05/24/84	06/03/84	13	Flop

Number of New Hits   = 1
Number of New Flops   = 9
Number of Revival Hits   = 1
Number of Revival Flops = 4
TOTAL NEW SHOWS   = 10
TOTAL REVIVALS   = 5
Pre-Broadway Flops   = 1
Total Shows   = 16
Percent Flops   = 88%
Pre-Broadway Flops:
Per *Burns Mantle:* Chaplin

Broadway Musicals, 1984–1985

Title	Prod.	Theater	Open	Close	No. Perf.	End Result
Quilters	N	Jack Lawrence	09/25/84	10/14/84	24	Flop
The Three Musketeers	R	Broadway	11/11/84	11/18/84	9	Flop
Doug Henning and His World . . .	N	Lunt-Fontanne	12/11/84	01/27/85	60	Flop
The King and I	R	Broadway	01/07/85	06/30/85	191	Hit
Harrigan 'n Hart	N	Longacre	01/31/85	02/03/85	5	Flop
Leader of the Pack	N	Ambassador	04/08/85	07/21/85	120	Flop
Take Me Along!	R	Martin Beck	04/14/85	04/14/85	1	Flop
Grind	N	Mark Hellinger	04/16/85	06/22/85	79	Flop
Big River	N	Eugene O'Neill	04/25/85	09/20/87	1005	Hit

Number of New Hits   = 1
Number of New Flops   = 5
Number of Revival Hits   = 1
Number of Revival Flops = 2
TOTAL NEW SHOWS   = 6
TOTAL REVIVALS   = 3
Pre-Broadway Flops   = 0
Total Shows   = 9
Percent Flops   = 78%

Broadway Musicals, 1985–1986

Title	Prod.	Theater	Open	Close	No. Perf.	End Result
Singin' in the Rain	N	Gershwin	07/12/85	05/18/86	367	Flop
Song and Dance	N	Royale	09/18/85	11/08/86	474	Flop

Title	Prod.	Theater	Open	Close	No. Perf.	End Result
Tango Argentino	N	Mark Hellinger	10/09/85	03/30/86	198	Hit
The News	N	Helen Hayes	11/05/85	11/09/85	4	Flop
The Mystery of Edwin Drood	N	Imperial	12/02/85	05/16/87	608	Flop
Jerry's Girls	N	St. James	12/18/85	04/20/86	139	Flop
Wind in the Willows	N	Nederlander	12/19/85	12/22/85	4	Flop
Jerome Kern Goes to Hollywood	N	Ritz	01/23/86	02/02/86	13	Flop
Uptown . . . It's Hot!	N	Lunt-Fontanne	01/28/86	02/16/86	24	Flop
Big Deal	N	Broadway	04/10/86	06/08/86	70	Flop
Sweet Charity	R	Minskoff	04/27/86	03/15/87	368	Flop

Number of New Hits   = 1
Number of New Flops   = 9
Number of Revival Hits   = 0
Number of Revival Flops = 1
TOTAL NEW SHOWS   = 10
TOTAL REVIVALS   = 1
Pre-Broadway Flops   = 3
Total Shows   = 14
Percent Flops   = 93%
Pre-Broadway Flops:
Per *Burns Mantle:* Sing, Mahalia, Sing, Babes in Arms, Leave It to Jane

Broadway Musicals, 1986–1987

Title	Prod.	Theater	Open	Close	No. Perf.	End Result
Honky Tonk Nights	N	Biltmore	08/07/86	08/09/86	4	Flop
Me and My Girl	R	Marquis	08/10/86	12/31/89	1420	Hit
Rags	N	Mark Hellinger	08/21/86	08/23/86	4	Flop
Raggedy Ann	N	Nederlander	10/16/86	10/19/86	5	Flop
Flamenco Puro	N	Mark Hellinger	10/19/86	11/30/86	40	Flop
Into the Light	N	Neil Simon	10/22/86	10/26/86	6	Flop
Oh Coward!	R	Helen Hayes	11/17/86	01/03/87	56	Flop
Smile	N	Lunt-Fontanne	11/24/86	01/03/87	48	Flop
Stardust	N	Biltmore	02/19/87	05/17/87	102	Flop
Les Misérables	N	Broadway	03/12/87		1285+	Hit
Starlight Express	N	Gershwin	03/15/87	01/08/89	761	Flop
The Mikado	R	Virginia	04/02/87	05/03/87	46	Flop
Barbara Cook: A Concert . . .	N	Ambassador	04/15/87	04/26/87	13	Flop

Number of New Hits   = 1
Number of New Flops   = 9
Number of Revival Hits   = 1
Number of Revival Flops = 2
TOTAL NEW SHOWS   = 10
TOTAL REVIVALS   = 3
Pre-Broadway Flops   = 0
Total Shows   = 13
Percent Flops   = 85%

Broadway Musicals, 1987–1988

Title	Prod.	Theater	Open	Close	No. Perf.	End Result
Dreamgirls	R	Ambassador	06/28/87	11/29/87	177	Flop
Roza	N	Royale	10/01/87	11/11/87	12	Flop
Late Nite Comic	N	Ritz	10/15/87	10/17/87	4	Flop
Anything Goes	R	Beaumont	10/19/87	09/01/89	804	Hit
Cabaret	R	Imperial	10/22/87	06/04/88	262	Flop
Don't Get God Started	N	Longacre	10/29/87	01/10/88	86	Flop
Into the Woods	N	Martin Beck	11/05/87	09/03/89	764	Flop
Teddy & Alice	N	Minskoff	11/12/87	01/17/88	77	Flop
The Phantom of the Opera	N	Majestic	01/26/88		1000+	Hit
Sarafina!	N	Cort	01/28/88	05/09/89	597	Hit
The Gospel at Colonus	N	Lunt-Fontanne	03/24/88	05/15/88	61	Flop
Oba Oba	N	Ambassador	03/29/88	05/08/88	46	Flop
Mail	N	Music Box	04/14/88	05/14/88	36	Flop
Chess	N	Imperial	04/28/88	06/25/88	68	Flop
Romance/Romance	N	Helen Hayes	05/01/88	01/14/89	297	Flop
Carrie	N	Virginia	05/12/88	05/15/88	5	Flop

Number of New Hits	= 2		Pre-Broadway Flops	= 1
Number of New Flops	= 11		Total Shows	= 17
Number of Revival Hits	= 1		Percent Flops	= 82%
Number of Revival Flops	= 2		Pre-Broadway Flops:	
TOTAL NEW SHOWS	= 13		Per *Burns Mantle:* Satchmo: America's Musical Legend	
TOTAL REVIVALS	= 3			

Broadway Musicals, 1988–1989

Title	Prod.	Theater	Open	Close	No. Perf.	End Result
Legs Diamond	N	Mark Hellinger	12/26/88	02/19/89	64	Flop
Black and Blue	N	Minskoff	01/26/89	01/20/91	824	Flop
Jerome Robbins' Broadway	N	Imperial	02/26/89	09/01/90	634	Flop
Chu Chem	N	Ritz	03/17/89	05/15/89	44	Flop
Welcome to the Club	N	Music Box	04/13/89	04/22/89	12	Flop
Starmites	N	Criter. Ctr. S. R.	04/27/89	06/18/89	60	Flop
Ain't Misbehavin'	R	Ambassador	08/15/88	01/15/89	176	Hit

Number of New Hits	= 0		Pre-Broadway Flops	= 1
Number of New Flops	= 6		Total Shows	= 8
Number of Revival Hits	= 1		Percent Flops	= 88%
Number of Revival Flops	= 0		Pre-Broadway Flops:	
TOTAL NEW SHOWS	= 6		Per *Burns Mantle:* Senator Joe	
TOTAL REVIVALS	= 1			

Broadway Musicals, 1989–1990

Title	Prod.	Theater	Open	Close	No. Perf.	End Result
Dangerous Games	N	Nederlander	10/19/89	10/21/89	4	Flop
Meet Me in St. Louis	N	Gershwin	11/02/89	06/10/90	253	Flop
Threepenny Opera	R	Lunt-Fontanne	11/05/89	12/31/89	65	Flop
Prince of Central Park	N	Belasco	11/09/88	11/11/89	4	Flop
Grand Hotel	N	Martin Beck	11/12/89	04/26/92	1018	Hit
Gypsy	R	St. James	11/16/89	01/06/91	477	Hit
City of Angels	N	Virginia	12/11/89	01/19/92	878	Hit
Aspects of Love	N	Broadhurst	04/08/90	03/02/91	377	Flop
Truly Blessed	N	Longacre	04/22/90	05/20/90	33	Flop
A Change in the Heir	N	Edison	04/29/90	05/13/90	16	Flop

Number of New Hits   = 2
Number of New Flops   = 6
Number of Revival Hits   = 1
Number of Revival Flops = 1
TOTAL NEW SHOWS   = 8
TOTAL REVIVALS   = 2
Pre-Broadway Flops   = 3
Total Shows   = 13
Percent Flops   = 77%
Pre-Broadway Flops:
Per *Burns Mantle:* Annie 2: Miss Hannigan's Revenge, Durante, The King and I

Notes

Preface

1. Harold Prince, *Contradictions.*

1. Broadway Musical Show Biz and Rising Costs

1. Deems Taylor, foreword to Stanley Green, *World of Musical Comedy*, xiii.
2. Alfred L. Bernheim, *Business of the Theatre.*
3. Brooks McNamara, *Shuberts of Broadway*, 3–58; Bernheim, *Business of the Theatre*, 64–71.
4. Oscar Hammerstein, *Lyrics*, 47.
5. Bernheim, *Business of the Theatre*, 3.
6. Gerald Schoenfeld, "The Broadway Theatre circa 1983," 1–2.
7. "Broadway Theatre Managements, Bookings, Receipts," *Variety*, June 6, 1984.
8. Bernheim, *Business of the Theatre*, 113.
9. Hilary de Vries, "New Paths for Regional Theaters," *New York Times*, September 3, 1989.
10. Because variations from year to year are so large, we have taken an average number for each three-year interval. The total yearly average is based on all the separate years.
11. Bernheim, *Business of the Theatre*, 208.
12. Bernheim's data are based on all the shows on "Broadway," including nonmusicals. We suggest, however, that this includes what we now call Off-Broadway and that his criteria for a "failure" are different from those used today.

Season	Number of New Productions	Percent of Success	Failure
1923–24	170	33%	67%
1924–25	192	28	72
1925–26	193	30	70
1926–27	195	29	71
1927–28	197	31	69
TOTAL	947	30%	70%

13. Bernheim, *Business of the Theatre,* 208.

14. The *New York Times* reported on June 26, 1925, that on "Broadway . . . of the pieces produced nearly 75% have been financial failures." The theater magazine *Billboard* reported on June 15, 1929, that "a checkup reveals that forty musical productions made their bow on Broadway between August 1, 1928 and last Saturday. . . . Of these . . . 31 have opened and closed" (about 75 percent flops). On October 31, 1932, the *New York Times* quoted the *Billboard* Index, which defined a failure as a show that runs less than one hundred performances, that during the 1931–32 season of 176 total new productions, 150 were "dramatic," of which 86 percent were "failures"; twenty-six were "musicals," of which 67 percent failed. By June 5, 1935, *Variety,* which had already adopted its present definition of a flop (not "breaking even" or losing investors' funds), headlined "13 hits and 95 flops in '34–'35 . . . producers bat .208 . . . odds against a show are 5 to 1." The base for these odds was *all* the "Broadway" shows, not just musicals.

15. We have averaged across all the years from 1945–46 to 1989–90 to arrive at a total yearly average.

16. Revivals have a slightly higher rate of flops: 78 percent, compared to the average new musical flop rate of 73 percent. If you include new musicals, revivals, *and* preopening flops (many of which are not recorded) in the total count of seasonal Broadway musicals, from 1945 to 1990, then the *general* flop percentage was 76 percent: about three out of four shows (an approximate figure) fail to recoup while on the Broadway run. More probably, *the flop rate is about eight out of ten,* if you include *all* abortive preliminary projects that have, to date, not been systematically defined and recorded.

17. Prince, *Contradictions,* 231.

18. "The Learning Annex," August 1983 bulletin.

19. Thomas C. Hayes, "Hollywood, in Tumult, Booms," *New York Times,* September 29, 1984.

20. Schoenfeld, "The Broadway Theatre circa 1983," 1.

21. Letters, George A. Wachtel to Catherine B. Lanier, September 28, 1982.

22. Elizabeth I. McCann, quoted in William D. Hartley, "The 'Last Hurrah' for Old Broadway?" *U.S. News and World Report,* December 13, 1982.

23. Alfred Harding, "A Brief History of the Actors' Equity Association," in Bernheim, *Business of the Theatre,* 132.

24. Glenn Collins, "The Daunting Task of Preventing Theft at Theater Box Offices," *New York Times,* March 25, 1992.

25. Cecil Smith and Glenn Litton, *Musical Comedy in America,* 290–291.

26. Cy Feuer, quoted in "Backers Want Fast Payoff," *Variety,* April 11, 1984.

27. Gerald Schoenfeld, quoted in ibid.

28. Mervyn Rothstein, "Spectacles Raise the Stakes for Today's Broadway Musicals," *New York Times,* January 8, 1989.

29. Christopher Jones, " 'Starlight' Tour Ready to Roll: 325g Guarantee Matches 'Miz'," *Variety,* November 1, 1989.

30. Smith and Litton, *Musical Comedy,* 300–348.

31. "B'way in '83–'84: Quantity Drops, Quality Registers Marked Gains," *Variety,* June 6, 1984.

32. Samuel G. Freedman, " 'Kean': A Case Study of the High Cost of Theater on Broadway," *New York Times,* January 15, 1984.

33. "Broadway Theater Managements, Bookings, Receipts," *Variety,* June 6, 1984.

34. Mervyn Rothstein, "The Musical Is Money to His Ears," *New York Times,* December 9, 1990, VI, 86.

2. The Fall and Rise of Broadway in the Eighties

1. Samuel G. Freedman, "Broadway Economic Season Is Called Worst in a Decade," *New York Times,* May 20, 1985.

2. In the fifties and sixties on Broadway there was marked neighborhood and architectural deterioration. The Broadway area, Times Square and its environs, persisted into the eighties in a drug-drenched atmosphere, filled with junkies, pushers, hookers, muggers, porn palaces, and other such deterrents to theatergoing. Entrepreneurs, women's groups, and politicians saw the threat. Unable to blink it away, they mobilized in a war on blight with belated support from the city, the state, and private enterprise.

One of twenty-four districts in the city, the Times Square Business Improvement District is an organization (which includes the League) that was formed in January 1992 and is now deploying a security force of forty-one to patrol the twelve blocks of the Broadway turf in two daily shifts of twelve people each. This effort, along with the new community court system, will help handle the special problems peculiar to an area that is awake twenty-four hours a day, and is visited by twenty million tourists each year.

There is also an ambitious clean-up of the area such that porn will diminish as its purveyors move elsewhere in the metropolis. Plans call for more high-rise hotels, office buildings, and other such wonders throughout the nineties. One even hears that these planned alterations have gone too far. Many felt that they would miss the little theaters or that they would not be able to stroll about in an atmosphere of the *belle époque.* Critics said that 42nd Street, Times Square, and 8th Avenue around the Broadway turf would become like Wall Street, with new buildings so massive as to dwarf mere pedestrians. Plans were then altered to include eight theaters (see appendix 3), and large buildings were redesigned with sidewalk amenities and "mile-high" neon signs. The plans are in, and the city, hand-in-glove with a number of private enterprises, large developers, theater owners, the state, and even the banks, are cooperating to do the clean-up, making the new Broadway turf if not aseptic, at least far less raffish—and, all the while, creating jobs. Of course, a downturn in construction and real estate during a time of fiscal jitters would put a temporary damper on much of this plan; but major changes have already begun.

3. The respondents were fifteen hundred men and women, eighteen years of age or older, constituting a probability sample of metropolitan residents living within fifty miles of Manhattan. Twelve hundred of the respondents were theatergoers who received mail questionnaires in May and June of 1979. Three hundred non-theatergoers were interviewed by telephone. The report, "A Study of the New York Audience for the Broadway Theater" (April 1980), was prepared by George

Wachtel, Research Director for the League, with data collected by Consumer Behavior, Inc.

4. "A Study of the New York Audience for the Broadway Theatre," 10.

5. Ibid., 23.

6. Ibid., 12.

7. Ibid., 14–21.

8. Alex Witchel, "As Others Fold, One Show Just Keeps Tapping Along," *New York Times,* August 29, 1990.

9. "Season Boxoffice Totals," *Variety,* June 6, 1990.

10. William Baumol, Edward Wolff, and Hilda Baumol, "Ticket Prices in the Broadway Theatre."

11. Bernard Jacobs, quoted in Sandra Salmans, "Last Season's Ticket Sales Get a Mixed Review," *New York Times,* July 19, 1983.

12. Similarly, returns must be reasonable to the authors. The option money to lease a play from its authors in the new contract trebled, from around six thousand to eighteen thousand dollars. Furthermore, authors could now take advances that they did not need to repay. Since the contract of 1985, when the show runs they are guaranteed a minimum each week, *viz.,* three thousand dollars, which is split among the authors—lyricist, bookwriter, and composer. They are also allowed to take as much as 2 percent of the capitalization, but no more than sixty thousand dollars. The authors have compromised on only one item. Instead of taking 6 percent up front, they agreed to 4.5 percent at the show's start and up to the point at which the investors were paid off. In other words, they were and are initially taking less. But when the investors are paid off, the authors return to 6 percent. Other devices have come into play so that investors receive their due. Instead of the old fifty-fifty split between producer and investors, some current contracts provide 70 percent to the investors for a period of time, and then again, when they are paid off, the percentages are rearranged as before.

13. *Variety* reported the trend: "It's now common for Off-Broadway shows to be capitalized at $400,000, which about five years ago was the approximate cost of a Broadway play." *Variety* listed some Off-Broadway shows scheduled for transfer to Broadway (they didn't make it) and their initial cost figures: *Pacific Overtures* (1984 revival) at the new Promenade, for four hundred thousand dollars; *Three Guys Naked from the Waist Down* (1984) at the Minetta Lane Theater for $495,000. The $430,000 cost of Lanford Wilson's *Balm in Gilead* was partly a result of its large cast, but half that sum went for advertising and marketing. (Richard Hummler, "Off-B'way Production Costs Climbing: 400G and Up Now Common," *Variety,* July 25, 1984.)

In 1984, Prince opened *Diamonds,* with baseball as its theme, at the Circle in the Square on "downtown, low-cost" Bleecker Street, to the tune of six hundred thousand dollars. His interest in authenticity led to expenditures like those connected with bringing original bleacher seats from New Jersey. By 1987, the usual production costs for Off-Broadway musicals were two hundred thousand to seven hundred thousand dollars, and rising. In 1989, *The Heidi Chronicles,* a straight play, cost $175,000 to produce Off-Broadway at Playwrights Horizons, but it cost about $850,000 to move to Broadway's Plymouth Theater, a few blocks and several worlds away. (Laurie Winer, "In Moving Uptown, A Hopeful 'Heidi' Takes a

Gamble," *New York Times*, March 12, 1989.) (It was a hit.) According to *Variety*, more Broadway managements were becoming active Off-Broadway not only because of lower production costs but also because of lower break-even figures. Break-even can occur at about 50 percent of capacity Off-Broadway, while that point on Broadway might be reached at about 70 to 75 percent of capacity.

14. Smith and Litton, *Musical Comedy in America*, 347.

15. Ibid.

16. "Channing, Brynner Lead List of Original-Cast Touring Stars," *Variety*, January 11, 1984.

17. "Season Boxoffice Totals," *Variety*, June 14–20, 1989.

18. Witchel, "As Others Fold" (see note 7 above).

19. "Channing, Brynner Lead" (see note 16 above).

20. Richard Barr, quoted in a 1985 press release from Harvey Sabinson and the League of New York Theatres and Producers.

21. "Channing, Brynner Lead" (see note 16 above).

22. "Shubert, New Haven, Registers $187,415 First Quarter Deficit," *Variety*, April 25, 1984.

23. David Patrick Stearns, "Tinkering with B'way on Tour," *USA Today*, April 4, 1984.

24. Porter Anderson, "The Great White Freeway: Broadway Maps Out the Yellow Brick Road to Success," *Theater Week* 4 (September 17–23, 1990): 20–29.

25. Ibid.

26. Freedman, " 'Kean': A Case Study" (see chapter 1, note 32).

27. Richard Hummler, "David Merrick Hits a B'way Homer: '42nd Street' Owner Grosses 500G Per Week," *Variety*, April 25, 1984.

28. Hummler, " 'Les Miz' at $18–Mil Profit, Netting Huge 600g a Week," *Variety*, May 3–9, 1989; "Fat 'Cats' Hits Record Profits," *Variety*, February 13–21, 1989.

29. Mervyn Rothstein, "For 'Cats,' Nine Is the One to Celebrate," *New York Times*, October 7, 1991.

30. Mandelbaum, *Not Since Carrie*.

31. N. R. Kleinfeld, "The Money Song from *Nick and Nora*," *New York Times* Sunday Arts and Leisure section, November 3, 1991, 29.

32. *Variety*, January 11, 1984.

33. However, in 1982, of the 159 theaters listed in *Theatre Profiles*, a guide to nonprofit (Off and Off-Off-Broadway) professional theaters, not one was devoted exclusively to musical theater. And of the ninety-four nonprofit theaters in the Alliance of Resident Theaters, only two were devoted solely to musical theater. But by 1987 Off Broadway and regional theaters were beginning to originate and to develop more new musical plays, largely because of record local box office returns from running Broadway musicals that had originated there. The first (and still only) university program in the nation to train lyricists, composers, and bookwriters together to create musical plays originated at New York University in 1981.

34. Jim Hardiman, "Dreamgirls Pulls $5.1–Mil in Japan at $93 Top Ticket," *Variety*, December 31, 1986.

35. Sanjay Hazarika, "Broadway Musicals Are Big in Bombay," *New York Times*, December 31, 1988.

36. Rothstein, "Spectacles Raise the Stakes" (see chapter 1, note 28).

37. Richard Bernstein, " 'Aspects,' the Musical That Had Everything, and Lost Everything," *New York Times,* March 7, 1991.

38. Mandelbaum, *Not Since Carrie,* 351.

39. Rothstein, "Spectacles Raise the Stakes" (see chapter 1, note 28).

40. Thorstein Veblen, *Theory of Business Enterprise,* 47–48.

41. Ibid., 36–37.

42. Hummler, "Jerry Weintraub Makes Deal for Joe Nederlander Shares; Six B'way Theatres Involved," *Variety,* September 26, 1984.

43. Veblen, *Theory of Business Enterprise,* 41–42.

44. Bernard Jacobs, quoted in Carol Lawson, "Broadway Is in Its Worst Slump in a Decade," *New York Times,* January 3, 1983.

45. Rothstein, "A Box-Office Record for the 3d Season in a Row," *New York Times,* June 6, 1990.

3. Collaboration of Top Executives

1. Chester Barnard, *Functions of the Executive.*

2. Bernard Rosenberg, *Province of Sociology,* 33–42.

3. Barnard, *Organization and Management,* 15.

4. Barnard, *Functions of the Executive,* 235.

5. Ibid., 232.

6. Agnes de Mille, *And Promenade Home,* 194–203.

7. Samuel G. Freedman, "How 'Big River,' a Story Begun in a Car, Made It to Broadway," *New York Times,* July 16, 1985.

8. Quoted in Ibid.

9. Barnard, *Functions of the Executive,* 21.

10. William Goldman, *Adventures in the Screen Trade,* 39.

11. Max Weber, *Sociology of Religion.*

12. Ernst Troeltsch, *The Social Teaching of the Christian Church,* 2:993–97.

13. Barnard, *Functions of the Executive,* 217.

14. Ibid., 44.

4. Top Executives Score the Action

1. Frances Fergusson, introduction to *Aristotle's Poetics,* 11.

2. Ibid., 68.

3. Ibid., 92.

4. Ibid., 69.

5. Ibid., 61.

6. Ibid., 92.

7. Ibid., 67.

8. Kurt Weill, "The Alchemy of Music," originally published in *Stage* (November 1936); reprinted in *Kurt Weill Newsletter* (Fall 1986) 4: 2, 8.

9. E. Y. "Yip" Harburg, "Lyrics and Lyricists," presentation at the 92nd Street Y, December 20, 1970.

10. Harvey Schmidt, quoted in "Theater Music: Seven Views," in Otis Guern-

sey, ed., *Playwrights, Lyricists, Composers, on Theater,* 142, hereafter referred to as *Playwrights.*

11. Fergusson, introduction, 9–10 (see note 1 above).

12. "Never Was Born," *Bloomer Girl* (1944), lyrics by E. Y. Harburg, music by Harold Arlen.

13. Jerome Kern, quoted in Green, *World of Musical Comedy,* 58.

14. See Deena Rosenberg, *Fascinating Rhythm.*

15. *Aristotle's Poetics,* 91.

16. Jule Styne, quoted in "Theater Music: Seven Views" (see note 10 above).

17. Yip Harburg, interview with Deena Rosenberg, December 1980.

18. Hammerstein, *Lyrics,* 19.

19. Ibid., 15.

20. Jerry Herman, "The American Musical: Still Glowin', Still Crowin', Still Goin' Strong," in *Playwrights,* 133 (see note 10 above).

21. Hammerstein, *Lyrics,* 15.

22. Green, *World of Musical Comedy,* 186.

23. Harold Meyerson and Ernest Harburg, *Who Put the Rainbow in "The Wizard of Oz?",* Chapter 5.

24. *Aristotle's Poetics,* 64.

25. Stephen Sondheim, "Theater Lyrics," in *Playwrights,* 91 (see note 10 above).

26. Alan Jay Lerner, "Lyrics and Lyricists," presentation at the 92nd Street Y, December 12, 1971.

27. Herman, "The American Musical; Still Glowin'," in *Playwrights,* 131 (see note 10 above).

28. Lerner, "Lyrics and Lyricists" presentation (see note 26 above).

29. Ethan Mordden, *Broadway Babies,* 72.

30. *Aristotle's Poetics,* 88.

31. Hammerstein, *Lyrics,* 15.

32. Rouben Mamoulian, quoted in Aljean Harmetz, *The Making of "The Wizard of Oz",* 68.

33. Sondheim, "Theater Lyrics," in *Playwrights,* 74 (see note 10 above).

34. "Robert Brustein on Theatre: Expanding Einstein's Universe," *New Republic,* January 28, 1985, 23.

35. Frank Rich, "Stage: 'Tracers': Drama of Vietnam Veterans," *New York Times,* January 22, 1985.

36. Ibid.

37. Ibid.

5. Producing the Musical Fabric

1. *Aristotle's Poetics,* 107.

2. Fergusson, introduction to ibid., 33.

3. Sondheim, "Theater Lyrics," in *Playwrights,* 71 (see chapter 4, note 10).

4. Lawrence Kramer, *Music and Poetry,* viii.

5. Sondheim, "Theater Lyrics," in *Playwrights,* 75 (see chapter 4, note 10).

6. "Theater Music: A Discussion," in *Playwrights,* 156 (see chapter 4, note 10).

6. The Critics and the Audiences

1. Elizabeth Burns, *Theatricality*, 190.
2. Ibid., 188.
3. Ibid., 189n.
4. Ibid., 187.
5. Ibid.
6. Ibid., 190.
7. Ibid., 191.
8. Ibid., 195.
9. Henri Peyre, *Writers and Their Critics*; Nicholas Slonimsky, *Lexicon of Musical Invective.*
10. "25 Shows in the Money: 13 Hits and 95 Flops in '34–'35," *Variety,* June 5, 1935.
11. "Dramatic Critics' '34–'35 Score," *Variety,* June 5, 1935.
12. " 'Variety' Boxscore Winners," *Variety,* June 7, 1944.

7. Conflict and Collaboration

1. Hammerstein, *Lyrics,* 47.
2. "Robert Brustein on Theatre: The Promise of Permanent Companies," *New Republic,* August 15 and 22, 1983, 26.
3. Donald Farber, *Producing Theatre.*
4. Frank Rich, "Stage: 'Marilyn,' Musical about Monroe's Magic," *New York Times,* September 21, 1983.
5. Yip Harburg, "Lyrics and Lyricists" presentation (see chapter 4, note 9).
6. Samuel G. Freedman, "Playwrights Must Often Defer Royalties to Get Plays on Stage," *New York Times,* October 3, 1983.
7. Ibid.
8. Ibid.
9. Ibid.
10. Ibid.
11. Ibid.
12. Robert Anderson, quoted in Freedman, "Playwrights Must Often Defer" (see note 6 above).

8. The Anatomy of Collaboration

1. Chris Argyris, *Approaches to Effective Leadership.*
2. Maier, *Problem Solving and Creativity.*
3. L. Richard Hoffman, Ernest Harburg, and Norman R. F. Maier, "Differences and Disagreements as Factors in Creative Group Problem Solving," *Journal of Abnormal and Social Psychology* 3 (1962):206–14.
4. Barnard, *Functions of the Executive,* 232.
5. Richard Rodgers, "A Composer Looks at His Lyricists," in *Playwrights,* 98 (see chapter 4, note 10).
6. Richard Rodgers, *Rodgers and Hart Song Book,* 3.

7. Isaac Goldberg, *George Gershwin,* 201–2.

8. Lawrence D. Stewart, "Ira Gershwin and 'The Man That Got Away',"
unpublished paper, UCLA, 15.

9. Burton Lane, interview with Ernest Harburg, Brad Ross, and Art Perlman,
July 10, 1984. E. Y. ("Yip") Harburg Collection, Billy Rose Theatre Collection,
New York Public Library for the Performing Arts, Lincoln Center.

10. Ibid.

11. "End of a Beautiful Friendship" (© 1976), E. Y. Harburg and Harold Arlen,
unpublished.

12. Kurt Weill, "The Alchemy of Music," *Kurt Weill Newsletter* 4:2,8.

Epilogue

1. Robert Merton, *Social Theory and Social Structure,* 128.

2. Elizabeth McCann, quoted in Hartley, "The 'Last Hurrah,' " *U.S. News and
World Report,* December 13, 1982.

3. Bernheim, *Business of the Theatre,* 208.

Selected Bibliography

Argyris, Chris. *Approaches to Effective Leadership: Cognitive Resources and Organizational Performance.* New York: John Wiley, 1987.

Aristotle's Poetics, Trans. S. H. Butcher. Introduction by Francis Fergusson. New York: Hill & Wang, 1961.

Barnard, Chester. *The Functions of the Executive.* Cambridge: Harvard University Press, 1938. Repr. 1968.

———. *Organization and Management: Selected Papers.* Cambridge: Harvard University Press, 1949.

Baumol, William J., and William G. Bowen. *Performing Arts—the Economic Dilemma: A Study of Problems Common to Theatre, Opera, Music, and Dance.* Cambridge: MIT Press, 1966.

Baumol, William J., Edward Wolff, and Hilda Baumol. "Ticket Prices in the Broadway Theatre: Perspectives on Their Rates of Increase." The League of American Theatres and Producers. January 1986.

Bernheim, Alfred. *The Business of the Theatre.* New York: Actors' Equity Association, 1932. Repr. New York: Blom, 1964.

Best Plays series, various editors. Boston: Small Maynard, 1920–1925; New York: Dodd, Mead, 1916–1987; New York: Applause Theatre Book Publishers, 1987–.

Bordman, Gerald. *American Musical Theatre: A Chronicle.* New York: Oxford University Press, 1986.

Burns, Elizabeth. *Sociology of Literature and Drama: Selected Readings.* Harmondsworth, England, and Baltimore: Penguin, Books, 1973.

———. *Theatricality: A Study of Convention in the Theatre and Social Life.* London: Longman, 1972.

Contemporary Theatre, Film, and Television, Vols. 1–8. Detroit, Michael Gale Research, 1981–1990.

de Mille, Agnes. *And Promenade Home.* Boston and Toronto: Little, Brown, 1958.

Dryden, John. *The Conquest of Granada by the Spaniards; in Two Parts.* London: Herringman, 1672.

Farber, Donald. *Producing Theatre: A Comprehensive Legal and Business Guide.* New York: Drama Book Specialists, 1981.

Ferguson, John. *Aristotle*. New York: Twayne, 1972.

Fiedler, Fred. *Increasing Leadership Effectiveness*. Melbourne, Fla.: Krieger, 1983.

Gershwin, Ira. *Lyrics on Several Occasions: A Selection of Stage and Screen Lyrics Written for Sundry Situations; and Now Arranged in Arbitrary Categories. To Which Have Been Added Many Informative Annotations and Disquisitions on Their Why and Wherefore, Their Whom-for, Their How, and Matters Associative*. New York: Knopf, 1959.

Goldberg, Isaac. *George Gershwin: A Study in American Music*. New York: Simon & Schuster, 1931.

Goldman, William. *Adventures in the Screen Trade: A Personal View of Hollywood and Screenwriting*. New York: Warner, 1983.

———. *The Season*. New York: Harcourt, Brace & World, 1969.

Green, Stanley. *Broadway Musicals Show by Show*. Milwaukee, Wis: Leonard, 1985.

———. *The World of Musical Comedy: The Story of the American Musical Stage as Told through the Careers of Its Foremost Composers and Lyricists*. 4th ed. New York: Da Capo, 1980.

———, ed. *Rodgers and Hammerstein Fact Book*. New York: Lynn Farnol, 1980.

Guernsey, Otis, ed. *Playwrights, Lyricists, Composers, on Theater: The Inside Story of a Decade of Theater in Articles and Comments by Its Authors, Selected from Their Own Publication, The Dramatists Guild Quarterly*. New York: Dodd, Mead, 1974.

The Gulls Hornbook, ed. R. B. McKerrow. London: De La More, 1904.

Hammerstein, Oscar. *Lyrics*. New York: Simon & Schuster, 1949.

Harmetz, Aljean. *The Making of "The Wizard of Oz"*. New York: Knopf, 1977.

Henderson, Mary C. *The City and the Theatre*. Clifton, N.J.: White, 1973.

Kramer, Lawrence. *Music and Poetry: The Nineteenth Century and After*. Berkeley and Los Angeles: University of California Press, 1984.

McNamara, Brooks. *The Shuberts of Broadway: A History Drawn from the Collections of the Shubert Archive*. New York: Oxford University Press, 1990.

Maier, Norman Raymond Frederick. *Problem Solving and Creativity in Individuals and Groups*. Belmont, Calif.: Brooks/Cole, 1970.

Mandelbaum, Ken. *Not Since Carrie: Forty Years of Broadway Flops*. New York: St. Martin's, 1991.

Merton, Robert. *Social Theory and Social Structure*. Glencove, Ill.: Free Press, 1957.

Meyerson, Harold and Ernest Harburg. *Who Put the Rainbow in "The Wizard of Oz"? Yip Harburg, Lyricist*. Ann Arbor: University of Michigan Press, 1993.

Mordden, Ethan. *Broadway Babies: The People Who Made the American Musical*. New York: Oxford University Press, 1983.

Notable Names in the American Theatre. Clifton, N.J.: White, 1976.

Peyre, Henri. *Writers and Their Critics*. Ithaca, N.Y.: Cornell University Press, 1944.

Prince, Harold. *Contradictions: Notes on Twenty-Six Years in the Theatre*. New York: Dodd, Mead, 1974.

Rodgers, Richard. *The Rodgers and Hart Song Book: The Words and Music of*

Forty-Seven of Their Songs from Twenty-Two Shows and Two Movies. New York: Simon & Schuster, 1951.

Rosenberg, Bernard. *The Province of Sociology: Freedom and Constraint.* New York: Crowell, 1972.

Rosenberg, Deena. *Fascinating Rhythm: The Collaboration of George and Ira Gershwin.* New York: Dutton, 1991.

Ross, Laura, ed. *Theatre Profiles 5: The Illustrated Reference Guide to America's Nonprofit Professional Theatres.* New York: Theatre Communications Group, 1982.

Roszak, Theodore. *Where the Wasteland Ends: Politics and Transcendence in Postindustrial Society.* Garden City, N.Y.: Doubleday, 1972.

Schoenfeld, Gerald. "The Broadway Theatre circa 1983." The League of New York Theatres and Producers, 1983.

Slonimsky, Nicholas. *Lexicon of Musical Invective.* New York: Coleman-Ross, 1953.

Smith, Cecil M., and Glenn Litton. *Musical Comedy in America.* New York: Theatre Arts Books, 1981.

"A Study of the New York Audience for the Broadway Theatre: A Membership Report." The League of New York Theatres and Producers. April 1980.

Theatre World. Ed. Daniel Blum, 1945–1964; ed. John Willis, 1965–. New York: Blum, 1945–1948; New York: Greenberg, 1950–1957; Philadelphia: Chilton, 1958–1964; New York: Crown, 1965–.

Troeltsch, Ernst. *The Social Teaching of the Christian Church.* 2 vols. Trans. Olive Wyon. New York: Macmillan, 1981.

Veblen, Thorstein. *Theory of Business Enterprise.* Repr. Clifton, N.J.: Kelly, 1975.

Vogel, Harold L. *Entertainment Industry Economics: A Guide for Financial Analysis.* 2d ed. Cambridge: Cambridge University Press, 1990.

Weber, Max. *The Sociology of Religion.* Trans. Ephraim Fischoff. Boston: Beacon, 1963.

Who's Who in America. 45th ed. Wilmette, Ill.: Marquis Who's Who, 1988.

Zadan, Craig. *Sondheim and Co.* 2d ed. New York: Harper & Row, 1986.

Periodicals Consulted

The New York Times
Newsday
Playbill
Theater Week
Variety
Women's Wear Daily

Index

Page numbers in **boldface** refer to figures and illustrations.